# ADIVASI RIGHTS AND EXCLUSION IN INDIA

This volume examines the processes and impacts of exclusion on the Adivasis (tribal or indigenous people) in India and what repercussions these have for their constitutional rights. The chapters explore a wide range of issues connected to the idea of exclusion – land and forest resources, habitats and livelihoods, health and disease management, gender relations, language and schooling, water resources, poverty, governance, markets and technology and development challenges – through case studies from different parts of the country.

The book argues that any laws intended to safeguard the fundamental rights of Adivasis must acknowledge the fact that their diverse and complex identities are not homogenous, and that uniform laws have failed to address their systemic marginalisation since the colonial era. This work appeals for a serious and meaningful political intervention towards tribal development.

The volume will be useful to scholars and researchers of tribal and Third World studies, sociology and social anthropology, exclusion studies and development studies.

**V. Srinivasa Rao** is Associate Professor at the Centre for Regional Studies, School of Social Sciences, University of Hyderabad, India. Earlier he was Assistant Professor and Research Associate in the Centre for the Study of Social Exclusion and Inclusive Policy at the University of Hyderabad (2009–17) and Maulana Azad National Urdu University (2007–9) respectively. Prior to this, he undertook research while working with CARE-India on education, health, food security and livelihood activities in the tribal areas of northern Andhra Pradesh on the Sustainable Tribal Empowerment Project (STEP) assisted by the European Union (2002–7). He has published the book *Primary Education in Tribal Areas in India: A Study of Community Participation in Sarva Shiksha Abhiyan*. He has also published his research findings in peer-reviewed journals including *Economic and Political Weekly*, *Journal of Educational Planning and Administration* and *Indian Journal of Public Administration*.

A valuable addition to the literature on different forms of dispossession of Adivasis – where even supposedly inclusive policies lead to dispossession of languages and cultures.
—**Dev Nathan,** Visiting Professor, Institute for Human Development, New Delhi, India; Coordinator, GPN Studies, New Delhi, India; and Visiting Research Fellow, Center on Globalization, Governance and Competitiveness, Duke University, USA

Indian Adivasis have been victim of imperial as well as internal colonialism in post-Independent India, with them losing their resources for livelihood and cultural moorings and experiencing exclusion even from welfare programmes. The volume with an interdisciplinary perspective highlights multiple issues that cause their exclusion.
—**Ghanshyam Shah,** Former National Fellow, Indian Council of Social Science Research, New Delhi, India

# ADIVASI RIGHTS AND EXCLUSION IN INDIA

*Edited by V. Srinivasa Rao*

LONDON AND NEW YORK

First published 2019
by Routledge
2 Park Square, Milton Park, Abingdon, Oxon OX14 4RN

and by Routledge
711 Third Avenue, New York, NY 10017

Routledge is an imprint of the Taylor & Francis Group, an informa business

© 2019 selection and editorial matter, V. Srinivasa Rao; individual chapters, the contributors

The right of V. Srinivasa Rao to be identified as the author of the editorial material, and of the authors for their individual chapters, has been asserted in accordance with sections 77 and 78 of the Copyright, Designs and Patents Act 1988.

All rights reserved. No part of this book may be reprinted or reproduced or utilised in any form or by any electronic, mechanical, or other means, now known or hereafter invented, including photocopying and recording, or in any information storage or retrieval system, without permission in writing from the publishers.

*Trademark notice*: Product or corporate names may be trademarks or registered trademarks, and are used only for identification and explanation without intent to infringe.

*British Library Cataloguing-in-Publication Data*
A catalogue record for this book is available from the British Library

*Library of Congress Cataloging-in-Publication Data*
A catalog record for this book has been requested

ISBN: 978-1-138-27991-9 (hbk)
ISBN: 978-0-429-43707-6 (ebk)

Typeset in Sabon
by Apex CoVantage, LLC

# CONTENTS

| | |
|---|---|
| *List of illustrations* | viii |
| *Notes on contributors* | x |
| *Foreword* | xiv |
| SHANTHA SINHA | |
| *Preface* | xvii |
| *Acknowledgements* | xix |
| *List of abbreviations* | xxi |
| Introduction: conceptual framework | 1 |
| V. SRINIVASA RAO | |

## PART I
## Dichotomy of rights and exclusion: Adivasis in-between — 25

1 Isolation, inclusion and exclusion: the case of Adivasis in India — 27
VIRGINIUS XAXA

2 In between inclusion and exclusion: the changing face of health and disease management practices among Gonds in a central Indian village — 41
S.N. CHAUDHARY

3 Abandoned by the nation: 'adverse possessions' and the denial of tribal rights to habitat in Indo-Bangladesh border — 70
SAJAL NAG

## CONTENTS

4 Inclusions and exclusions of Adivasi women: subsuming challenges from the past, present and future in Chhattisgarh    93
ILINA SEN

5 Expropriation of land and cultures and the rise of the radical Left: the Odisha story and beyond    108
SUBRAT KUMAR SAHU AND MAMATA DASH

6 Kidnap of the collector in Odisha: the question of tribal exclusion    132
G. HARAGOPAL

7 Tribal rights and big capital: critical reflections on the growing dichotomy and role of corporate media    142
SUDHIR PATTNAIK

### PART II
### Untouchability, atrocities and marginalisation: an unspoken empirical veracity    153

8 Understanding Adivasi dispossession from their land and resources in terms of 'investment-induced displacement'    155
FELIX PADEL

9 Livelihoods of Adivasis in India: continuing marginalisation    178
G. MURALIDHAR

10 Adivasis water exchange and caste-based water lords: a case of groundwater market in a village of Gujarat, India    196
FARHAT NAZ

11 Atrocities against Adivasis: the implicit dimension of social exclusion    217
G.C. PAL

## CONTENTS

12 Exclusion and persistence of poverty among Adivasis in India: a disaggregated analysis    242
AMARESH DUBEY

## PART III
## Inclusive policies: myth or reality    267

13 An unbroken history of broken promises: exploration from a tribal perspective    269
PRADIP PRABHU

14 Language and schooling of Adivasi children in India: issues relating to their right to education    297
V. SRINIVASA RAO

15 Developmental challenges of nomadic and denotified tribes of India: with special reference to Andhra Pradesh    311
MALLI GANDHI

16 Decentralised governance and implementation of PESA in tribal areas: evidences from the western tribal belt of India    332
YATINDRA SINGH SISODIA AND TAPAS K. DALAPATI

*Index*    348

# ILLUSTRATIONS

## Figures

| | | |
|---|---|---|
| 11.1 | The trend of registered cases of the total and PoA crimes against Adivasis, 2001–14 | 220 |
| 11.2 | States with percentage contribution of registered crimes to all India crimes against Adivasis | 222 |
| 11.3 | Disposal of crimes committed against Adivasis by Police and Courts | 225 |
| 11.4 | Trend in the disposal of crimes against Adivasis by the Police and Courts, 2001–14 | 226 |

## Tables

| | | |
|---|---|---|
| 2.1 | Treatment: then and now (multiple response) | 49 |
| 2.2 | Diseases and treatment | 53 |
| 2.3 | Name of the diseases and treatment methods | 54 |
| 2.4 | Food grains provided by PDS at Pathai | 57 |
| 2.5 | Age- and month-wise number of patients who accessed treatment at the PHC | 59 |
| 2.6 | Number of patients registered at Sahpur CHC during January–December 2008 | 61 |
| 10.1 | Net area irrigated by source in Gujarat (area in '00 hectares) | 200 |
| 10.2 | Increase in water price over the course of ten years | 207 |
| 11.1 | State-wise percentage share of the PoA crimes to the total crimes over the years | 223 |
| 12.1 | Distribution of population STs across districts (census) | 244 |
| 12.2 | Sample size by population distribution of STs | 247 |

ILLUSTRATIONS

| | | |
|---|---|---|
| 12.3 | Mean consumption and inequality | 248 |
| 12.4 | Average annual change in mean per capita consumption | 249 |
| 12.5 | Poverty incidence during 1993–94, 2004–05 and 2009–10 (in per cent) | 250 |
| 12.6 | Mean consumption and disparities in consumption | 252 |
| 12.7 | Incidence of poverty (in per cent) | 255 |
| 12.8 | Decomposition of change in head count ratio | 257 |
| 12.9 | HCR and by socio-religious groups and sector (in per cent) | 262 |
| 12.10 | Annualised growth of MPCE by socio-religious groups and sector (in per cent) | 263 |
| 12.11 | State and districts | 264 |

# CONTRIBUTORS

**S.N. Chaudhary** is Rajiv Gandhi Chair Professor in Rajiv Gandhi Chair in Contemporary Studies, Ministry of HRD, Government of India, Barkatullah University, Bhopal, India. He has written, edited and translated 32 books and 62 research articles. His research interests include tribal indebtedness, impact of technology transfer on tribes, land reforms and empowerment of rural women, suicide among tribal farmers in Madhya Pradesh, trafficking of tribal girls and development and displacement with reference to tribes of Madhya Pradesh.

**Tapas K. Dalapati** is Assistant Professor at M. P. Institute of Social Science Research, Ujjain, India. He is also Associate Editor of *Madhya Pradesh Journal of Social Sciences*. His areas of research include tribal land alienation, tribal movements, agrarian labour relations and changing facets of Hindu marriages.

**Mamata Dash** works in the domain of human rights and justice in India, and has been involved in several democratic rights platforms and movements. She is based out of New Delhi, India.

**Amaresh Dubey** is Professor of Economics at the Centre for the Study of Regional Development, Jawaharlal Nehru University, New Delhi, India. His publications include four co-authored and co-edited books, over 60 articles and papers in national and international journals and edited volumes and 34 research project reports, and he has also commissioned policy papers and several opinion pieces in the national newspapers. Dubey's ongoing research includes international collaborative research projects with the University of Maryland, College Park, Manchester University, the University of East Anglia and the University of Tokyo.

CONTRIBUTORS

**Malli Gandhi** is Professor of History at Regional Institute of Education, NCERT, Mysore, India. His books include *Development of Denotified Tribes: Policy and Practice* (2006); *Denotified Tribes: Dimensions of Change* (2008); *Tribes under Stigma: Problems of Identity* (co-authored with V. Lalitha, 2009); *Denotified Tribes: Retrospect and Prospect* (2014); *Educating Tribal Children: Issues, Concerns and Remedies* (2014) and *Tribal Culture in Andhra and Telangana: Tradition and Change* (co-authored with V. Lalitha, 2015). His areas of interest lie in nomadic, semi-nomadic and denotified communities.

**G. Haragopal** is Visiting Professor in National Law School of India University, Bangalore, India. He was earlier Visiting Professor at Indian Institute of Advanced Studies, Shimla, and an ICSSR National Fellow with the Tata Institute of Social Science (TISS), Hyderabad. He has been published in *Economic and Political Weekly* among other places, written for both the Telugu and English press on human rights and politico-economic issues.

**G. Muralidhar** is Chief Mentor at Akshara Livelihoods and Editor-in-Chief of its journal *livelihoods*. He has contributed significantly to New Thinking and Practice in Livelihoods Domain and evolved and managed Livelihoods Framework.

**Sajal Nag** is Netaji Subhas Chandra Bose Distinguished Chair Professor in Social Science and History at Presidency University, Kolkata, India. Earlier, he has been Senior Fellow at the Nehru Memorial Museum and Library, New Delhi; Commonwealth Fellow at Queen's University, Belfast, and Charles Wallace Fellow at the Centre for South Asian Studies, University of Cambridge.

**Farhat Naz** is a Post-Doctoral Researcher at the Wageningen University, Wageningen, Netherlands. She is a development sociologist by academic training and earned her PhD in Development Studies from Centre for Development Research (ZEF), University of Bonn, Germany.

**Felix Padel** is a sociologist and anthropologist based in India. He has earlier taught at Indian Institute of Health Management Research (IIHMR), Jaipur; Visva Bharati, Shantiniketan, and at Jawaharlal Nehru University, New Delhi. He is the author of *Sacrificing People: Invasions of a Tribal Landscape* (1995), *Out of This Earth: East India Adivasis and the Aluminium Cartel* (co-authored with Samarendra Das, 2010) and *Ecology, Economy: Quest for a*

CONTRIBUTORS

*Socially Informed Connection* (co-authored with Ajay Dandekar and Jeemol Unni, 2013).

**G.C. Pal** is a Senior Research Fellow and Director at Indian Institute of Dalit Studies, New Delhi, India. To his credit, he has a book, and over 30 research papers published in edited books and academic journals, besides several monographs. His research interest includes issues related to human development with a special focus on marginalised groups; areas of cognition and education; social exclusion; identity-based discrimination and violence; disability and inter-sectionality, and inclusive policies.

**Sudhir Pattnaik** is Chairman of *Samadrusti* Media Group which is based out of Bhubaneswar, India. He has worked with Dalit and tribal victims of involuntary displacement and also heads the *Madhyantara* Video news magazine. The group runs an open school that imparts free education to Dalit and Adivasi students wanting to learn grassroots journalism in India.

**Pradip Prabhu** has been a tribal rights advocate and activist for Kashtakari Sanghatana, India, for the past 40 years. He has previously been associated with the Expert Group on Tribal Land Alienation and Restoration (GOI), The Committee on Inter-Sectoral Issues Relating to Tribal Development (PMO), Technical Resource Group for Drafting Bill on Forest Rights Act in India, The Central Employment Committee of MGNREGA, Extension of PESA 1996 to Scheduled Areas, and with the Steering Committee on Tribal Empowerment for XI Plan.

**Subrat Kumar Sahu** is an independent researcher, filmmaker, journalist and writer based in New Delhi, India. Apart from producing-directing documentary films on social, political, cultural and environmental issues, he keeps contributing to various magazines, newspapers and other publications. He is currently working on a project of filmmaking engaged with the issues of cultural appropriation and internal economic colonisation.

**Ilina Sen** is Professor at Advanced Centre for Women's Studies, TISS, Mumbai, India. Her research, writing and action have focused on women's politics and livelihood issues, as well as issues of sustainable development, agro-biodiversity and peace. She has earlier been Senior Fellow at the Nehru Memorial Museum and Library, New Delhi. Her major publications include *Inside Chhattisgarh: A Political Memoir* (2014), *Sukhvasin: the Migrant Woman of Chhattisgarh*(1995) and *A Space Within the Struggle* (1990).

CONTRIBUTORS

**Shantha Sinha** is an anti-child labour activist of international reputation. She is the Founder Secretory Trustee and Chief Programme Advisor of M.V. Foundation in India. She was a former Professor and Head in the Department of Political science in the University of Hyderabad. She was nominated by the Government of India as the first Chairperson of the National Commission for Child Rights (NCPCR) in the year 2007 and served two terms in that position until 2013. In 1998 she won the Rotary India Award for Elimination of Child Labour, Rotary Awards for service to Humanity (India) Trust. The same year she was awarded the Albert Shankar International Award by Education International in recognition of outstanding personal contribution for education, at Washington, D.C. In 1998 she was awarded the Padma Shri by the Government of India, which is one of the highest civilian awards, and also won the Ramon Magsaysay Award for Community Leadership in 2003 that is considered as Asia's Nobel Prize. She was awarded the "Goldene Feder "Award by Bauer Publishing House, Germany, in 2007.

**Yatindra Singh Sisodia** is Professor and Director at M. P. Institute of Social Science Research, Ujjain, India. His books include *Democratic Governance and Human Development: Stocktaking and Future Strategies* (2013), *India's Development Scenario: Challenges and Prospects* (2009), *Experiment of Direct Democracy* (2007), *Rural Development: Macro-Micro Reality* (2007), *Functioning of Panchayat Raj System* (2005) and *Tribal Issues in India* (co-edited with D.C. Sah, 2004). Besides these he has authored 5 monographs and published more than 60 research papers in journals of repute and in edited volumes. He is the Editor of *Madhya Pradesh Journal of Social Sciences*. His areas of interest are democracy, decentralised governance, tribal issues and developmental issues.

**Virginius Xaxa** is Pro Vice-Chancellor at Tata Institute of Social Sciences (TISS), Guwahati, India. He has earlier taught Sociology at Delhi School of Economics at the University of Delhi. He is the author of *Economic Dualism and Structure of Class: A Study of Plantation and Peasant Settings in North Bengal* (1997) and *State, Society, and Tribes* (2008). He has also co-edited a volume with Dev Nathan entitled *Social Exclusion and Adverse Inclusion: Development and Deprivation of Adivasis in India* (2012). His area of expertise in the field of academic research is the issue of Adivasi exclusion in India.

# FOREWORD

It is my privilege to write the Foreword for the volume edited by V. Srinivasa Rao entitled *Adivasi Rights and Exclusion in India*. It is one more special addition to the scholarly literature on Adivasis in contemporary times. It sees how exclusion and rights are two sides of the same coin and how the Adivasis are consistently pushed out and get excluded by the State and market even as they are promised autonomy and rights. Through in-depth analysis of several distinct Adivasis groups and their experiences, the volume gives insights into the gross injustice done to them in contemporary society in India. The chapters in the volume do not homogenise the Adivasis as one entity but each goes into the depth of the specificity of each of the Adivasi communities and the challenges they encounter. Thus, it is a contribution to the understanding of the predicament of the tribal community across states.

It examines the contentious issues on how the paternalistic attitude of the State has always regarded them as subordinate citizens in spite of the affirmative action of the Constitution of India under Schedule V and Schedule VI that provides entitlements to them. In the areas that come under Schedule V there is little presence of the public institutions like health, education and other civic facilities. The only face of the State was the forest guards who exploited them for using the forest produce as the land and forests did not belong to the Adivasi communities as a matter of property right.

The presence of Maoists and their contact with the Adivasis across states gave them the strength to confront the local officials in the ideological framework of armed struggle. The initial response of the State was to suppress the movement through police and paramilitary action. The tension in the area got aggravated causing loss of lives, land, displacement, fractured families, trauma and total exclusion of the Adivasis. The worst affected were women and children. This led to the

# FOREWORD

delegitimisation of the State and its apparatus in the area. It is at this juncture that there were attempts of the State to introduce development programmes and policies to wean away the Adivasis from the Maoists and to restore the legitimacy of the State. The State intervention was a means to solve the problem of Maoists and the wellbeing of the Adivasis was not seen as an end in itself. They were still excluded as they had no say in the development process.

At the same time these Scheduled Areas in which the tribal community is located are rich in precious minerals and natural resources which are much needed by the market to explore and exploit. Thus, the Adivasis were pitted against the multinational corporations. Earlier the struggles of the tribal community were against the forest guards, usurious moneylenders and non-tribal land-grabbers. This time it is against far too powerful forces, which are invisible, inaccessible and as far as the Adivasis are concerned, the impact of the multinationals on their ecology, environment and on their lives was devastating. The tribals had to pay heed to the State to resolve the issues and the leadership had to build alliances with civil society partners, political parties and their leaders, the media and even some individual pro-tribal officials. This brought them to engage with the State and civil society in a far more sophisticated fashion.

Under such circumstances State perforce introduced radical legislations such as 'The Provisions of the Panchayats (Extension to Scheduled Areas) Act', 1996 for ensuring self-governance through traditional Gram Sabhas for people living in the Scheduled Areas of India. In order to protect their land from the multinational corporations 'The Scheduled Tribes and Other Traditional Forest Dwellers (Recognition of Forest Rights) Act', 2006 was enacted wherein the Gram Sabha has been given the authority to decide whether they consent to part with their land and also the terms and conditions of the transaction in lieu of such a displacement.

The impact of laws and polices has been complex. There were attempts to make the Adivasis subjects to be part of the decision-making process from a position where they were looked at as objects having little or no say in the development process. Further in response to the weak implementation of these enactments new forms of struggles evolved through the assertions of the Adivasis. A stage of negotiating and bargaining with the State mediated by civil society ensued, and tribal exercise of agency began in the process. At the same time the dichotomy between exclusion and enjoyment of rights remained unresolved.

# FOREWORD

The chapters in this volume have shown how there has been increasing exclusion and exploitation of the tribal in the name of inclusive development protection of their rights. This has been a uniform pattern across several cultural, environmental, livelihood, language and other diversities.

While there are some laws and policies that cut across all states, considering the fact that each state is bound by its own set of challenges the responses of the states too have been complex. Just as the tribal communities are not homogenous and have distinct characteristics, the states' response too is bound by its institutional structures and the history of tribal revolts as well as the predicament of the Adivasis in that area.

There are also other issues that the volume examines with sensitivity regarding loss of traditional knowledge even in the uses of herbs which have been effective as medicines, local wisdom on flora and fauna, culture and language, deterioration of gender equity with introduction of patriarchy.

At the same time the volume discusses the challenges faced by Adivasis groups in the states of northeast India wherein there is a constant tussle among the Adivasis groups and the Adivasis and the Indian State. It discusses how the Adivasis groups on the Indo-Bangladesh border who have always interacted as one homogenous community and lived as one culture have been divided on either side of the India and Bangladesh border, disturbing their traditional networks and relationships and causing an irreconcilable identity crisis between citizenship of a nation and as a member of an Adivasi group. They are now forced to belong to either India or Bangladesh which is so unnatural. This tension adds richness to the debate on exclusion and rights of Adivasis. Indeed this is true of the tribal groups, for example the Gonds who are now divided between Andhra Pradesh, Orissa and Maharashtra and are having to deal with their diversity of languages and governance procedures across the states while all of them belong to the same cultural zone.

This volume covers a range of challenges faced by the Adivasis and has consistently used the word 'Adivasi' to describe them as distinct from scheduled tribe. This gives authenticity to their identity as subjects and as those who are conscious citizens of India struggling for their legitimate claims as equal citizens of India.

**Shantha Sinha**
Professor, University of Hyderabad, India

# PREFACE

It was in the early 2000s when I realised the dichotomy between rights and exclusion while working with Care-India – an international Non-Governmental Organisation (NGO) – to implement the Sustainable Tribal Empowerment Project (STEP) in northern Andhra Pradesh funded by the European Union (EU). Even though I was not quite familiar with the term 'exclusion' as in academic discourse during my association with the organisation between July 2002 to June 2007, I had been working for the 'rights' of the tribal community in the project based at Rampachodavaram agency area in Andhra Pradesh for some time then. Most of the tribal communities in the project area were not aware of their rights, and found themselves disconnected with the so-called developments that have been happening in their geographical area.

The Gram Sabha is a body empowered by PESA to pass resolutions on matters concerning the village/panchayat. However, in an overwhelming number of cases, it is observed that the Gram Sabhas are not aware of the provisions in the PESA. Therefore, in most cases implementation of certain constitutional safeguards and subsequent policy provisions in the area has become a challenging task. This has emerged as one of the important points to label Adivasi communities as being ignorant and illiterate. The so-called development activists, some of whom were accessing funding for the development of these tribes, and the personnel working in these organisations, too were of the same opinion.

However, while it is a fact that in actuality, legislation often cannot be implemented in Adivasi areas, it is not because of the ignorance of this community. Entitled to rights, and still subject to exclusion, reflects that justice and rights are working in opposition. The influence of outsiders, including the state, is one of the main reasons for this grim situation that many tribal areas are not able to implement various constitutional provisions. This is revealed from various instances

# PREFACE

in tribal areas across the country. It is also a reality that the tribals in India continue to lag behind in all development indicators, even though they are provided with more constitutional rights and policy provisions in comparison to other social groups.

In this given reality, even a layperson may be led to ask: Why do Adivasis continue to lag behind even though they have sufficient rights? The present volume seeks to address this question. The central idea of the present volume is to bring various issues that have been bothering many of us with reference to tribal exclusion in India.

In 2007, after I joined academia, I got an opportunity to read extensively on the concept of 'exclusion' in academic discourse. The Centre for the Study of Social Exclusion and Inclusive Policy (CSSEIP) in the Maulana Azad National Urdu University (MANUU) provided me with a platform for my research. Later, after working for nearly two years at MANUU, in 2009, I moved to the same centre in the University of Hyderabad for teaching and research on the subject. As part of my research, in 2012, the Centre for Human Rights in the University provided me with the opportunity to co-ordinate a national seminar on the subject. Looking back into my past experience in the development field between 2002 and 2007, and my academic experience thereafter, I decided to hold a National Seminar on the theme 'Adivasi Rights and Processes of Exclusion in India' at the University of Hyderabad on 15 and 16 February 2012.

After working for nearly eight months on the seminar theme before it could be convened, finding scholars working from the point of view of rights and exclusion with reference to Adivasis in India was a major challenge. Several important publications have, in the recent past, dwelt on a range of issues affecting tribals. It was then that I realised that there was a relative dearth of research connecting the two concepts – rights and exclusion – in the context of the Adivasis. The discussions during the seminar by eminent scholars on their own subject field with reference to Adivasi rights and exclusion has attempted to reduce that gap. The present volume, *Adivasi Rights and Exclusion in India*, brings together a selected set of academic papers from the seminar. I hope this volume will deepen the discussion on 'inclusive growth' of tribal communities in the context of rapid economic changes and lack of social welfare policies for the past two decades and more. The volume lends a context to continue the discussion on how new economic policies and the state's 'financial interest' erodes the rights of tribals that results in their exclusion.

# ACKNOWLEDGEMENTS

This volume is the result of collaboration and coordination of research centres and scholars in the field. I am more than delighted to name some of them in my acknowledgements. I would like to start by thanking Prof. G. Sudarshanam, the then Coordinator, Centre for Human Rights (CHR) in the University of Hyderabad (UoH), for his timely initiative in giving me this opportunity to hold the national seminar on the theme *Adivasi Rights and Processes of Exclusion in India*. This helped me to collaborate with the Centre for the Study of Social Exclusion and Inclusive Policy (CSSEIP) in UoH where I had been teaching until 2017. I am thankful to Dr. Sreepati Ramudu, my colleague in the Centre, for his encouragement and guidance during the post-seminar period for sustaining my objective until this volume comes out. I particularly take this opportunity to thank all the scholars who have contributed their intellectual discussions in the form of research papers for this volume. The staff of the Centre, P. Ramakrishna, Umadevi, Mehjabeen, Chandu, contributed most of their time and energies during the seminar and even transcribed some of the seminar papers during the publication period. The research scholars in the Centre who selflessly contributed to and were involved during the seminar include Venkatesh, Ashok, Himabindu, Prashanthi, Madhava. Thanks to Prof. Bhangya Bhukya, Dr. S. Shaji, Dr. Soumya Vinayan, for their valuable academic suggestions in this volume. Special thanks to Prof. Dev Nathan and Prof. Ghanshyam Shah for patiently reading the manuscript to write endorsement to this volume. I also would like to acknowledge Prof. N. Sudhakhar Rao for his initiative and support. I thank my teacher and guide Prof. Shantha Sinha for immediately accepting to write foreword for this volume.

I wish to thank Dr. Shashank S. Sinha and his team at Routledge for their jet-speed work and additional academic comments while it was

## ACKNOWLEDGEMENTS

in review. Similarly, their valuable inputs and suggestions helped me to have more focus on the theme of this volume.

Last but not least, I appreciate my wife Pushpavalli, daughter Deevenasri and son Sriraj for their patience and encouragement during my busy schedule with the seminar and also while I was working on the publication of this volume. Of course, I am indebted to my mother.

# ABBREVIATIONS

| | |
|---|---|
| AAY | Antyodaya Anna Yojana |
| ACHR | Asian Centre for Human Rights |
| AGP | Asom Gana Parishad |
| AICTEC | All India Criminal Tribes Enquiry Committee |
| AIDS | Acquired Immune Deficiency Syndrome |
| AIR | All India Radio |
| AK | Anganwadi Kendra |
| AMAS | Adivasi Mulya Adivasi Sangha |
| AMPL | Adani Minerals Private Limited |
| ANM | Auxiliary Nurse Mid-wife |
| AP | Adverse Possession |
| AP | Andhra Pradesh |
| APCTE | Average Per Capita Consumption Expenditure |
| APL | Above Poverty Line |
| AR | Annual Report |
| BBC | British Broadcasting Corporation |
| BBJM | Bisthapan Birodhi Jan Manch |
| BCEC | Backward Class Enquiry Commission |
| BDR | Bangladesh Rifles |
| BJP | Bharatiya Janata Party |
| BMO | Block Medical Officer |
| BoP | Balance of Payment |
| BoR | Board of Revenue |
| BPL | Below Poverty Line |
| BSF | Border Security Force |
| CAVOW | Committee Against Violence on Women |
| CD | Community Development |
| CEP | Chhattisgarh Energy Policy |
| CES | Consumer Expenditure Survey |

# ABBREVIATIONS

| | |
|---|---|
| CFM | Community Forest Management |
| CHC | Community Health Centre |
| CM | Chief Minister |
| CMAS | Chasi Mulia Adivasi Sangh |
| CMHO | Chief Medical Health Officer |
| CMP | Chhattisgarh Mineral Policy |
| CMSS | Chhattisgarh Mines Shramik Sangh |
| CPI | Communist Party of India |
| CPI | Consumer Price Index |
| CPM | Communist Party of India (Marxist) |
| CRPF | Central Reserve Police Force |
| CSE | Centre for Science and Environment |
| CSR | Corporate Social Responsibility |
| CTA | Criminal Tribes Act |
| DC | Dossier Criminals |
| DC | District Council |
| DDAUY | Deen Dayal Antyodaya Upchar Yojna |
| DDMH | Deen Dayal Mobile Hospital |
| DID | Development-Induced Displacement |
| DKDA | Dongria Kandh Development Agency |
| DMO | District Medical Officer |
| DNT | Denotified Tribes |
| EAS | Employment Assurance Scheme |
| EGS | Employment Guarantee Scheme |
| EIA | Environment Impact Assessments |
| EMC | English Magna Carta |
| EPA | Environment Protection Act |
| FAO | Food and Agriculture Organisation |
| FDP | Forest Department Personnel |
| FFDA | Finding Documentation and Advocacy |
| FRA | Forest Rights Act |
| FWP | Food for Work Programme |
| GA | General Assembly |
| GCC | Girijan Cooperative Corporation |
| GDP | Gross Domestic Product |
| GE | Gross Enrolment |
| GIAHS | Globally Important Heritage System |
| GoI | Government of India |
| HCR | Head Count Ratio |
| HIV | Human Immunodeficiency Virus |
| IAP | Integrated Action Plan |

## ABBREVIATIONS

| | |
|---|---|
| IAS | Indian Administrative Service |
| IFC | Iron Folic Acid |
| IID | Investment-Induced Displacement |
| IILS | International Institute of Labour Studies |
| IIP | Industrial Investment Policy |
| ILO | International Labour Organisation |
| INR | Indian Rupees |
| ITDA | Integrated Tribal Development Agency |
| ITDP | Integrated Tribal Development Project |
| JFM | Joint Forest Management |
| JGS | Jyotirgram Scheme |
| JRY | Jawahar Rojgar Yojna |
| JSY | Janani Suraksha Yojna |
| KBK | Kalahandi – Balangir – Koraput |
| MADA | Modified Area Development Approach |
| MBBS | Bachelor of Medicine, Bachelor of Surgery |
| MGNREGA | Mahatma Gandhi National Rural Employment Guarantee Act |
| MHA | Ministry of Home Affairs |
| MLA | Member of Legislative Assembly |
| MNC | Multi-National Companies |
| MNREGS | Mahatma Gandhi National Rural Employment Guarantee Scheme |
| MOU | Memorandum of Understanding |
| MP | Madhya Pradesh |
| MPCE | Mean Per Capita Expenditure |
| MRD | Ministry of Rural Development |
| NALCO | National Aluminium Company Limited |
| NCC | National Counterterrorism Centre |
| NCH | North Cachar Hills |
| NCHRR | National Commission of Human Rights Report |
| NCRB | National Crime Record Bureau |
| NCST | National Commission for Scheduled Tribes |
| NE | North-East |
| NEFA | North-East Frontier Agency |
| NEHU | North-Eastern Hill University |
| NEP | New Economic Policy |
| NGO | Non-Governmental Organisation |
| NGY | Nirmal Gram Yojna |
| NHRC | National Human Rights Commission |
| NIRD | National Institute of Rural Development |

## ABBREVIATIONS

| | |
|---|---|
| NPE | National Policy on Education |
| NREGS | National Rural Employment Guarantee Scheme |
| NREP | National Rural Employment Programme |
| NRHM | National Rural Health Mission |
| NRLM | National Rural Livelihood Mission |
| NRM | Natural Resource Management |
| NSA | Non-State Actors |
| NSSO | National Sample Survey Organisation |
| NSTC | National Science and Technology Commission |
| NSTFDC | National Schedule Tribes Financial Development Corporation |
| NT | Notified Tribes |
| NTFP | Non-Timber Forest Produce |
| NVDP | Narmada Valley Development Project |
| NWB | National Wildlife Board |
| OBC | Other Backward Castes |
| OGH | Operation Green Hunt |
| OSATIP | Orissa Scheduled Areas Transfer if Immovable Property Regulation |
| OTAC | Orissa Tribal Advisory Council |
| OTH | Other |
| PAD | Platform Against Displacement |
| PCR | Protection of Civil Rights |
| PCTE | Per Capita Total Expenditure |
| PDS | Public Distribution System |
| PESA | Panchayats Extension to Scheduled Areas Act |
| PHC | Primary Health Centre |
| PL | Planning Commission |
| PLSI | People's Linguistic Survey of India |
| PM | Prime Minister |
| PO | Project Officer |
| PoA | Prevention of Atrocities |
| POA | Programme of Action |
| POSCO | Pohang Iron and Steel Company |
| PR | Panchayat Raj |
| PRA | Participatory Rural Appraisal |
| PRI | Panchayat Raj Institutions |
| PTG | Primitive Tribal Group |
| RCDC | Regional Centre for Development Cooperation |
| RCNC | Report Card of National Coalition |
| RGNIYRD | Rajiv Gandhi National Institute of Youth and Rural Development |

# ABBREVIATIONS

| | |
|---|---|
| RLEGP | Rural Landless Employment Guarantee Programme |
| RTE | Right to Education Act |
| RVUNL | Rajasthan Vidyut Utpadan Nigam Limited |
| SA | Scheduled Area |
| SC | Scheduled Caste |
| SC | Supreme Court |
| SDB | Sahpur Development Block |
| SEZ | Special Economic Zone |
| SGRY | Sampurna Gramin Rojgar Yojna |
| SGSY | Swanjayanti Gram Swayrojgar Yojna |
| SMO | Sector Medical Officer |
| SPO | Special Police Officers |
| SRS | Sample Registration System |
| SSC | South Sea Company |
| ST | Scheduled Tribe |
| STD | Sexually Transmitted Disease |
| STFB | Scheduled Tribes Forest Bill |
| TB | Tuberculosis |
| TDCC | Tribal Development Cooperative Corporation |
| TFDA | Traditional Forest Dwellers (Recognition of Forest Rights) Act |
| TISS | Tata Institute of Social Sciences |
| TRIFED | Tribal Cooperative Marketing Developing Federation |
| TSC | Total Sanitation Campaign |
| TSP | Tribal Sub Plan |
| TSR | Tripura State Rifles |
| UDHR | Universal Declaration of Human Rights |
| UDRME | Universal Declaration of the Rights of Mother Earth |
| UIP | Upper Indravati Reservoir |
| UN | United Nations |
| US | United States |
| USA | United States of America |
| USAID | United States Agency for International Development |
| VDC | Village Development Committee |
| VO | Voluntary Organisation |
| VSS | Vana Samrakshana Samiti |
| WB | World Bank |
| WHO | World Health Organisation |
| WSF | World Social Forum |
| WSS | Women Against Sexual Violence and State Repression |

# INTRODUCTION
## Conceptual framework

*V. Srinivasa Rao*

Rights and exclusion are quite opposite in nature. They do not co-exist with one single person or a group of persons. If rights are ensued, it is done to address exclusion. If somebody is excluded, it means that their rights remain unrecognised. In that case, the excluded would certainly demand for a proper implementation of their rights or lay claim on their rights. The question which arises here is: are there Indian citizens who have constitutionally been ensured rights and subsequently been supported through policy provisions by the highest decision-making body, i.e. the parliament, but are still subject to exclusion? The answer is *yes*.

Dr. Manmohan Singh, during his tenure as prime minister, had commented on the systemic failure to provide Adivasis a stake in the modern economic processes, which have been invading their living spaces, resulting in the alienation of Adivasis over the decades, and is now taking a dangerous turn in several parts of the country (Prime Minister 2009). Over the last 70 years, as the prime minister stated, Adivasis have been marginalised due to exclusionary and encroaching practices. Such a trend has placed them in a state which is often characterised as 'underdevelopment'. Paradoxically, Adivasis are periodically forced to sacrifice their land, resources and labour for the development benefits of the mainstream society; yet they remain excluded from the benefits of such 'development'.

The present prime minister, Narendra Modi, has stated that his government's *Stand Up India* initiative will transform the lives of Adivasis along with the Dalits and women in the country and noted that the 'job seekers' will become 'job creators' in this scheme (IANS 2016). The Adivasis in the country have been less anxious about seeking new livelihood opportunities and more concerned to protect their land and resources. Therefore, the government should prioritise the proper implementation of the existing schemes and safeguarding their constitutional rights, instead of launching more 'flagship programmes' for electoral gains. The resources such as land, forest and water are valuable to the Adivasis for their self-sustainability. But these resources, in most cases in the liberalisation process, have been diverted in the name of development. As a result, the Adivasis experience alienation and exclusion.

Multiple, interrelated factors contribute to Adivasis' deprivation, which include physical segregation, dispossession from the land and forests they have depended on for centuries, exploitation by the mainstream society and various forms of *internal colonialism* (World Bank 2011). The World Bank has observed that the Adivasis are lagging 20 years behind in the realm of poverty levels when compared to most other social groups in India. The extent of deprivation among India's Adivasis is such that they can be ranked among the 25 most-deprived communities of the world, along with inhabitants of Sub-Saharan Africa.

In a society such as India where tradition is the most dominant influence on processes of exclusion and inclusion, the opportunities created through market reforms are mostly utilised by already affluent groups, whose competition over increasingly scarce resources further excludes the traditionally marginalised groups (Chalam 2011: 1–11). Thus, in the era of globalisation, the market, along with the state, has played a key role compounding Adivasi exclusion. Adivasi alienation from land and forests, due to national and globalised development initiatives, has proved deeply detrimental to their interests.

In the light of this systemic marginalisation and exclusion, the fundamental rights aimed at addressing their deprivation need to be questioned since it is clear that their constitutional rights and the subsequent policies which followed have failed to end the processes that have excluded them since the colonial era. The discussion in the present volume intends to understand the intensity of Adivasi exclusion on a range of aspects relating to their life systems. Before moving on to a detailed discussion on this, let us challenge/discuss some of the concepts that are significant in providing clarity on the focused theme.

## Rights

The issue of human rights is as old as the existence of human beings. In the process of its journey, the issue of rights is associated not only with

INTRODUCTION

the human beings, but also with the human environment. Therefore, we debate not only human rights, but also ecological and animal rights. Hence, the concept of rights is applied to everything that is associated to the life of living beings in this universe. These rights are of various kinds. The modern concept of rights is traced through the English Magna Carta (1215) – the document constituting fundamental guarantee of rights and privileges – to the United States Declaration of Independence (1776) and the French Declaration of the Rights of Man and Citizen (1789). These declarations recognised the rights of common people who were unrecognised till then and had made strong foundations in the history of human rights movement at the international level.

In continuation to the historic recognition of rights of human beings at various platforms, on 10 December 1948 the General Assembly of the United Nations proclaimed a Universal Declaration of Human Rights (United Nations 1949) which included the right to 'life, liberty and security of person' (Article 3), 'recognition everywhere as a person before the law' (Article 6), 'freedom of movement and residence' (Article 13), 'a nationality' (Article 15), 'freedom of thought, conscience and religion' (Article 18), 'freedom of peaceful assembly and association' (Article 20), and 'freedom to take part in government' (Article 21) in its Charter. These provisions, which intended to safeguard the rights of human beings and were incorporated in various conventions and declarations at the international level, reveal that the state and civil society should give top priority to protecting the basic rights of individuals or groups of individuals irrespective of their identity in society. These human rights are essential to ensure a more stable society. With the advent of the global village and liberal economy, these universal principles to protect human dignity received momentum not only to protect human beings but also to guarantee an equal share of benefits across all human beings irrespective of their social identity and economic status.

In the specific context of India, with reference to human rights and dignity, the founding fathers of the Indian Constitution understood the importance of a just society and they rendered their vision into reality through the Constitution. Their vision is primarily incorporated in the Preamble, the Fundamental Rights and Directive Principles of State Policy in the Constitution. Hence, it has become the major responsibility of the state to ensure that it provides what it has promised in the Constitution. The realisation of this promise becomes very vital in the wake of a liberal economy in India since it was introduced in the early 1990s.

The rights of people for the last 25 years, especially after the introduction of the free market economy in India, have become one of the main agenda points in the civil liberties discourse. However, this approach in India suffers an important setback. In the course of the human rights struggle, the economic and cultural rights of the people have not received much attention. Most activists emphasise civil and political rights but overlook economic, social and cultural rights. These rights are equally significant for a country such as India, which is affected by feudalism, casteism, communalism and gender discrimination (Roul 2015). With these existing pitfalls in India, the new economic policy has further become an added deterrent to the rights of common people. In the process of the new economic policy implementation, the state and private firms are witnessed as a major threat to human rights in India. Of late, the media, which has been considered as the fourth estate, has become an active partner to this group set against the interest of the already peripheral communities. The major perpetrator and leading agency is the state as it impinges upon the dignity of the common man time and again. This has been noted by J.S. Verma, the former Chairman of the NHRC, who observed that the state has been found to be the major violator of human rights in numerous cases in the country, even when the greatest responsibility to protect and safeguard the rights of its citizens lies with the state itself (Mittal 2010). What further evidence is required to expose the real face of the state with reference to the protection of common people's rights in India?

Specifically, on the point of protection of the rights of Scheduled Tribes, various commissions appointed by different governments have emphasised the need of greater stake of Scheduled Tribes in their own development and accentuated the role of land- and forest-based products. In the process of recognising their self-rule, the Indian Parliament passed the Panchayats Extension to the Scheduled Areas Act (PESA), 1996, in which it recognised various traditional community rights over natural resources. PESA grants authority over matters such as sale of non-timber forest produce and acquisition of land to the Gram Sabhas. Likewise, it further designates a larger role of the Gram Sabhas in environmental clearances in the case of mining explorations. The Scheduled Tribes and Other Traditional Forest Dwellers (Recognition of Forest Rights) Act, 2006 too emphasises a rights-based perspective by strongly pointing to the rights of Scheduled Tribes over natural resources in the areas which they inhabit.

INTRODUCTION

However, one comes across frequent violations of these Acts. For the first time in ten years since the Forest Rights Act (FRA) was introduced in India, the Chhattisgarh government has annulled forest rights allotted to tribals of Ghatbarra village in Surguja district. In an order issued on 8 January 2016, the state forest department stated that the village residents were using their rights to oppose mining in coal blocks. This may be the first instance on record where the state government cancelled the rights of Scheduled Tribes granted to them by an act of Parliament; however, there are several such evidences where tribal groups have been witnessing violation of the act off the record. These instances are termed 'open violation' of the provisions of the PESA Act by Sharma (2012: 20). The violator here is the state. The state has been violating its own rules and regulations to protect the interest of private firms and corporates. The approach of the Chhattisgarh government to annul the forest rights of tribals to benefit Rajasthan Vidyut Utpadan Nigam Limited (RVUNL) and Adani Minerals Private Limited is one of the current instances in this direction.

## Exclusion

The term 'exclusion' was originally coined in France in the 1970s while referring to the most disadvantaged people during that time. The term was popularised when the state was slowly withdrawing its social welfare measures by replacing labour with machines to enhance its economy in European countries. As a result, the concept 'new poverty' emerged during the time. The term – exclusion – in those days was at the centre of reference in argument for new poverty in social science discourse in Europe. The subsequent journey of the term – social exclusion – within the social science discourse has been expanded across all continents with the research initiatives of international bodies such as International Institute of Labour Studies (IILS), United Nations (UN) and so on. There is much literature on this concept attributing with specific regional experiences and outcomes. However, there is limited research on this concept in the context of the Indian experience of social exclusion (Appasamy *et al.* 1996; Chalam 2011; Nayak 2012; The World Bank 2011; Thorat and Attewell 2007; Nathan and Xaxa 2012).

Realising the fact that certain sections of the Indian community have been explicitly excluded for various reasons, the Government of India has introduced the concept of 'inclusive growth' in its Tenth Five Year Plan to address the exclusion of certain communities. The earlier concept of 'development' has been replaced with the term 'growth' in the process of new economic reforms. Ever since liberalisation has been introduced, it is the Adivasi community whose rights are totally neglected and hence these communities are discriminated against and excluded. The process and nature of their exclusion in various domains has been discussed at length by the scholars in the following chapters of this volume.

The concept of social exclusion has been defined by scholars in Europe as 'not simply as an economic or political phenomenon, but as a deficiency of "solidarity" or a rupture of the social fabric' (Silver 1994: 10) that resulted in the emergence of a 'new poverty' (Room 1990). The concept is defined variously based on the context of particular regions; further, its definition changes from time to time and from region to region. The definition of exclusion is contextual in nature. I maintain that exclusion is an umbrella term which covers debates on terms such as alienation, deprivation, discrimination, injustice, underdevelopment, untouchability and so on. However, this concept in the Indian context has been viewed in three different perspectives in relation to three specific social groups. A study by the World Bank (2011) identified Dalits, tribes and women in India as excluded and noted that exclusion 'has its roots in historical divisions along lines of caste, tribe, and the excluded sex, that is, women' (p. 2). Further, the study observes that the reasons are 'rooted in a philosophical tradition that justifies these through religious texts that provide systematic rules for exclusion' (p. 2).

Thus, 'social exclusion' is not an outcome that is calculated based on consumption, income or education alone, but on relations that compel individuals or group of individuals from achieving these outcomes (cited by the World Bank 2011 from de Haan 1997). A methodical strategy to eliminate certain groups to limit their capabilities has been scientifically implemented in India. This 'scientific elimination' of certain social groups in India has been based on three important parameters. These indicators include caste, gender and geographical conditions. As the World Bank study has rightly synthesised, social exclusion in India is not about outcomes alone, but more about the processes that result in these outcomes (The World Bank 2011). Therefore, identifying the processes of social exclusion is an important consideration when we study issues associated to social exclusion. The concept of social exclusion must therefore be understood within the context of Indian tradition and governance instead of bringing in the European attribution. Theoretically, one of the basic features of social exclusion is its

## INTRODUCTION

dynamism. The notion of exclusion keeps changing its characteristics based on the geographical area where the excluded people live, the identity of an individual or group of individuals, the social status and hierarchy, the accessibility to resources to certain groups, hegemony and political representation. Hence the attribute of social exclusion in India changes with reference to the particular social group being referred to. Social exclusion is thus very specific to individuals, groups and communities for the reasons of exclusion could differ when we apply them to a particular individual, social group or geographical area. In order to understand its existence in a particular context, we need to study the history or the historical developments on which the particular society is built and the processes adopted in order to build the particular society.

Adivasi exclusion by itself is dynamic in nature. Exclusion of Adivasis in one aspect further results in their exclusion in multiple areas given the nature of their geographical establishment. Therefore, rights play an important role to control the exclusion of these communities. However, I assume that both the acts – providing rights by an act of legislation and violation of the same rights – go much beyond the will of the state. Since the intentions are not genuine and honest to protect the basic life system of the Adivasis, there is always a rift and violation in order to safeguard their rights even though they are constitutionally guaranteed. The life basis of Adivasis is their association with nature. This includes the rich resources available in the area where they live. The Adivasis' way of using them, the structure and process of self-governance to facilitate their use and to protect them from exploitative forces, are all considered as part of their life system. The Adivasi identity is not uniform across India. There is a lot of diversity within the tribal society and among various tribal communities. This diversity is evident in their language, health systems, livelihood processes, culture, geographical locations, gender relations, village settlements, income-generation activities and so on. If this is the reality, then how can a uniform law or act help them to address their diverse issues? Whatever acts or laws are made to address the tribal issues in India are uniform in nature. Except for the Fifth and Sixth Schedule to divide tribal India into the Northeast and the rest of the country, no effort has been made to address their issues in a community- or region-specific manner by the Indian government. This division too was only to geographically segregate them for political purposes rather than to address their social and economic challenges. These realities clearly expose the lack of intention and insight of the various governments since Independence in bringing equity to Adivasis. No political party in governance has explored any meaningful solutions to reduce the severity of Adivasi problems. No uniform law or act can serve any real purpose considering the diversity inherent among the Adivasi communities in India. This, therefore, implies that the intentions of various governments since India's Independence have been to retain the status quo in affairs related to tribal development. The intention to keep the Adivasis away from the mainstream society has resulted in their exclusion in different aspects of their life.

In view of disturbances in tribal life across India, particularly as part of the post-liberalisation process, it becomes imperative on the part of social activists and researchers to explore the different actors responsible for Adivasi exclusion and critically review the status of Adivasi constitutional rights and subsequent policy initiatives that have so conspicuously failed to address their exclusion. The exclusion of Scheduled Tribes in India is not a new phenomenon. As rightly observed and commented by Guha (2011), M.K. Gandhi worked hard to abolish untouchability and even harder to bring about Hindu–Muslim harmony; however, he did not seriously plan any programmes of social development for this forest community. As Guha observed, there has never been an Adivasi Ambedkar to represent their issues at the policy level. National media too invariably neglect the issues of Adivasi concern and focus more on the problems of Dalits and the Muslim issues. The process of Adivasi exclusion is not a new phenomenon, but had been witnessed since much of the early period of British rule. This has further intensified during the post-Independence period. As Guha (ibid.) rightly observed:

> the situation of the adivasis who lose their lands to mines and dams, the adivasis deprived of access to schools and hospitals, the adivasis who are ignored by the media and the political parties, the adivasis who are massively under-represented in the professional classes and in the upper reaches of the bureaucracy, the adivasis subject to violence by State and insurgent alike.

The fact of the matter of Adivasi *development* is that they have gained least and lost most from India as a free and democratic country (ibid.). This fact has been witnessed in various instances from South to North and East to West in India. This marginalised group, due to their demographic isolation, has been perceived as most powerless not only in terms of making a difference through powerful vote banks in Indian politics,

INTRODUCTION

but also in protecting their rich natural resources such as rivers, land and rich reserves of iron ore and bauxite from the powerful social forces including the state. These *aboriginal* facts did not allow the Adivasi community to claim its constitutional rights to further its development like any other social group in the development processes of the country. These factors helped others to dominate this geographically segregated group in order to grab their resources by excluding them. This exclusion has been established as a regular phenomenon in the hands of state and non-state actors to push them further back and worsened their condition in terms of social, economic and political development.

### *Why exclusion is so important to discuss with reference to Adivasis*

The concept of exclusion so far remains dominantly associated or attributed to Dalits in India because of their non-touchability through the *Varna* system proposed by the traditional Hindu society. The existing studies (Jodhka 2015; Teltumbde 2017; Thorat and Sabharwal 2010) on this aspect emphasise this fact. The single issue that causes exclusion of the Dalits is untouchability which is based on caste discrimination. Whereas in the case of Adivasis in India, it is not one, but multiple issues that cause their exclusion. Issues such as geographical segregation, home language, culture and tradition, dependence on forest for their livelihood, inaccessibility to education and health facilities are a few among many other such issues. Therefore, in the context of multiplicity of factors and in the theoretical framework of exclusion, it becomes imperative to discuss the issue of exclusion in relation to Adivasis in the Indian perspective.

Scholars in this volume discuss multiple issues that have caused Adivasi exclusion. Virginius Xaxa, while narrating how historically Adivasis have been pushed out of the Indian larger system, states that the Adivasis are viewed more as economic and political rather than social and cultural entities. Access to various life-support systems such as forests, rivers, land and water that contribute to their daily sustenance have been systemically denied to this community since the colonial period. In his chapter which explains the nature of exclusion in the case of Dalits and Adivasis, Felix Padel observes that while Dalits were forced into slavery by the dominant castes, Adivasis resisted their domination most radically by retreating to inaccessible regions.

Adivasis, as the Dalits, are vulnerable to different forms of atrocities. However, atrocities against Adivasis are less discussed. G.C. Pal discusses that the issues related to atrocities against Dalits have been a dominant theme in the discourse of human rights and social exclusion, whereas in the case of Adivasis, their atrocities have been more implicit, very often kept stubbornly in place and get less percolated to mainstream society. This is because of consolidation of the 'Dalit' factor and segregation of 'Adivasi' identity. The exclusion is more operational in the case of Adivasi issues and cannot compare in its intensity with the exclusion of any other social groups, including Dalits in the Indian context. Along with these factors, other issues such as inaccessibility to infrastructure and violation of their cultural, economic, political and traditional rights by the so-called mainstream society including the state in the name of development, form part of the aspect of exclusion. The Adivasis in India have been guaranteed constitutional rights in order to protect their life systems; however, the same rights are often violated by the state and non-state actors. This results in compounding their exclusion in multiple areas of their living aspirations. Therefore, it is important to discuss the concept of exclusion in relation to the Adivasis in India.

## Issues beyond scope

Like every other volume which express certain limitations while consolidating various issues on a subject, the present volume too limits its subject pertaining to rights and exclusion of Adivasis. Again, while discussing the rights and exclusion of the Adivasi, issues with reference to agriculture, governance, forest and forest-based income have not figured in this volume. Nearly 70 per cent of Adivasis depend on agriculture-related activities for their livelihood. Since agricultural land of the Adivasis has been withering day by day due to so-called developmental programmes, their dependence on casual labour within agriculture and their migration for work in non-agricultural occupations has been increasing. In this process they get distanced from their homeland on the one hand and losing their right to cultivate their land on the other. Losing one of the major income sources, which comes from their landholding, leads to multidimensional negative consequences in their life cycle.

Thus the process of liberalisation, privatisation and globalisation is a setback to the traditional Adivasi society. Introduction of free market and state-sponsored investment caused Adivasis to lose their existence in the free market economy. The traditional life management system of Adivasi society has been adversely affected as their natural resources are under threat due to violation of constitutional guarantees. This has led to deprivation of their rights in Scheduled Areas. One also observes adverse effects of inclusion of these communities (for more details Nathan and Xaxa 2012) due to their displacement caused by modern development.

The governance of allocating various resources in the Scheduled Areas is not followed properly in most instances. For example, the implementation of Panchayats Extension to Scheduled Areas (PESA) Act 1996 has not been implemented in its true spirit. The act has delegated extensive powers to the Gram Sabha on matters pertaining to local governance. The consent of the Gram Sabha is necessary while allocating any of the local natural resources to outside individuals or agencies including the state. However, in many instances across India, the autonomy of local people through their Gram Sabhas is not recognised, and their rights of control are bypassed while their natural resources are diverted. The natural resources such as land, water and forest have decided their life cycle for ages and protected them from external exclusion. Due to the free market in the liberal economy, these natural resources have come under severe threat as many of the local governance principles are violated, further pushing the Adivasis into a state of deprivation and homelessness. These issues have not been covered in the discussions in the volume which may be viewed as a limitation. However, the present volume focuses critical attention to much debated current issues pertaining to Adivasi exclusion and rights.

## Major areas dealt with in this volume

In the pursuit to explore the nexus between rights and exclusion in relation to the Adivasis in India, this volume offers a fairly comprehensive account of a wide range of issues. This volume consists of 17 chapters including this *Introduction*. These chapters bring together various Adivasi issues in a multidisciplinary format spanning a range of disciplines such as anthropology, ecology, economics, history, political science, social work and sociology. The issues discussed in this volume cover a range of themes including education, health, livelihood, food security, globalisation, displacement, rights over natural resources, minority rights, cultural genocide, atrocities, untouchability, self-governance, poverty, media and so on. These multifaceted issues are particularly focused on in order to understand the dichotomy between rights and exclusion with reference to the Scheduled Tribes.

This is possibly the first attempt to understand the exclusion of Scheduled Tribes from a rights perspective. However, this volume does not exclusively focus on a discussion of Adivasi rights. Rather, its emphasis and focus is to understand the processes of exclusion by highlighting the existing rights. It is hoped that the arguments within this framework will reduce the gap in existing literature regarding the dichotomy between rights and exclusion related to the Scheduled Tribes in India. The central idea of each chapter in this volume is to delve into how Adivasis are excluded by different agencies even though they are entitled to rights over certain basic resources. These rights are guaranteed by the Indian Constitution and through various act(s) of legislation. In a nutshell, this volume identifies various processes of exclusion from a rights perspective. This publication essentially aims to initiate an intense and meaningful engagement among academics, policymakers, administrators, media and social activists with Adivasis, both at the policy level and grassroots interventions.

## Themes

In keeping with the already discussed aims, the content in the present volume has been distributed into three important thematic categories:

1 Dichotomy of Rights and Exclusion: Adivasis in-between.
2 Untouchability, Atrocities and Marginalisation: An Unspoken Empirical Veracity.
3 Inclusive Policies: Myth or Reality.

These thematic divisions will help the reader to consolidate the major contributions and develop the discourses in a meaningful pattern.

### *Dichotomy of rights and exclusion: Adivasis in-between*

Globalisation can justly be viewed as a primary cause of Adivasi marginalisation. 'Isolation, Inclusion and Exclusion: The Case of Adivasis in India' by Virginius Xaxa explains that the Scheduled Tribes in India have been exploited with twin colonial processes, one of the British rule and administration and the other of the non-tribal population. He argues that the tribes who once had control over land, forest and other resources and enjoyed autonomy of governance got pushed to the margins of the new political and economic system that resulted in exclusion in the form of loss of access and control over livelihood as well as over the decision-making process. The chapter emphasises how certain rights have been granted to the tribes and plan allocations made to address their exclusion. However, as the author observes, in terms of the trade between the state and the Adivasis, the Adivasis lost more since Independence. Large-scale development projects and a policy of denial of access to forest resources contradict the affirmative action programmes for the welfare of Adivasi people.

Moving to the issue of health and disease management practices among Gonds, S.N. Chaudhary presents empirical data on how traditional disease management practices are excluded by replacing them with modern health institutions as an inclusive measure in tribal areas. The author establishes in his study the importance of traditional or local health practices by providing evidence from various existing literature. He observes that the traditional health practices have been developed in keeping with the local social, economic and ecological conditions and the carrying capacity of local tribes. This traditional health practice has been maintained with no difference between its practitioners and users in social and economic terms. However, as the study examines, gradually with the establishment of the modern nation-state, the state and other stakeholders endeavoured to modernise and homogenise the field of health and disease management. This resulted in the establishment of Primary Health Centres (PHC) and Community Health Centres (CHC) in tribal areas. These health institutions were projected as an inclusive measure with the intention to deliver treatment to all. The processes of exclusion of tribal traditional health practices have been affirmed in the name of inclusive health practices in modern India. The study observes that as a result of establishment of these institutions, the traditional system was made fragile and the modern system retained its distance in terms of access and delivery. The claims are established with empirical evidence from Pathai village of Shahpur Development Block of Betul district of Madhya Pradesh. The author concludes his study by making suggestions for ensuring true inclusive health management for tribal society.

Adivasi rights in areas like Northeast India were undermined during the demarcation of Hindu and Muslim homelands, a process which ignored the interests of small Adivasi communities and sacrificed their habitats along the Indo-Bangladesh border. Sajal Nag, while exploring the historical facts on tribal rights to habitat on the Indo-Bangladesh border, found that Adivasi groups as the Khasi, Garo, Hajong, Koch, Chakma and tea-tribes live in enclaves that remain misclassified. His study observes that although Partition of India and displacement of

Hindus and Muslims are much highlighted, the displacement and dispossession of these Adivasi groups is not talked about. The study, while talking about 'adverse possessions' and denial of homeland rights to Indian tribals during partition, found that in the process of state formation the Indian nation had other spin-off effects which actually violated the very principles of nationalism on which the hundred years of the nationalist movement was based. In other words, the nationalist movement attempted to create a nation by unifying all Indians; however, in reality, it ended up dividing and distancing its own people. In this background and reality, the author concludes that the tribal people on the border area of Indo-Bangladesh are abandoned by both nations, with non-recognition of their citizenship and thus rejection of their basic rights. Even after seven decades of Independence and partition, a large number of Adivasi communities remain in a no-man's land, surrounded by hostile foreign powers and denied their basic rights, waiting for the two countries to settle their uncertain future.

The chapter by Ilina Sen is on gender inequity within Adivasi society, a result of globalisation. The author discusses processes that undermine the role of tribal women presently by undertaking a micro-level study of the Gond community in Chhattisgarh. The cultural creation of *dependent wife* is itself a production of the cultural integration of Chhattisgarh into mainstream India. The chapter strongly argues that globalisation, with its pressures for acquisition and industrialisation in indigenous areas, has brought its own patriarchal and dowry package. Further, the provisions of Panchayat (Extension to Scheduled Areas) Act, 1996 (PESA) such as participation of women remain poor in the official Gram Sabhas, thereby hitting at values of gender equity. While talking about various processes that undermine the role of women in tribal society, the author establishes that the processes of globalisation and market economy have negatively contributed by reducing/compromising the role and status of women in their traditional society. This has further resulted, the chapter reveals, in rendering women completely absent from the decision-making processes in their community's social bodies as well as constitutional bodies such as the Gram Sabhas. The author in her conclusion raises questions for the larger society.

In their chapter titled 'Expropriation of Land and Cultures and the Rise of the Radical Left: The Odisha Story and Beyond', Subrat Kumar Sahu and Mamata Dash emphasise cultural genocide and economic colonisation of Adivasis as the first steps towards appropriation of their resources. The authors discuss the various processes

INTRODUCTION

of expropriation of Adivasi cultures, resources and territories from pre-colonial to present in three different stages. In the pre-colonial phase, mainstream Hindu society often adopted Adivasi deities and cultural practices. During the colonial phase, Adivasis started to be dispossessed from their territories in large numbers under economic pressures aimed at increasing land revenue. The Adivasis are often rich in terms of natural resources while poor in household income. This chapter reminds one of *Rich lands poor people* (CSE 2008), which presents the paradox that wherever large-scale extraction of mineral resources on Adivasi lands been rampant, it has led to a massive increase in their poverty levels. This is quite in contrast to the promised prosperity. *Unbroken History of Broken Promises* (Sharma 2010) encapsulates this history. The study further emphasises how people's political activism has gained momentum since the onset of liberalisation in 1991 when the state and corporations tried to grab the rich natural resources of Adivasis in Odisha. While concluding their study, the authors also remind us that democratic movements have a huge task to take upon themselves, which is to reflect upon their failures within a broader frame of Adivasi rights rather than rejoicing over the limited successes they have achieved so far.

The abduction of the Malkangiri district collector, Vineel Krishna, by the Maoists in Orissa state has been viewed as an impact of exploitation of natural resources by top multinational companies in the tribal areas. As the author, G. Haragopal, reminds us, the Maoists placed a charter of demands before the government to release the district collector. Of the total eight demands, the demand regarding cancellation of the mining leases and withdrawing of the Memorandum of Understandings (MoUs) with various multinational corporations (MNCs) in tribal areas is important to understand the context. The author rightly puts the entire episode within the domain of development or welfare. The author views that giving pattas to the tribals and restoring back the land from non-tribals is not a simple task for the government to handle. The chapter is based on the author's own role as a mediator between the Maoists and state government to bring the district collector back to the office. The author analyses the pitfalls of the media for not building proper public opinion to address the deep crisis, thus compromising its own values and integrity. The chapter rightly puts this as a serious implication to the working of the liberal framework of Indian democracy. Finally, the author observes that the abduction caused a debate on Maoists' concerns and their approach to the development model in tribal areas. The author also suggests that the Maoist party should rethink on the method of kidnapping sympathetic civil servants who work for the poor, and observes that the state should develop a healthy law-abiding culture when dealing with sensitive cases that involves human lives. The chapter concludes that the model of development that the present state has been following has undoubtedly trapped the tribals in a vicious circle. This vicious circle is another manifestation of exclusion in the name of modern development by the state which involves multinational companies sacrificing the lives of tribal people by expropriating their rich natural resources.

Another important chapter in this volume, 'Tribal Rights and Big Capital: Critical Reflections on the Growing Dichotomy and Role of Corporate Media' by Sudhir Pattnaik exposes the relationship between the mainstream media and capital. The chapter argues that the media, referred to as the *fourth estate*, has become an integral part of big capital. The author, while reviewing various arguments, observes that scholars have outlined patterns of pro-corporate interpretations propagated by mainstream media, which tend to sideline Adivasi movements and voices or depict them falsely as Maoists. The author begins by observing that tribal identities and tribal rights are presently passing through a period of serious crisis, often giving rise to conflicting assertions and confusing interpretations. Aggressive media slants on events in Adivasi regions facilitate the entry of private capital into resource-rich regions, further marginalising Adivasi rights and viewpoints. The dichotomy between rights offered and rights realised by Adivasis is widening at an unprecedented rate. The chapter says that since the national media is grabbing most of the advertisement revenues, this is leading to an unholy competition between the national media and the regional media. Therefore, in the conclusion the author suggests that the role of media and journalists, who take risks to bring out the Adivasi perspective, is therefore crucial in order to stop these processes which seriously affect the rights of Adivasis.

### Untouchability, atrocities and marginalisation: an unspoken empirical veracity

Felix Padel in his study entitled 'Understanding Adivasi Dispossession from their Land and Resources in Terms of *Investment-Induced Displacement*' says that for many, the Adivasis are enjoying the privilege of more rights than most other groups through constitutional safeguards and various policy initiatives. However, he questions this view by asking, why then do Adivasi remain so marginalised despite the

INTRODUCTION

safeguards and policy proclamations? It is evident that the Adivasis, along with their lands and resources, are seen through the prism of market forces. According to Padel, *investment-induced displacement* is the most appropriate term for expressing Adivasi alienation from their land and communities. For construction of new dams, mining activity and factories have lowered their standard of living drastically and therefore, for them, these activities constitute the antithesis of real development. He argues that displaced Adivasis find that almost none of the benefits promised to them materialise, and that they lose immeasurably in terms of food security, livelihoods, richness of their social life and natural environment. While citing examples of the displacement caused by the upper Indravati hydropower project, the author substantiates his views with facts. Many Adivasi families are uprooted from their natural habitats and contemporary documentaries as DAM-*aged* (filmed by Subrat Kumar Sahu) capture the social melancholy emanating from this process. This study views cultural genocide and economic colonisation of Adivasis as the first step towards appropriation of their resources. The processes of Adivasi exclusion in India are explained in three phases by the author. First, in the pre-colonial phase, mainstream Hindu society often adopted Adivasi deities and cultural practices. Second, during the colonial phase, Adivasis began to be dispossessed from their territories in large numbers under financial pressures aimed at increasing land revenue. Third, internal colonisation sums up the present phase of rapid appropriation of the rich resources which Adivasi communities have sustained over centuries. The author sums up by saying that the Adivasis are often rich in terms of natural resources while are extremely poor in terms of household income.

In another chapter on rich livelihood sources of Scheduled Tribes and their continuing marginalisation, G. Muralidhar explains how the rich resources of Scheduled Tribes are appropriated so that they are excluded from their traditional livelihood practices. The study finds that in the wake of a market-driven economy, agriculture has been rapidly commercialised with profound and adverse consequences for Adivasi livelihoods. Farmers who traditionally cultivated crops for their own consumption have been compelled to shift to cash crops for survival whose market is skewed against them.

The author argues that with declining forest cover and not-so-good returns for NTFP, large sections of Adivasi communities have been forced to look for new livelihoods outside their traditional environment. Adivasis today constitute about 25 per cent of the total MGNREGA workforce. The study highlights some of the important findings in MGNREGA data on changing trends in the traditional livelihood practices of Adivasis. It appears that many Adivasi households, more than any other social group in the country, are looking towards MGNREGA as a livelihood option. The danger is that they are giving up their traditional livelihood practices and becoming dependent on casual wage labour for sustenance. In the process, they lose their skills, knowledge as well as traditional rights. Exemplifying some of the late studies on livelihood practices in Adivasi areas, the author cites important research findings. According to the author, scholars have traced the roots of the decline of Adivasis' traditional communitarian system in Jharkhand to the penetration of capital and huge mining activities in the Adivasi areas initiated during the colonial period. As a result the tribal communities are living in economic distress despite endowment of rich natural resources, social resources and spiritual resources. They are thus subject to resource alienation (forests, commons and lands), financial exclusion and market exclusion. Their identity and cultural capitals are being eroded and there is an increased disruption of their social fabric and loss of their resource endowment. They are not receiving at par with what the mainstream could access in return. Therefore, the author in his conclusion, suggests that it is important to find ways to globalise time-tested tribal ways of living (with minor modifications, if warranted), instead of trying to push them into mainstream ways of living.

Even though the issues of discrimination and untouchability are largely attributed to Dalits, contemporary incidents and developments indicate that Adivasis too are equally subjected to these unethical practices of exclusion. Farhat Naz in her chapter on Adivasi water exchange and caste-based discrimination and groundwater market in Gujarat emphasises how the upper-caste population discriminates against the Adivasi people. In this micro-level study the author finds that the drinking water is used as a tool to reproduce untouchability practices and discrimination against Adivasis in the state of Gujarat. Rules pertaining to drinking water access are clearly defined through caste hierarchy, regulated by concepts of pollution and purity. The processes of exclusion of Adivasis are based on discrimination on the grounds of accessibility of water and treating water as an economic resource by the upper-caste communities. The Thakores, who form the upper-caste population in the village, do not buy drinking water from Adivasi water-sellers. Discrimination against Adivasis is practiced at every level and has even been ruthlessly 'polished' in the idiom of modern-development-culture. The author concludes the study by stating that the groundwater market in Mathnaa village is dependent on social structure, social norms and practices deeply embedded in caste and its interplay with irrigation and drinking water developed at the village level.

The chapter by G.C. Pal, 'Atrocities against Adivasis: The Implicit Dimension of Social Exclusion', exposes certain evidences on atrocities against Adivasis in India. This chapter compiles various data sources to present evidences where the state has remained silent on atrocities against Adivasis. The study presents the evidence from officially registered cases of atrocities against Adivasis, compiled by the National Crime Record Bureau, to reflect upon the patterns and potential trends of atrocities against Adivasis. The high number of instances of crimes against Adivasis registered in most states shows a clear violation of human rights. The inability of the state to control these incidents exists side by side with its modern economic reforms package. The author presents recent instances in support of his arguments. Evidences in Alubaka forest area in Andhra Pradesh are definitive indicators to denial of justice to many victims of atrocities and raise serious concerns about the security of the Adivasis. In another incident, the forest officials set on fire nearly 40 huts of migrant Adivasis, originally hailing from the border areas of Chhattisgarh, following an alleged demolition drive conducted by them to evict Adivasis at Mothey village in Burgumpadu mandal of Andhra Pradesh. The author observes that, although a large section of Adivasis and Dalits have been subjected to atrocities, the problems of Adivasis remain distant for various qualitative reasons such as their geographical location and availability of natural and rich resources. The study observes that the denial of justice to many victims of atrocities raises serious concern about the security of Adivasis. When some of the main perpetrators are members of security forces and are not brought to justice, this further alienates Adivasis from mainstream society and drives them in desperation towards the Maoists. These processes to exclude the Adivasis to the extent of pushing them to an inferior status is only another strategy to grab their resources.

Poverty is another major issue confronting Adivasi families. Recent literature sheds light on the fact that Adivasis are at the bottom on a range of development indicators including consumption and poverty. As the author Amaresh Dubey observes, disparities between Adivasis and other social groups are reported to be worsening and these disparities indicate the high extent of deprivation of Adivasis in this country. The chapter on poverty analysis among Adivasis in India shows that benefits of growth have been cornered more by affluent population groups and less by marginalised social groups. The natural concomitant of this disfigured growth is a steep increase in inequality. Economic reforms introduced in the early 1990s largely excluded Adivasis both by appropriating their natural resources for private firms, and also by not allowing them to steer their own development process. Analysing various indicators by using existing data, the chapter points out that the deprivation levels among Adivasi residing in major states and with less than majority Adivasi population appear to be the most vulnerable groups among all Adivasis. The data presented in the chapter indicates that the incidence of poverty in excess of 50 per cent is seen among the districts with substantial Scheduled Tribes population in states such as Gujarat and Maharashtra, which are recognised as the most investor-friendly and have reflected rapid growth. This suggests the non-participation of Scheduled Tribes in the current episode of economic growth. The process of exclusion has been continuous irrespective of the strong voices raised by the Adivasi community against their deprivation. In these cases the poverty of Adivasis remains constant and growth of the advanced classes continuously increases.

## *Inclusive policies: myth or reality*

Pradip Prabhu draws attention to the fact of how the promised rights of tribal people have been systemically ignored since the pre-colonial period to present times. In his chapter titled, 'An Unbroken History of Broken Promises: Exploration from a Tribal Perspective', the author presents facts based on a careful participant learning from a long history of tribal struggles, both recorded as well as drawn from the oral tradition of a large number of Adivasi communities. The author has endeavoured to explore how the tribal geographical areas and their traditional rights have been overlooked by British as well as independent India at every step. While presenting the example of construction of roads to link tribal areas to the larger society, the author notes that this largely helped the non-tribal community to lay claim on natural resources from tribal areas and building a huge mass of middlemen. The chapter brings to light facts about how the financial allocations for tribal development made in Five Year Plans are diverted and how the establishment of ITDAs have proved to be ineffective in this direction. The study finds that 'development' has turned into a process of expanding liberties and license for the elites to appropriate the survival resources of the Adivasis. The author is critical of the processes

## INTRODUCTION

of development which have led to the creation of elites. It is in this background that Prabhu reminds that every promise made to the Adivasi people in the Nehruvian Panchsheel was ironically made to be broken subsequently.

As has been established, language is not a mere medium of communication; it constitutes domination and subordination and reflects power relations. Srinivasa Rao in his chapter on language and schooling of Scheduled Tribe children reviews the relationship between the role of language in schooling and implementation of the Right to Education Act (RTE) in tribal areas. The author underlines that language is a major concern when it comes to Adivasi education. Almost every Adivasi community has its own language or dialect. But these languages are not considered fit to be mediums of instruction in school education as they do not have scripts, although it is constitutionally binding to use the mother tongue in early years of school education. The chapter argues that script is not a key criteria; a language can be written in any script. The national language and official language of India, that is Hindi and English, have no script. However, they are taught as compulsory languages in schools as first and second languages. They are taught simply because they are languages of the majority language speakers. Since the teachers do not adopt the tribal languages as a medium of instruction for communicating with tribal children, this results in poor performance and dropping-out of children from school. This chapter examines how the Adivasi right to education is being denied by imposition of an alien language, particularly in the context of implementation of the recent Right to Education Act for tribal children.

Malli Gandhi in his chapter on 'Developmental Challenges of Nomadic and Denotified Tribes of India: With Special Reference to Andhra Pradesh' narrates how some of the Adivasi communities got labelled as Criminal Tribes during British colonial rule in India. While explaining the process of designating certain tribes as criminals, the author draws upon important historical evidences to elucidate how the state and non-state actors have played a role in their marginalisation. The chapter discusses livelihood practices of the some of the ex-Criminal Tribes known as Denotified Tribes in post-Independent India. According to Gandhi, traditionally these tribes worked as vegetable sellers, plantation workers, stone quarry workers, earth workers, baggage carriers, food grain transporters, basket-makers, rope weavers and other skill-based professions. However, the process of modernisation and development constituted a threat to their identity and human dignity. Their traditional livelihood practices in the process have slowly been rendered irrelevant. This has led them to shift their livelihood sources. Even government efforts to support their cause has led to little improvement in their condition. The author strongly recommends the need for a socialisation process to integrate the Denotified Tribes with the larger society.

Decentralised management of natural resources (land, water and forest) is one of the core objectives of PESA, besides conservation and protection of traditions, rituals and cultural identity. A research chapter based on empirical data by Yatindra Singh Sisodia and Tapas Kumar Dalapati attempts to find out the processes and mechanisms which operate in the implementation of PESA in the Scheduled Areas of Central India as Madhya Pradesh, Rajasthan and Gujarat. The authors mainly focused on how effectively the Gram Sabhas and Gram Panchayats are functioning to gain control over natural resource management and conservation and protection of traditions and rituals in the study area. The study very interestingly finds that Adivasi participation in Gram Sabhas in the western Adivasi belt of Madhaya Pradesh, Rajasthan and Gujarat is anything but encouraging. This is mainly due to the domination of non-Adivasi members under the influence of local bureaucracy. According to the study, non-tribal leadership has been very strong in tribal regions. They work as middleman/agents for the development schemes. They have established a strong network with local bureaucracy and influence the decision-making process in their favour by negating the tribal leadership at the grassroots level. These findings, largely borne out by contemporary social activists and researchers, reveal a huge gap between macro-level decisions and grassroots-level social realities in the Scheduled Areas. Another setback for the poor functioning of these grassroots bodies, as found by the authors, is that the state governments have not yet given full powers to these village-level bodies as per the provisions laid down in the PESA. These deterrents posed by the government as well as non-Adivasi are the main hurdles for poor functioning of PESA in Scheduled Areas.

This volume thus covers a range of Adivasi issues under various thematic sections focusing on Adivasi exclusion and rights in the Indian context. While doing so, each chapter attempts to focus on the current state of Adivasi exclusion from the rights perspective. It has been established from the discussions in these chapters that Adivasis are excluded and adversely affected by various developmental projects which overwrite their natural and constitutional rights. Thus,

INTRODUCTION

the so-called constitutional and legislative 'rights' have been unable to ensure inclusion of Adivasis in line with other social groups. The promises made to the Adivasi people in the Indian Constitution with respect to preserving the distinctiveness of their civilisations and various subsequent policies to promote their integrity and safety should be respected and implemented in their true spirit. If the state and people fail in this, the Adivasi community, which is more than 8 per cent of the total population in India, would be pushed to further 'adverse exclusion' from their already current state of 'exclusion'.

It is believed that the discussions in the volume with reference to Adivasi exclusion and their rights would provide a platform to both policymakers and civil society for dialogue and intervention. The final purpose of such an analysis is to provide reasons and direction to policymakers to address the issues discussed in this volume. Most chapters presented in this volume identify key exclusionary practices pertaining to a range of Adivasi issues. These issues are closely connected to their rights, either constitutional or otherwise. Therefore in their discussions, each scholar while contributing to facts, has strongly pointed out that upholding the ethos of Adivasis is one of the means to address their exclusion. The distinctness of Adivasi culture and values would be a great asset in nation building, if their issues are properly connected to the larger civil society.

## References

Appasamy, Paul, S. Guhan, R. Hema, M. Majumdar, and A. Vaidyanathan. 1996. *Social Exclusion From a Welfare Rights' Perspective in India*. Research Series 106. Geneva: International Institute of Labour Studies.

Centre for Science and Environment. 2008. *Rich Lands Poor People: Is 'Sustainable' Mining Possible?* New Delhi: Centre for Science and Environment.

Chalam, K. S. 2011. *Economic Reforms and Social Exclusion: Impact of Liberalisation on Marginalised Groups in India*. New Delhi: Sage Publications.

de Haan, A. 1997. 'Poverty and Social Exclusion: A Comparison of Debates', *PRUS Working Papers 2*, Poverty Research Unit. Sussex: University of Sussex.

Guha, Ramachandra. 2011. 'Lost in the Woods', *Hindustan Times*, 14 August. www.hindustantimes.com/StoryPage/Print/733328.aspx (accessed on 24 August 2011).

*The Hindu*. 2012a. 'Forest Officials Destroy Huts of Migrant Adivasis', Hyderabad, 29 March.

*The Hindu*. 2012b. 'Two Tribal Youths Injured in "Crossfire"', Hyderabad, 17 March.

IANS. 2016. *PM Narendra Modi Launches 'Stand UpIndia' Initiative to Empower Women Entrepreneurs*, 6 April. www.bgr.in/news/pm-narendra-modi-launches-stand-up-india-initiative-to-empower-women-entrepreneurs/ (accessed on 25 August 2016).
Jodhka, S. S. 2015. *Caste in Contemporary India*. New Delhi: Routledge.
Mittal, Deepesh. 2010. *Human Rights Violation*. Pune: Bharati Vidyapeeth University, 9 November. www.legalindia.com/human-rights-violation/ (accessed on 12 December 2015).
Nathan, Dev and Virginius Xaxa. 2012. *Social Exclusion and Adverse Inclusion: Development and Deprivation of Adivasis in India*. New Delhi: Oxford University Press.
Nayak, Pulin. 2012. *Economic Development and Social Exclusion in India*. New Delhi: Critical Quest.
*Prime Minister's Address on 4 November 2009 in Chief Ministers' Conference on Implementation of the Forest Rights Act*. http://pib.nic.in/newsite/erelease.aspx?relid=53809 (accessed on 10 March 2012).
Room, Graham. 1990. *'New Poverty' in the European Community*. London: St. Martin's.
Roul, Kamalakanta. 2015. 'Foster Culture of Respect', *Orissa Post*, Saturday, 12 December: 8. www.orissapost.com/epaper/121215/p8.htm (accessed on 15 December 2015).
Sharma, B. D. 2010. *Unbroken History of Broken Promises: Indian State and Tribal People*. New Delhi: Freedom Press.
Sharma, B. D. 2012. 'Rights of Tribals at the Core of Maoist Conflict', *The Hindu*, Correspondent Mohammad Ali, 6 May.
Silver, Hilary. 1994. 'Social Exclusion and Social Solidarity: Three Paradigms', *Discussion Paper No. 69*. Geneva: International Institute for Labour Studies. http://staging.ilo.org/public/libdoc/ilo/1994/94B09_187_engl.pdf (accessed on 22 December 2015).
Teltumbde, A. 2017. *Dalits: Past, Present and Future*. New Delhi: Routledge. (Forthcoming).
Thorat, S. and P. Attewell. 2007. 'The Legacy of Social Exclusion: A Correspondence Study of Job Discrimination in India', *Economic and Political Weekly*, 42(41): 4141–5.
Thorat, S. and N. S. Sabharwal. 2010. 'Caste and Social Exclusion: Issues Related to Concept, Indicators and Measurement', *Working Paper Series*, 2(1). New Delhi: Indian Institute of Dalit Studies and UNICEF. www.dalitstudies.org.in/images/stories/Unicef_IIDS_Working_Paper_Volume_2_No1.pdf (accessed on 8 October 2016).
United Nations. 1949. *United Nations Universal Declaration of Human Rights 1948*. http://watchlist.org/wordpress/wp-content/uploads/Universal-declaration-of-human-rights.pdf (accessed on 10 December 2015).
The World Bank. 2011. *Poverty and Social Exclusion in India*. New Delhi: Oxford University Press.

# Part I

# DICHOTOMY OF RIGHTS AND EXCLUSION
## Adivasis in-between

# 1
# ISOLATION, INCLUSION AND EXCLUSION
## The case of Adivasis in India

*Virginius Xaxa*

The idea of social exclusion and inclusion stems from a value premise that every member of a group or society be treated as equal or as having full membership of a group or society in reference. Outside of this value, a group or society cannot be problematised in the framework of social exclusion and inclusion. Underlying the idea of social exclusion and inclusion then lies the idea of citizenship, which is the status of equality though status has invariably been associated with the idea of inequality (Béteille 1996). Social exclusion means denial to or deprivation from things valued in the society. It is denial to the full membership of the society.

Things valued in society and from which certain groups are denied or excluded fall broadly into three distinct categories. These are wealth/income, power and status. In a sense then social exclusion is rooted in social inequality, which can broadly be discerned in four forms, that is, class, caste, race/ethnicity and gender. At times, religion too assumes the form of social exclusion. In India the major form of social exclusion has been identified as caste, tribe/ethnicity and religion.

Social exclusion has been a pervasive feature of societies historically. This is so with all class-ridden society. Marx's classification of the type of societies points to this in the strongest manner possible. Indian society is no exception. And yet social exclusion for a long stretch of history was not seen as a problem. This is not to say that there was no challenge to it. There have been resistance, movements and revolution against this. However, hierarchy, inequality continued to remain the dominant values of society.

Since the 18th century, such an ideology and system began to be questioned. There was replacement of the value of hierarchy and inequality with the value of equality, freedom and justice. However, such a value in itself may not present the phenomenon of social exclusion and inclusion as problematic until that value becomes the dominant value or ideology in the society. Indeed, for a long stretch of history of humankind, the value that has been dominant in society has been the value or ideology of inequality. There was then harmony between the dominant ideology viz. that of inequality and the existing social structure. It is with the idea or ideology of equality assuming dominance in society characterised by inequality and hierarchy that brought to the surface the phenomena of social exclusion and inclusion in society.

Such a perspective emerged for the first time in Europe. This came due to the ascendancy of the ideology of freedom and equality in place of constraint to freedom and equality. The shift also led to a new notion of justice. The emergence of such an ideology in Europe as the organising principle of society spread to other parts of the world as well and India has been no exception to this. Such ideology as an organising principle of society did catch the attention of the educated elite and nationalist leadership. The British did introduce certain measures, legal, administrative and even economic, which to a limited extent broke the constraint to freedom and equality inherent in the traditional social structure. Of these the most important were legal measures that subjected the people irrespective of their caste and creed to the same law – civil and criminal, which was not the case in the traditional social context. Administration as well as new employments brought about during the British rule was theoretically open to all segments of the population unlike what was in practice in the traditional society. The post-Independence India took this matter even further. The provisions made in the Indian Constitution bear testimony to it. To begin with, all irrespective of caste, class, creed and race, were brought under the same law. They were conferred the status of citizenship, which entitled them to civil, political and social rights.

## Historicising social inclusion and exclusion in the context of tribes in India

The critical idea underlying the concept of social exclusion has further been explored and expanded and today it has assumed a place of critical significance in social science literature. Though the concept has mainly been deployed to examine the existing social structure, the concept has also been used to examine the society in reference historically. Needless to say that much of social inequality and social exclusion that characterised the society at its present stage is in fact a product of historical processes. Now, if we take Indian society as reference and explore it historically in terms of the concept of social exclusion, tribes would not have space for analysis for much of the historical past, as they were outside of what has generally been considered as constitutive of Indian society. Hence it is important to historicise the process which makes it possible to examine tribes as a part of the structure of Indian society.

It was under the British rule that tribes were drawn into the structure of the larger Indian society. To begin with, the British rule brought tribes and non-tribes under one single political and administrative authority. With some exceptions here and there, they were subjected to the same laws, rules, regulations and administrations. The same was the case in the economic sphere. Through land, labour, credit and commodity market, they were all brought under a single economic order. Tribes thus came to be part of the same political and economic system that the larger Indian society was. However, the position the tribes came to occupy in the new politico-administrative system was one characterised by steady erosion of their control and access to land, forest and other resources. In this, both the colonial administration and the non-tribal population, especially traders, merchants and moneylenders, were responsible. Tribes have thus to go through the process of twin colonialism, one of the British rule and administration and the other of the non-tribal population. Tribes who had control over land, forest and other resources and enjoyed autonomy of governance got pushed to the margin of the new political and economic system. There was thus the process of integration/inclusion of tribes into the larger system under colonial rule but a process of inclusion that came to be intertwined with the process of exclusion in the form of loss of access and control over livelihood (economic rights) as well as control over decision-making processes in determination of their own life.

The loss of land in the form of alienation of land from tribes to non-tribes that began under the colonial rule got accelerated with the consolidation of the British rule on the one hand and extension of roads, railways, trade and commerce that facilitated the movement of the population from the plains to the tribal areas in search of new avenues of livelihood, income and profit. The tribal land moved from tribes to non-tribes mainly through usury and indebtedness. Force and fraud, however, were not altogether absent. These processes led to social differentiation in the tribal society in the form of the emergence and rise of landlessness, bonded labour and dwindling size of farm holding. The process of proletarianisation brought about by exogenous processes transformed the remaining landholders into what in the literature is termed as the middle class, a phenomenon that came by default.

While on the one hand tribal society was marked by an unprecedented process of dispossession, no steps whatsoever were taken to train and equip them for new avenues of employment, howsoever limited they may be, which were emerging under colonial rule. The colonial administration needed manpower to man the expanding colonial administration in tribal areas but no steps were taken to fill them with tribal people. In fact, modern education critical to man the administration was not even given thought to in tribal areas. These were left to the Christian missionaries. At best they gave some grants to the missionaries for spreading education among the tribal population. And so was case with modern health institutions. Neither did they take any initiative to augment agricultural production in the form of extension of modern systems of agricultural practice. Rather, even the access they had over the various life-support systems such as the forest and rivers that provided a part of their daily sustenance came to be denied to them.

Tribes as part of the structure of Indian society were more of an economic and political entity rather than a social and cultural one. As a social and cultural entity, they remained outside of the larger Indian society. Due to increasing contact and interaction with the non-tribal population because of the extension of roads and railways, growth of trade and commerce, expansion of the administrative structure, all of which attracted a non-tribal population in tribal areas, there was of course an influence of the larger Indian society leading to some degree of acculturation in the form of Sanskritisation among them. Despite that, socially and culturally, they remained independent of the structure of the larger Indian society. Some among them integrated themselves socially and culturally with the structure of the larger society, and thereby moved in the direction of becoming caste rather than remaining tribes. Hence at the dawn of Independence, although integrated economically and politically with the larger Indian society, socially and culturally, they remained outside of it. They spoke languages other than the languages spoken by the dominant linguistic communities that inhabited the different parts of India, were outside of the structure of caste that permeated these linguistic communities and represented a social and a cultural form that were markedly different from those of the dominant linguistic communities. Dominant linguistic communities comprised many castes and were characterised by division along caste lines, but they represented cohesiveness and solidarity as a distinct linguistic, religious and cultural identity. They treated tribes as different and outside of their collective self. The division between the dominant linguistic community (whose defining feature was caste) and tribe had come to be well entrenched and became the basis not only of domination and exploitation but also of discrimination in the post-Independence nation building.

In short, what marked tribal society at the dawn of Independence was rampant dispossession from their land, forest and other life-support systems by the colonial state as well as the larger population. Whereas the colonial state laid the legal and administrative structure for the process of dispossession, the non-tribal population took advantage of the structure in dispossessing tribes from their land. Much of the deprivation that characterised tribal society at the eve of Independence was brought about by the active role of the state and its collaborators who happened to be the larger Indian population. At the same time, new avenues that were opened up by the forces of modernisation that the colonial state initiated were systematically kept outside the purview of the tribal society. These were the twin problems that marked the tribal society at Independence, which the Indian state aimed to address in the post-Independence era.

## State agenda of building an inclusive society

As a part of the process to address the problem referred above and thereby build an inclusive society, many provisions were made for the tribal people in the Indian Constitution. To begin with, tribals were given the same rights and status as those accorded to members of the larger Indian society in the form of the right of citizenship. Citizenship is a status which entitles an individual to full membership of a community. It confers on individuals an array of rights and obligations. The citizenship rights in the words of Marshall comprise three components, that is, civil, political and social rights. Civil rights are composed of rights necessary for individual freedom. Political rights mean rights to participate in the exercise of political power. Social rights mean rights to a modicum of economic welfare and security to the right to participate fully in the social heritage, which means the right to live a life of a civilised being according to the standard prevailing in the society (Marshall 1977: 78–91).

In addition to rights as citizens, tribals along with Dalits were also given certain special rights, which the other citizens were not entitled to. The special rights granted to them was meant to compensate for the disability they suffered for centuries either due to systemic discrimination (in the case of the Dalits) or historical exploitation and isolation (in the case of tribes) and thereby ensure their effective enjoyment of citizenship rights enshrined in the Constitution. The special rights so enshrined in the Constitution come closer to what may be termed in social science literature as social rights. The special rights meant for the tribals have been of various kinds. There have been rights which were protective in the sense that they aimed at safeguarding and protecting the interest of the tribal people. Then there were rights which aimed at providing them a certain share of participation in state institutions. Towards fulfilment of these rights a certain percentage of seats were reserved for them in state institutions such as parliament/state legislatures, governments and institutions of higher learning. The rights so provided in the Constitution are more popularly known or described as the reservation facilities. Finally there are provisions in the Constitution which aim to uplift the tribal people from their existing social backwardness and underdevelopment. The special treatment given to a certain category of people in order to protect their welfare and interest and promote their development may be broadly termed as the affirmative action programme in India.

## Affirmative action programmes

Affirmative action programmes are interventions that aim primarily to address the issues faced by disadvantaged groups. Possible interventions according to Myron Weiner are broadly of four types. One is a wide range of policies, which aim to reverse social inequality but which are racially/ethnically neutral. The second concerns policies directed at eliminating barriers to entry to jobs, universities etc. by ending legal and official barriers. The third type of intervention is one which aims to improve the quality of the pool (creating abilities) from which individuals are recruited. Reservation or quota fixation for the disadvantaged is the other possible intervention (Weiner 1983).

All of these possible interventions in different measures have been at work in the context of India. However, what has received wide attention and generated public debate is the reservation. The debate on reservation has not so much been on the political reservation but on the reservation in government employment and admission to institutions of higher learning, especially medical and technological institutions. Reservation in employment and educational institutions has been at work for about 50 years. Tribes have no doubt taken advantage of these provisions. This is evident from the fact that they are now found at all levels of government service. It is a different story that in terms of their share or quota, the position is far from adequate, especially at the upper echelon of government service. In fact, even by 1999 the share of the tribes in Classes I and II central government services, for example, stood at a mere 3.39 and 3.35 per cent respectively. Even in the case of Class III (6.07 per cent) and IV (7 per cent) services, the percentage fell short of the stipulated 7.5 per cent. What is important to note here is that the tribals are yet to approximate the quota stipulated for them. The scenario is the same in the sphere of higher educational institutions as well. It is to be noted that the concern and urgency to fill in the stipulated quota is much stronger at the central government services. The same concern and urgency in general is lacking at the state levels. Unfortunately, data at state levels are not easily forthcoming.

The debate in India on reservation has been so intense that the attention to other forms of affirmative policies/interventions pursued by the Indian State has been completely glossed over both by the critics as well as protagonists of the reservation. Critics have always been arguing that rather than pursuing the system of reservation, the state must target at capacity and capability building of the disadvantaged section of the population such as the scheduled caste and scheduled tribe. Indeed, in the argument against reservation, reference to these is again and again made in the debate on the reservation policy. Those opposed to the reservation policy do not altogether rule out the affirmative policy that is aimed at enabling the disadvantaged to acquire the required skills and abilities. Needless to say, the filling in of quotas in job and educational institutions is itself contingent upon acquiring certain qualifications and skills for which special programmes for the disadvantaged do exist. Some of these programmes are provisions of scholarship, book grants, hostel facilities, remedial classes in addition to a host of other facilities. Yet no serious attempt has been made to understand the way these measures have worked and the difference/impact they have made on the disadvantaged. Now the question is, how effective and adequate have these affirmative action programmes been?

In addition to the above, there have been other forms of affirmative action programmes. These programmes are geared towards improving the economic and social condition of the tribal people. The assumption was that the improvement in their economic and social well-being would help them to take advantage of the benefits extended for them by the state. To this end, special considerations were made for the welfare and development of the tribal people and special allocation of resources were set aside in the plan outlay. As a first step to developmental initiatives, special multipurpose development projects as supplements to the community development projects were introduced in the tribal areas. It is to be noted that the general development programmes in the case of tribes were so designed as to adequately address their special needs and that special provisions were used for securing their additional and more intensified development. Accordingly, the community development programme approach – the general approach to development in India – was reoriented keeping in mind the special problems of the tribal people. This approach continued till the fourth five-year plan. Since the approach failed to serve the interests of the tribal people, a new approach in the form of a tribal subplan was adopted in the fifth five-year plan, which continues till this day.

The fifth plan is taken as a landmark in the task of tribal development. Not only did it mark a shift in policy perspective from welfare to development, but it also introduced a new concept of the tribal subplan and integrated tribal development projects. The plan entailed a separate budgetary head for the purpose. The immediate objective of this strategy was to eliminate the forms of exploitation that existed in the tribal areas and accelerate the process of development. The tribal subplan thus primarily focused on area development with the goal of improving the quality of life of the tribal communities. Its main components were the Integrated Tribal Development Project (ITDP), Modified Area Development Approach (MADA) and pockets and primitive tribal group projects. Over 74 primitive tribes were identified who required special care for their development both at the level of planning and of implementation.

Under the broad strategy of the tribal subplan a number of schemes have been introduced from time to time with a view to uplift the condition of the tribal people. Broadly the schemes fall under two categories – economic and social. Social development has been pursued along two lines – education and health which take up the issue of women and children as well. For promotion of education, in addition to introduction of schools of various levels, various schemes have been worked out to give a boost to education among tribal children. Some of the key schemes have been residential schools, vocational education, scholarships, book grants, free uniforms, mid-day meals etc. In the sphere of health, emphasis has been placed on extending and improving health infrastructure such as PHC, CHC etc. as well as prevention and control of communicable and non-communicable diseases. Many of the schemes under health and education exclusively deal with women and children issues. In the case of economic development, the issues taken up include mainly activities such as employment and income generation, credit and market support mechanisms, skill and vocational training etc. Under such activities, important schemes have been Integrated Tribal Development Projects (ITDP), Employment Guarantee Scheme (EGS), Food for Work Programme (FWP), National Rural Employment Programme (NREP), Rural Landless Employment Guarantee Programme (RLEGP), Employment Assurance Scheme (EAS), Jawahar Rojgar Yojna (JRY), Sampurna Gramin Rojgar Yojna (SGRY) and Swanjayanti Gram Swayrojgar Yojna (SGSY). National Rural Employment Guarantee Scheme is latest addition to address the problem of employment and poverty in rural areas including tribal areas. All such programmes constituted affirmative action programmes for the tribal people.

The development schemes under the TSP have been at work for about 36 years by now. Yet the results are still very depressing. The percentage of tribal cultivators has steadily been in decline. It decreased from 68.15 in 1961 to 54.5 in 1991. Conversely the percentage of agricultural labourers has increased from 19.71 in 1961 to 32.69 in 1991. An equally important point to be noted is that as large as 42.9 per cent of the operational holding of the tribes belong to a category of marginal farmers, which means that they hold less than 1 hectare. Another 24.1 per cent are small cultivators with a holding of 1 to 2 hectares. Only 2.2 per cent of households have holdings of more than 10 hectares. Such a scenario has far-reaching consequences for the livelihood of the tribal population.

In 1993–94, the proportion of the tribal population falling below the poverty line was 51.14 per cent, as compared with 35.97 per cent for the country as whole. By 2004–05 the share of the tribal population living below the poverty line had declined to 46.5 per cent, as compared with 27.6 per cent for the population as a whole (Mathur 2008). Thus, although there has been a decline, the level of poverty in the tribal population is still much higher than the national average and the gap between the two continues to be one of the major issues of concern in poverty discourse in India. The same is the case in regard to other indicators of social development such as education and health.

In 1991 the literacy rate of the scheduled tribes was 29.60 per cent as compared to 57.69 per cent for the general population. The gap between the two was as high as 28.09 per cent. By 2001 the literacy rate for the general population had jumped to 68.81 per cent as compared to 47.10 per cent for the tribal population. The gap between the two has been somewhat bridged but the difference of 21.71 per cent is still very large Government of India 2007). The picture is no different in respect of health of the tribal population. The infant mortality as per NHP-2002 was 84.2 per cent as compared to 67.6 per cent for the total population, child mortality was 46.3 per cent as compared to 29.3 per cent and under age five mortality as high as 126.6 per cent as compared to 94.9 for the total population. The percentage of institutional deliveries was a mere 17.1 per cent in the case of tribes as compared to 33.6 per cent for the total population. As for ANC check-up, the figure was 56.5 per cent for the tribal population, the same being 65.4 per cent in the case of the total population (ibid.).

A number of factors seem to account for this shoddy state of affairs. Firstly, the resources earmarked for tribal development, though having undergone an increase, had been far from adequate. At no point in time did the plan allocation go beyond 3.7 per cent. The only exception was the eighth plan period when the allocation was the highest at 5.2 per cent of the total outlay. It is important to note that plan allocation under Tribal Plan is meant for area and not for tribes per se. Hence the benefit of such allocation accrues to everyone living in the region and not to the tribal population alone. That means that actual allocation meant directly for the tribal people is far short of what is stipulated in the plan allocation. Given the inadequate funds earmarked for tribal development, could anything tangible be expected in tribal communities? In fact, in the first four five-year plan periods, the allocation was just around 1 per cent of the total plan outlays. That explains partly why the lack of infrastructure such as schools and health centres as well as personnel to staff them are so inadequate in tribal regions. The ineffective implementation of the programmes is seen as another line of argument by which the issue of social development among tribals is explained. In this discourse, the thrust of the solution lies in accelerated and effective implementation of state-sponsored development programmes and schemes, whether these pertain to livelihood/ income-generation activities or education or health or communication facilities. The third set of argument is built around traditional sociocultural aspects of tribal life. That is, if tribals suffer from low income and poor educational and health status as well as various kinds of diseases, these are often attributed to their tradition and style of life. A way out to this problem is discussed in terms of adoption of new ideas, knowledge and values. This is the modernisation perspective, which has been in currency the world over in discussions of modernisation of traditional societies. This is an argument which is applicable for the whole of Indian society. However, this has been sharply problematised in the context of the tribal society as if the rest of the Indian society has already become modernised. While there is some relationship between the lack of development and traditional social structure and culture, this aspects needs to be further probed and carefully examined.

There is no denying the truth that certain aspects of traditional social structure and culture do constrain the development programme, but it is equally pertinent to ask why, even after over 60 years of national reconstruction processes, there is still a large tribal population which has not been connected with social infrastructure or why there is still poor implementation programmes or delivery mechanisms in tribal areas. This is a question which needs to be problematised and explained. Much of the answer to this lies in the relation between tribes and the larger society, especially in the regional context. The larger society has always viewed tribes as those who are alien to their society and hence there is an overall indifference towards their cause and development. Rather the relation between the two historically and even today is one of appropriation of resources of the tribal community by the larger society. The state administration too is not untouched by such an attitude and that explains why there is a problem of implementation as well as a failure of extending programmes in tribal areas.

More important than the failure to push development programmes in tribal areas due to inadequate resources or ineffective implementation or even tribal tradition and social structure is the larger question of national and regional development, which is tied with the interests of the larger regional and linguistic communities. The national and regional development has invariably been in the form of large-scale development projects such as dams, irrigation, power plants, roads, railways, industry and mineral exploitation. The latter invariably took the form of appropriation of tribal land, forest and other resources that had begun under colonial rule and has continued in the post-Independence era, except that in the post-Independence era this has gone under the garb of national and regional development. The benefits of this development, which Jawaharlal Nehru, the country's first prime minister, described as the temples of modern India, did not accrue to the tribal people. These were interventions detrimental to the interest of the tribal people and in the process affected their access to affirmative action programmes. After all, through no fault of their own, they were steadily being taken away from their control over and access to land, forest and other resources due to state-sponsored projects of national development on one side and alienation of land from tribes to non-tribes on the other. Between 1951 and 1990, a little over 21 million are estimated to have been displaced by development projects (dams, mines, industries and wildlife sanctuaries) in India. Of the total displaced population, over 16 million have been displaced by dams, about 2.6 and 1.3 million by mines and industries respectively. A little over 1 million has been displaced by other projects, wildlife sanctuaries being the most important among them. Of the total displaced, as large as 8.54 million have been enumerated as the tribals. Tribals have thus come to constitute as large as 40 per cent of the displaced population, though they constitute less than 8 per cent of the total population. Their share in the displacement from projects such as mines, wildlife sanctuaries and dams has been to the tune of over 52, 75 and 38 per cent respectively. It is only in respect of industrial and other unspecified projects that the size of their share does not exceed 25 per cent. And yet even here the proportion is much higher than the proportion of their population to the total population of the country. Of over 21 million displaced, only 5.4 million have been resettled, out of which 2.12 million are stated to be tribals. This means that only about 24.8 per cent of displaced tribals had been rehabilitated. For a very large chunk of the population, rehabilitation still remains an elusive phenomenon. Further, land alienation from tribes to non-tribes, an endemic phenomenon for centuries, continues on a wide scale even to this day.

Even more paradoxical has been that the benefits of such developments have hardly accrued to the people who have made possible these projects by their sacrifice. In Jharkhand by 1996, for example, 8 major and 55 medium hydraulic projects along with many more minor projects had come up. Needless to say, these had displaced a large number of households. Yet the area under irrigation in Jharkhand constituted only 7.68 per cent of the net sown area and households electrified was mere 9.04 per cent. As many as 201 large- and medium-scale industries have come up in Jharkhand, displacing a large number of families on the one hand and providing employment to thousands of people on the other. Yet the benefits of these did not go to tribal people of Jharkhand or to the displaced tribals. This can be vividly illustrated by citing the case of coal mine industries. Between 1981 and

1985, the industry had displaced 32,750 families but had provided jobs to only 11,901 heads of households. The gravity of this situation is compounded by the fact that the displaced until very recent years were hardly thought of in terms of rehabilitation. They were summarily dismissed by cash compensation. Yet even here the state has been found faltering in its responsibility. It was found out in 1988 that after 30 years of filling in of Hirakund reservoir, the compensation amounting to 15 crore rupees was due for payment to 9,913 claimants who had lost their land. In the case of the Machkund Hydroelectric project, even when they have been rehabilitated, benefits of the project in general had hardly accrued to the displaced. In terms of irrigation, electric power, tourism, pisciculture and other schemes for economic development, the government, for example, justified the Upper Kolab project. However, the rehabilitated displaced had none of these benefits. In the process of the development of these projects, a large number of tribal people have been displaced from their land and other sources of livelihood. Neither have they been given adequate compensation nor have they been provided proper rehabilitation.

An equally important aspect that adversely affected the tribal population was the policy that restricted the access to forest resources. Tribes were greatly dependent on the forest for their food, shelter, instruments, medicine and even clothing in some cases. As long as tribes were in control of the forest in the sense of unrestricted use of the forest and its produce, they had no difficulty meeting these needs. The entry of the British, however, drastically altered this relationship. To the British the forest was an important source of revenue and commercial exploitation. Hence the forest policy that was enunciated by the British introduced state control over forest resources and imposed curtailment of rights and privileges over the forest resources. The policy pursued by the British was continued in the post-Independence era of economic development with even stricter regulation and enforcement. All these were justified on the ground that these were necessary for the wider and national public interest. However, this had and still has serious consequences on access to basic necessities of life such as food, shelter etc. for the tribals. Not only that, but forest law also turned them into encroachers under constant threat of eviction and violence.

The large-scale development projects and policy of denial of access to forest resources were interventions of greater magnitude and scale than reservation and other affirmative action programmes developed for the welfare of the tribal people. Such intervention offset all that was desired to be achieved by affirmative action programmes. The latter, the state has displayed as a post-Independence sign of tribal development. In close introspection, however, affirmative action in the case of tribes tends to be no longer affirmative action, as it does not tend to lift them from the given social base in which they were traditionally located. Rather, affirmative action has been pushed through alongside the larger processes of development that kept on uprooting tribes from their economic and social base, thereby further deteriorating their existing social and economic condition and exposing them to even greater vulnerability than before. Hence, there is nothing affirmative about affirmative action programmes in the case of tribes in India. Rather, there has been a term of trade or exchange between state and tribes, a term of trade that has been exploitative of tribes. The state has gained much more out of this trade than it has given to tribes.

This being the dominant pattern of development in the case of tribes, those in northeast India in post-Independence India, and if we are to place it in the frame of social exclusion and inclusion, then the concept/category that captures this reality best is not that of 'tribe' but of 'Adivasi', the indigenous peoples. Tribe as a concept/category points to difference, not only in regard to language and culture but more importantly the state of development, but it does not capture the relations producing social exclusion. In contrast, Adivasi as a concept/category does. It is a concept rooted in features of exploitation, domination and discrimination and this is the framework that captures better the state of tribal development in India.

# References

Béteille, Andre. 1996. 'The Mismatch Between Class and Status', *The British Journal of Sociology*, 47(3).
Government of India. 2007. *Report of the Working Group on Empowerment the Scheduled Tribes for the Eleventh Five Year Plan (2007–2012)*. New Delhi: Ministry of Tribal Affairs.
Marshall, Thomas Humphrey. 1977. *Class, Citizenship and Social Development*. Chicago: University of Chicago Press.
Mathur, Ashok. 2008. 'An Overview of the Jharkhand Economy and Perspectives for Human Development', Background paper read at the *National Seminar onGrowth and Human Development in Jharkhand: Perspectives and Policies*, 4–5 July, Ranchi, India.
Weiner, Myron. 1983. 'The Political Consequences of Preferential Policies: A Comparative Perspective', *Comparative Politics*, 16(1): 35–52.

# 2

# IN BETWEEN INCLUSION AND EXCLUSION

The changing face of health and disease management practices among Gonds in a central Indian village

*S.N. Chaudhary*

In order to understand health and disease, from the historical perspective, especially among tribes, scholars have heavily relied on subjective interpretation across the world. Clement (1932) documented five fundamental reasons of disease as perceived by primitive people. These are sorcery, breach of taboo, object intrusion, spirit intrusion and soul loss. Most of these reasons are related to spirit or what may be called 'ghost'. Hence, primitive people in particular, living across the globe, have faith in ghost and its ugly face. Under subjective interpretation experience-based narratives and opinions of people have been elaborated. Their views about both health and diseases differ from culture to culture and from one social group to another. In India, also subjective interpretation of health and diseases have dominated in both rural and tribal societies. There are a large number of studies on individual tribes, across the country, which disclose their fatalistic interpretation of health and disease. Kurian and Tribhuwan (1990) studied perception of the Thakur tribe of Raigad district of Maharashtra. They found that causes of diseases, as attributed by them, were supernatural i.e. visitation of gods and goddesses, wrath of gods and goddesses, evil eye, possession by evil spirits, witchcraft and sorcery, breach of taboo and failure to perform divine duty or rites (ibid.: 253). According to Chaudhuri (1993) among HOs of Bihar (now Jharkhand) there is the Deuri or religious headman and Deonwa or the spirit doctor. The Deuri worship the deities and if epidemics or diseases are there, they offer a sacrifice at the sacred place. They depend on benevolent deities. The Deonwa, often through magical performances, controls the malevolent spirits. According to Mathur (1982) among the Diyan tribe of Kerala the 'goddess Mariamma cause epidemic like smallpox, chickenpox, measles etc. Turmeric powder, a bundle of Neem leaves, coconut plantain and five Panams are generally given as the main offerings of Mariamma for curing the above mentioned diseases' (ibid.: 297). Among the Gonds of Baster, diseases are perceived as the legacy of god. Chaudhary (1998) observed that a number of diseases are attributed to the wrath of some deity or spirit or are believed to be due to the violation of some norms, i.e. committing adultery or incest. To cure these diseases they seek the help of Valpa who diagnoses the cause and prescribes the remedies. They indeed make some distinctions between physical injuries, the cause for which is very obvious and which are not generally attributed to the wrath of the god or spirit, and others which are attributable to the gods (ibid.: 50).

It is true that the subjective approach is largely based on perception but it has also helped in the emergence of healing mechanisms of all varieties i.e. magic, religion and science. Of course functioning of the former two dominates in the tribal societies, which is claimed to be relatively simple, forest- and mountain-ridden, geographically and socially relatively isolated from non-tribal society, but this does not mean that the latter is completely invisible among them in modern times. In all societies, even at a given point in time, more than one variety of treatments is found. And as societies move from tradition to modernity or from a relatively homogeneous to a relatively heterogeneous situation, importance and practice of science (modern medicine) gradually increases. Modern health management institutions become popular. And with this, the scope and implications of objective interpretation of health increases. Development of this variety have also taken place in the tribal world. Here today one can see a radical departure from *Jhar-Phuk* practice to the massive use of herbs and medicinal plants. According to Joseph (1989) in Madhya Pradesh and Orissa, the tribal use is 156 applications of mammals and their products, 32 of birds, 30 of reptiles, 10 of fish etc. The use of the blood and meat of pigeons is widespread in Orissa for the treatment of paralysis. Derivatives of bear, bat, tiger, wild boar, also cow's urine, goat's liver, hen's eggs, honey, snake fat, flesh of earthworms, and bones of elephants are used for various diseases. Lal (1987) attempted to know the role of herbs and medicinal plants to cure bone fractures among the tribes of Mandla, Sidhi, Raipur, Baster, Dhar, Bilaspur and

Balaghat of undivided Madhya Pradesh. To him there are 21 important medicinal plants belonging to 21 genera and 16 families which are used for the treatment of bone fractures in the case of both human beings as well as cattle. These plants are well known to the local medicine men. They are known by different names among different tribal groups throughout the state. These findings reveal that tribes have not jumped directly from the use of magico-religious prescription to modern medicine. Rather they have been simultaneously using herbs and medicinal plants for treatment. But gradually with the change in their mindset coupled with the decreasing availability of local herbs, medicinal plants and also the decreasing number of reliable medicine men and the so-called popularisation of Primary Health Centre (PHC), Community Health Centre (CHC) and other institutional interventions, tribals' dependence on traditional practices is decreasing. Media, dominant public opinion, institutional arrangements like Panchayats, Self-Help Groups, Schools and NGOs are encouraging tribals to depend on modern health institutions even at the cost of traditional practices. Needless to say, the traditional treatment system was completely local. It was constructed in the light of local social, economic and ecological conditions. It was also as per the carrying capacity of local tribes. Local culture contributed to this system. There was no difference between its practitioners and users in social and economic terms. The relationship was based on trust and reciprocity. Cash payment had no role to play. The treatment method was transmitted from generation to generation through oral tradition. The role of felt experience played a significant role in its sustenance for generations. From the tribal perspective, it was inclusive because their experience, requirements and carrying capacity played vital roles in the adoption and sustenance of treatment systems. There was no discrimination.

But gradually with the establishment of the modern nation-state, particularly after Independence, the modernisation model of development was popularised in the country. Tradition was perceived as an inhibiting factor for development. Hence, all efforts were made by the state and other stakeholders to modernise all aspects of our culture – both material and non-material in a specific direction. It was an effort to homogenise the society. In the field of health and disease management also it was perceived that traditional treatment methods are inferior and backward and modern/Western methods are superior, scientific and the latest word. Over time this thinking became dominant at the local and at the national level. And with this, the traditional system got the back seat. According to the modern interpretation of health which claims to be objective, whether a person is healthy or not is determined by the modern, qualified and degree-holding health practitioner. The bases of such determination is claimed to be scientific i.e. test of different organs and components of the body on a scientific basis. According to Lewis (1954), if the various organs work well enough not to draw attention to themselves and their owner is free from pain or discomfort, he usually supposes that he is in good health. This criterion is then a subjective one. But if he avails himself of the mass x-ray service and in consequence learns that his lungs show strong evidence of tuberculosis disease, he ceases to consider that he is in good health: the criterion now he adopts is an extraneous one viz. the assertion of a physician who relies on objective or pathological data (ibid.: 111). According to the modern interpretation, health refers to a state of complete physical, mental and social well-being. And this well-being needs to be reflected at two levels, firstly, at the society level where one can call a person healthy if he/she is able enough to perform social roles assigned to them i.e., if able to participate in the reproduction of society. Secondly from the standpoint of the individual, where he/she is normally able to maximise growth and happiness. WHO defined the concept of health as 'a state of complete physical, mental and social well-being and not merely the absence of disease and infirmity'. Modern treatment methods came with their own class bias. They are not available to poor tribes who mostly live in remote villages. Their carrying capacity is not as per the terms and conditions of the modern treatment system. State leaders promised to provide health facilities, but at the implementation level, remained insensitive and non-responsive for longer periods. Hence, tribal people were massively excluded from the new system. Tribes at large became almost like a straw man. The traditional system was no longer there to help them and the modern system was at a distant place to them. However, even under the given framework, which operates in the top-down model, thousands of tribes are today associated with the modern system. And gradually the number of tribes availing themselves of modern health facilities is increasing and it is further likely to increase. The roles of the new Panchayat system and NGOs are significant in this context. But it has made beneficiaries dependent-prone. And many of them are still excluded because of social, psychological and economic barriers. In short, from the point of view of availing themselves of modern health facilities, tribes at large are in between exclusion and inclusion. The present chapter is a case study to explain the functioning of traditional and modern health institutions from an exclusion and inclusion perspective with reference to the Gond tribe living in a central Indian village.

The chapter is divided into three parts. The opening part deals with the perception of the Gonds about different aspects of health and diseases. It also deals with common diseases in the area and tribal response to these diseases. The second part examines the role and status of both traditional and modern health practices to understand health status as well as techniques adopted to deal with health- and disease-related issues. Towards the end, some steps have been suggested to manage health and disease among tribes in an inclusive and sustainable manner.

## Methodology

The study was conducted in Pathai village of Shahpur Development Block of Betul district of Madhya Pradesh. The logic behind selecting Sahpur Block was numerical preponderance of tribal population (64 per cent). Needless to mention that the Development Block under study falls under Schedule V. In Pathai village more than 99 per cent of the population is of tribe. They are Gond. The entire area of Sahpur is dominated by the Gond population but in some villages the Korku tribe resides. Gond is the second-largest tribal population in Madhya Pradesh. Pathai is located at a distance of about 4 km from Sahpur Development Block office and Betul-Itarsi National Highways. There are 200 households in Pathai and all of them participated in the study.

Pathai village is numerically dominated by illiterates, poor and non-workers; 25 per cent of households do not have land and villagers depend on wage-work, farm work or both for their livelihood. The village is near to a forest. Historically tribes have been dependent on the forest for their requirements. Even today a significant number of tribal women collect firewood from the forest in order to meet their day-to-day requirements. But in the broader sense the forest is now no more an important source of livelihood for the villagers. Of 38 basic facilities required, only 11 are available in Pathai. These are Panchayat Office, Primary Health Centre (PHC), metal road, electricity, Anganwadi Kendra, primary and middle school, kirana shops, PDS shop, flour mill, hand pump, tubewell and Jharphunk facility.

An Interview Schedule, interview guide and case study were the three specific techniques used to collect data. Those who participated in the study were Head of the Household (usually male), Anganwadi Worker working at PHC, Traditional Medicine Men (Bhagat), private practitioners working at Sahpur and functionaries working at CHC,

Shahpur. Information was also collected from secondary sources especially from records provided by PHC, CHC and Mobile Health facility working under Deen Dayal Antyodaya Upchar Yojna. Fieldwork was carried out during 2007–09.

I

## Perception about health and disease

Perception of both villagers, doctors and other health workers working in Pathai and Sahpur was mapped to get a comprehensive and comparative picture of different aspects of health and disease. Tribes have their own perception about health and healthy persons. To them a healthy person is one who eats properly, looks pleasant, has a thin body, roams here and there, looks neat and clean, is active in day-to-day life, performs hard physical work, avoids alcohol and has a glowing face. A happy life, consumption of vegetarian food and straight posture of body are also indices of good health. Interpretation about roots of diseases in Pathai is also based on objective consideration. Fatalistic or metaphysical interpretation is today largely absent from the scene.[1] For instance, most of the diseases – both simple or complex – are perceived as due to lack of cleanliness. Here cleanliness refers to cleanliness of one's body, clothes, houses, use of pure and safe drinking water, clean cooking utensils and so on. Many villagers said that people become ill because their food habit and meal time is not properly managed. Increasing use of chemical fertiliser in agriculture also contributes to illness. Carelessness, consumption of rotten food, use of meat and regular consumption of Mahua liquor, which is very common in Pathai, and lack of proper and in-time medical check-ups on a frequent basis also contribute to illness. The role of black magic or religion was hardly rated by any respondent as a key indicator of disease and illness. Hence, all the villagers expressed objective views about indices and roots of both health and disease.[2]

According to doctors some of the common diseases found in the Sahpur area in general and Pathai village in particular (as narrated by 2 MBBS doctors who are practicing at Sahpur) are fever, vomiting and loose motion, malaria, joint-ache, cough and cold, body-ache, swelling in leg, swelling in liver, TB, chickenpox, throat infection, pile, skin disease, STD, jaundice, abortion, anaemia, habit of eating soil, snake bite, delivery related problem, fracture, teeth pain, wound, cut, itching and so on. Such diseases occur primarily because of malnourishment, lack of vitamins in food, poverty, wastage of time with Bhagat, lack of awareness about health, lack of sufficient treatment facility at Sahpur hospital, lack of de-worming scheme and so on. Tribes not only delay approaching a doctor/proper health service provider, but also there is total lack of follow-up on the part of patients.[3]

Tribals hesitate to revisit doctors even when they are advised to visit twice or thrice. As a result, the treatment remain incomplete which in many cases results in re-appearance of some of the diseases, especially malaria, in a complicated form, after a few weeks or months. It was reported that in many cases most of the patients suffering from common ailments do not complete the course of treatment as prescribed by doctors. Needless to mention that cataracts, itch, ulcer and malaria are the very common diseases in the entire district for a long time.[4]

On the basis of these interpretations it may be said that both experts and villagers have more or less similar perceptions about types of diseases as well as factors and conditions responsible for these diseases. Tribal perception about health and diseases in an objective manner clearly refers to the fact that the days of magico-religious explanation of disease and illness are now gone. This development has taken place because of numerous exogenous factors, especially due to the state-initiated health management institutions at the village and at the district level.

## II

## Treatment: then and now

Since the explanation of disease is now largely objective in nature, the history of which is not very long, and although both traditional and modern healing mechanisms are followed, the wind is now blowing in favour of modern health practices. This is clear from the following description.

## Traditional treatment

To deal with most of the diseases historically tribes of Pathai have practiced traditional medicine, which includes medicine made out of herbs and medicinal plants as practiced by local medicine men (Bhagat). Lakra (1997) conducted a study on the Khairwar tribe of Surguja district of Madhya Pradesh. According to her 99 per cent families have deep faith in traditional folk healing and generally follow traditional methods of delivery. This is partially due to their poor economic conditions and the major cause being the tribes residing far away from

PHCs in the interior areas. These parameters determine the medical facilities which the tribal people can access and thus directly affects their health status. Due to the far location of PHCs the women are unable to get PHC services during the delivery time and the untrained Dias attend them. Again the absence of modern health management institutions has also encouraged tribes to depend on traditional medicine, besides their dependence on the Jhar-Phuk technique. According to Kurup (2000) over 600 wild medicinal plants are often used for various diseases by tribal communities. Plant species like canarium evphyllum (Andamans), Paeonia obovata (Western Ghats) and Euphorbia acualis of Madhya Pradesh are found to be very effective against rheumatoid arthritis and inflammation. Similarly, adina cordifolia and andrographis paniculata collected from the forests of Madhya Pradesh are found to have remarkable hepato-protective and immunostimulant activities.

But today the wind is blowing in favour of modern medicine. Table 2.1 clearly refers to the use of treatment methods then and now.

On the basis of table 2.1 the following interpretation may be made. Barring snake bite, villagers' dependence on treatment of all types of diseases has drastically increased on doctors, hospitals and modern medicine. In the same proportion their dependence on traditional practices has significantly decreased. This refers to expansion of a modern health management system among them. But these modern practices are exterior to many of them. It has made beneficiaries dependent-prone. The traditional practices which were indigenous, cost-effective and available at any time at their doorstep are now a thing of the past. Such traditional practices might have been semi-scientific but they have a long history. Persons who carried on such practices had social acceptance and cultural legitimacy. They were insiders. But the new health management system is costly, not available at their doorstep and it contributes to psychological and cultural conflict in the life of many patients who try to adopt it. It forces them to make delays in approaching modern health practices. Poverty, lack of sufficient health facilities at the local level and apathy on the part of health workers force them to keep away from modern health services.

In the past villagers used to depend on practices like ojha and traditional medicine men. The number of these traditional practitioners has significantly decreased. And with this, treatment alternatives have also been reduced. For instance, to get rid of a fever they had eight alternative techniques in the past, but today they only follow five such techniques. About 25 years ago, the juice of Jari-buti, other herbal medicine,

Table 2.1 Treatment: then and now (multiple response)

| S. no | Disease name | Then (20–25 years ago) | | | | | Today | | | | |
|---|---|---|---|---|---|---|---|---|---|---|---|
| | | Traditional[5] | Modern[6] | Both[7] | Nothing | No response | Traditional | Modern | Both | Nothing | No response |
| 1 | Snake bite | 194 | 5 | | | | 194 | 6 | 0 | 0 | 0 |
| 2 | Fracture | 158 | 2 | | | | 0 | 157 | 38 | | 5 |
| 3 | Stomach problem | 167 | 10 | | | 47 | 90 | 92 | 19 | | 1 |
| 4 | Headache/body ache | 160 | 10 | | | 22 | 31 | 149 | 20 | | |
| 5 | Children's illness | 249 | 16 | | | 36 | 10 | 190 | | | |
| 6 | Delivery | 182 | 14 | | 96 | 32 | 41 | 179 | | 9 | |
| 7 | Teeth formation | 158 | | | 49 | | 23 | 151 | | 26 | |
| 8 | Teeth pain | 317 | | | 40 | | 19 | 176 | | | |
| 9 | Dehydration/Vomiting | 149 | 9 | | 28 | | | 179 | 5 | 14 | |
| 10 | Feet | 156 | 17 | | 30 | | 26 | 169 | | 6 | |
| 11 | Fatigue | 149 | 15 | | 46 | | 81 | 98 | | 31 | |
| 12 | Fever | 144 | 11 | | 25 | | 15 | 187 | | | |
| 13 | Sleeplessness | 97 | 45 | | 101 | | 32 | 94 | | 76 | |
| 14 | Wound | 163 | 6 | | 17 | | 12 | 188 | | 6 | |
| 15 | Cut | 176 | 21 | | 13 | | 5 | 181 | 10 | 7 | |
| 16 | Itching | 164 | 11 | | 21 | | 20 | 180 | | 7 | |

Source: Based on the narratives of the villagers.

help of Bhagat, patti of cold water on forehead, rest, consumption of Mahua liquor, consumption of kutki and Samma daliya, the help of a doctor/hospital was taken. Significant numbers of respondents were not using any method with the assumption that the ailment will disappear automatically. But today a maximum number of them (187) take the help of the doctor/hospital. They do not leave diseases unattended. Those who used to take rest, use Mahua liquor, take the help of Bhagat and body massage of coconut oil etc.; their number have decreased today. Also, to control dehydration and vomiting they used to depend on eight techniques but today they depend on only three techniques. Hence, with the passage of time, the degree and amount of villagers' dependence on modern health management practices have increased and the number of alternatives of treatment has significantly decreased.

The number of patients who could not access any type of treatment during sickness in the past has decreased significantly. For instance, in the case of sleeplessness 101 persons did not seek any treatment about 20–25 years ago but today the number of non-treatment seekers for this disease has decreased to 76. Similarly, in the case of dehydration and vomiting, 28 respondents could not access any treatment about 20–25 years ago, but the number of patients suffering from such diseases has also decreased today to 14. This trend shows increasing amounts of awareness among tribes regarding health and disease as well as their inclination in favour of modern health management practices being run especially by PHC and CHC at the local level. Treatment methods adopted in the case of some of the diseases today as presented below support this explanation.

1   Prenatal Death – During 2007 harvesting of soybean crop was in progress. A pregnant Gond woman of 24 years of age was also engaged in harvesting. All of a sudden she experienced labour-pain. She immediately rushed to Sahpur Community Health Centre for safe delivery. In the course of treatment the doctor found it a critical case and it was immediately referred to the government hospital in Betul. Betul is about 30 km away from Sahpur. For want of money the patient could not go to Betul hospital. The next day, after managing money, she went to Betul District hospital. In the course of treatment at Betul, it was found that the expected infant was dead. Therefore, it was aborted. Needless to mention that in this case the patient was not dependent at all on Bhagat. But she was too late to approach the hospital. Her total

dependence was on a trained doctor but due to delay in treatment she had to suffer. Had she accessed a proper medical facility in time especially at Sahpur CHC, the life of the expected infant might have been saved.

2. Skin Disease – Asam Uikey is a five-year-old boy. During 2007 he had wounds and itching on different parts of the body. He was suffering from pain and body-ache. Initially his parents approached the village Bhagat and followed Jharphuk technique but there was no relief. After a few days the local medicine men asked him to take a bath with neem leaf juice mixed with water. This method was followed for several days but this technique also could not extend any relief to the patient. Subsequently the patient approached Sahpur CHC. At CHC proper treatment was provided. But this effort also could not succeed. Even today on occasions like a full moon night and a full dark night, there is itching on such wounds and by itching, these wounds become alive. The family does not have faith in Bhagat at all. To date the family has spent about Rs. 500/- on treatment.

3. Pneumonia – Shubhan is a four-year-old boy. About one and half years ago the upper part of his backbone was not functioning well. His parents are wage-earners. Initially his parents approached Bhagat Shankar Lal Dhurve. Dhurve adopted Jharphuk technique and massaged the affected part of the body with the help of egg liquid. But such efforts did not succeed. Subsequently the patient visited Shahpur CHC, where a blood test was made. But the parents felt that the treatment was not proper and therefore, they approached a private doctor at Bhawra. Here proper treatment was made for a continuous 10 days. The parents had to spend about Rs. 1,500/- which they had earned from wage-work. Now the patient is free from this disease.

4. TB – Genda Lal Dhurve, 70 years old, was suffering from TB for the last 15 years. Initially he sought treatment from the government hospital and he felt relief. He thought that he was free from TB and therefore, he discontinued treatment. But in the real sense he was not free from TB. After a few months, TB reappeared. Instead of approaching the doctor he consulted Bhagat for treatment. Bhagat treated him in his own way, locally known as Dana Uthana in which grains of rice or wheat are taken from the patient's family and by uttering mantras it is thrown. It is thrown with the assumption that with this the disease will also disappear. But at the same time, on an infrequent basis, he also continued

treatment in the government hospital. Since the treatment was infrequent and he continued taking inferior quality food for want of money and therefore, even after spending about Rs. 10,000/- he could not survive and ultimately he died in 2007.

5   Accident – Ravindra Dhurve was 45 years old, when he met with a road accident in 1998. He is in a government job. He also owns cultivatable land. His monthly salary is around Rs. 5,000/-. He has two wives. From the first wife, he has one daughter and currently she is living with her daughter at her maternal place after the separation. Ravindra is living with his second wife and two small kids. His father was serving in the Forest Department. He died during the job period. Rs. 2 lacks was paid to Ravindra's mother as a compensation. Ravindra was provided a job in forest department on compassionate ground. He purchased one new motorcycle out of the compensation amount. He was habituated to consume Mahua liquor every now and then. One day he was going to Ghoradongri town by motorcycle. He was drunk. On the way he had a serious road accident. His motorcycle was totally damaged and he had multiple fractures. He was in hospital constantly for three months. He went through a number of surgical operations. In the course of treatment he had to spend about Rs. 75,000/- from the amount of Rs. 2 lacks which he had received as a compensation. During the course of treatment his salary was paid to him but his wife was forced to work as wage-earner. She was also forced to collect and market fuel-wood to maintain the family and continue the children's study. Today he is doing his job but every now and then he suffers from pain.

On the basis of these five cases, it may be said that gradually people's inclination towards traditional health services have been replaced by modern health services provided by the state and private players. This does not mean that traditional healers have totally disappeared from the scene. A few of them are still found although they are at the stage of extinction. The following two examples support this observation.

### *Shankar Lal Dhurve*

Shankar Lal Dhurve is Gond. He is 55 years old. He belongs to a relatively well-to-do family. The family economy is primarily based on farming. He is practicing Jharphuk technique as well as herbs and medicinal plants for treatment. He has been engaged in this

*Table 2.2* Diseases and treatment

| Diseases | Treatment |
|---|---|
| Tonsils | Paste of Bhasm khand is applied on the affected part of the body several times |
| Phunsi | Paste of Bhasm khand is applied on the affected part several times |
| Cut | Paste of Neem tree kin is applied on the affected part several times |
| Jaundice | Mixed juice of Amerbel and Jangli Haldi is both consumed and applied on the body. Mustard oil is also applied on the body. Jhar Phunk technique is also followed. |
| Fever | Juice made out of Kadu jeera is consumed continuously for two to three days |
| Headache/ body ache | Massage with kerosene oil is made |
| Dehydration/ vomiting | Mixed juice of Phudina and lemon is consumed several times |

Source: Compiled from field data.

work for the last 10 years. He could not receive any formal training for this work. Rather he learnt it in day-to-day life from the villagers. Usually he treats eight types of diseases with the following techniques.

Shankar Lal said that most of the patients are affected by fever, tonsils and jaundice. They all are from Pathai itself. No fee is charged for treatment. However, once they get a cure they offer coconut, and agarbatti etc. to the Bhagat. He claims to be a follower of God Vishnu, and he observed that by using both local herbs and mantras related to Vishnu, he provides treatment to villagers. However, he said that tribals are now no longer interested to visit him. They prefer to visit doctors. If doctors are absent, if they have no money or if they are fed-up with doctors, then only they prefer to visit him.

### Bihari Batke

Bihari Batke is an 85-year-old Gond of Pathai. He hails from Gyaki Dhana. He uses both Jharphuk and Jari-buti since the age of 15 years for treatment. His father was also engaged in this work. But his father died when Bihari was a child. Today Bihari treats about 20 diseases.

As the interpretation of health and disease have become largely objective, coping mechanisms have also become by and large objective.

Table 2.3 Name of the diseases and treatment methods

| S. no | Disease | Treatment |
|---|---|---|
| 1 | Stomach problem | Paste made out of silkajhar and Jaramtadi is applied on stomach as well as halwa/tablet made out of it is consumed by patient continuously for 3 days and the patient gets cured. |
| 2 | Sukhi Bimari | Paste made out of Barahmas is applied on body as well as smoke created by burning raw barahmas is inhaled for 3 days to get relief. |
| 3 | Cough and cold | Tea made with the mixture of Phasi Jhar is consumed to get relief. |
| 4 | Asthma | Paste made out of Phasi Jhar is eaten as well as applied on body several times to get relief. |
| 5 | Jaundice | Mixture made out of Ani dhara (hathikan) and Am ras are mixed together and it is both eaten and pasted on different parts of the body. Also Jharphuk technique is used with the help of mustard oil and Dub grass. |
| 6 | Cancer | A tablet made out of leaf of Chatar goti and flower is consumed. 3 tablets are taken each day for 90 continuous days with some food-related restrictions. |
| 7 | TB | The above medicine used in the case of cancer is also used to cure TB. |
| 8 | S.T.D./piles | Root of Ramratan mixed with water is taken for 15–30 days. |
| 9 | Pneumonia | A tablet made out of Harra/root of Pulsa and root of hatikan is taken two times each day for 10 continuous days. |
| 10 | Fit | A raw mixture made out of Pudina, Tulsi, Long and peppermint is consumed 2–3 times each day for a few days to cure the disease. |
| 11 | Headache/body ache | A tablet made out of the mixture of Silka tree and part of Thingsaw is taken for few days. |
| 12 | Period disorder | A tablet made out of the mixture of Ghatharu tree and skin of Khendua Chal is consumed continuously for 8–10 days. |
| 13 | Itching | A liquid made out of Ghatharu tree mixed with coconut oil is fried for a few minutes and it is used on affected part for several days to get cure from this disease. |

| | | |
|---|---|---|
| 14 | Teeth-related problem of children | A dust made out of the mixture of root of Khara, a mango seed and skin of Kaira is mixed with milk and children are asked to drink it several times. |
| 15 | Fracture | A paste made out of Hadjor and Rajkarna fruit is used on the affected part for several days. Besides strengthening bone it also reduces swelling. |
| 16 | Snake/scorpion Bite | For scorpion bite liquid made out of leaf of Barahamas Khakara is applied on the affected part. Similarly in the case of snake bite the patient is asked to eat leaf of Bharu Cherota. |
| 17 | Fatigue | Dust made out of seed of Mudhari mixed with water is taken to get rid of fatigue. |
| 18 | Wound/cut | A paste made out of the dust of root of Raj karula and Hadjor is applied on the affected part. |
| 19 | Tooth ache | Paste made out of Tin Patiea Bela is applied on the affected part. |

Source: Compiled from field data.

Tribal dependence on modern health management institutions like PHC, Anganwadi Kendra and CHC etc. have increased during the last few years. Health-related coping mechanisms may be explained at two levels i.e. preventive and actual treatment. While the former creates an environment at the family and at the village level to take a number of precautions to escape air and water borne diseases, because these are the two major sources of diseases in the village, the latter provides treatment facility of different types. Both these steps are, however, interlinked. Under these two measures the following efforts are in progress in the studied village. Both these measures are institutional in nature. It shows increasing importance of the state in health management in tribal villages.

## Preventive measures

At the family level many of the villagers take regular baths, use soap in baths, follow modern teeth-cleaning instruments, take food in time, consume so-called clean water, wash hands after using the toilet, and most of them also do physical labour. At the village level efforts are made by Anganwadi worker to make villagers aware of the importance of environmental cleanliness and names and reasons for air and water borne diseases; villagers are also advised to take precautions in their day-to-day lives in order to escape diseases. In the recent past a number of efforts have been initiated at the village level in order to improve the health status of villagers. Important among these are the following measures.

## Total Sanitation Campaign

Total Sanitation Campaign (TSC), also known as Nirmal Gram Yojna, is an intervention for environmental upgradation. This project is directed to provide modern toilet facilities in all households. It is also directed to encourage cleanliness in the village and teach the lesson to keep cooking places and spaces clean in and around the house and the place where drinking water is kept. So far as Pathai is concerned, here during 2007–08 in more than 50 per cent of households toilet facility was provided. It was promised that this facility will be extended to other households in due course. It was assumed that villagers will use this facility and help each other in the environmental upgradation, which will subsequently keep them healthy.[8]

## Safe drinking water

There are 11 handpumps in Pathai. However, during 2006–09, 28 wells were constructed under NREGS, of which 18 are properly working today. These wells satisfy the domestic requirement of water. In the past, villagers at large used to face drinking water problems.

## Public Distribution System (PDS)

In order to address the problem of food insecurity and malnutrition there is a special provision for the poor. Blue and yellow ration cards have been issued to obtain food grain at the cheaper rate from the local PDS shop. For instance, while APL (Above Poverty Line) card holders receive wheat at the rate of 7 rupees per kg, BPL (Below Poverty Line) and most poor (Antyodaya Anna Yojana) card holders (Yellow Card) receive at the rate of only 3 rupees and 2 rupees per kg respectively. Other food grains are also provided to them at the cheaper rate.

## Social forestry

During 2007–08 efforts were made by Panchayat to undertake plantation work in Pathai and Nishana village. In Pathai 27.5 acres of government land were undertaken for this purpose. Similarly in Nishana village 32 acres of land came under the social forestry project. Altogether Rs. 0.13 million was spent during 2007 and 0.15 million in 2008 for plantation purposes. By doing this Panchayat created

*Table 2.4* Food grains provided by PDS at Pathai

| Category of family | Item | Quantity (in Kg/Litre) | Price (per Kg/Litre) |
|---|---|---|---|
| APL (white card) | Wheat | 10Kg | 7/- |
|  | Kerosene oil | 4Lt | 10/- |
| BPL (blue card) | Wheat | 20Kg | 3/- |
|  | Rice | 4Kg | 6.50/- |
|  | Sugar | 2Kg | 13.50/- |
|  | Kerosene oil | 5Lt | 10/- |
| Antyodaya Anna Yojana (AAY) (yellow card) | Wheat | 31Kg | 2/- |
|  | Rice | 4Kg | 3/- |
|  | Sugar | 2Kg | 13.50/- |
|  | Kerosene oil | 5Lt | 10/- |

Source: Compiled from field data.

7,875 man-days of employment under NREGS. Towards the end of 2007 it was found that about 40 per cent of the seedlings had dried. To fill up the gap, new seedlings were planted in 2008. Since this is a social forestry project, in due course, besides environmental upgradation, this project is also supposed to meet the needs of fuel, fodder and non-timber forest produce to villagers.

## Treatment

A number of institutional and non-institutional agencies/bodies are working both at the village and at the Block level to provide modern health facilities to tribals. Most of these arrangements have been made by the government. Important among these are the following.

## Primary Health Centre (PHC)

PHC is working in Pathai since the middle of 2008. It covers four villages namely Nishana, Pathai, Bhagthandhana and Palaspani. The Centre has one trained health worker (ANM). Besides serving at the Centre, the worker also moves in each of the villages for awareness generation as well as for extending treatment facility to the needy. Some of the important assignments performed by the PHC are free distribution of medicine, refer complicated cases to Sahpur Community Health Centre, assist villagers to understand procedures to take medicine as prescribed by CHC, awareness generation relating to preventive measures and so on. Some of the diseases commonly treated at PHC are fever, cough, dehydration, stomach pain, knee pain, vomiting, eye ailment, cough and cold, headache, breast pain, teeth pain, pneumonia, wound, ear ailment, itching and so on. In the case of failure or partial success, the case is referred to the CHC.

During one year (October 2008 to September 2009) PHC treated altogether 1,013 patients belonging to Pathai village. Most of the patients were between the ages of 6 to 35 years. July and August were the peak months during which the maximum number of patients received treatment.

In spite of the fact that on an average 84 patients were treated in each month during 2008 and 2009, PHC and the ANM (Auxiliary Nurse Mid-wife) is facing some of the fundamental challenges in its day-to-day functioning. These challenges are of two types viz. challenges at the place of work and challenges relating to procedural mechanisms. While the former includes resistance by husbands or

*Table 2.5* Age- and month-wise number of patients who accessed treatment at the PHC

| Months | Age | | | | | | Total |
|---|---|---|---|---|---|---|---|
| | 0–1 | 2–5 | 6–14 | 15–35 | 36–60 | 60+ | |
| Oct. 08 | 07 | 8 | 24 | 40 | 19 | 01 | 99 |
| Nov. 08 | 11 | 16 | 16 | 15 | 20 | 05 | 83 |
| Dec. 08 | 05 | 13 | 22 | 21 | 07 | 10 | 78 |
| Jan. 09 | – | 13 | 10 | 16 | 14 | 06 | 59 |
| Feb. 09 | 03 | 19 | 28 | 12 | 17 | 03 | 82 |
| March 09 | 06 | 33 | 16 | 16 | 16 | 04 | 91 |
| April 09 | 01 | 09 | 07 | 05 | 04 | 03 | 29 |
| May 09 | 02 | 11 | 05 | 15 | 06 | – | 39 |
| June 09 | 03 | 12 | 09 | 22 | 06 | 06 | 58 |
| July 09 | 01 | 16 | 29 | 26 | 17 | 10 | 99 |
| Aug. 09 | 04 | 38 | 74 | 68 | 33 | 13 | 230 |
| Sep. 09 | 06 | 15 | 18 | 13 | 10 | 04 | 66 |
| Total | 49 | 203 | 258 | 269 | 169 | 65 | 1,013 |

Source: Compiled from field data.

other male family members in the case of permanent sterilisation of women, confusion among women that sterilisation will contribute to a number of ailments in due course such as weakness, illness and fatness, problems of interaction between the ANM worker who knows the Marathi language and villagers who do not know this language and so on. The latter category includes shortage of essential medicines which PHC receives from CHC, lack of essential treatment facility and lack of instruments like delivery-related package, pathological test facility and lack of helping hands. Today the catchment area is big and the PHC worker has also to attend the weekly meeting on Saturday at CHC, as a result she is not available at PHC on that particular day.

## Anganwadi Kendra

Anganwadi Kendra (AK) is working in Pathai since 1996. There is one Anganwadi worker and one helper posted at the Centre. Anganwadi worker is responsible to encourage villagers to follow institutional delivery, adopt family planning devices, immunisation and other modern health management methods. In order to strengthen the health status of infants and children, Iron Folic Acid (IFC) is frequently distributed among them. From 2007 to 2009, 61 children were provided this tablet. Because of increasing health awareness among villagers, the number of children suffering from malnutrition is lower in comparison to normal children. For instance, of 143 children up to five years in Pathai during 2009, 96 (67.13 per cent) were normal, 35 (24.47 per cent) were malnourished and the remaining 12 (8.39 per cent) were severely malnourished.[9] However, the problem of malnourishment is more serious among girls in comparison to boys. This is largely because of the spread of patriarchy and its values in the studied village.

The immunisation programme carried out by the Anganwadi Kendra is popular in the village. All the alive children of the specific age group are provided this facility. During 2007, 2008 and 2009, 31, 36 and 30 children were covered under the immunisation scheme respectively. Because of the immunisation project the number of infant deaths has significantly decreased. During 2007, 2008 and 2009 there were deaths of three, four and two infants respectively. But in spite of this facility the rate of infant death is higher in comparison to death among other age groups. For instance, between 2006 and 2009 a total of 30 deaths occurred in Pathai, of which the maximum deaths (16) were of infants i.e. 10 male infants and 6 female infants. Also, in all the age groups the rate of death is higher among men (19) than women (11). There was no case of any maternal mortality during 2006 to 2009. This clearly denotes the increasing atmosphere in favour of safe delivery.

## Community Health Centre (CHC)

Community Health Centre located at Sahpur is headed by Block Medical Officer (BMO). Besides running a 30-bed hospital, the Centre is also managing Janani Suraksha Yojna (JSY) and Deen Dayal Mobile Hospital (DDMH). At Sahpur CHC hospital most of the time beds are engaged. For registration, APL patients have to pay 2 rupees but for BPL patient registration is free. There are three doctors working at this Centre. Some of the common diseases for the treatment of which patients at large visit CHC are fever, cough, cold and headache. Also delivery facility as well as for family planning operation.

During 2008, a total of 32,665 patients visited Sahpur CHC for treatment. In Pathai there are about 1,400 people, of which 896. patients visited this hospital. If we see month-wise variation, it is evident that during the months of July, August and September the maximum number of patients visited this hospital for treatment.

During these three months the number of patients from the CHC catchment area was also highest. This shows that during these three

*Table 2.6* Number of patients registered at Sahpur CHC during January–December 2008

| Month | Sahpur block | Pathai |
|---|---|---|
| January | 2,292 | 52 |
| February | 2,014 | 38 |
| March | 1,948 | 51 |
| April | 1,606 | 67 |
| May | 1,886 | 65 |
| June | 2,350 | 71 |
| July | 3,508 | 153 |
| August | 4,424 | 165 |
| September | 4,569 | 116 |
| October | 4,659 | 56 |
| November | 2,559 | 40 |
| December | 850 | 22 |
| | 32,665 | 896 |

Source: Compiled from field data.

months the number of patients increases not only in Pathai but also in the entire catchment area.

## Janani Suraksha Yojana (JSY)

This scheme was introduced to provide an opportunity of safe and institutional delivery to women from below the poverty line. Under this scheme economic assistance is provided to the expectant mother at the time of delivery. Earlier Rs. 700 was paid to the concerned woman but today the amount has been increased to Rs. 1,400/-. From 2005 to 2007, 74 women from Pathai village have availed themselves of the institutional delivery facility and have received the support of Rs. 68,100/- under this scheme. Success of JSY may be realised from the fact that between 2006 and 2009 altogether 142 births took place in Pathai, of which 96 took place at the hospital and the remaining 46 at home. While in the case of the former, the service of a nurse was received, in the case of the latter, Dai (both trained and untrained) played crucial roles. This data also reflect increasing interest in favour of institutional delivery.

## Deen Dayal Mobile Hospital (DDMH)

Deen Dayal Mobile Hospital (DDMH) is directed to work in the Development Blocks which are numerically dominated by SC and ST populations.

Most of the expected beneficiaries are poor, having poor access to a modern health facility. This facility is extended to them free of cost. In Madhya Pradesh this scheme was introduced on 26 May 2006 in a phased manner. Today this facility is in operation in 86 Tribal Development Blocks, having 92 Mobile Units. If we see the statistics, it is obvious that from its inception (26 May 2006) to date (February 2009) 4,375,414 patients have received treatment. During 2008–09 alone at the state level a sum of Rs. 11.78 crores was spent under the scheme.

Some of the health management activities done by DDMH are as follows:

1. Medical advice to patients, first aid and free distribution of medicine.
2. Health Check-Up before and after delivery and free distribution of medicine.
3. Collection of blood and spittoon sample relating to malaria and TB disease.
4. Identification of serious patients in villages and refer them to CHC and other hospitals.
5. Launching awareness programme relating to various family planning devices, welfare schemes and education.

In Sahpur Development Block (SDB) a Delhi-based NGO named Jagran Solution (An Unit of Jagran Prakshan Private Limited) is running this project since October 2007. There is MOU between the NGO and Health Department of Government of Madhya Pradesh for three years, which may be extended for another two years after review. Under this scheme a properly equipped vehicle moves in villages, attends all weekly markets and other common places. It has to follow a route chart prepared and provided by the Block Medical Officer (BMO). The vehicle moves between ten in the morning to six in the evening to provide treatment, free medicine and free advice. The mobile hospital examines 100 patients each day and 300 pregnant women in each month. This target is pre-decided. Besides the facility of GPS, table for diagnosis, BP test instrument, instrument relating to treatment of pregnant women, IUD kit, contraceptive pills and other material, oxygen mask, blood counter, first aid kit, the vehicle is also loaded with instruments relating to the popularisation of population education such as TV, DVD, white board, chart, loud speaker and so on. The mobile van receives medicine from CHC free of cost and it also distributes the same without any charge.

Besides these facilities in each mobile van there is a facility of a pathological lab, one oxygen cylinder and stature, one MBBS doctor, one pharmacist, one trained ANM, one supervisor and one driver. The mobile hospital moves for six days in a week and on an average 26 days in a month. In the beginning of the month the route chart prepared by BMOs in consultation with field staff is provided to the mobile hospital in-charge. In most of the cases this chart is followed.

Sector Medical Officer (SMO), BMO, DMO, CMHO, Janpad Panchayat etc. are the important institutions which have been entrusted to examine the functioning of the mobile hospital.

In short, roughly about 1,950 patients are examined and treated in each month in the villages of Sahpur. Making comments on the achievement, dresser of this mobile hospital R.K. Pandegra said:

> In spite of lack of ECG machine and spittoon slide in the mobile hospital, this project has reduced the cases of disease among poor dalits and tribals in a significant manner. People at large know about mobile hospital and they eagerly wait for its arrival in their villages. Its intervention have provided health facility at their door step.

### Private doctors at Sahpur

There are six chemist shops and private practitioners at Sahpur. The chemist shops provide advice to the patients on demand and accordingly they also prescribe medicine for various ailments even on credit. In different Kirana shops also medicines for minor ailments are prescribed and sold. Similarly there are six Allopathic doctors and two Homoeopathy doctor private practitioners at Sahpur. Villagers frequently visit them for treatment.

### III

The above observation clearly denotes that today tribes at large are no longer dependent on their traditional healing practices. Only for snake bite, which is rare, they are still dependent on the traditional system. Villagers' dependence on state-initiated health management mechanisms like PHC and CHC have significantly increased. Efforts and initiatives taken by CHC are very popular among them. More or less similar is the situation with PHC. The ever-increasing number of patients registered for treatment at both the centres is a testimony to this observation. Also, the number of schemes managed by CHC is very popular in tribal villages. Villagers do not hesitate to consult these formal institutions in need.

But this is one side of the coin. The other side needs introspection and overhauling of the total health management mechanism, especially in light of the scattered and poorly connected geographical space where tribes are located with having their limited psychological and economic carrying capacity. In spite of the presence of traditional medicine men in many tribal villages, tribes prefer to go to institutional arrangements. But the question is to what extent these institutions, especially PHC, are well equipped? Neither the ANM is properly trained to diagnose, nor the centre has sufficient infrastructural facilities. Catchment area of ANM is vast. Most of the time ANM is in the field and during this time at the PHC, the visitors are unattended. Besides providing treatment the ANM worker has also to do a number of official assignments. In case the ANM is an outsider and also from a different cultural background and mindset, they do not associate themselves closely with villagers.

CHC has become popular over time, but neither it is well equipped nor easily available to poor tribals in need. Even in the critical situation safe delivery is not possible at the CHC for want of needful facilities.[10] Patients are referred to the district hospital. The mobile hospital is neither well equipped nor very frequent in the catchment area. There is no proper and frequent monitoring of its functioning. Medicines prescribed by the chemist shop is one of the testimonies to this state of affairs.

It is true that tribal dependence on modern health management institutions has increased over time but still there are some traditional healers.[11] For treatment of some of the diseases villagers still go to them. There is no effort to modernise and capacitate these traditional healers. Traditional knowledge possessed by these healers will disappear with their death because traditionally they rarely share this knowledge with the new generation and the new generation is not interested to learn this knowledge. Hence, in the future the health-related traditional knowledge system is likely to disappear. And with this century old intangible cultural heritage will disappear from the scene.

In the light of these findings it can be said that modern health management initiatives have become very popular in tribal villages. It is functioning largely in an inclusive manner. But its introduction and functioning is at the cost of the traditional healing system. It has made villagers dependent-prone. Under the given situation if there is reluctance and apathy on the part of the state and its initiatives pertaining to effective functioning of health management schemes, if there is apathy on the part of health workers, working at the micro-level, nobody is there to take care of the health-related needs and requirements of poor tribals. The traditional practices, whether scientific or not, will not be there to save them from ailments. This will be a critical situation for poor tribals. This calls for formulation of an action agenda in such a manner that it can ensure inclusive health management for tribal masses.[12]

Some of the steps that need to be undertaken in this direction are the following:

1. Since the tribal economy revolves around their basic need and if their health status deteriorates even for a few days their basic need of food, income etc. will be adversely affected; therefore, their health and nutrition condition has to be improved and retained. For this purpose there is a need to ensure proper and fruitful functioning of all the preventive measures initiated at the community level, such as supply of safe and sufficient drinking water, proper functioning of schemes like the public distribution system, immunisation programme, total sanitation campaign, social forestry scheme and so on. These interventions, if properly managed, will directly or indirectly create enabling environments which in turn will improve their health status. However, functioning of all these initiatives can only be ensured provided beneficiaries at large are made aware about these schemes on a constant basis. And for awareness generation, besides PHC and CHC initiatives, services of other institutions such as primary schools, Gram Panchayats, self-help groups, NGOs etc. may be taken.

2. It is true that over time tribal dependence on traditional healing methods has decreased, and it is further likely to decrease but on this basis alone its contribution in the past cannot be undermined. Nobody can undermine the cultural legitimacy and ecological foundation of this practice. Nobody can ignore scientific and social values of herbs and medicinal plants. Hence, instead of accusing it as traditional and outdated and on this basis discarding it, there is a need to document and preserve this knowledge in different local languages and dialects to make properties of each of the available herbs and medicinal plants popular among the masses for its wider use. There is a need to capacitate and

modernise the traditional healers by linking them with modern health institutions. If properly linked and managed, they can be an integrating force between tribal masses and the modern health practices. We have to remember that modern medicine and treatment is a new entrant in the tribal world. There is also a need to organise, modernise and capacitate Jhola-chap doctors who are found in large numbers in villages. They are easily available, culturally accepted and many of them extend services even on credit. They have face-to-face relationships with poor clients.

3 There is a need to activise and strengthen PHC and CHC. Such institutions exist at their doorstep. Tribal dependence on these institutions has increased over time. This trust has to be popularised, retained and strengthened. PHC is neither properly equipped nor the ANM is able and capable enough to create needful environments. ANM numbers need to be increased at all the PHCs. Similar effort needs to be taken in the case of CHC. During the peak season (July–September) the number of doctors and supporting staff needs to be increased. Also, an organised, structured and well-equipped training and capacity-building package needs to be formulated and implemented for them.

## Notes

1 Patel (1991) studied traditional health management practices among the Baiga primitive tribe of Madhya Pradesh. He documented the number of religious beliefs, supernatural powers, unhygienic food habits, faith in the concept of sin and virtue, birth and re-birth, violation of taboos etc., which were held responsible by Baigas for various diseases. He also found the number of traditional treatments like worship, magic, herbs and medicinal plants etc. being used by them for treatment. There was no role of modern medicine used for the treatment of about 44 diseases among them.
2 According to Khera (1990) 'The Baiga are fully acquainted with the mosquitoes, the deadly cerebral malaria that infests the region as well as other poisonous insects and have developed special protective measures for it as well as for snake bite, bear bite, dog bite etc. It is their knowledge about medicinal plants and herbs that has made them famous. Indeed, a Baiga is sought after as the healer of the area'.
3 Chaudhary and Singh (2006) observed a similar narrative made by the local medicine man which inhibits patients to approach modern health institutions at the earliest. The healer narrated: 'If somebody is bitten by a scorpion, crushed Kapur is applied on the bitten part to remove poison. If it fails, which usually not, then Jhar-Phuk technique is used. If bitten by snake like Kobra, Kaili, Padmani and Patalhari, both Jhar-Phuk technique and very small tablet made out of poisonous Kalihari Kund is taken with water. If it fails then only patient is brought to hospital at Tamia'.

4 People do not take very kindly to the operation of extraction of the lens, though evidence of successful operations is forthcoming in a large number of villages. They quite cheerfully undergo the dislocation performed by the native Sathyas, though these practitioners destroy about 80 per cent of the eyes operated on by them (Gazetteer of India 1907, reprint 1999: 228).

5 Traditional Treatment: Black magic, herbal treatment, massage treatment by Bhumka, soil plaster, massage with garlic/soil, massage with boiled Mahua, consumption of Mahua liquor, consumption of raw bel leaf, consumption of mahi, consumption of root of banana plant, lemon water with sugar, kerosene oil massage, consumption of fried Mahua, use of copper wire, consumption of jamun gutli, consumption of peepal leaf juice with milk, inhaling of lakh smoke, jhar-phunk, use of chandan, hot papaya juice, hot water massage, turmeric powder massage, use of leaf of akau tree, steam of junglee bringal, hot juice of guava leaf, lemon juice, massage with cow ghee/inhaling of cow ghee, consumption of kutki and sama dalia, sing song, pestering of neem leaf dust, juice of amla plant, bath in front of statue of god, paste of soil mixed with cow dung, bath with neem soap.

6 Modern Treatment: Through trained and untrained doctors in the market, PHC and CHC and direct treatment by medical store.

7 Both: Initially traditional treatment but subsequently modern treatment as per the requirement or both are adopted side by side.

8 But the picture is altogether different in 2009. Most of the toilets were not in a working condition. Length and breadth of the toilet room is small and villagers hesitate to use it because of its narrow size. In certain cases it was used only by children. There are other inhibiting factors. The village is surrounded by forest and there is no paucity of open space. Therefore, by habit villagers prefer to defecate in the open space and the so-called awareness programme initiated by PHC and Gram Panchayat totally failed to change the mindset in favour of environmental upgradation. Also, villagers prefer open space because it requires less amount of water in comparison to their home-based recently constructed toilets. In some of the households, however, people used their toilet in the rainy season. It is needless to mention that in a large number of houses Mahua liquor is prepared for their own consumption as well as for market. Some of the toilet rooms are either used for storage or for preparation of Mahua liquor. Villagers at large do not know the negative implications of huge consumption of Mahua liquor on their health. They also do not know the positive impact of the use of family-based toilets on their health and environment.

9 Indicators of malnourishment are both gender- and age-specific as per the indicators and guideline prepared by the WHO. For instance, female infants of less than 6.5 kg and male infants of less than 7 kg are called severely malnourished. Similarly, female infants between 7 kg and 8.75 kg and male infants between 7.75 kg and 9.5 kg are termed as normal infants, respectively.

10 According to Rao (1998) vacancies in hospitals are high in tribal areas. Even if doctors and other health workers are posted there, many of them remain on leave or are found absent. Doctors and technical staff find tribal areas difficult as family stations because of the poor infrastructure, and

few states have a sustainable personnel policy for placing medical personnel in these areas. Placements in tribal areas are often perceived as punishment postings that are assigned to non-performers.
11 Such healers are also active in other parts of the world. According to Munguti (1997) despite the introduction of Western medicine many Kenyan communities, including Tugen, follow traditional medicine because it is cheap, easily available, commands faith, while Western medicine is very costly. It is beyond the reach of many.
12 By sustainable development we mean development which is productive especially in the output and benefit sense of the term, stable even after formal withdrawal of the project by the state and other implementing agencies and equitable which can honestly and continuously take care of needs and concerns of even those who are at the end of the queue.

## Reference

Chaudhary, D. 1998. 'Conserving Genetic Heterogeneity in North-East India', in M. K. Ruha and A. K. Ghose (eds.), *North-East India's: The Human Interface*. New Delhi: Gyan.

Chaudhary, S. N. and R. P. Singh. 2006. *Tribes of Pachmarhi Biosphere Reserve and their Indigenous Knowledge*. Bhopal: Indira Gandhi Rashtriya Manav Sangrahalaya.

Chaudhuri, B. 1993. 'Health, Culture and Environment: The Tribal Situation in India', in M. Miri (ed.), *Continuity and Change in Tribal Society*. Shimla: Indian Institute of Advanced Study.

Clements, Forrest E. 1932. 'Primitive Concept of Disease', in *American Archeology and Ethnology*. Berkeley: University of California Press, 185–252.

Joseph, A. N. T. 1989. 'Ethnozoology of Reptiles in Relation to Health Care Among Tribals in Madhya Pradesh', *Social Action*, 39(4): 405–22.

Khera, P. D. 1990. 'The Baiga and the Sal Forest', *The Eastern Anthropologist*, 43: 241–58.

Kurian, J. C. and R. D. Tribhuwan. 1990. 'Traditional Medical Practitioners of the Sahyadri', *The Eastern Anthropologist*, 43(3): 251–8.

Kurup, A. M. 2000. 'Indigenous Knowledge and Intellectual Property Rights of Tribals: A Case Study', *Yojana*, 5–9.

Lakra, Indumati. 1997. 'Health Status of Women of Khairwar Tribe of Surguja District', *Bulletin of the Tribal Research and Development Institute*, 35(2).

Lal, Brij. 1987. 'Traditional Remedies for Bone Fracture Among the Trials of M.P. India', *Bulletin of the Tribal Research and Development Institute*, 40(1–2).

Lewis, A. 1954. 'Health as a Social Concept', *British Journal of Sociology*, 6: 109–24.

Mathur, P. R. G. 1982. 'Anthropology of Tribal Medicine: Disease and Curing Techniques Among the Tribals of North Wayanad (Kerala)', *Man in India*, 62(3): 295–312.

Munguti, K. 1997. 'Indigenous Knowledge in the Management of Malaria and Visceral Leishmaniasis Among the Tugen of Kenya', *Indigenous Knowledge and Development Monitor*, 5(1): 10–12.

Patel, G. P. 1991. 'A Study of Traditional Healing Practices Among Baiga Tribe of Madhya Pradesh', *Bulletin of the Tribal Research and Development Institute*, 19(1 and 2).

Rao, K. S. 1998. 'Health Care Services in Tribal Areas of Andhra Pradesh: A Public Policy Perspective', *Economic and Political Weekly*, 33(9): 481–6.

# 3

# ABANDONED BY THE NATION

'Adverse possessions' and the denial
of tribal rights to habitat in
Indo-Bangladesh border

*Sajal Nag*

Two hundred years of colonial rule, the clinical experimentation of divides et impera, the nature of appropriation of the nationalist discourse and the communal mobilisation had succeeded in dividing India even before it was free. But imagining two separate nations and actually carving out two separate national territories out of a single space was a different task altogether. The accomplishment of this arduous task was assigned to Sir Cyril Radcliffe who was to head a Boundary Commission constituted on 30 June 1947 vide order no D50/7/47R by the Governor General. The terms of reference of the commission were 'to demarcate the boundaries of the two parts of Bengal on the basis of ascertaining the contiguous areas of Muslim and non-Muslim. In doing so it will also take into account other factors' (Grover and Aurora 1997: 313–14). There were two such commissions – one for Bengal and the other for Punjab which were to be divided. The other members of the Bengal Commission were Justice Bijan Kumar Mukerjee, Justice C.K. Biswas, Justice Abu Saleh, Muhammed Akram and Justice S.R. Rehman. The time given to the commission was short and even its composition was not representative. Moreover, the terms of reference of the commission did not specify its assignment vis-à-vis areas outside Bengal. For example, Sylhet was administratively a part of Assam but the Boundary Commission found it imperative to deliberate on it for partition. There were princely states like the 25 Khasi states or the state of Coch Bihar, Rangpur and Tripura where paramountcy had lapsed and the states were given the option to decide their future but which could not escape being affected by the partition. Some of these states were planned to be partitioned even before they had actually decided on joining or not joining either of the dominions. The commission was dealing with real people but the terms of reference of the commission was to partition territories based on the religious affiliation of the people without taking into account their will. Hence they set out to do their job by simply drawing a line on the map. It was this line which created partitioned territory, created nations, divided homes, cut off people from their livelihood and left behind a permanent source of conflict. Radcliffe constructed a line on the map of India that decided how the two countries were going to be partitioned into India and Pakistan. The objective of the commission was to demarcate Hindu-majority areas in Eastern India and Muslim-majority areas of Western India. The decolonisation and state formation process across the globe, not just South Asia, had in fact divided people instead of integrating national groups into one political space. The process had been started by the colonialists through political manoeuvres beginning with Ireland. It was followed by the partition of India, Palestine, Korea, Malaysia, Yemen and Vietnam whereby not only kinsmen have been divided but their habitat partitioned. It even resulted in hostilities and created enemies out of former brethrens. This is contrary to the avowed principles of unity of national groups inherent in the nationalist discourse. The Partition of India had created two and later three major sovereign states in South Asia. Homogeneity of population was created by displacement and exchange of population. States are formed on the basis of a definite territory. This territory is defined by a boundary. The boundary is created not on the basis of national considerations but by drawing a line across the map which is later actualised by fencing or deployment of frontier check posts. Thus in South Asia we have the Radcliff Line, McMohan Line and so on. The line while demarcating areas between the Hindus and Muslims actually divided various tribal groups between the two states and also displaced them from their permanent habitat. These tribals were neither Hindus nor Muslims nor were participants in the acrimonious communal politics that the subcontinent witnessed during the colonial period but were mostly practicing their indigenous faith while some of them had just been converted to Christianity by European missionaries. The displacement was not only between the two states, but a new category of displacement occurred by the emergence of what is now an adverse possession. Although partition of the country and displacement of Hindus and Muslims are greatly talked about, the displacement and dispossession of these tribal groups are not talked about at all. Not only because they are tiny tribal groups but also in the competing discourse of nation-states, marginal groups were sacrificed without compunction. These tribals were denied their legitimate to right to live in their ancestral habitat, systematically displaced and then encroached upon by the majority non-tribal communities under the patronage of a partisan state and even sought to be completely wiped out, if not physically but culturally. This chapter is about such tiny tribal groups who lived in various autochthones in India and were divided between the two countries or displaced by the partition of the country. Even after Independence and partition a number of tiny tribal groups remain in enclaves surrounded by a hostile foreign power, denied their basic rights and access to subsistence and waiting for the two countries to settle their uncertain future. This chapter is about the plight of these unfortunate tribal populations of various ethnicities who were unsung victims of nation formation.

## Dividing kinsmen

The objective of the Radcliffe Line was to demarcate two territories of Muslim- and Hindu-majority as these two were the aggrieved parties. But while drawing this line Radcliffe divided many groups who were not aggrieved parties, meaning neither Muslims nor Hindus. They were divided as their habitat fell along the line of partition. Thus, the Khasi, Jaintia, Garo, Hajong and Chakma tribes were divided between India and Pakistan (Bangladesh) though the objective was to divide only Hindus and Muslims. In a similar situation the Khasi and Garo tribes had been divided between India and Bangladesh. Reports indicate that the Khasi and Garo tribesmen face tyranny from both the Bangladesh administration as well as the Bangladeshi majority. Pressurised by a population explosion, the Bangladeshis are trying to push the tribes out of their habitats and take possession of it themselves. The Bangladesh Government itself had been supporting the move. As recently as 2003 the Bangladesh Government launched a project to evict the Khasi and Garo tribals from their ancestral habitat in Madhupur Reserve Forest in Borlekha (Maulavi bazaar District of Sylhet) to develop an ecological park. The 10,000 Khasi and Garo were to be forcefully evicted by the administration. However, due to international pressure and resistance from the tribes themselves, the project had to be abandoned for the time being (*The Asian Age* 2003; *The Times of India* 2003). Surprisingly, the better-off Khasi and Garos of India did not voice the slightest of protests to these moves of the neighbouring government, though despite the preferential treatment of the government, Indian Khasis often launched violent movements against non-tribal migration to their area. There were few protests from the political elite or urban Khasis when the affected people of the Khasi-Jaintia borderlands protested that, while fencing the boundary between India and Bangladesh along their territory, huge chunks of Khasi and Jaintia lands were being transferred to Bangladesh (*Shillong Times* 2005).[1]

The Khasis not only experienced persecution across the frontier but also within India. Besides the Meghalaya state they also have a presence in the State of Tripura, Karbi Anglong and Cachar districts of Assam. In both places they are a small minority against the dominant Karbi and Bengalis respectively. In all these places they are primarily occupied in the production of pan leaves in which they have specialised proficiency. But they are also subjected to extortion, eviction and threats of genocide, especially in the Karbi Anglong District. In Cachar district of Assam the Khasi pan growers often face Bengali musclemen attempting to frighten them to migrate to Meghalaya so that their lands could be occupied by them. In the Vairangte subdivision of Mizoram there is a small Khasi population of about 2,000 people who are denied even citizenship rights by the Mizoram Government. The underground Karbi outfits Karbi National Volunteers and United Democratic Peoples Solidarity to try to oust them from their habitat so that land could be occupied by their tribe. A similar situation is also in North Cachar area from the Dimasa outfit Dima Haloi Daoga as well as by the Hmar outfit of the Hmar Peoples Convention. The Khasi and Garo people of India who have powerful political voices in the State of India strangely have been silent over the plight of their kinsmen in those areas. Even the Khasi and Garo underground outfits (Achik National Volunteers Council and Hynnewtrep National Liberation Council) who claim to fight for the liberation of their kinsmen were silent about the persecution of their people both in India and Bangladesh.

Similarly when the British sought to separate Burma from the Indian empire it divided the Naga, Mizo and Arunachali tribes between the two countries. It is evident that state formations out of national groups not only divide people but even reduce the sentiments of kinship substantially. As can be seen, the better-off section of the people develop indifference and even antipathy towards the less fortunate section who remain in other territories. The Nagas for example has been fighting a secessionist war against the Indian state for half a century. In this war they have always talked about their Naga kinsmen who had remained in the State of Myanmar. Currently they are in the process of negotiating with the Indian State about the possibility of integrating all the Nagas dispersed in different provinces of India into one single political unit. But in these negotiations the question of Nagas living in Myanmar has ceased to figure. In fact the Nagas of Myanmar are in a terrible condition and are subjected to untold oppression under the military regime there. The Myanmarese Nagas need the support of their ethnic counterparts in India more than anything else. But realising that the inclusion of Myanmarese Nagas in their political agenda would be futile, the Naga apex organisation, the National Socialist Council of Nagaland (IM), seems to have decided to leave the former to their own fate.

The Mizos had launched a Zo Reunification Movement in the 1970s with the objective of unifying and integrating all Mizo people similarly dispersed in different territories in India, Bangladesh and Myanmar in one single province. The movement had gained immediate support and enthusiasm of all Mizos. So much so that though Myanmarese Mizos were as much a foreigner as an American in India, they were allowed to cross over and settle in Mizoram province of India. It was illegal but the empathy of the Indian Mizos and the unofficial support of the Mizoram government allowed the settlement to continue. It was neither reported officially nor illegalised. But once Mizoram was granted the status of separate statehood, a murmur began about the unabated migration of Myanmarese Mizos in this Indian state leading to scarcity in land resources, shrinkage of employment opportunities, spurt in criminal activities, increase in drug and small arms peddling, spread of HIV and AIDS and intensification of anti-national movements in this border state. There was discussion to initiate some regulation over their unabated infiltration. The murmur developed into a chorus in the 1990s. The Myanmarese are generally poverty-stricken, uneducated and victims of oppression and deprivation by the majority Myanmarese as well as the government. They migrate to India to work as maid servants, wage labourers, small time vendors, shop keepers and smugglers of contraband goods and items. In contrast the Indian Mizos due to their advancement in educational pursuits (Mizos have one of the highest literacy rates in India) and State Preferential Policy are relatively well off. The Indian Mizos still believed that their Myanmarese kinsmen were slowly taking away their entrepreneurship and employment opportunities, spreading the drug culture in the region thereby paralysing the younger generation and increasing crimes like theft, robberies, murder and, most important, rape. Most important was the fear that the Myanmarese Mizos would soon outnumber the indigenous Mizos, thereby taking over political power from them. There was a growing hostility towards the Myanmarese Mizos which prompted the government to attempt regulation of their migration. The peoples' hostility found expression in newspaper articles and occasional attempts at assaulting these hapless migrants. In June 2003, however, there was a Quit Call to them by the Mizo Students Union – a powerful body in the state over the incident of the rape of a minor girl reportedly by a Myanmarese Mizo youth. It asked all the Mizo migrants from the neighbouring state to leave the state by a stipulated date. Frightened by the fear psychosis it created, most Myanmarese Mizos left for their abandoned home fearing an ethnic riot. The activists of the Reunification Movement tried to interfere and calm down the leaders of the Quit Movement without much success. In fact now the Indian Mizo expressed their indifference to the unification endeavour. There was such a strong antipathy against them in Mizoram that they would not dare return. It is difficult to understand why a people who started a Reunification Movement to unite with their kinsmen under one administration suddenly forcefully began to expel the same kinsmen from their territory, ruthlessly fearing numerical dominance. Although the administration stepped in calm the tension, it too joined the fray firstly by asking for official papers from suspected Myanmarese nationals, failing which they were deported and secondly tightening up the border vigilance so that further infiltration could be checked.

## Sacrificed at the altar of nations: the Chakmas

The Chittagong Hill tracts did not figure in the Pakistan scheme of Muslim League. But in their haste to effect the transfer of power, the national leadership preferred to ignore such details. The Chakma and Hajong – two major tribes inhabiting the hills – made desperate appeals to the central Congress leadership not to alienate them as part of India. But such pleas fell on deaf ears. The Chittagong Hills went to East Pakistan after partition. Thenceforth, it was a story of systematic deprivation and atrocities on these small Buddhist and animist tribes by the majority community as well as the successive Pakistani and Bangladeshi regimes.

The Chakmas are an Indo-Mongoloid tribe and one of the very few professing Buddhism. Confined largely to the hills, they generally lived on primitive cultivation tactics. The population explosion and extreme land scarcity in the present Bangladesh from the 1950s made inroads into the tribal lands. Gradually even the state sponsored such usurpation of tribal lands. To force the tribals out of their land often coercive methods amounting to atrocities were applied on the tribal population. During the military regimes of the 1960s such coercion compelled the Chakma and Hajong people to seek refuge in India for security and safety. In 1964 more than 40,000 of these tribal communities entered India through the northeast frontier and were settled in the North East Frontier Agency (Present Arunachal Pradesh) by the Government of India. Since then the trickle continued. For example, due to the displacement caused by the Kaptai Hydel Project 4,000 more Chakmas were settled in the area. The rest of these frightened people were given shelter in the neighbouring states of Tripura and Mizoram. The size of the refugee population has grown tremendously since then. In Arunachal Pradesh itself, the 40,000 refugees grew to be more than 100,000 during three decades.

The weak demographic and economic structures of the states where the refugees were settled soon began to feel the pressure. The xenophobic tiny indigenous tribal population of Arunachal Pradesh began to consider the refugees as 'encroachers'. The limited means were to be shared by both the groups which created acute tensions. The politicisation of demographic issues, so typical of Northeast India, soon generated a fear that the Chakma refugees might at a certain point outnumber the indigenous tribals thereby usurping the political hegemony of the latter. The hostility towards the refugees intensified with the declaration of the Centre's intention of granting these refugees Indian citizenship.

In 1992, in response to a query from Lacta Umbrey, MP from Arunachal Pradesh, the then Minister of State for Home Affairs, M.M. Jacob, informed 'being new immigrants viz. refugees from Bangladesh who came to India between 1964 and 25 March 1971, the Chakmas and Hajongs are eligible for citizenship. In fact a large number of them have already been granted citizenship. Further, a large population of these refugees who have been born in India and therefore, automatically entitled to Indian Citizenship'. Therefore, the deportation of Chakma and Hajong refugees from Arunachal Pradesh was ruled out. But after this declaration came the Supreme Court verdict on 27 April 1993 (Khudiram Chakma versus State of Arunachal Pradesh case) which was quite opposite to the politics of the Union Government. Although the Union Government did not comment on it, it because clear the government was going to changes its policy when the Minister of State for Home Affairs, P.M. Sayeed, informed the Rajya Sabha Member from Arunachal Pradesh, Nadek Yonggam, that according to the Indira-Mujib pact of 1972, the Chakma and Hajong refugees who came to India from erstwhile Pakistan before 25 May 1971 will be considered for the grant of Indian citizenship.

The fear of a permanent presence of a growing refugee population and the failure of the provincial politicians to safeguard the interests of the indigenous tribals made the student community (All Arunachal Pradesh Students' Union) take up the issue when their demand of setting the refugees outside Arunachal Pradesh was not implemented. They asked the Chakmas to quit the state on or before 30 September 1994. Since there was no response to it from the Chakmas, another deadline was given – 31 December 1995. The students' agitation gained momentum, when even the Chief Minister of the State, Gegong Apang, lent support to the demand. Simultaneously there were economic blockades and persistent intimidation to the refugees.

The Centre's silence over the issue compelled the National Human Rights Commission to intervene. It moved the Supreme Court after failing to obtain a response from the Centre on the issue of prosecution and forcible eviction of the Chakmas in Arunachal Pradesh. The Supreme Court in a judgement of far-reaching consequence directed the Government of Arunachal Pradesh to counter all moves to evict the Chakmas forcibly and ensure their protection from being shunted out of their homes and occupations. A Division Bench comprising Chief Justice A.M. Ahmadi and S.C. Sen made it clear that 'except in accordance with law the Chakmas shall not be evicted from their homes and shall not be denied life and comfort therein'. Also, that the state government shall not evict or remove the concerned persons from his occupations on the ground that he is not a citizen of India until a competent authority has taken a decision in that behalf. On the citizenship question the bench said that applications of the Chakmas in this respect should be entered in the Register maintained for the purpose and the same should be forwarded by the Collector or District Collector to the Central Government for its consideration. On the issue of the 'Quit Notice' given to the Chakmas, the bench said that it amounted to threats to the life and liberty of the Chakmas and should be dealt with in accordance with the law.

There was widespread dissatisfaction on the Supreme Court verdict. The All Arunachal Pradesh Student Union which spearheaded the movement and the Arunachal Pradesh Home Minister accused the

NHRC of being biased in favour of the Chakmas. Facing rebellion from the State Government run by the Congress the Union Government finally formed a 'high power' core group to break the continuing deadlock over the Chakma refugees under the supervision of the Prime Minister himself.

It is indeed unfortunate that a matter which should have been settled years ago purely on humanitarian considerations should reach such a stage of crisis. The Chakma refugees of the 1964 batch were given an understanding that they would be granted Indian citizenship. The Chakma people form the second-largest tribe in Mizoram, after the Mizos. They originally belonged to the Chittagong Hill Tracts (CHT) of Bengal presently in Bangladesh. The Chakmas of the Mizo Hills migrated mostly from the Chittagong Hill Tracts of Bengal to the Mizo Hills in different periods and settled on its western fringes. The history of the Chakmas in Mizoram can be traced back to the time when 'a group of Chakmas, beyond the river Thega, i.e. the western bank of the river, fled to the Lushai Hills (now Mizoram), when this part was separated from Bengal and made a district of Assam Province during the British period. However, when the North and South Lushai Hills were amalgamated into a single administrative unit in 1900, a revision of the territorial boundaries also followed. The boundaries of the territory of Rani Kalindi was revised and a portion of the east including the place called Demagiri (Tlabung) with a population of about 1500 was transferred to the Lushai Hills' (Bareh 2001: 234). The areas inhabited by the Chakmas became part of Mizoram after the partition of the Indian subcontinent in 1947. The Chittagong Hills Tract did not figure in the areas demanded by the Muslim League for Pakistan as it was not a Muslim-majority area. In fact it was inhabited by the Chakmas, Magh and Mizo tribes. Yet the Radcliffe Commission allotted those areas to Pakistan. The Chakmas appealed to Nehru, but there was no hearing. With the partition of the Indian subcontinent in 1947, the Chittagong Hill Tract became part of East Pakistan, which was against the will of the local inhabitants. While the entire Chittagong Hill Tract was transferred to East Pakistan, some parts of it adjoining Lushai Hills remained in India due to lack of proper boundary demarcation. This is how the Chakma-inhabited territories became a part of Mizoram. Since this land was contiguous to Lushai Hills, it was administered as a part of that district. The total Chakma population in Mizoram was about 120,000 in 2001. They are mostly concentrated in the three districts of Lawngtlai, Lunglei and Mamit where more than 90 per cent of them live. In fact, Chakmas have formed a majority in the Lawngtlai district where they make up about 52 per cent of the district population. In fact the Chakmas who were settled in Mizoram have been granted a District Council and even have an MLA in the State Assembly. But as the Centre failed to evolve a uniform Refugee Rehabilitation Policy and vacillated too long over the citizenship issue, the settled Chakmas of Mizoram also have now become the target of anti-foreigner agitation. The successive Union Governments have failed to implement its commitment to the refugees made decades ago. It is high time the position of the Chakmas and Hajongs be legalised. If Arunachal Pradesh refuses to let the Chakmas settle in their state, it is the state's responsibility to settle them elsewhere in the country.

## Nations in enclaves: the nowhere people

The state formation process of the Indian nation had other spin-off effects which actually violated the very principles of nationalism on which the hundred years of nationalist movement was based. In other words the nationalist movement strived for creating a nation by unifying all Indians but eventually it ended up dividing and distancing its own people. The Radcliffe Line that drew the boundary between India and Pakistan, which later became Bangladesh, was inconclusive and had failed really to create two definite territories. Some Indian territories remained within Pakistan and vice versa. These territories were called Adverse Possession (AP). It was a term borrowed from Europe. In the United Kingdom for example, some Welsh territories are in the adverse possession of England. The case of Alsace-Lorrain, a French territory under German occupation on the eve of the First World War, was also a similar example. In simple terms AP are territorial parts of a country controlled by another country. Since Partition, a large tract of Indian territories has been under the possession of Bangladesh (earlier Pakistan). Similarly, parts of Bangladeshi territory are also controlled by India due to non-resolution of boundary problems by the two states. These tracts of land are neither geographically contiguous to each other nor lie in the same stretch but small chunks in different points of the porous border. Hence these are called Enclaves. Essentially these AP were the results of thoughtless demarcation of the border to partition the country by Cyril Radcliffe who was completely ignorant of the cultural and territorial features of the area through which the line was drawn. As a result the border cuts through the middle of several villages and in some cases, while one section of the house is in one country, another is in the other. The India-Bangladesh boundary is no ordinary one. Hastily constructed in the dying days of British colonialism, it was the longest international boundary created during the age of decolonisation. The border was intended to separate a contiguous majority area of Muslims from that of non-Muslims – but for only about a quarter of its length does it separate a Muslim-majority in Bangladesh from a Hindu-majority in India. As many as 162 tiny enclaves (111 Indian and 52 Bangladeshi) dot a section of the frontier: in the extreme an Indian enclave sits within a Bangladeshi enclave, itself situated within a larger Indian enclave, all surrounded by Bangladeshi territory. Shifting rivers, mapping errors and 'adversely possessed lands' – that is, lands unwittingly encroached upon and (illegally) occupied by both countries – added to the maze of identity, loyalty and insecurity along the Bengal borderland.

After Independence when the demarcation of the boundary was undertaken by Indian and Pakistan in the mid-1960s there were disputes regarding these areas which led to the rise of Adverse Possession areas. In West Bengal, for instance, there are more than 100 villages located right on the zero line and in many villages there are houses where the front door is in India and the rear door opens into Bangladesh. For instance, Hilli in the Malda district of West Bengal is located right on the border and a row of houses in this town have their front doors in India and their rear doors opening onto the railway platform of Hilli in Bangladesh. Several such houses exist in areas of Tripura state bordering Bangladesh (Rammhoan 2002; Lakshman and Jha 2003). Then there are problems of enclaves. Enclaves are isolated strips of land or villages, which are surrounded on all sides by the neighbouring country. There are 43 such enclaves belonging to India but controlled by Bangladesh and over 47 enclaves belonging to Bangladesh but controlled by India. In total there are 161 such AP in the 4,096 km of border between India and Bangladesh, of which 6.5 km are yet to be demarcated. Of these, 111 enclaves are Indian territories (17,158.1 acres) but are in the control of Bangladesh. As against this there are 51 Bangladeshi enclaves (7,110 acres) which are under Indian control. These enclaves are like islands surrounded by foreign and sometimes hostile country, all four sides without any access to their own country. Incomplete demarcation created these problems of enclaves. The population figures of these enclaves are not available as no access to the Indian enclaves in Bangladesh territory has been provided by Bangladesh for census operations (Khanna 2003). The Land Boundary Agreement between the two countries in 1974 laid down procedures for joint demarcation of boundaries. Although the survey authorities of the two countries have completed demarcation of over 4,000 km of the India-Bangladesh boundary they have not been able to resolve differences in demarcation of approximately 6.5 km of land boundaries in the states of Tripura, West Bengal and Assam (Krishnan 2001). The two countries have set up two Joint Boundary Working Groups to resolve all pending issues relating to the implementation of the Land Boundary Agreement of 1974, including exchange of enclaves. In the Bangladesh-Meghalaya border there are nine Adversely Possessed areas (559.7 acres) of Bangladesh under the occupation of India (Meghalaya) and two Indian enclaves (52.15 acres) held by Bangladesh. Among these are Pyrdiwah, a Khasi village officially Bangladeshi land, is in the adverse possession of India as well as Nongken, a Jaintia village, demarcated as Bangladeshi land is in the possession of India. These areas are mostly Khasi villages known as Khasi punjis, the people of which want to be united with their people in India. It is strange that the partition of the country which was implemented on the basis of the two-nation theory also divided habitats of tribals like the Khasis in Pyrdiwah, Jaintias in Nongken and Jaintianpur, Manipuris and Khasis in Karimganj and Garos in Boraibari in Mankachar in Garo Hills. This was despite the assertion in the Radcliffe Report that 'In my view the question is limited to the district of Sylhet and Cachar, since the other districts of Assam that can be said to adjoin Sylhet neither Garo Hills nor the Khasi and Jaintia hills nor the Lushai hills have anything approaching a Muslim majority of the population in respect of which a claim could be made' (Grover and Aurora 1997: 313–14).

In the Karimganj subdivision there are about 11.432 km. It falls in the Nilambazar area from Baropunji to Ballia (Khasia punji). Within it a stretch of about 800 m is inhabited by the Khasi inhabitants of Bangladesh and is under intense *jhum* cultivation, and betel leaf farming. This possession also includes Madonpur tea estate as well as some *patta* and *khas* lands. The second stretch starts from Madonpur tea estate adjacent to the Madonpur BSF outpost, a length of about 4.5 km out of which 600 m is under adverse possession of Bangladesh-owned Komashail tea garden. In the same stretch Bangladeshis exploit some tracts of Indian forestland. A portion of betel leaf farmland is controlled by Bangladesh. The third stretch in this sector has Kalair Mokam, which is located inside Indian Territory but is controlled by Bangladeshis. This stretch also includes a two km tract of forestland known as Ballia. In the adjacent region Khasi hamlets are found. A tract of land belonging to Promodenagar tea estate which is owned by an Indian is under adverse possession of Bangladesh. Out of the 11.432 km stretch of adversely possessed area 7 km is termed as Adverse Part I in Border Roads Circle official papers. The remaining 4.435 km is known as Adverse Part II. Most of these tracts are inhabited by Bengali Muslims as well as Hindus, Manipuris and Khasis. The Government of India has undertaken the border fencing which is almost complete barring the adversely possessed area. Curiously the fence is erected 137 metres inside the Indian Territory away from the border.

Technically, however, out of the 4,096 km stretch of the India-Bangladesh border there is acrimony over only three patches with a total of 6 km. On the map at least the rest is well defined and one can make out which area belongs to whom. Out of the three patches the first is near Muhuri River at Comilla district of Bangladesh adjacent to Tripura state in India along the Indo-Bangla border. Both the Radcliffe Line of 1947 and Indira-Mujib Pact of 1974 agreed that the boundary should be the mid-point of the river. But the disputes persist at least in the 2 km area of this river where Bangladesh insists on keeping the river completely in its territory. For the villagers and fisherman, the riverbed is important for their survival and that is the bone of contention for both sides. The second area of dispute where the joint survey team has not been able to find out a mutually agreed path is another small place called Lathitilla in Karimganj district of Assam, which is inhabited by Manipuri people but they have been paying taxes to Bangladesh out of compulsion. Interestingly, the original map, prepared during the British time, is reportedly missing and hence no settlement could be done without it (Sharma 2001: 14). The Indian authority has been insisting that the Bangladesh must show the original map likely to be available in Sylhet District Archives. The third area of dispute lies in the Bangladesh-West Bengal border and the root of the dispute is the change of the course of a small river. In other words along the 4,096 km of international boundary with Bangladesh three stretches involving 6 km are yet to be demarcated. These un-demarcated stretches included 1.5 km at the Muhari river in the Belonia (Tripura) section, 3 km in the Lathitila-Dumabari sector (Assam, Karimganj) and another 1.5 km in Daikhata area (Cooch Bihar, North Bengal). Sixty years have elapsed since independence of the country but the state has been able to resolve this problem of 6.5 km and hence huge populations who are citizens of one country continue to live in another country deprived of all basic amenities that any ordinary citizen enjoys.

In the AP areas like Lathitila and Dumabari in Karimganj district of Assam the Indian lands are in the control of Bangladesh. The people of these areas are in possession of land *patta* issued to them by the Karimganj land settlement office but they have to pay their annual revenue to the Bangladesh Government. These villagers cast their votes in every Indian election but cannot claim to be Indians as their 1,200 *bighas* of land lies in the AP of Bangladesh. These two *mouzas* were shown as Indian territories in the map during Partition but for some unknown reason the Indian administration failed to take possession of them. As a result both *mouzas* were annexed first by Pakistan in 1965 and then by Bangladesh in 1971 (*The Telegraph* 2003a). In the same area there are entire Indian tea gardens which are in the control of Bangladesh. The change in ruling party in either country, especially Bangladesh, often created further problems. For example in April 2003 after the Bangladesh Nationalist Party came to power in 2002, the Bangladesh Rifles objected to agricultural farming, especially tea in the AP areas like Bholaganj and Mankachar in Meghalaya and Belonia in Tripura (*The Telegraph* 2003b). The people of these areas live a miserable existence with no security of life and property, no protection legal or political, no social life, no economic rights, no future or any certainty. There is a constant threat of foreign invasion. The unofficial invasion from the neighbouring nation is of course common and regular. But from the respective government there is lack of concern. India and Pakistan gained independence in August 1947 but this problem was not even addressed up to 1958. The problems of all other AP lands continue to plague both the governments. Since these were small pieces of lands containing a fraction of the total population of the two countries, no efforts were made to resolve the issues. Over the years the Assam government was maintaining that about 500 acres of Assam land was under the adverse possession of Bangladesh but the latest report from the Deputy Commissioners of Dhubri and Karimganj districts have however pointed out to more areas of Assam under the adverse possession of Bangladesh and the total areas of such possession was not 500 acres but 684.93 acres and that no areas of Bangladesh were under the possession of India. According to reports at Boraibari, which is a part of the Revenue village Thakuranbari under Mankachar Revenue circle in Dhurbri district, 189.06 acres of Assam land have been under the adverse possession of Bangladesh. In Pallatal Tea Garden, 330.58 acres under boundary strip sheet no 225 and in Patharia Forest 'B' Block and Promod Nagar Tea Garden 165.29 acres under Bomla sheet no. 226 in Nilam Bazar Revenue Circle in Karimganj district have been under the adverse possession of Bangladesh. While Boraibari has about 200 households comprising a population of

4,000, Pallatal Tea Garden has a Khasi population of 20,000 in Bangladesh. The Patharia Forest 'B' Block and Promod Nagar Tea Garden are under forest cover (*The Sentinel* 2010).

## Life in the enclaves

The enclave has an interesting population composition. Most of the enclaves in the border that lie along the Assam and Meghalaya border with Bangladesh are mostly tribal. In other words it was the tribal autochthones locally called punjis that lie in the adversely possessed areas. For example in the Bangladesh-Meghalaya border it was mostly Khasis, Jaitias and Garos. Pyrdiwah, one of the major AP under Bangladeshi possession, was a traditional habitat of the Khasi tribe of Meghalaya. Similarly in Nongken and Jaintianpur it was the Jaintias. In Lungkhat I, II and III it was the War people – a conglomerate tribe of the Khasis. In Tamabil and Naljuri I and II also it was mostly Khasis mixed with some non-tribal Hindu and Muslims populations. The Rongkhon, Amjalong, Amki, Kurribnallah and Muktapur AP are the traditional autochthones of the Jaintias which were adversely possessed by Bangladesh. Interestingly even in the APs of Assam-Bangladesh border it was mostly the Khasi and Garos whose habitats were absorbed by a foreign country. There are Meithei and Khasis in Karimganj and Garos in Boraibari and in Mankachar in Garo Hills. In the Karimganj subdivision there are about 11.432 km. It falls in the Nilambazar area from Baropunji to Ballia which includes a number of Khasia punji meaning Khasi villages. These are Khasis of Bangladesh. In fact during their migratory movement the Khasi tribals had developed a number of settlements which fell in the states of Brahmaputra Valley of Assam, Barak Valley of Assam, Meghalaya, Mizoram, Karbi Anglong and North Cachar Hills of Assam and Tripura and pockets of Sylhet in Bangladesh. Hence it is not correct of assume that Khasis are found only in the state of Meghalaya. Their settlements were spread over a large area in Northeast India where they formed their villages along the migratory route. Around the settlement they had developed their democratic polity and a social fabric. Their economy basically centred round slash and burn locally known as *jhum*. But interestingly they were involved alongside with a significant cash crop cultivation of betel leaf farming. It is curious that the entire betel leaf farming in Northeast India is a virtual Khasi monopoly. A good proportion of this farming is carried out in the AP areas. In Bholaganj it is mostly the Khasi and Boraibari, which is a part of the Revenue village

Thakuranbari under Mankachar Revenue circle in Dhurbri district, 189.06 acres of Assam land have been under the adverse possession of Bangladesh it is the Garo tribals who were trapped in. Here too the tribals are involved in jhum farming along with other cash crop like betel leaf and raw cotton farming and trade. The adverse possession also includes Madonpur tea estate as well as some patta and khas lands. Lathitilla in Karimganj district of Assam is inhabited by Meithei people who practice settled rice cultivation and related trade. The Pallatal Tea Garden has a Khasi population of Bangladesh along with some tea labour population. The Patharia Forest 'B' Block and Promod Nagar Tea Garden are under forest cover. It is also inhabited mostly by tribal and tea labour populations like the Santhal, Munda who were brought to the region through indentured labour. Besides being tribal, who are marginal people in either the state of India or Bangladesh, these people are also stateless.

Life however was not easy for these stateless people in the enclaves. They do not have a single piece of paper – except for the land deeds that identity them as residents of enclaves. Each time they step outside their village, they worry about being arrested by Indian police who accuse them of being Bangladeshi and often try to push them back to Bangladeshi thinking they are illegal migrants to India. The opposite too happens they move to Bangladesh. The enclaves have no schools, electricity or hospital. They have to go to nearby Indian hospitals for treatment. It is not easy for women of the enclave to give birth to a child as nearby hospitals are in India where they cannot go. Most of the Bangladeshi enclave residents had never been to Bangladesh and even married a girl from the neighbouring Indian village and vice versa.

Although these territories belong to one country, they are under the possession of another country. The people of these areas are citizens of one country but have no rights to speak of. In the Palathal-Madanpur region these two enclaves are actually two tea estates. Madanpur tea estate remained in India during partition but Palathal went to Pakistan. When Bangladesh was formed Madanpur became a part of Bangladesh. Since then people of the estates, including the plantation labourers, were given Pakistani and eventually Bangladeshi citizenship and were granted other facilities by the respective governments. During the land survey in 1976 Bangladesh asked India to surrender its claim over the land. In fact during the survey it was found that the actual land under Bangladeshi occupation was 455 acres. Despite the fact that their names are there in the Indian voters' list, the people are treated as Bangladeshis simply because they live in the adverse possessions.

They are deprived of all facilities provided by the Indian government. For the 17,000-odd people, living in the Bangladesh enclaves is not an option. Having lived within India for years they feel they have become Indian by heart. These people lived in Bangladesh enclaves for generations and considered India as their country. They grew up and earned their livelihood, selling paddy and vegetables in the Indian markets next door. Most of them had never been to Bangladesh and even married a girl from the neighbouring Indian village. It can be seen that the enclaves are not just pieces of disputed landmass. They contain people who continue their social, economic and political practices in these lands. By not resolving the dispute the people have been denied their right to their ancestral habitat, cut off from the linkages and kinsmen, harassed by the executive machinery of the respective states and their total life has been disrupted for last 60 years.

## Conflagration over adverse possession

In June 2002 however the problem of AP sparked a violent confrontation between India and Bangladesh, indicating the delicate nature of the problem. The Pyrdwah village of Bangladesh, inhabited by the Khasi tribe on the border of Meghalaya state, which is under the adverse possession of India, was attacked by Bangladeshi peasants aided by the Bangladesh Rifles. These intruders tried to illegally construct roads and erect structures in the village, which sought to have the invasion stopped by the Indian Border Security Force. But while the intruders withdrew from this area they attacked the Indian forces in another AP in the Assam-Bangladesh border – Mankachar – killing a number of Indian soldiers. This sparked a violent encounter between the two armies, threatening to become a full-scale war. The timely diplomatic initiative restored peace, but the tension in this area continued for a long time, compelling the two governments to strengthen their deployment in the region.

The course of events went as follows. Pyrdwah was a disputed territory and was under the possession of East Pakistan since the 1960s. The Indian forces took possession of it during the 1965 war with Pakistan. This was the place from where, during the war of liberation in 1971, the Bengali freedom fighters with the active support of the Indian military carried out several operations against Pakistani forces. After the emergence of Bangladesh, it claimed that Pyrdwah be returned to Bangladesh as per the Indira-Mujib Pact of 1974. Both India and Bangladesh had agreed to settle the dispute through the institutional mechanism of the Joint Working Committee on Boundary Disputes. In July 1999 the BSF had allegedly detained a large Bangladesh Rifles patrol when the latter entered the area to check the pillars. There was also a brief exchange of fire between the two border forces in 2000 which was normalised after a deputy director general level meeting. The Pyrdiwah issue came up once again at the director general level meeting of the two border forces held in New Delhi on 2 April 2001, which was inconclusive. On the night of 15–16 April 2002 troops of the Bangladesh Army and Bangladesh Rifles, after violating the international border agreement, laid a seize to Pyrdiwah, situated around 5 km from Dawki. The Bangladesh troops took the entire BSF outpost with 32 BSF men and one Assistant Commandant, S.S. Rawat. There was heavy exchange of fire between both security forces. Backed by the Bangladeshi forces, more than 1,000 Bangladeshi residents entered Pyrdiwah village and ransacked it. The nightlong plunder and attack by the Bangladeshis compelled the Pyrdiwah villagers – mostly Khasi and Santhal tribals – to vacate the village and take shelter in the jungle. The BDR's contention was that Pyrdiwah was India's adverse possession so it needed to be taken back. As the BSF men remained trapped at Pyrdiwah, reports were that Bangladesh was amassing BDR reinforcements along the border and that the Bangladesh Army was also being alerted for the next course of action. The Indian response was slow because neither the intelligence nor any tension was there to anticipate the trouble. As they realised the situation, a decision was taken to attack Boraibari in Mankachar, 300 km west of Pyrdiwah, which was a Bangladeshi adverse possession 'to ease the pressure on Pyrdiwah and divert Bangladeshi army's attention to a new site' (Gaur 2001). Once it was decided to attack Boraibari, the BSF's deputy commandant B.R. Mondal was asked to lead the charge. Mondal was in the area for a long time and had developed a good rapport with the villagers on both side of the border. But he was perhaps too complacent about his familiarity with the people and the terrain of the region. He had not reckoned with the changed sentiments on the other side. As he moved into the territory he and his 15-member team were taken hostage by a combined group of Bangladeshi villagers and BDR troops and then killed in cold blood. It seemed a full-fledged war with Bangladesh was on the verge of breaking out. In addition to the killing of 16 BSF troops in Mankachar, the Bangladeshi troops also took over 200 acres of Kakripara in the Assam-Meghalaya border. Five civilians were seriously injured and one civilian died on the spot due to mortar shelling. Fear psychosis among the villagers along the

Assam-Meghalaya border mounted. Panic-stricken villagers numbering 50,000 moved towards the safety of the Garo Hills sector. There was a wave of displaced persons from these villages to the nearby Indian outposts. Flag meetings were immediately held and trade and commerce suspended. A hurried and hectic diplomatic parley was able to ease the situation and maintain the status quo.

## Epilogue

The Government of India and Bangladesh signed a bilateral agreement on 6 September 2011 in Dhaka, in which there was broad agreement in transferring the disputed enclaves to the respective countries. The two governments agreed that there were four disputed zones along the Indo-Bangladesh border. These were the Palathal-Madanpur region, Noyagaon-Niyamura region, Lathitila-Dumabari region and Boraibari-Thakurianbari region. When the agreement was ratified by the parliament of the two countries and implemented, Bangladesh would own the 111 Indian enclaves that lie in its territory with an area of 17,160 acres, while 51 Bangladeshi enclaves stretching across 7,110 acres would merge with India. The two countries carried out a joint survey along the border in July 2011 and conducted a headcount determining that 51,000 people lived in the 162 enclaves that would change hands once the border pact took effect. Under the 2011 agreement, families living in the 162 enclaves locally known as Chhit or Chhitmahal would be asked to choose their nationalities. For instance, a man living in an Indian enclave in Bangladesh could opt for Bangladeshi citizenship and stay on in that enclave once it is handed over to Bangladesh. Or he can leave the enclave and come to India and become an Indian citizen. In that case he will be allotted a plot in India.

As far as Meghalaya was concerned, Bangladesh had conceded the seven areas of land under adverse possession located in the state. The areas which Bangladesh conceded in Meghalaya were Lungkhat I, II and III, Pyrdiwah, Tamabil and Naljuri I and II. It mentioned that ten areas are claimed to be under adverse possession of India in Meghalaya, including Pyrdiwah, Lynkhat I, II, III, Kurinallah, Tamabil, Naljuri I, II and III, Rongkhon, Amjalong, Amki and Muktapur. On areas Amki, Amjalong, Rongkhong, Kurrinallah and Muktapur a joint survey was not undertaken because of the fact that it was not possible to establish India's legal rights, physical possession or cultivation in these areas, adding that the agreement was very much in favour of the people of the state. But the people of these areas were aghast that they were not consulted before entering into any such agreement. They alleged that landowners, traditional institutions and district councils were not also consulted. They asserted that they would not cede even an inch of their land to Bangladesh and even threatened to seek the intervention of the UN if the deal was not in their favour. In fact they informed that they were not even aware that such an agreement had already been signed (*The Telegraph* 2011b: 1). The secretary of the Federation of Ri War Mihngi Local Darbars, which comprises 132 villages, said that the joint border survey projected only 193 acres for Pyrdiwah against 220 acres it holds now. In Lyngkhat I the Khasis were likely get only 4.75 acres instead of 6 acres and in Lyngkhat sector II and III, the projection is less than an acre. In Lyngkhat sector III instead of 11 acres the border survey has proposed 6.5 acres. They wanted the rest of the land that has been left undecided (*The Telegraph* 2011a: 1).

The opposition to the treaty appears most vociferous in Assam, which shares a 262 km border with Bangladesh and is now ceding 357.5 acres to it. Creating an emotive opposition to the land transfer is an obvious attempt to regain lost political ground, raking up latent anti-Bangladeshi sentiments and playing on the fears of the Assamese of being marginalised to a minority by 'Bangladeshi' design and Congress acquiescence. Backed by a vitriolic vernacular media, the shrill rhetoric is sure to sway at least a section of the population that harbours a deep suspicion of anything Bangladeshi and a constant sense of victimhood and alienation from India. Therefore, ceding 357.5 acres of it to Bangladesh is absolutely unacceptable. The hyperbole has reached such proportions that a few of the AGP and BJP worthies have even termed it as the 'Second Partition of India'.

## Conclusion

The state formation process of the Indian nation had other spin-off effects which actually violated the very principles of nationalism on which the hundred years of nationalist movement was based. In other words the nationalist movement strived for creating a nation by unifying all Indians, but eventually it ended up dividing and distancing its own people. The Radcliffe Line that drew the boundary between India and Pakistan, which later became Bangladesh, was inconclusive and had failed really to create two definite territories. Some Indian territories remained within Pakistan and vice versa. These territories were called Adverse Possession (AP). Thus the partition of the country not only divided the territory and created two separate nations; it also separated a huge community of tribal people who were neither Hindus nor Muslims. While two major nations were created, small tribal autochthones were partitioned and kinsmen divided, a number of such groups were abandoned in enclaves as stateless citizens. In the struggle of creating nations and nation-states for majority communities, tiny tribal communities were denied their basic right to their habitat. Habitats are not just territories. It comprises of landscapes, ecology, water bodies, all of which are part of the peoples' consciousness. There are memories associated with it, legends emanated out of the process of its formation and myths and folklores have sprung out of it. It has memories of migration, settlement, polity formation, community formation, invasions and attacks, victories and defeats, violence and peace, famines and times of plenty which are preserved for generations. These memories, myths, legends and folklores constitute the 'tradition' of the community. There are memories of ancestors and their remains which are the inheritance of the community. Most of these communities believe that the souls of their ancestors still hover around this habitat and protect them from evil and adversities. There are lores, ballads and songs which ancestors have handed down to them. There were legendary lovers whose pining still haunts the area. The tribals have their own gods and goddesses, witches and demons, spirits and fairies who also live in this land. If the tribals are displaced, these deities and spirits are also displaced. Prolonged collective living has generated certain common practices which constitute their culture. It is these cultures that determine their civilisation. Hence displacing, partitioning, evicting or disrupting the tribals from their habitat means a disruption and displacement of a huge tradition, a civilisation. But nations in their arrogance of demographic strength rarely respect the rights of small communities. Displacement of marginal groups and sacrificing the peripheral tribal habitats are a part of the nation-formation process. The partition of India and creation of two separate nations for the majority religious groups were no exception. The above narrative of the plight of the tribal groups in this weird concept called adverse possession is a testimony to this. Besides the Khasi, Garo, Hajong teatribe, a large section of the poor Hindu and Muslim farmers live in the adverse possessions and fight for everyday survival. Targeted by border guards of both countries, they live in constant danger of being shot dead or deported. They have no right to land or any rights which even the poorest of citizens enjoy in the mainland. They are stateless. The mighty state has no right to deny the marginal communities their right to their habitat. Displacement, division, eviction or placing them in another country is denial of that right. Since Independence India as a new nation-state strived to evolve a polity which is non-discriminatory and responsive to the needs of its multi-community structure. Tribals were often assured of their rights and granted autonomy. But Pakistan neither evolved any democratic polity nor was protective of its marginal tribal groups. Bangladesh since its birth has been notorious for displacing and dispossessing the tribals. The Indian tribals under the adverse possession of Bangladesh were the victims of such systematic oppression. Since these AP were small pieces of lands containing a fraction of the total population of the two countries, few efforts were made to resolve the issues. The case of the Adverse Possessions and its people is one example which elucidates the neglect and abandonment of marginal people by the nation-state. Once it attained its independence and nation-state-hood, it conveniently forgot its own people who were left within another country, without any basic human rights. The nation even found it convenient to forget that these adverse possessions were its own citizens who were in their present plight not due to any of their own faults but the creation of the nation itself. They are people truly abandoned by the respective nations.

## Note

1 See Letters to the Editor in *Shillong Times*, Shillong, 29 October 2005. Around this time the regional newspapers were full of reports that the rural tribals were protesting that their cultivable lands were being transferred to the other side of the fence between Bangladesh and India. Some such lands also fell in the mandatory 'no-man's land'. They were therefore against the construction of the fence and wanted the status quo to be maintained as regards the boundary.

## References

*The Asian Age*. 2003. Gauhati, 16 and 11 June.
Bareh, Hamlet. 2001. *Encyclopaedia of NE India, Volume V (Mizoram)*. New Delhi: Mittal Publication.
Gaur. 2001. *Outlook*, May 7: 23–4.
Grover, V. and Ranjana Aurora (eds.). 1997. 'Report of the Bengal Boundary Commission (Radcliffe Report) 1947', Appendixed in *India 50 Years of Independence*, Volume 1. New Delhi: Deep & Deep, 313–14.
Khanna, V. 2003. 'Statement of Union Minster of State for External Affairs in the Rajya Sabha', *Unstarred Questions No. 3660*, April 24. http://164.100.24.219/rsq/quest.asp?qrep=80014.

Krishnan, K. 2001. 'Policing the Indo-Bangladesh Border', *Strategic Analysis*, 25(5): 665.
Lakshman, Kanchan and Sanjay K. Jha. 2003. 'India-Bangladesh: Restoring Sovereignty on Neglected Borders', *Faultline: Writing on Conflict and Resolution*, 14(July): 123–58.
Rammhoan, E. N. 2002. *USI Journal*, 132(550), October–December, p. 496, cited in Lakshman and Sanjay, 'India-Bangladesh'.
*The Sentinel*. 2010. 'More Assam Land Under Bangladesh Possession'. Silchar, 5 August.
Sharma, S. N. 2001. 'Questionable Possessions', *North East Sun*, 1–14 May: 14.
*Shillong Times*. 2005. Shillong, 29 October.
*The Telegraph*. 2003a. Gauhati Edition, 15 April.
*The Telegraph*. 2003b. Gauhati Edition, 9 July.
*The Telegraph*. 2011a. 'Border Land Deal Creates a Divide'. Guwahati, 9 September.
*The Telegraph*. 2011b. 'Dhaka Land Deal Sparks Furore'. Guwahati, 8 September.
*The Times of India*. 2003. Gauhati, 8 June.

# 4

# INCLUSIONS AND EXCLUSIONS OF ADIVASI WOMEN

Subsuming challenges from the past, present and future in Chhattisgarh

*Ilina Sen*

Issues of Indigenous communities, the challenges facing them in today's globalised world, and especially the voices of indigenous women, often get marginalised and lost in the social and political discourse today. It is essential to focus on these questions since the political resolution of the problems associated with tribal development, central to the polity of the nation today, desperately need critical engagement by academia. There are many reasons why we need a gendered analysis of the crisis in Indigenous (read *Adivasi*) society and development urgently at the present juncture. Even a preliminary listing of reasons would include the following:

- The category of the Indigenous/Tribal women is often read in tandem with Dalit women following the administrative clubbing of the SC/ST in our academic vocabulary. And just as SC/ST often becomes a footnote to the discourse on the 'regular' population, within the SC/ST classification, the ST, and particularly, the tribal woman, often becomes the smallest footnote in the entire discourse.
- The economic and political aspects of tribal women's reality, their struggles, representation, as well as vulnerability, while having a rich history, are barely on the fringes of serious social science scholarship, barring colonial anthropological accounts.
- The issues around the mainstream representation of the 'tribal' entity, their reality and the essential representation of tribal women

themselves are little understood and need to be urgently unpacked in a world spiralling into change.

The Indigenous/Adivasi communities in India are concentrated in the North East, Central India, Western states and the South. The history of their integration into mainstream and colonial historiography has been different in each area and among the different tribes in an area, based on many factors. However, despite differences, certain broad generalisations are apparent. The indigenous women's relationship with land, forest and nature has been special and has informed the stuff of the sustainability discourse and eco feminist debates. Although individual tribes have followed different forms of social organisation (e.g. matrilineal like the Khasi, patriarchal like the Gond), patriarchy as a social system does exist in tribal societies, and is reflected in certain aspects of what are called customary laws as well as familial relationships. This is often unacknowledged in debates around autonomy and customary rights, and some of these confusions have carried over into governance debates and spaces like the Fifth and Sixth schedules of the Constitution. Scholars and administrators who have been strong advocates for the customary rights of tribal communities have not always had the sensitivity to understand and articulate a gendered understanding of the rights of tribal women. At the same time, the strong participation of Adivasi women in tribal resistance struggles in history conveys an impression of women's agency that is not an uncomplicated one. The fact that the Indigenous areas in many parts of the country are today epicentres of struggles around the paradigm of development adds some urgency to our enquiry.

The present chapter is a small attempt to address some of the issues of Adivasi women's inclusions and exclusions in the context of these larger questions. It is rooted in original fieldwork in Central India, mostly among different subsets of the Gonds, largely in the state of Chhattisgarh, ongoing for the last two decades. Although the context is specific, there are some common analytical frameworks that can be drawn from this. There is no effort to dilute the enormous variation and diversity in the lives and experiences of tribal women in different contexts. However, it is certainly an attempt to capture some common threads that do perhaps transcend the different experiences.

The basic premises are simple. Tribal and Indigenous women have made a major contribution to the sustainability of land and forest, yet remain unrecognised in their own communities and in larger society. Processes underway in the larger society and political economy marginalise and exclude them even further. This chapter is also an attempt to locate patriarchy in Adivasi societies, and to deconstruct some glib generalisations about Adivasi women with which many of us grew up. These relate to the so-called full equality of women with men in Adivasi societies.[1]

## Gender issues in tribal societies

Many (particularly non-tribal) scholars as they come out of universities are impressed with the gender equality that is apparent in tribal societies. It is true that tribal women are not secluded and veiled, and are far more visible in public life than women in mainstream Indian society, and that gender ratios in districts with predominantly Adivasi populations show better survival of women. To give an example from Chhattisgarh, in 2012 according to the SRS analytical average (GoI 2012), the gender ratio in the state was among the best in the country. While the overall sex ratio in Chhattisgarh was 979 women per 1,000 men, it was 1,002 for the rural areas, and it was 956 for the urban population. The child sex ratio (0–6), the bête noire of demographers today, was 972 and 932 respectively for rural and urban populations. Chhattisgarh ranks third in overall gender ratio among the states in India, after Kerala (1,084) and 979 (Tamil Nadu). The figures from the Census of India are similar, with Chhattisgarh having a sex ratio of 991 women to 1,000 men, holding its own after Kerala, Puducherry, Tamil Nadu and Andhra Pradesh (GoI 2011). In 2011, Chhattisgarh had a tribal population of approximately 31 per cent of its total. It is clear that in terms of certain survival and visibility indices, the situation of tribal women stands well vindicated.

However, it is perhaps time to look beyond these generalisations. Firstly it is important to understand that Adivasis and Adivasi women are not homogenous categories. It is also true that Adivasi women participate fully in the economic life of the family and community, and are often central to these institutions. Yet we see, with examples from Gond society, that women are singularly absent from the traditional political structures and remain less than fully integrated in modern structures of representative government. There is also a strong tendency to codify and interpret traditional social norms on sexuality and personal life along fundamentalist premises that tend to push women into the margins and destroy the fragile equity that exists in the economic sphere. The last process is aided by the forces of globalisation and market liberalisation.

ILINA SEN

# The economic life of tribal women: women's role in food production and other livelihoods

In many ways, the Adivasi women of Chhattisgarh enjoy a unique position within the country. The sex ratio is universally acknowledged as an indicator of women's well-being, survival and status, and in this the position of Chhattisgarh ranks high among states in the country and well above the national average. Unlike women in many other parts of India where the culture of exclusion and seclusion seems to prevail, women in Chhattisgarh are articulate, visible, and play a major role in all aspects of the livelihood systems.

The Indigenous communities of Chhattisgarh have been food sovereign in ways not fully comprehended by the scientific community right up to the present time. To make an attempt to understand this reality, one has to understand Chhattisgarh's food production and distribution systems in some detail. Chhattisgarh has had an amazing variety of food production systems. It is one of the last places on the earth to have a remembered history of an enormous diversity of food resources. These food resources include many kinds of rice germ plasm, a wide range of millets and other dryland crops, pulses, oilseeds, fruits, edible flowers, tubers, mushrooms and other gathered foods. Many of these are dependent upon access to and close proximity of the forests.

The role that women have played in maintaining these systems is relatively little understood. In Indigenous Chhattisgarh, women are the major agricultural workers. They work in each and every aspect of crop production, preservation and storage. In certain parts of the state like Abujhmar and Sihawa, women are also known to use the plough, a function that is tabooed and prohibited for them in almost all other parts of the country. Apart from crop weeding, maturing, harvesting, women are the leading players in all post-harvest and storage operations. Women also play a major role in the collection and processing of the many kinds of uncultivated foods found in Chhattisgarh. Many of these foods are collections from the forest, and women use them for maintaining household food security and nutrition needs outside the market system.

Women are the primary gatherers of all uncultivated foods, and inheritors of an ancient knowledge system about food biodiversity. They are also the gardeners and herbalists with primary knowledge and responsibility for maintaining the home gardens, the *baris* and the *bakhris*. Again, it is the women who take the produce to the primary markets and barter or trade in the items related to primary food needs. Women are also the keepers of the seeds and are responsible for all post-harvest operations. An important aspect of these is the preservation of the seeds of biodiversity. In traditional Chhattisgarh, the crop to be harvested as seed is identified in the field of standing crop, and women take special care while reaping these. A wide variety of seed storage structures are used in subsequent stages, and the exact storage structure used for seed depends on the length of time the seed is to be stored away, the moisture content and other factors. Some seeds like rice are stored in bamboo *dholgi* (or dhongi), thatched and sealed with cow dung, and kept away. These can last for up to three years. Other seeds like the minor millet seeds or vegetable seeds are stored in Sal leaf containers, and often hung up in the kitchen above a wood fire, so that the smoke can act as a pesticide and preservative. The extremely complex knowledge of seed storage and preservation, including its technical aspects, is in the hands of the women.

The important economic position of women in the traditional area of food security spilled over into the mining sector as this developed in the state and can be seen also among migrant workers from Chhattisgarh who are major contributors to the construction industry nation-wide. Many of the metropolitan highways, buildings and national industries have been built by the migrant workers from Chhattisgarh, and the women of Chhattisgarh have been more than equal contributors in these efforts. In the case of mining (Chhattisgarh is the most mineral-rich state in the country), the entire operation of manual mining makes it necessary for men and women to work in pairs, with one breaking the freshly blasted rock into handleable-sized nuggets and the other carrying head loads away to the transport point. The viability of this symbiotic relationship could be seen in any of the open cast mines and quarries that dot the landscape in Chhattisgarh and other parts of central India. In the iron ore mines of Dalli Rajhara, in Durg district, in the captive mines of the Bhilai Steel Plant, Chhattisgarh's flagship industrial undertaking, major struggles by the workers' organisation Chhattisgarh Mines Shramik Sangh (CMSS) were waged at the turn of the century over the issue of the issue of women's right to work. The threatened displacement of women from the workforce as the mine management sought to modernise technology and do away with manual mining became a major industrial dispute issue in the late 1970s. Women workers strongly resisted attempts to lay them off, and went to the extent of questioning labour and technology policies in a labour-surplus economy like that of India. The most important contribution to both the Labour and Women's questions by the women workers of Dalli Rajhara was their insistence on women's equal right to a productive life.

ILINA SEN

## The social world of Adivasi women

When we extend this discussion to the social position of Indigenous women, some of the complexities of the situation begin to be noticed. The position of women in the Indigenous society of Chhattisgarh is at the same time extremely strong and yet vulnerable.

Highlighting the socially accepted positive contribution of women in the Indigenous society of Chhattisgarh must in no way be taken as a plea for an unqualified glorification of the fabulous situation of women's empowerment in the Indigenous world. We are only now getting sensitised to the issue of patriarchy within Indigenous communities. There are huge gaps in our knowledge and understanding, yet some general conclusions are possible from the experience of working Gond Adivasis in the Raipur, Dhamtari and Kanker districts. For convenience we can structure this discussion into the three areas of civil rights, spiritual life world and regulation of sexuality relationships.

### *Civil rights and citizenship issues of Indigenous women*

Women are completely absent from the decision-making systems and processes in either the community social bodies or structures like the village grain banks (*charjaniha*) that have helped communities to tide over food scarcity situations in the past. Traditionally Gond women, in particular, the Dhruv Gond women I have worked with for many years, do not have any inheritance rights in land or other forms of movable property. Lineage and property are both transmitted through the male line. Single women do have residence rights in their parental/marital homes, and there is limited knowledge or acceptance of constitutional rights in this regard. In traditional Gond society, governance is through a body of community elders (*siyan*s) who are all male. This body traditionally adjudicates in cases of personal/civil dispute as well as dispute among or between villages, or between the domains of various deities (*devta*s). Being a scheduled area, the provisions of the PESA are operative; however women's participation in 'official' Gram Sabhas remains poor, and this indicates that there is little internalisation of constitutional values of gender equity and full participation in civil society.

### *The faith and spiritual world: women and witchcraft*

The Gond spiritual life world is regulated by the many devtas and a wide supernatural realm of magic and the dark world that casts its effect on the day-to-day well-being of humans. The devtas include several mother goddesses, like Kumrahin, Kankalin, Alsahin, and others. It is to be noted that up to fairly recent times, the term 'devta' was used interchangeably for male and female deities. Today, the terminology is beginning to include the word '*devi*' to indicate female goddess shrines. All devi shrines have the wooden replica of Angadev (who lacks human form but indicates the eternal power behind creation) in the courtyard leading up to the sanctum sanctorum. In a sense, Angadev gives us access to the mother goddess and is the gateway to her power. Angadev, however, is male, as are all the priests (*baigas*) of the female goddesses. It is the baigas who are custodians of the flag (*jhanda*) and weapons of the goddess, with which they join the ritual processions and perform the rites of worship on behalf of their patron whenever the devi is invited to a *madhai* in a neighbouring village or to a large gathering like the Bastar dashera darbar. It is clear that female spiritual power, while recognised, is mediated through and controlled by the male.

Coming to the realm of magic and the dark arts, this configuration becomes clearer. There is universal belief in supernatural power, but there is a difference in the way it is conceptualised for men and women holders of supernatural power. All baigas have supernatural power, and they are universally propitiated for this reason. In sickness, the ill are taken by relatives to the baigas, and gifts of alcohol and chicken are made to him, seeking his intervention with the magical world on behalf of the sick. There is a shared belief that the baiga can intervene on behalf of the needy to facilitate a positive result. The belief system in the case of women is starkly in contrast to this. There is widespread belief in witchcraft, and an understanding that a *Tonhi* (witch) can cause sickness and death through the use of black magic. The Tonhi in tribal Chhattisgarh is a figure of fear and hatred and young children are taught to avoid her like the plague. Female access to supernatural power is never for the good of human kind and can cause only destruction and harm according to tradition. The actual identification of a Tonhi is often done by a baiga in the context of an actual mis happening in the village, and once identified, a Tonhi is subjected to the cruellest torture and social ostracism.

### *The regulation of women's sexuality*

The regulation of sexual relationships among the Gonds is interesting. Traditionally, there were many variants of a formal marriage – the *barbihav* (first marriage of boy and girl at the bride's house), *lagin bihav* (the same, but at the groom's house), *paithu bihav* (feast to give community recognition to the marriage of a boy and a girl who have eloped together and returned to the community after an absence), *bhowji churhi* (where a younger brother-in-law marries the wife of a deceased brother to keep her in the family), *churhi pahinava* (formal community recognition to a second or subsequent marriage of the female partner solemnised by her male partner putting bangles on her hand) and *harras*, where an unmarried girl who is pregnant, is granted legitimacy for herself and her child through a community meeting in which the siyans invite a suitable proposal for her. In the latter case, preference is given to the biological father of the unborn child, but, in case of his inability to marry the woman, proposals are usually received from widowers or others who may have need of a female companion and homemaker. Once a harras marriage is conducted, there is no difference in the status of the woman married through this process as compared to one married through any other form. The child is accepted as the child of the mother's husband. One glimpses here a tolerance and acceptance of the plurality in the regulation of sexuality that is absent from mainstream Hindu society. Recent tendencies among Gond *Mahasabhas* (assemblies) from Kanker and Dhamdha to codify their customary laws have, however, derecognised and discouraged most forms other than the *bar bihav*. Paithu is allowed with heavy penalties and fines to the community, and one can notice a definite loss of plurality and space for personal preference. Whatever have been women's rights and entitlements in Indigenous society, processes responsible for their interpretation and codification are not working today in the interests of women.

The changing scenario can be illustrated with reference to the report of an incident that shook Gond village society to the core in the year 2000 in Chhattisgarh's Dhamtari district, and made for social friction between patriarchal constructions of female sexuality among Gond social patriarchs and pesky Raipur journalists, keen to report and write on 'human rights abuses'.

In August 2002, all newspapers in Chhattisgarh carried the sensational headlines of a teenage girl's suicide following her auction in village Gohannala of Dhamtari. The *Indian Express* of 21 August reported that a young girl, Kesari Bai, of Gohannala had committed suicide after a being auctioned to the highest bidder for Rs. 551 by the elders of her community following the 'discovery' of her unwed pregnancy. A week before her auction, Kesari was allegedly caught sleeping with a local youth, Bhuru, who runs a shop in the village.

The village elders, who took exception to her conduct, first asked Bhuru to marry the girl. When Bhuru refused, the matter went to the Adivasi Mahasabha, a body represented by 16 villages. The Mahasabha held on 14 July summoned Bhuru and Kesari. Charges were framed against them for indulging in immoral activity not permitted in the Gond society. "While Kesari denied having ever approached him, Bhuru claimed he was under the influence of liquor and couldn't recollect how he landed up with Kesari", recalls Kamla Vati.

'Halal Singh Netam, head of the Mahasabha, rejected their explanation. He asked Bhuru to pay a fine of Rs. 2,500 and put Kesari on auction. Six prospective grooms participated in the bidding. Babulal, the highest bidder, was told to take Kesari away. But the humiliation was too much for Kesari and she decided to end her life' (*Indian Express* 2002).

Similar reports appeared in vernacular-language newspapers, and online news portals. It transpired that some 'social workers' from Gohannala had approached Raipur-based Subhash Mahapatra, head of an NGO named Fact Finding Documentation and Advocacy (FFDA), with details of the incident, and he had taken cognisance of this case. The newspaper reports were on the basis of the press release he had put out. These reports and the resulting invasion of the village by the press, the police and the administration caused deep disquiet and anger in the village about the role of 'outsiders' in the *samajik* (social) matters of the community.

What happened at Gohannala, the harras marriage, was the community's way of finding a partner for an unmarried girl who is pregnant out of marriage. Once the pregnancy is discovered, usually by a family member, the matter is taken to the local chapter of the *samajik mahasabha* (social council) that effectively translates as a group of elders and patriarchs, the siyans. The latter usually organise a social meeting, in which all interested parties are expected to be present. In the event, the male partner of the girl is otherwise eligible to be her marital partner (i.e. he is not from the same clan as the girl), he is requested to marry her. In case he is not eligible, or unwilling to marry the girl, other interested and eligible men are invited to offer marriage. In this way, out of a number of offers of marriage, the girl is asked to choose the one she considers most suitable, and the community asks for a contribution and feast from the prospective groom, and the matter is settled. The cash transaction that takes place is called the *neng* (offering) to the deities and the community, and not quite the auction that the city-bred activists and journalists had projected the matter to be.

It is always difficult to take a position on the political correctness of the social practices of a community. In the event, I was surprised to find that several elderly couples residing peacefully in Gedra and Gattasilli villages adjoining village Gohannala had come together initially through a harras marriage. The codification of social rules that have taken place in many branches of the Gond Mahasabha (several of these came to hand) prohibit or strongly discourage the paithu, *bhowji*, churhi and harras forms of marriage, as part of the process of Sanskritisation. The system no doubt does not offer an option of foeticide, horror of horrors, when we recall the spate of female foeticides across cultures and national borders! Or single parenthood to a girl with a premarital pregnancy, and it is no doubt traumatic for a young girl to have to deal with the end of a first love. However, the liberality of traditional Gond society in which there is an attempt to deal practically with youth sexuality, in which a man accepts the social and legal paternity of a child not biologically fathered by him, is rare in any patriarchal society, and must also be appreciated.

## Sanskrtisation, integration and mainstreaming

Modernisation and globalisation have affected Indigenous women in Chhattisgarh, as in other places, and this has not necessarily been for the better. In recent years we find that not only are incidents of violence and crimes against women in Chhattisgarh on the rise, traditional society's attitude towards women is also changing for the worse. Caste/Tribe Panchayats have emerged as severely patriarchal bodies of siyans (elders) and in several cases have meted out severe punishment to women transgressing what are perceived to be customary laws. These trends are in keeping with hardening attitudes to female morality among male-dominated groups of community elders in many parts of the country. Dowry at the time of marriage was an almost unknown phenomenon 20 years ago, but with the coming of sections of the Indigenous population into the service sector, with the money inflow for government servants through implementation of successive Pay Commissions, it has become standard for the lower middle and middle classes to hand out and receive the customary dowry package of refrigerator, TV set, motorcycle at the wedding of a daughter or a son. Certain provisions of customary law like the 'Churhi Pratha', which once gave women the freedom to end an unpleasant relationship and contract another that is more compatible to their being, are today being used by men to throw out economically dependent and vulnerable wives and children and contract subsequent relationships. The cultural creation of the 'dependent' wife is itself a product of the cultural integration of Chhattisgarh into mainstream India.

In this context, the experiences after the new state of Chhattisgarh was created in 2000, in a grand exercise at supposed 'decentralised responsive governance' is worth studying. Chhattisgarh was carved out of Madhya Pradesh's 16 eastern-most districts, with borders to Jharkhand, Uttar Pradesh, Odisha and Maharashtra apart from the parent state. Government development policy aimed at 'women's empowerment' drafted by high-flying consultancies[2] revealed no special sensitivity to the issues of tribal women in the state, and used practically the same language as used in any state or location of the country. There is no indication or regard apparent in the document regarding any local structures of empowerment that may have existed earlier. A quick look at the Chhattisgarh Women's Policy (*Chhattisgarh Mahila Neeti* 2000) may be instructive. The policy document proclaimed that its objectives included steps to:

- Facilitate a conducive environment to enable women to realise their full potential and promote self-reliance.
- Achieve equality in access to economic resources including forests, common property, land and other means of production.
- Ensure participation of women in social, political and economic life of the state.

While the Women's Policy was a 'social sector' Policy, the major policy documents created after Chhattisgarh's statehood related to the development of industry, mines and energy. The Chhattisgarh Industrial Policy (2004–09) set the tenor for many of the other policy documents in the state. Work on it began soon after the state was born, but it took three years for it to become operational. Recognising that Chhattisgarh is endowed with abundant natural resources, the policy document stated as its main objective the addition of maximum value to these natural resources while creating maximum employment opportunities by setting up industries in all districts of the state. Within this larger objective, the secondary but important objectives of creating an enabling environment for increased industrial production, promotion of private sector partnership for the creation of industrial infrastructure in the state, and the establishment of the competitiveness of industrial investment in Chhattisgarh vis-à-vis other states in the country were placed. The Chhattisgarh Mineral Policy announced in 2001 is a precursor and in many ways intricately linked to this Industrial Investment Policy. The Chhattisgarh Energy Policy (*Chhattisgarh Urja Neeti* 2001) complements the industrial and the mining policies.

As far as women are concerned, there appears to have been total oblivion in the overall understanding of policymakers that even the limited objectives listed in the Women's Policy were inconsistent with the policy of aggressive industrialisation which the state was adopting, policies that displaced communities engaged in primary production and affected women's traditional livelihoods the most.

## The current crisis in development and the impact on Adivasi women

In so many ways, the effects of the simmering crisis in 'development' in the Indigenous areas put Adivasi lives, Adivasi heritage and aspirations at the centre of the discourse on our political future in this country. The gender dimension of this discourse is important, and necessary to take into account for understanding and responding to the issues politically, culturally, and in our role as academics. Let us engage with these questions in the upcoming paragraphs.

It is a truism today that the birth of the new state of Chhattisgarh at the turn of the new millennium took place very much in the context of globalisation and the liberalisation of the Indian economy in the decades following 1991. The forces set in motion with these processes were extremely violent, and caused deep trauma to the fabric of Indigenous societies that existed there. In unimaginable ways, it has transpired that tribal women have been at the centre of this trauma, and our larger society today needs to understand why this has been so.

Following the birth of the new state of Chhattisgarh and the inking of several mining industry projects in the mineral areas of south and north Chhattisgarh, there was evidence of widespread resistance to land acquisition and the displacement of centuries-old Indigenous populations that was an expected corollary from many parts of the state. Public opinion and political discourse got sharply polarised between those wanting 'development' in this backward state, and those who argued on the grounds of constitutional provisions of the Fifth and Sixth Schedules to the Constitution as well as the newly enacted Panchayati Raj (Extension to Scheduled Areas) Act. These acts stipulated that any development project needed to safeguard constitutional guarantees of self-governance to the tribal population, and according to major exponents of tribal rights like Dr B.D. Sharma (Sharma 2010), ensuring their actual implementation has been extremely tardy.

In 2005, the state of Chhattisgarh launched its controversial 'Salwa Judum' (Purification hunt) programme, a state-supported vigilante force that was supposedly a 'peoples' initiative against violent revolutionary resistance aimed to overthrow the Indian state. There were enough indications that this was actually a ground-clearing exercise to vacate large areas for mining and industrial development and to crush any opposition to official development plans (Sen 2006). Without getting into a debate about the Salwa Judum, it is a fact of the matter that the combination of Salwa Judum, burning of 'hostile' villages, displacement, strategic hamletting and the sheer scale of militarised conflict that emerged in the south Bastar area of Chhattisgarh after 2005 completely destroyed normal life in the region. Social services including health services stand dismantled, agriculture and livelihoods do not exist in large parts of the area, and the education of children is only now beginning to be taken up today, more than ten years later.

## What did all this mean for women?

As the Central Indian tribal areas become engulfed in conflict due to the hardening battle lines between the 'sharks' of development and the multifaceted resistance of the Adivasis, it is tribal women are often subjected to the worst forms of sexual violence from the militarised forces that are called into the area to 'control' the law and order situation. A 2006 study (CAVOW 2006) on the impact of the conflict on women documented some of the many ways in which sexual violence against women has been used as a tool of area domination by the vigilantes and the security forces alike. Some landmark instances that have drawn public attention to this phenomenon nationally include the cases of Soni Sori and Meena Xalkho. Soni Sori, an Adivasi school teacher, was arrested on charges of being a Maoist supporter (illegal according to Chhattisgarh's Special Public Security Act of 2005), was brutally tortured in police custody, and an independent medical examination found her complaint of stones being inserted in her rectum and vagina to be correct. It is a symbol of the patriarchy of the state that her torturer, a police officer, was decorated with a gallantry award for counter-insurgency operations by the president on Republic Day in 2010.

Meena Xalkho, a 16-year-old tribal girl from Karcha village in the state of Chhattisgarh, was gang raped and killed in the forest close to her village by an armed police search party in 2011. The security forces subsumed Meena's horrible rape and murder within the terms of a 'laudable mission', one that managed to neutralise all rage against police atrocities, by claiming Meena to be a Naxal and by claiming her to be fatally wounded in an encounter that night against a larger party of Naxalite cadres. Sustained public pressure forced the appointment of a judicial enquiry into the case, and the report of the commission of enquiry became public in 2015. The judicial enquiry report categorically dismissed claims of the state government that Meena was a Naxalite and she was killed in an encounter with the police. Forensic reports have confirmed presence of semen on her body and clothes, directly putting the blame on police for gang rape and brutal murder. The single-member judicial commission, headed by retired district and sessions judge Anita Jha, had submitted its report over the incident in 2015, which recommended the state government to reinvestigate the incident and take necessary action into it. The report had also pointed that a police bullet had killed Xalkho.

Thereafter, the state CID had registered a murder case into the incident in the same year based on the findings of the judicial inquiry and launched a probe. A total of 25 police personnel were named in the report, and to date only one of them has been arrested prior to being released on bail.

## Conclusion

We have attempted in this brief chapter to review Adivasi women's economic and social life worlds within the confines of traditional Gond society in Chhattisgarh; a society that was fairly rooted, although changing slowly, in the matter of being in contact with and influenced by mainstream caste society in the areas where they lived. Both the rootedness, as well as the interaction, had gender dimensions; there was at no time absolute lack of patriarchal control for women, although, in comparison to mainstream caste society, the situation of women seems to have been favourable in many respects. In the late 20th century, because of larger political and economic forces that overtook the habitats of the tribal population, the pace of change increased dramatically. At this time, challenges of governance, power relations and differences with regard to development choices spiralled the Adivasi heartlands in Central India into conflict, and in many ways, the bodies of Adivasi women became symbols of contestation and assertion of power. Sexual violence on Adivasi women's bodies became the currency of power and nation building – we are living with this situation all around us today. No one is sure whether at any time in the foreseeable future the (graded) advantages that tribal women enjoyed, in their own society and in the larger community of women, will ever again be recalled except in terms of a world that we have lost. No one is sure which way the dynamics of state, power and the violence of development will shape out in the immediate future. The challenges are enormous, both in terms of the discourse on gender equity, and the preservation of the fabric of a society that is still holding together. If this chapter has provided at least a space where some of these questions have been flagged and thrown open for debate, the effort will have been more than justified.

## Notes

1 The words 'Indigenous', 'tribal' and 'Adivasi' have all been used more or less interchangeably in this chapter. Unless categorically stated, there is no intention of attributing difference in this usage.
2 In the case of Chhattisgarh, the Vision Document for the new state as drafted by the firm of Price, Waterhouse Cooper in 2000.

## References

*Chhattisgarh Mahila Neeti.* 2000. 'Chhattisgarh Sarkar Jan Sampark Vibhag', in *Nai Rajya Nayi Neetiaan*, 2005, Raipur.
*Chhattisgarh Urja Neeti.* 2001. 'Chhattisgarh Sarkar Jan Sampark Vibhag', in *Nai Rajya Nayi Neetiaan*, 2005, Raipur.
CAVOW. 2006. *Salwa Judum and Violence on Women in Dantewara*. Chhattisgarh: Report of a Fact-Finding by an All India Women's Team.
Government of India. 2011. *Provisional Population Totals*. New Delhi: Census Data.
Government of India. 2012. *SRS Report*. New Delhi: Registrar General and Census Commissioner, Ministry of Home Affairs, 19 April 2014.
*Indian Express*. 2002. Raipur Edition. 21 August.
Sen, Ilina. 2006. 'Ground Clearing With the Salwa Judum'. *Himal Southasia*.
Sharma, B. D. 2010. *Unbroken History of Broken Promises: Indian State and the Tribal People*. New Delhi: Sahayog Pustak Kutir.

# 5

# EXPROPRIATION OF LAND AND CULTURES AND THE RISE OF THE RADICAL LEFT

## The Odisha story and beyond

*Subrat Kumar Sahu and Mamata Dash*

In a state like Odisha in which Dalit and Adivasi communities constitute about 47 per cent of the total population (Prasad 2001), it is apparent that the issue of 'access' to resources (land, forests, water, etc.) is at the nerve-centre of most conflicts – social, economic, political and cultural. For traditional communities, 'access' is directly linked to civilisational paradigms and cultural ethos, which rather decide their 'economics', and not the other way around that may be true to modern, techno-centric civilisations. In traditional milieus – especially with Adivasis – 'culture' is the larger umbrella under which social and economic behaviours come early as precious, binding lessons to each member of the community that lives as a 'collective' rather than as a complex set of individual schemes as in modern societies. Therefore, the chain of production and consumption in Adivasi societies repeats in a balanced cycle – and, at times, in upward spiral mobility – in which the available resources (natural resources) must be consumed in such religious manner that ensures their sustainability for posterity. And, such practices bind the community and nature (resources) in an ideal symbiotic relationship.

So, in traditional milieus, denial of 'access' to resources not only results in their cultural degradation, it also directly impacts their 'food security'. It is no wonder that most hunger deaths reported from the state – under Independent, democratic India – during the past three decades are those of Adivasis and Dalits. Most mainstream discourses of history and politics have, however, tried to locate the crisis in the absence of 'appropriate state interventions'. But, a dig into the social history points to deeper roots of the crisis: denial of access and ownership through various social and political processes over centuries, which rather intensified after the entry of the 'welfare state'. On the other hand, myriad spontaneous responses by communities suffering the assault for centuries have also been either strategically undermined in mainstream political discourses, or repressed – most often brutally – and excluded from history writing.

### Odisha: a random outline

- 75 per cent of tribal and 67 per cent of Dalit populations live below the poverty line.
- Poverty in South Odisha (Koraput) with higher tribal population has increased in the past three decades: 87 per cent below the poverty line.
- 44 per cent of the area of the state is marked as Schedule-V area.
- In the Schedule-V districts: the state holds 74 per cent of the land; 65 per cent are small and marginal landholders in possession of only 13 per cent of the land; non-Adivasis (15 per cent hold 13 per cent of the land; the rest 20 per cent are landless). In Gajapati district: 93 per cent of the households (comprising small and marginal farmers and the landless) hold only 9 per cent of the land.
- The average size of landholdings among Adivasis across the state is only 1.10 standard acres.
- The average holding size for marginal Adivasi landowners is only 0.45 standard acres.

(Kumar *et al.* 2005)

### Deconstructing history: how 'access' is denied

*Cultural appropriation leading to dispossession*

Cultural practices of Indigenous folks are strictly guided by the laws of nature. They religiously consider themselves as part of nature, and worship Mother Earth in various forms depending on the belief system of the specific tribal group involved. These practices and beliefs, in turn, decide their economic cycles and sustenance – judiciously relying on the resources available at hand and, at the same time, dutifully ensuring that the resources sustain for posterity. Therefore, the relationship between Adivasis and land (including forests and water) is implicitly symbiotic in nature. It is no wonder that any distortion to this relationship has often spelt doom for the Adivasis as well as other traditional communities.

Invasion into the forests of central and eastern India by hordes of communities and clans from north and west India and adjoining states in the mediaeval period witnessed fierce battles over resources and lands. However, with the natives deeply rooted to their cultures, which decided their economic and ecological behaviour as religious tenets, economic colonisation was not possible – despite the blood – without colonising them culturally. And this was done broadly in two ways: (1) patronise and adopt the existing cultural practices of Adivasis and gradually take control of them and their resources; and/or (2) impose your own cultural and religious tenets by using royal power or by intimidating them by propagating the divine 'superiority' of a new god, such as the spread of the Jagannath cult in which thousands of temples have come up in remote, forested hinterlands of Odisha. The latter has been, over centuries, the single most lethal process of cultural colonisation in Odisha – covertly helped by the dominant political order of any given day – that continues to dispossess traditional communities of their economic bases and sustainable lifestyles even today.

Sindhekela village in Balangir district, for instance, presents the microcosm of the first type of cultural appropriation leading to economic colonisation. The local Adivasis here have been worshipping Goddess Duarseni since time unknown. There was no idol earlier; what they actually worship is what they call *badan khaal* (badan = body, khaal = trench), which is in fact a natural tunnel, believed by the locals to be several kilometres long. To the Adivasis here, the badan khaal symbolises progeny, production and continuity – the 'soul of the soil' that nurtures life, culture and identity in and of the land and forests of the Adivasis.

But, one does not have to make an effort to notice that their very life-support system – the forests – have vanished since then; and a little probing would also have one discover that the ownership of the vast stretches of farmlands all around (where a dense forest stood earlier) are now with non-Adivasis, including Brahmin landlords and *Marwadi* traders. The world of the Adivasis, as though, has shrunk into a space as much that of as the badan khaal acquires.

A peep into the socio-cultural history of the region unravels the paradox a bit further. About a century and a half earlier, the erstwhile king of the princely state of Patna (now Patnagarh) sent one of his kin to rule the region. But, the bloody history of valiant battles over

# EXPROPRIATION OF LAND AND CULTURES

'controlling resources' between tribes – and more often between tribes and non-tribal groups – in mediaeval central India had the rulers enlightened about a precious lesson in practising feudalism: instead of confronting physically, take control of the 'culture' of Adivasis, and then their 'resources' are yours!

So, the first task the new ruler took upon himself was to 'patronise' the rituals of Duarseni in the guise of an upholder of Adivasi culture. Gradually – and predictably – the Kondhs were debarred from the village. A religious legend was created in which, 'Kondhs cannot own land, nor can they build houses and stay there in the village, barring a few – the *Dal Kondhs* (the Kondh priests)'. So, you do not find them now within a radius of 5km from the Duarseni temple. With the economics of the rituals falling into alien hands, the political economy of natural resources underwent huge alterations. Communities of all hues arrived here and usurped the land and forests of the Adivasis. And, to accommodate the 'outsiders' in the existing belief systems (meaning, in the share of the resource-loot), roles were defined for sundry communities while only a tiny section of Kondhs – the Dal Kondhs – were allowed to stay back so as to perform the main rites.

(Interestingly, along with the Kondhs, Muslims have also been debarred from the village. It is said that the war-force of the dynasty that ruled the region from Patna was joined by a huge contingent of Muslim soldiers who were brought by the king from north India a few centuries back. Now their descendants are settled in various parts of the region, though very few in numbers. Since Muslims are considered great warriors – and so are the Kondhs – it is rather obvious for them to be debarred as well, especially for the fact that the new king in Sindhekela with a weak war-force would not have liked to have the presence of any such community that could potentially revolt and effectively defeat him.)

Post-Independence, the onset of 'democracy' rather opened up new opportunities for landlords and traders. As their social and political dominance gained legitimacy with the abolition of kingship, their grip over the Adivasi culture further tightened up. And, the biggest casualty was the disappearance of the dense forests – 'in which tigers used to jump', as Halu Thanapati, the *patdehri* (chief priest) of the Duarseni temple says – which was cleared on massive scales to make way for more farmlands for the new lords. The 'dark and dense jungle' was relegated into mere images – intriguing though – in folklores, and so was the very livelihood base, let alone self-reliance, of traditional communities.

Although the ecology that was directly linked to the tradition now stands decimated, the Adivasis have tried their best to keep it alive. Today, the Adivasis walk up about 75 km for three days to the Chhattardandi forest and walk back for as many days in the process of collecting one specific kind of bamboo stick essential to the annual rituals. The *Ganher* trees, branches of which are used by the locals to make a delicious cake – one of the 16 items offered to the goddess – are now few and far between. So, ironically, what Goddess Duarseni once stood to protect and sustain for posterity for all life forms is today metamorphosed into vast tracts of revenue-generating assets, owned by a tiny set of individuals. Even hundreds of hectares of land originally attached to the Duarseni temple are now owned by landlords and traders whereas those who had a cultural and symbiotic relationship – existential imperatives – with the land possess very little or nothing.

There are countless such examples so as to understand the whole political economy of cultural appropriation in India as a tool for not only resource-grab but also 'internal economic colonisation'. If we go back farther in history, the imperatives of 'resource-control' – after the Aryans' invasion into India's hinterlands – had become so impeccable that communities who actually were in possession of lands, and were arguably the original farmers, had to be completely forced out of the new socio-political order and space, and were labelled 'untouchables'. Ages later, in 'democratic' India, they are still denied that space!

In the second type of cultural appropriation, the main weapon of subjugating the natives was not only in establishing Hindu shrines (such as Jagannath temples) as the new 'power centres', it also involved manufacturing new myths around existing religious beliefs of the natives in attempts to homogenise all traditional communities into the mainstream Hindu hierarchy. In the KBK (undivided Kalahandi – Koraput – Balangir) region in Odisha, Brahmins had already made their ways into kings' *durbars* (courts) as advisors or ministers centuries back, thereby forming a lethal alliance between the ruling class and the elite gentry, which not only took control – by force or sly measures – of the whole of people's resources, it also ruthlessly imposed on the natives cultural behaviours that destabilised the strength of the latter and strengthened the dominance of the former.

Apart from these Brahmins in kings' courts, influx of the 'outsiders' – non-Brahmins as well as non-courtier Brahmins – to the region had, however, intensified in the beginning of the 19th century. It is no wonder that, in the second half of that century, this region endowed with rich natural resources and advanced farming practices was hit by famine for the first time in history, which has become a routine feature thereafter. And, the precise reason was cultural appropriation leading to change of hands in controlling local resources around the new 'power centres' – always in agreement with the dominant political order of the day, which, in turn, strengthened and widened the process of internal economic colonisation by introducing the natives to a kind of 'market' that they could not comprehend fully, let alone have a hand in controlling it, and by making inroads for modern tools, such as railway links. This resulted in sudden dispossession and perpetual deprivation of the natives. Today, the affluent communities of the region are those who have migrated there during the past two centuries. And it is a travesty of history that the natives – Adivasis, Dalits and OBCs (other backward castes) – are the ones who now lend the region the dark identity of being 'hunger-ridden' and 'backward'. Ironically, this was the region believed to be where the rice seed was first invented by the natives through traditional farm practices!

Post-Independence, myriad development projects added further woes to the wounds, by accelerating the rate of ecological distress. Appropriation of cultural ethos of traditional communities not only translates into decimation of natural resources, it also makes way for modern tools to come in to multiply profits, leading to irreversible ecological damage, which, in the process, impels pauperisation of traditional communities – akin to cultural genocide! (Sahu 2011).

### *The British, the kingship and the resource-grab*

It was not easy for the British to take control of the land and resources where traditional communities resided – especially central India, which included most of tribal Odisha – without taking the existing feudal structure on their side. So, the kings and *zamindars* – who had been spearheading the process of cultural appropriation along with Brahmins – became the obvious allies of the Raj in the structural assault on traditional communities and their resources. Under the British rule, which made its presence in the state in the second half of the 18th century, there were broadly three systems of 'revenue assessment', essentially meaning 'resource-control':

1  The *zamindari* system: most of the coastal Odisha and Angul district – landholder could sublet the land to tenants, the latter with no legal protection.

2   The *ryotwari* system: Sambalpur region – rights of the landholder were controlled by the executive.
3   The domain of princely states: 24 princely states in Odisha – the same *zamindari* system with the supreme power in the hands of the kings.

(Patnaik 2008: 10)

However, it was the Permanent Settlement Act of 1793 that gave the hardest blow on the traditional economic structure. Till then, traditional communities did not know of the concept of 'individual' land-ownership. The act simply shattered the social and cultural exigency of collective living and the sustainable, 'inclusive' economic structures traditional communities had long established, drawing wisdom from the laws of nature. With a single stroke, the very livelihood basis of traditional communities was turned into 'assets' as defined by the state and 'ownerships' attached as decided by the state. More importantly, overnight, women – who naturally played equal roles in all walks of social and economic systems – were rendered second-class citizens, because the land – if entitled to – was recorded in the name of the man of the household. Many tribal groups are still not in acceptance of this concept of individual ownership, as they cannot accept Mother Earth being torn into pieces, with each piece demarcated by a boundary all around and sanctified by a piece of paper.

The 1793 Act, on the other hand, opened up a dream-door for non-Adivasi landlords and traders to swarm into the Adivasi heartland to usurp resources using the act, as traditional communities neither were very receptive of this concept nor were equipped to go through the process of official formalities to have their land recorded in their names. So, land actually in possession of Adivasis and Dalits in most places officially fell into the hands of non-Adivasis who grew into being very influential in the changing socio-political scenario post-Independence. In the tribal heartland of Odisha, mostly these landlords are the ones who now represent both the legislatives and the executives, and also the intelligentsia. So, democracy, in a way, sanctified the historical process of cultural appropriation and land-grab, and further alienated Adivasis and Dalits from the much-celebrated 'welfare nation-state'.

### *Cultural and resource appropriation, post-Independence*

While the process of cultural appropriation of the Adivasis continued in Independent India, land-grab – both forced and by means of sly measures – did not stop either. The feudal tyranny that existed under kingship during the British Raj only got a cosmetic makeover and continued in various forms after Independence. While earlier the local rulers could impose their diktats at will on the natives, post-Independence they (even though they were no longer called 'rulers') were joined by various state agencies meant for welfare works to promote Brahmanic power centres and, thereby, economic colonisation.

In Mursing village in Balangir district, for example, a Jagannath temple built only in recent years has further been refurbished using JFM (Joint Forest Management) funds, in the name of 'forest protection'. Since the temple is now 'protecting' the forests, which are the livelihood base of local Adivasis, the latter are unwittingly sucked into an alien temple system. Suddenly deprived of their cultural space, the Adivasis are fast drawn away from their sustainable ways, thereby losing their life-supporting grounds – including farmlands to non-Adivasis. And, while mainstream Hindus from far-flung places rush the temple to offer prayers putting extra burdens on the local resources, the forest is being clear-felled by timber traders, right under the nose of the Forest Department.

The story of Rampur village in Sonepur district is striking in the sense that it tells the story of most villages in India. A century and a half ago, the village demography was characterised by Adivasis (mainly *Saoras* and *Binjhals* among others) and Dalits (*Ganrhas*). Social history, as corroborated by many residents, says that, by 1935, more than 75 per cent of the village farmlands still belonged to Adivasis and Dalits. This is besides the forest that addressed past livelihoods. During the past century, two major events have turned the wheel in different directions: first came a Jagannath temple, and then, in the 1960s, came irrigation water from the Hirakud Dam. As a result, five major changes swept the village: continuous influx of non-Adivasis (*Kuilta, Sunrhi, Brahmin*, etc.) who settled there for good; the forest disappeared; Goddess Chandlipat, the local deity, was replaced by Lord Jagannath as the dominant religious phenomenon in the collective psyche; hooch made available; cash crops took over traditional crops.

Today, Adivasis and Dalits own only 2 per cent to 5 per cent of the village farmland. Farmland to the tune of tens of acres is attached to the Jagannath temple alone, 'managed' by a few Brahmin families. Adivasi population in the village has been reduced substantially, indicating the degree of dispossession and destitution they have suffered after being thrown off their traditional economic life.

Koraput offers rather a starker mirror to the travesty. If you stand atop a hill and look down to the hilly Koraput town, what is most prominent in the landscape is a towering Jagannath temple right in the middle; and, more conspicuously, the absence of any sign of an Adivasi milieu that would have ever existed there. To the right is the Upper Kolab Dam that has drowned nearly 12,000 hectares of primary forests and the livelihood base of tens of thousands. To the left is a never-ending stretch of the Panchpat Mali hill range that has gone barren after NALCO started digging for bauxite some 30 years back. And the result: the local ecology that had sustained millions of life forms for thousands of years has vanished forever and the natives – Adivasis and Dalits – have been pauperised into subhuman living conditions!

In the process of cultural appropriation leading to dispossession of land, the introduction to and spread of cooked country liquor – hooch – among Adivasis and Dalits have always played a major role. The bootleggers – mainly the *Sunrhi* community – would take up the task of replacing traditional drinks such as toddy, *salpa*, etc., with hooch, which the Adivasis would 'buy' from the former. Once addicted to such alien spirits, the production of which is not in the control of the Adivasis, their lives eventually come in control of the bootleggers. Moreover, such alien drinks do not go well with the food habit of the Adivasis and Dalits and, therefore, the addiction becomes strong and results in health hazards. All this sets a perfect trap for the traditional people to come under tremendous economic pressure, for primarily two reasons: (1) the imperatives of spending money for the liquor, which was not the case with the traditional drinks they themselves used to cook earlier; and (2) the expenses for the treatment of unknown ailments that come with the addiction of the alien spirit. And, such economic pressure leads to borrowing money from landlords and moneylenders, which eventually leads to giving away land to the bootleggers or the landlords or the moneylenders – completing a cycle of exploitation in which Adivasis and Dalits end up in complete dispossession and perpetual deprivation.

However, amidst the loot of resources of traditional communities, the state has continuously posed itself as the benign saviour by putting in places various rules and legislations. None of them, of course, has been put to practice in letter and spirit.

Some important land legislation in Odisha is the following:

- *Odisha Estate Abolition Act, 1952*: *zamindars* were allowed to keep up to 33 acres of land; no protection of the rights of tenants.
- *Odisha Scheduled Area Transfer of Immovable Property Regulation, 1956*: no monitoring.

- *Odisha Survey and Settlement Act, 1958*: large areas of land still not surveyed – 640,752 acres, as per state records – but settled as government land anyway; 30000 sq km of areas under shifting cultivation by Adivasis not at all surveyed, but declared government land.
- *Odisha Land Reforms Act, 1960* (amended in 1965, 1973, 1974): did not address the problem of share-cropping; no provision to record concealed tenancy.
- *Odisha Government Land Settlement Act, 1962*: to the extent of 70 per cent of land the state holds is meant to be distributed among the landless; very little progress, especially since 1980 and almost non-existent since economic reforms in 1991.
- *Odisha Prevention of Land Settlement Act, 1972* (amended in 1982): penalty on encroacher and subsequent eviction; penalty was hardly a deterrent; massive scope for corruption.

After Independence, a land ceiling was imposed to acquire land to be distributed among the landless. In Odisha, about 160,000 acres of ceiling-surplus land has been distributed among about 140,000 landless, of which about 100,000 were Adivasis and Dalits. Likewise, under the *Bhoodan* movement, the state had acquired about 640,000 acres of land as donation, and distributed about 580,000 acres of land to the landless (Patnaik 2008).

However, these projected efforts were overshadowed by the state's lack of actual willingness to benefit the landless, as:

- Land records in most of the cases were not properly done.
- Large numbers of powerful landholders could easily conceal their assets and still keep holding to large areas of land.
- Most of the beneficiaries could not till the land given to them as the original owners later took it back by means of force or sly measures.
- Those who could till the land could not benefit because of poor quality of the land given.
- The state remains a mute spectator to such rampant exploitation, akin to being a direct partner in this structural crime.

A study by RCDC–NIRD (2006) states:

> that the much talked about re-distribution of ceiling-surplus land has remained far from being impressive. Over the years,

> the poor and landless, especially the tribals, have not been able to benefit much from the ceiling-surplus land that has been transferred to them under various schemes. As per the survey conducted in three blocks of Koraput, the landless are not an improved lot even after re-distribution of the ceiling-surplus land. For, as much as 16 per cent of the beneficiaries continue to struggle to get physical possession of the land allotted in their favour. Similarly, 30 per cent of beneficiaries have record of rights for land, which is not suitable for cultivation. While 42 per cent beneficiaries are cultivating their land, 6.6 per cent have either sold or mortgaged it. . . . This goes on to show that most beneficiaries are not deriving any actual benefit from the land they legally own. . . . It is interesting to note that, though allotted during 1976/77 and paying the cess regularly, the beneficiaries are still not in possession of the allotted land. The previous owners use their money and muscle power to regain possession over the surplus land. Besides this, there are problems of land acquisition (4 per cent) and sale and mortgage of land (7 per cent).
>
> (Patnaik 2008: 17)

In many cases, the beneficiaries are made to pay tax, even though they do not have physical possession of any land. As per records of the state revenue department (2006), there are about 460,000 landless in the state and about 540,000 acres of land still available to be distributed among them. Going by past experiences, even if these available lands are 'officially' distributed among the landless, the benefit will certainly go to landlords.

## Various land-rights movements in Odisha

In the fight to protect their cultures, resources and identities, the natives in Odisha have retaliated against the takeover of their resources in an organised way as early as the first half of the 19th century: Rendo Majhi not only lives on as a legend, his fight back against cultural appropriation and political aggression by the British and local landlords then is now lending tremendous courage and strength to various Adivasi movements in the state. Chakra Bisoyi, Laxman Majhi and other historical figures are doing the same too. However, the mode of repression by the state has not changed much since the past 200 years. If the revolts led by Rendo Majhi and Chakra Bisoyi were crushed using the pretext of ending *Meriah* – human sacrifice – as believed by the British, today there is a massive campaign – both political and legislative – to end 'animal sacrifice' to deities of Adivasis, Dalits and OBCs, which is an obligatory part of their rituals. And, what is threatening to replace the Indigenous rituals in the state are Brahmanic practices – such as *yangya, jaagran, naam prahari, kirtan*, chanting of *Gayatri mantra*, etc., – alien to the Indigenous communities, promoted not only by right-wing Hindu groups but also by organisations affiliated to parties such as the Congress and the ruling Biju Janata Dal, with overt support from part of the elite intelligentsia. If successful, such cultural assaults on Adivasis would eventually lead to their further pauperisation; for, they will straightaway lose control of their own cultures and thereby their life-sustaining resources, as experienced in cases of Sindhekela, Mursing and Rampur. However, encouragingly, Adivasis and Dalits in many districts are now consolidating their collective strength around these issues, which will have bigger ramifications in coming times.

Besides, the natives have exhibited various ways of resistance – both organised and sporadic – in various points in time against the myriad forms of assaults on their cultures and resources. Some are discussed here.

### *Reclaiming the commons: people's forests*

Odisha has a remarkable history of community initiatives in protecting, nurturing and taking control of community resources (forests, village commons, water) since the turn of the 20th century. After being thrown off their natural homes – forests – by the British following the establishment of the Imperial Forest Department in 1964, communities had fought violently with the state, but without much success in regaining their grounds. With the state taking over forests as an entity to be 'scientifically managed', the forest dwellers – mostly Adivasis – overnight became 'intruders' in their own homeland. Their livelihood practices, such as hunting-gathering and shifting cultivation, were termed unscientific and social evils. They were, in many instances, forced to take the plough or rendered bonded labourers or simply driven out of the forests into uncertain futures. How it amounted to 'cultural genocide' is evident in an account of anthropologist Verrier Elwin (1939), who lived many years researching with the Baigas in Central India, that 'the Baigas were reluctant to take to the plough, as it was akin to tearing the breasts of your Mother, the Earth'.

The repressive mandates bestowed upon the Forest Department effectively criminalised forest and rural communities, for their livelihoods depended on forest resources. Verrier Elwin demonstrated the incriminating process by quoting a forest officer as saying, 'Our laws are of such a kind that every villager breaks at least one forest law every day of his life'. So, most of rural India had little choice but to become 'criminals' in the course of their daily existence. For having resisted the takeover of their livelihood bases, tribes were even branded 'born criminals' by the British government and were made to be on the run. Post-Independence, they are still on the run, tagged as the 'denotified tribes of India'.

The unbearable pressure of survival in such situations forced many tribal communities to finally take the plough even though it was blasphemous to them. By the turn of the 20th century, however, many forest communities also realised that they had no options other than taking the mantle of – even though it was an alien concept to them – 'managing' their own forests, which the British could not foresee much of a problem in. Over decades, these communities took complete control over their commons and forests; and today in most community forests in Odisha, even the Forest Department can hardly exercise its *zamindari* or landlordism. Practically more than one-third (2 million hectares) of the state's total forest area is today under the control of these CFM (Community Forest Management) groups, which the Forest Department is trying hard to break by playing the JFM (Joint Forest Management) trick and pumping in humongous amounts of money. Conflicts between the Forest Department and communities continue over ownership of forests and lands (Sahu 2010a).

One of the major points of the conflicts has been the various unsustainable, commercial plantation and arbitrary harvesting projects being undertaken by the Forest Department in people's lands and forests, with direct impacts on the livelihoods of forest-dependent communities. The FRA (Forest Rights Act) 2006 – what the government calls a tool to correct 'historical injustices' meted out to forest communities – has so far been reduced to be a joke by the Forest Department in the state. Consider this: as recently as June 2010, the Forest Department forcibly undertook commercial plantation even on the 104.87 acres of land that 47 families of the Talaraidiha village of the Juang *pirh* (domain) in Keonjhar district now own, after being legally entitled to under the FRA 2006! Not only that, as a result of a massive protest by the locals on 30 July 2010, forest officials visited Talaraidiha village on 11 August and told the 47 families that they would now get another piece of land elsewhere! And, the new piece of land they are talking about is some 10 km away from the village and is actually a dense *sal* forest. Rabindra Juang, a local Adivasi, said, 'So, now what it means is that the Department will not go back on planting its chosen species for commercial purposes forcibly on people's land, and that the dense *sal* forest will be destroyed too!' (Sahu 2010b).

Do we call it a 'travesty', or unbridled 'despotism'?

Conflicts were in fact compounded when the Forest Department came up with the JFM scheme in the 1990s and tried to appropriate community ownership of forest lands, much the same way as the Hindu 'power centres' have been doing to the Adivasi milieus. Of late, with the Green India Mission and REDD waiting to 'unlock a treasury' – in the words of Union Minister Jairam Ramesh – for private bidders in India's forests, conflicts over ownership of land and forests are poised to take 'dangerous' turns.

## First armed, militant land-rights movement by the Left

Just as forest communities of Odisha found wisdom and ways in taking 'control' over their forests, Adivasis in many parts of the state during the past five decades started reclaiming their lands lost to non-Adivasis. The form of their struggle has been both armed and non-armed in specific cases.

The first coordinated, political movement in the state on the issue of 'land to the tiller' involving small and marginal farmers, the landless, and Adivasis began in early 1960s in various parts of Odisha, especially in South Odisha. This was supported by the then CPI (Communist Party of India). In 1962, a project called 'food liberation' was launched by the movement in the Gunpur subdivision of Koraput district and Paralakhemundi area of Ganjam district and thousands of hectares of farmland was 'liberated' from landlords. The movement instantly spread to even other far-flung areas. One example is the Rampur village of Sonepur district, mentioned earlier, in which about 20 acres of farmland was liberated from the *zamindar* and distributed among a few Dalit families in 1962–63. (However, later, these Dalit families again lost the land to one of the *zamindar's* kin in a court case.)

In 1967, after the multiple splits of the CPI, the movement in Odisha joined the faction called the All-India Coordination Committee of Communist Revolutionaries – later, the CPI (Marxist-Leninist) – and formed the Odisha State Coordination Committee in 1968. It is after that only the movement, particularly the Chitrakonda Labour

Movement, a constituent group led by Nagabhushan Patnaik, took to armed militant methods in attempts to restoring lost lands and livelihoods of the poor in the region. However, after the merger of the Odisha committee with its counterpart in Andhra Pradesh in 1969, it lost its tempo and approach. But, the armed land-rights movement continued until some top leaders were arrested in 1971 (Nayak 2006). Thereafter, even though this militant movement went on for decades, rather in a sporadic manner, its impact was not much visible until the turn of this century. The 1960s movement – though it achieved very little – had, nonetheless, sown the seeds for many militant uprisings, both armed and non-armed, in the tribal heartland – such as the Narayanpatna land-rights movement, which is on the boil at the moment.

## *The Narayanpatna land-rights struggle*

Since 1994, the CPI (ML)-Kanhu Sanyal group has been active in South Odisha on land-rights issues under the banner of CMAS (*Chasi Mulia Adivasi Sangh* – union of farmers, wageworkers and Adivasis). In 2004, Adivasis of the Narayanpatna block in Koraput district under the banner of CMAS started a campaign in the area to settle their land disputes with non-Adivasi landlords. In just five years of their struggle – till 2009 – they had succeeded in closing down liquor shops managed by landlords, hiking wage payments, stopping land-grab by non-Adivasis, restricting moneylenders and more importantly, 'liberating' more than 3,000 hectares of land that originally belonged to them. As this 'non-violent' movement was gaining strength and threatening to spread to other areas, untold brutal repression was unleashed by the state in 2009, directly steered by the non-Adivasi landlords and indirectly by mining companies waiting in hope to mine the nearby hill ranges for minerals. At least three leaders of CMAS were killed by the police and several hundreds of Adivasis were put behind bars; they are still languishing in jail without trial. The people's collective has been declared a Maoist outfit, only to legitimise the state repression on this historic land-rights movement. Many of the Adivasi leaders are still on the run while the rest are living under untold fear and intimidation.

When large-scale exploitations by the powerful are ignored for decades and democratic resistances to them are treated with state violence, the state sends out a clear message that the only language it understands is that of 'violence'. Merely asking for restoring one's fundamental rights is considered unlawful! All over Odisha, there are nearly 150,000 cases involving land against Adivasis and more than 45,000 cases of forest violations. So, what is the choice before the people?

### Non-violent, militant land-rights movement

Meanwhile, despite the split of the CPI (ML) itself, 'democratic' land-rights movements in Odisha are in full swing steered by the CPI (ML)-Kanhu Sanyal group, the CPI (ML)-Liberation, the CPI (ML)-New-Democracy, and many non-affiliated people's movements in many tribal pockets. These non-violent, militant land-rights movements have achieved tremendous success in the past decade in liberating thousands of hectares of usurped lands and have distributed them among Adivasis and Dalits in South Odisha, besides bringing them together on political platforms. This has not only empowered the Adivasis and Dalits to regain their socio-economic and cultural domains, it also has strengthened them to come together and fight back the forced takeover of their lands and resources by industries who are of late making a beeline to the tribal heartland of Odisha. One prime example of this is the strong resistance by the Adivasis and Dalits of Niyamgiri in Kalahandi and Rayagada districts.

### The Niyamgiri anti-mining struggle

The Niyamgiri struggle has now rather been very well known globally in which Adivasis and Dalits on the Niyamgiri hill range and its foothills are fighting a valiant battle against the possible takeover of their forests, hills, water sources and land by the mining giant Vedanta Resources PLC. '*Mining happiness . . .*' is the tagline of Vedanta's billboards clogging the urban landscape in Odisha! Just 10 years back, the whole Lanjigarh area on the foothills of Niyamgiri, comprising some 25-odd villages inhabited by the Kutia Kandh tribe and Dalits, was a serene landscape dominated by *sal* forests, intersected by the Vamsadhara River emerging from the Niyamgiri. Today, Vedanta's alumina refinery has turned their pristine and self-sufficient habitat into an industrial wasteland. Nearly 15,000 forest-dependent people have become refugees in their own homeland. Large tracts of forests have disappeared to make way for the factory, ash ponds, red-mud ponds, roads filled with hundreds of trucks, while the native forest dwellers are left scrambling for some livelihood option somewhere.

Arjun Chandi of Kadamguda village, close to the refinery, rather puts the situation in perspective, 'How can you call this *development*?

Someone else comes here, destroys your forests and lands, decimates your economic sources, pushes you onto the road, and makes a lot of money. Where is development? If you want development for us, first give our forests and lands back, and then talk about development' (Sahu 2010c).

However, after closely witnessing the devastation at the foothills, the Dongria Kandhs who inhabit the Niyamgiri mountains have put up strong resistance against the proposed mining of bauxite on Niyamgiri; successfully deferring Vedanta's 'mining happiness' to the past. The mining lease now stands cancelled by government orders. The fight of the Dongrias was supported and strengthened by many civil-rights and land-rights groups. After successfully trampling Vedanta's 'mining happiness', they have now intensified the struggle to have the refinery closed down, as they see 'enormous dangers' to their culture and livelihoods from its very presence in the area. But, the state has not relented from repressing the Adivasis there; even after the scrapping of the mining project, police and paramilitary forces have attacked Dongria villages many times over and have tortured the Adivasis. The state is trying to even declare Niyamgiri as 'Maoist-infested', in attempts to take complete control of the region. The locals say that the state is doing this only to open ways for Vedanta to start mining there in the future.

Apart from the struggle to protect Niyamgiri's ecology, cultural ethos and economic richness from an industry's onslaught, Niyamgiri offers many more travesties in the course of its existence especially with regard to being part of the sovereign state, which could be clues to the clinical methods employed by the state itself to culturally disintegrate tribal groups to make way for internal economic colonisation.

- The Forest Department continues to harass the Adivasis; they have in fact opened a timber-trading centre at the foothills. On the contrary, the reason for the forests on Niyamgiri still remaining dense and virgin is because the Dongrias worship Niyamgiri as their *Niyam Raja* – the supreme lord of laws – and therefore have kept the forests inviolate for ages. The Forest Department, however, sees revenue in its green spread.
- Non-Adivasis traders around the foothills who have migrated in from other areas of the state and also from adjoining states continue to exploit the Adivasis by intimidating and forcing them to sell forest produce at a dirt-cheap price, which the traders later sell at high prices in the local market that the Dongrias can hardly access.

EXPROPRIATION OF LAND AND CULTURES

- The DKDA (Dongria Kandh Development Agency) is the biggest of all exploiters in all possible forms.
    - The agency plays a major role in introducing and linking traders to the Dongrias, instead of protecting the latter from the former.
    - The agency is primarily responsible for the increasing disappearance of traditional seeds Dongrias are used to farming and introducing them to hybrid seeds, making them dependent on seed traders. This also impacts the nutritional intakes of the Dongrias, which is crucial considering their traditional lifestyle.
    - The agency runs programmes to motivate the Dongrias to adopt modern tools even though they do not need them, which only results in increasing their dependence on the market controlled by powerful strangers.
    - The schools run by the DKDA – many of them defunct – have been instrumental in subverting the cultural practices and identity of the Dongrias in the pretext of bringing them to the 'mainstream'. Cultural appropriation begins the moment a Dongria child is enrolled to a school. For example, if the child's name is Drika Pusika, he would be enrolled as, say, Deepak Pusika, as though the name Drika bears some sense of backwardness and needs to be sanitised! In the school, their traditional dress code is banned, food habit changed and cultural behaviours altered, alienating them not only from their society but in many cases from their immediate families. One Dongria youth once asked me, 'If P Chidambaram could go to Parliament wearing his traditional *dhoti* without being questioned by anyone, why am I denied to wear my traditional attires to school?'
    - The DKDA also work as an agent for Vedanta in motivating the Dongrias not to oppose the mining project.
- The success – so far partly though – of the Niyamgiri anti-mining movement has gained strength from the history of land-rights movements around the foothills for the past decades. First it was the CPI (ML)-Liberation that organised the landless Adivasis and Dalits in the 1990s to stake claim over hundreds of acres of land in and around Muniguda and Bissamkatak areas. The movement, however, soon fizzled out owing to the absence of effective leadership; the weakening of the movement also interestingly coincided with the entry of Vedanta. Then, the Lok Sangram Manch under the aegis of the CPI (ML)-New Democracy launched a militant, democratic land-rights campaign in the foothill villages of

Niyamgiri towards the beginning of this century. This movement, which is still in full swing, has so far reclaimed hundreds of acres of land usurped by landlords and distributed them among the native Adivasis and Dalits. It is this collective strength that later channelised into the fight against Vedanta and the state government to save Niyamgiri from mining. However, around Lanjigarh, Vedanta's alumina refinery today stands tall, due to the absence of such a movement with a clear political stance and goals so that the company could trample people's opposition and go ahead with the construction and operation of the plant.

Now that Vedanta is denied entry to the Niyamgiri hills, the local struggle group is looking into these issues, long ignored by civil-rights groups.

## People's resistance movements: the missing links

As the pressure on natural resources mounts in order to push farther up neo-liberal consumption, dubbed as 'national interests', there is a full-fledged 'war' out there! The state is, of late, at war with its own people. Economist Amit Bhaduri puts the situation in perspective:

> The political system of democracy is acclaimed for contributing to rising mass consumption by invading natural resources everywhere under various guises of legal and illegal trade, which trample on the democratic rights of those who cannot defend them. In post-colonial societies, decolonization merely changed the direction but not the goal of this violent hunt for natural resources. As countries that were once formal or informal colonies gain political independence, the more successful among them join the march of civilization in the name of 'development' only to become colonisers themselves. The irony of history does not end there. The formerly colonised countries are relatively new in the race, and handicapped by an inherited past of economic and military weakness in a world of stronger competitors. And so the direction and the target of the hunt change. If a lack of strength does not allow them to conquer other lands and people, regions inside the country are identified for the hunt of natural resources. Imperialism turns inwards; and the latecomers in the race wage war against their own citizens, but this time in the name of developing them.
> (Bhaduri 2010)

Land-grab through cultural appropriation that started centuries back (and that still continues) has thus taken a new and more dangerous form: large-scale resource-grab at one go by selling glittering, abstract dreams of growth and development. And, in the centre of this heinous game of selling out people's resources is the elite, middle class, which acts much like a 'comprador agency' to the bourgeoisie of the so-called globalised world, with its strong political dominance over the larger economic, societal and cultural domains enshrined in the 'system'. This 'comprador agency' is always busy erecting walls to safeguard the 'system' that is ever-evolving to suit the dominant political and economic order of the day and to ensure that people's political, cultural and economic domains stay outside the 'system', thereby making the process of resource-plunder uncontested and smooth. Trying to break this pattern, from outside the 'system', are two prominent phenomena: (1) democratic resistance movements, and (2) the armed Maoist movement!

Odisha has become the chosen laboratory for the Indian 'republic' to realise its neo-liberal misadventures, with the state government laying a red carpet for industries of all hues and profiles to come and take over people's lands and resources for profits. Odisha is also the state where people's resistance movements have successfully halted neo-liberal forces from realising their nefarious dreams to a large extent, despite brutal repression and even cold-blooded murders. Across the length and breadth of the state, there are voices of dissent by organised struggle groups: from Kalinganagar in Jajpur district to Kashipur in Rayagada; from the anti-POSCO movement in Jagatsingpur to the farmers against industrial colonisation of people's water sources in Sambalpur and Bargarh.

At the heart of the 'politics' of hundreds of these resistance groups is the sole objective: *restoring people's resources in people's hands*. Despite the spread of democratic resistance movements across the state with considerable success in stalling large-scale land-grab by corporations, however, what is disturbingly conspicuous is their inability to place 'land-rights' at the centre of the conflict. In the heat of fighting giant corporations, the fundamental issues of 'resource politics' within the society somehow have not made it to the larger agenda of most of these movements. The issues that are most strikingly ignored by most anti-industry/anti-dam/anti-development movements are the questions of the landless and the ever-perpetuating internal economic colonisation of traditional cultures, which are at the heart of the crisis that precedes corporate plunder of people's resources. This is the precise reason why democratic movements have so far failed to consolidate their efforts to provide a viable alternative to the political vacuum created by none other than the Indian State. And, this is also the reason why armed Left radicalism finds space to spread successfully, much to the delight of the state. For, democratic movements are supposed to be about 'democracy'; and it is 'democratic values and practices' that the state is so visibly scared of, and not so much of the guns of the rebels! Therefore, in order to keep 'dissent' alive in this democracy – meaning, to keep any hope of a political alternative alive within the democratic framework – it is of utmost importance that democratic movements do not lose touch with people's politics and their 'aspirations'.

## Spread of the Maoist movement

India's economic reforms in 1991 and their increasing impacts on the lives of the people thereafter had many a thing altered at various levels – especially in terms of political consequences and people's responses. The sudden and unprecedented attack on people's land and resources on a massive scale by the state and corporations stirred people's consciousness, leading to an unprecedented rise in people's political participation. For, this time the threats seemed to be enormous and final, which could wipe out their identities – and even existence – from the face of the earth. So, since 1991, grassroots India has been busy – as never before – in attempts to protect itself.

People's political activism during this period, as discussed, came in two dominant forms. One, thousands of democratic resistance groups confronted the state up front, questioning its 'anti-people' politics and 'anti-ecology' economics. As the resistance grew in intensity, state repression grew manifold – both in terms of physical violence and intimidation, using all sorts of state machineries. In the last ten years, more than 50 people – mostly Adivasis – in Odisha have been killed by police, thousands put in jail, and tens of thousands are being intimidated on a daily basis. The resistance, however, is still growing and spreading to newer areas and people.

On the side-line of this massive political upheaval on the ground, the armed radical Left – the CPI (Maoist) – is also silently and rapidly spreading its base to newer areas and people. This may seem a bit ironical as to how two different political domains gained ground simultaneously in the same geographic areas; but it certainly points to the fact that people's political consciousness and participation in political processes have increased unprecedentedly on the ground, especially in the Adivasi heartland.

## EXPROPRIATION OF LAND AND CULTURES

We will not go into details of the functioning and activities of these two political domains; rather we discuss briefly as to how this seemingly unusual political scenario was made possible to happen. Some of the observations are as follows.

- People on the ground who have suffered for centuries – and more so in 'democratic' India – are looking for 'definitive and viable political alternatives'. Neither rhetoric nor polemics works anymore.
- The state's blatant and open disregard for 'democracy' and constitutional values has had people disillusioned about the very idea of 'democratic processes' as defined by the state while choosing an alternative political space.
- The state's repression on democratic movements and the inability of democratic movements in coming together to fight back adequately and offer a 'definitive and viable political alternative' have many turning away from the so-called democratic processes. There are even instances in which democratic movements have not even shown the courage to own up to their own members after they were killed by the state in cold blood by labelling them Maoists. As a result, though this is not true to all democratic processes, many democratic movement groups are now intervened, if not controlled, by the Maoists with the wilful approval of local communities.
- Democratic movements are often driven by limited political agendas, such as simply to throw out a company or to fight for water-rights for dominant farmers; and they largely ignore age-old conflicts, such as the ones faced by the landless and small farmers in entrenched feudal settings, or the ones grappling forest communities or face the ruthless landlordism of the Forest Department for the past 150 years, or the cultural aggression and colonisation by Brahmanism over traditional communities.
- Democratic movements are, in many cases, also characterised by the 'aspirations' of a few leaders, instead of representing the larger 'aspirations' of the people and the political positioning of the entire collective they lead, creating disillusionment among the communities involved – thereby leading them to resort to 'radical' options.
- The weaknesses of democratic movements – and not to mention the terror of the state – opens up space for the radical Left to pitch in, who 'appears' to be offering 'definitive' political options – howsoever debatable they may be in intellectual and academic

- discourses – to people, by directly and purposefully 'engaging' themselves with the people, often with visible consequences.
- As people on the ground 'perceive', land-rights lies at the core of the Maoist agenda that naturally make their enemies common: feudal lords, traders, forest officials and the police, contractors, the mining and metal industry, or anyone who exploits the people – in a nutshell, the 'system'.
- So long as the state does not learn how to respect 'democracy' and/or democratic movements do not put in place a 'political agenda' that unambiguously reflects the larger 'aspirations' of the people and decisively challenge the 'system' from outside, with all its historicity and cultural continuity, it is certain that militant Left radicalism is in for a rapid rise in coming years. Whether it is good or bad, that is a different debate – and, a very critical one!

Meanwhile, democratic movements have a huge task to take upon themselves, voluntarily: to reflect upon their 'failures' on a broader frame, rather than rejoicing over the limited successes they have achieved so far. Without that, there cannot evolve any 'definitive and viable political alternatives' howsoever intensive and time-consuming are the political processes they are engaged in! People with their traditional resources are here pitted against the demonic might of the state, which has of late become war-hungry, covertly fed by the feudal and capitalist colonisers and overtly pushed by the imperialist economic powers of the so-called globalised world – all eyeing to plunder people's resources, at whatever cost! For them, democratic values are no longer sacrosanct; profit is! And, despite such a precarious situation, people on the ground seem ready to strike back in whatever way they know – that is the stark reality!

## References

Bhaduri, Amit. 2010. 'Recognise this Face?', *Economic and Political Weekly*, 45(47), 20 November. www.epw.in/commentary/recognise-face.html (accessed on 15 January 2011).

Elwin, Verrier. 1939. 'Civilising the Savage', in Ramachandra Guha (ed.), *Social Ecology*, 1998. New Delhi: Oxford University Press, 249–74.

Kumar, Kundan, P. R. Choudhary, S. Sarangi, P. Mishra and S. Behera. 2005. 'A Socio-Economic and Legal Study of Scheduled Tribes' Land in Odisha', *Paper Commissioned by the World Bank*, Washington, DC.

Nayak, N. 2006. 'Maoists in Odisha Growing Tentacles and a Dormant State', in K. P. S. Gill (ed.), *Faultlines: Writings on Conflicts and Resolutions*, Volume 17. New Delhi: Institute of Conflict Management, 127–51.

Patnaik, S. 2008. *Status Report on Land Rights and Ownership on Odisha*. New Delhi: UNDP India, 74.

Prasad, A. 2001. 'Hunger and Democracy: The Political Economy of Food in Adivasi Societies', *Frontline*, 18(20), 29 September–12 October.

Sahu, S. K. 2010a. 'The Taming of the Wilds', *Infochange* (online magazine). http://infochangeindia.org/Environment/Community-forests-of-Odisha/The-taming-of-the-wilds.html (accessed on 5 January 2011).

Sahu, S. K. 2010b. 'Treasure Hunt in the Kendujhar Forests', *Infochange* (online magazine). http://infochangeindia.org/201008288483/Environment/Features/Treasure-hunt-in-the-Kendujhar-forests.html (accessed on 5 January 2011).

Sahu, S. K. 2010c. 'Niyamgiri: Not the Last Battle of the Natives', *Hardnews*, May. http://www.hardnewsmedia.com/2010/05/3540 (accessed on 13 July 2018).

Sahu, S. K. 2011. 'Your Gods Are Mine', *Down to Earth*, 1–15 January: 58–9.

# 6
# KIDNAP OF THE COLLECTOR IN ODISHA
The question of tribal exclusion

## G. Haragopal

The kidnap of district collector R. Vineel Krishna and Pabitra Mohan Majhi, a junior engineer by Maoists took place on 16 February 2011 in the state of Orissa (now Odisha). The Odisha state is one of the poorer states in India with very rich natural resources, particularly water and mineral. They have some of the largest deposits of quality bauxite, the worth of which is estimated to be more than 2 trillion dollars, nearly twice that of India's GDP. In a very perceptive and insightful work 'Out of this Earth' Felix Padel and Samarendra Das brought out graphically the deepening crisis in the tribal areas of Odisha (Padel and Das 2010). The neo-liberal model of development that is out to loot has been slapped on the area, which is hitting hard the tribals who have been living in the region for centuries. The MNCs are dangerously engaged in the exploitation of natural resources in any corner of the globe and that has turned out to be a 'resource curse to the tribals of the region' (ibid.: xxiii) observe the writers. They also point out that as the earth is being ripped of its resources, the tribals are robbed of their life and livelihood. It is this brutal and naked exploitation of resources that led to tribal resistance. To put it in their words: 'Adivasis are not lying down and letting their age-old cultures just die any more' (ibid.). 'They add the trouble is, they face huge repression by security forces and company mafias, and their movements get confused in the popular imagination with the Maoist insurgency, which is growing in the region because of people's outrage at the increasing repression and exploitation' (ibid.). 'They argued driving the insane overexploitation of East India's resources is a ruthless capitalism, brilliant at making profits and demonic in its heedlessness of costs'. They hope 'If anything can save our earth for all of us, it's the uncompromising struggles of these Adivasi activists' (ibid.: xxiv).

It is in this backdrop the Malkangiri kidnap has to be analysed and understood. A sketch of this episode is to present the developments that followed the kidnap and see the democratic space available for mediation and peaceful resolution of the issues in an otherwise totally confrontationist volcanic situation.

In the wake of this kidnap, the Maoist party suggested three persons, R.S. Rao, G. Haragopal and Dandapani Mohanty, whom the media prefers to call 'interlocutors', to mediate on a charter of demands. The 'interlocutors' learnt about the mediation through the media. Varavara Rao, a well-known revolutionary poet, informed all three mediators about Maoist choice and advised that they partake in the mediation. The Odisha government through its Home Secretary conveyed its endorsement for mediation and mediators. The discussion on the demands between the three mediators and two government representatives (U.N. Behra, Principal Secretary, Home and S.N. Tripathi, Panchayati Raj, Secretary) commenced on 20 February 2011. The Maoist party nominated its two leaders, Sriramalu Srinivasulu and Ganti Prasadam, in Korput jail for consultation on behalf of the party. The Odisha government for its own reasons agreed for consultation with Ganti Prasadam and not Sriramulu Srinivasulu.[1] Not to lose time in the procedural rigamarole, the government of Odisha agreed to the proposal of the mediators that Ganti Prasadam be shifted from Koraput to Bhuvaneshwar jail for ready consultations.

The mediators, when they met with Ganti Prasadam in Bhuvaneshwar jail to discuss the technicalities and difficulties in the charter of demands, found that he took a broad democratic view and suggested that release of the tribals languishing in the jails be prioritised over the other demands. He also felt that demand for release of the leaders as a top priority may not be democratic as the leaders and activists can always voice their views and take recourse to legal battles while the voice of the tribals for whom their party was fighting was not often heard or remain unrepresented. He on his own, in addition to the charter of demands, suggested that a judicial enquiry into all the encounters of deaths could be added, not as a demand, but as his suggestion. This, in fact, made the task of mediators and the process of mediation easier and smoother.

As the charter of demands was taken up, the government representatives put them in such an order that they felt was easy to deal with.

The mediators chose not to object to the ordering of the demands. On 21 February, eight demands were taken up: these include: 1) Declaring Nookadora, Konda Reddy communities as Scheduled Tribes; 2) Stop Polavaram project; 3) Issue pattas to the tribals of Koraput, Malkangiri, Narayanapatnam and Vishakapatnam areas; 4) Construct a canal from Kotapalli to Maneguda; 5) Pay compensation to the families of tadangi Ganguluand Ratana Sirike who died due to torture in jail; 6) Release Central Committee member Sheela'di' and Padma due to their ill health; the seventh and eighth demands relate to cancellation of the mining leases and withdrawing MOUs with various MNCs.

One would realise that most of these demands would fall either in the development or welfare domain which the state government should be carrying on as its obligations to its own citizens. The state representatives obviously did not have much difficulty in readily conceding four to five demands. They not only agreed to the demand for recognising Nookadora and Konda Reddy Communities as Scheduled Tribes but informed that they already initiated steps by way of consultation with Odisha Tribal Advisory Council and recommended Konda Reddy/Reddi community to the Ministry of Tribal Welfare, Government of India for their inclusion in the list of Scheduled Tribes. It was promised that similar steps would also be taken up in the case of the Nookadora community and pressure the central government for early consideration of this proposal. With regard to Polavaram project that would submerge villages in Odisha and Telangana, the Odisha Assembly already unanimously passed a resolution opposing the project and also filed a case against the project in the Supreme Court.

The demand three about giving pattas to the tribals and restoring back the land from non-tribals was not as simple to handle as the earlier two demands. However, it was agreed to protect the land rights of the tribals and further agreed to constitute a high-level committee under the chairmanship of a senior officer (in the rank of Member, Board of Revenue) and post officers of the rank of Additional/Joint Secretary with statutory powers under the land laws to expeditiously dispose of the cases relating to land rights of the tribal persons.

In response to the demand relating to construction of a canal from Kotapally to Maneguda for providing irrigation facilities to Kalmela farmers, the government promised to construct an aqueduct for extension of the Kotapally Minor canal to Maneguda village, which can irrigate about 500 ha of additional land. Related to this issue was that of providing irrigation facilities to the left-out land of Manemkonda village; the government felt that it was not feasible because of higher elevation and difficult topography but promised that it would take up a lift irrigation project on a priority basis.

Demand five relates to payment of compensation to the families of Tadangi Gangaulu and Ratana Sirike who died due to torture by the Koraput jail authorities and neglect of healthcare. The government held that they died while under treatment in the hospital but not due to torture in jail. Since a writ petitions has been filed in the High Court by the family members, the government will abide by whatever order the Honourable High Court passes.[2] Demand six was about ill health of Sheela'di' and Padma. In the course of discussion it was learnt that they were not in Odisha jails. However, it was promised that the Odisha government would write to Chhattisgarh and Jharkhand state governments where these two were detained and request the respective governments to take care of their health.

The seventh and eighth demands taken up on the first day were difficult to negotiate: they relate to cancellation of mining leases and withdrawal of MOUs with various MNCs. This concerns the very development model. As a response to this demand, the government from its side promised to abide by all the relevant laws and rules such as PESA Act, Forest Conservation Act, Forest Rights Act and the Environment Laws in lieu of scrapping of the leases and MOUs. It was also promised that displacement of tribals would be confined to the minimum and adequate compensation and proper rehabilitation would be ensured to the affected persons. As mediators were not sure how far this demand could be stretched, it was thought that the response of the government under the given conditions was tolerable enough. This issue was taken up for a serious discussion when the mediators met the chief minister on 25 February.

This particular demand of Maoists has something to do with their political and ideological position on the brutal path of development that the Indian ruling classes, as stated earlier, have come to pursue during the last two to three decades. Almost all the political parties, irrespective of their allegiance to caste (including the oppressed castes), creed, colour, religion, region or subregion and proclaimed ideologies, have hammered out a consensus on the model of development. There is no single political party (except the left parties) openly opposed to the model as a part of their opportunistic politics. With the Singur and Nandigram episodes, CPM party also lost its credibility. The major failure of the left parties was that they did not mobilise the masses against the model. It appears that the political character of the elite either remained comprador or it got denationalised in the course of time. That the Maoists, located as they are outside the entire parliamentary politics, seem to be a political force to reckon with in opposing the model. In that sense this demand for cancellation of MOUs signifies their politics but goes beyond such negotiations.

The other six demands were taken up on 22 February: some of the demands were complex but have serious political import. The easier-to-handle demands were payment of compensation to the farmers of cut-off and submerged areas of Balimela reservoir and providing alternative facilities to the project-affected persons, and also providing justice to the displaced persons of Nalco project in Damanjodi (demands 10 and 11). The difficult case was that of the disappearance of Sitanna and the demand to indicate his whereabouts (demand nine). The other three demands (12, 13 and 14) were critical in the negotiations and much depended on the outcome of mediation on these demands. These were stop Green Hunt operations, release of central committee members and others, withdrawal of the cases against the tribals and Chasi Mulia workers in Koraput and Malkangiri Jails.

The response of the government to the payment of compensation to the farmers of cut-off and submerged areas of Balimela reservoir was that no complaints had been received from the affected persons. They promised that they would enquire into the matter and take action as per prevailing guidelines; with regard to the alternative facilities to be provided in view of the possibility of submergence, the government held that there was no proposal to raise the height of the dam and there need not be any apprehensions of further submergence of the villagers. Similarly, to the demand for justice to the Nalco-affected persons, there were no grievances reported but if any grievance was brought, the government would redress it.

In the case of disappearance of Sitanna, a tribal, the government not only flatly denied it, but said that Sitanna was very much alive and was in a hideout as he was afraid of the Maoist party which he chose to desert; it asserted that he was in constant touch with his wife and family members.[3] They agreed to order an administrative enquiry to investigate into this matter. On the crucial demand of stopping Green Hunt operations, the government agreed not to take recourse to coercive action as long as Maoists do not indulge in any unlawful activities. When mediators suggested for initiating peace talks on the lines of the Andhra experiment, they did not look enthusiastic.

About withdrawing the cases against the tribals (demand 13), it was stated that Odisha government has taken Suo Moto action for withdrawal of minor cases and in the past 9,013 such cases were dropped;

in keeping with this precedent, the government will initiate the process within 15 days, review the cases against tribals held on charges of Maoists activities and land-related disputes in Narayanapatna area and complete the whole process of release within three months. They agreed to the suggestion of the mediators that Prof. Radha Mohan, a well-respected Gandhian and Sudhakar Patnaik, a senior journalist from Odisha, will oversee the process of review and release of the tribals.

The last but important demand (14) was release of central committee member Ashtosh Sen and other members, Sriramalu Sreenivasulu, Gana Nayak, Jeevan Bose, Ganti Prasadam, Sirisha, Eshwari, Sarita and Gokul (the truck driver). In the mediation, as the other cases were far more complicated, the list was confined to Sriramalu Sreenivasulu, Ganti Prasadam and Sirisha, Eshwari, Sarita and Gokul (all the later five were a part of similiguda P. S. Case No. 78). The similiguda was a case where the three women and the truck driver were arrested when they were entering the forest to meet members of the Maoist party, Sirisha, alias Padma, was to meet RK (her spouse) who was the party secretary. The charge against Ganti Prasadam was that he facilitated their going into the forest. Mediators argued that this was no serious offence as the attempt to meet their family members was not a crime in itself. In response, the government agreed to take steps for withdrawal of the cases and all the five implicated in the case would be released soon. In the negotiation on this issue, Government of Odisha initially was favourably inclined to withdraw the cases against Sriramalu Sreenivasulu but backtracked on this promise.

As this agreement was finalised, keeping in view all the logistics, the mediators appealed to the Maoist party through a press conference held on the evening of the 22nd for release of Vineel Krishna, the district collector and Pabitra Majhi, the junior engineer in 48 hours. This appeal did not reach the Maoist party as the print and electronic media had no reach to these remote hilly tribal tracks. In the meanwhile, the Maoists released the junior engineer and sent a message with him that mediators should personally go to a venue suggested by them along with the freed Maoist leaders and other members when the collector will be freed. They also suggested the presence of Swami Agnivesh. Puzzled by this unexpected development, mediators took exception to the adding of new demands and sought advice and help of Varavara Rao and Ganti Prasadam. Both of them agreed that given the distance and other complications, it's not feasible at that stage. This was conveyed to the Maoists through All India Radio and BBC.

This message also reached them after 12 hours. It should, however, be noted that the Maoists expedited release of the collector to keep the word of the mediators and handed over the collector to media persons and local tribals two hours ahead of the set deadline.

The role of the media – print and the electronic – calls for deeper but separate analysis. The credibility and reliability of the entire national and regional electronic media came under deep erosion as they started telecasting on the evening of the 22nd that the district collector and junior engineer were released and the district collector had reached his residence. They started interrogating us on the news that they engendered and would not care to listen that the 48-hour deadline was set after considerable deliberation. In their competitive, sensational, 'first to announce' obsession, each channel committed the same blunder. We had to repeat again and again that that information was not correct. The next day morning, of course, some of the electronic channels apologised to the viewers. In the whole episode media did not conduct itself with self-respect and dignity, nor was it committed to transmit reliable information to build public opinion for peaceful resolution of a crisis. This approach of the media has serious implications to the making and working of the liberal framework of Indian democracy and promoting public reasoning and informed debate on sensitive issues.

The three-month period for taking action on the demands by the government lapsed on 24 May 2011. There have been questions from different quarters as to what happened to the agreement. When contacted the authorities sounded cool in enforcing the agreement.[4] The mediators had to address a letter to Naveen Patnaik, the Chief Minister, reminding him of the commitment he gave to the mediators on 25 February 2011. The letter stressed that 'non-implementation of the agreement will erode the confidence of the people in peaceful resolution of crisis which in turn adversely affects the credibility and legitimacy of the state power'.

In the meanwhile, the ceasefire agreement (Odisha government is not comfortable with this expression) was violated; both the parties blamed each other. To the letter to CM, a list of violations by the government brought to the notice of mediators was enclosed.[5] There is a large list of violations by the security forces during the last three months vitiating the overall atmosphere. There was also loss of human life. The Odisha government could have taken advantage of the opportunity to initiate peace talks on the lines that Government of Andhra Pradesh has done to avoid loss of human life on either side.[6]

On 24 May, after the three-month deadline lapsed, the mediators along with Varavara Rao, Prof. Radha Mohan and Sudhakar Patnaik met the chief minister and had a discussion on the 14-point agreement. The chief secretary and the home secretary recounted the steps that they initiated or propose to take. This time, to be more specific, the mediators prioritised four issues: 1) respect the peace agreement; 2) release Ganti Prasadam and others; 3) release the 600 tribals; and 4) protection of the land rights of the tribals. It was also suggested to bring a tribal land rights legislation on the lines of 1/70 of A. P. In fact, in the first meeting on 25 February, the devastation that the neo-liberal model has been causing was highlighted by the mediators. It was also pleaded that the Odisha government should shift the development paradigm and take tribals and their progress as the touchstone of any development. These concerns were reiterated in this meeting also.

The chief minister who sat all through the discussion lasting for two hours promised that Ganti Prasadam and four others would be released in two weeks' time and the release of at least 169 tribals detained in land-related and Maoist cases would be completed by the end of June. With regard to protecting the land rights of the tribals, they would abide by their promise to constitute a high-power committee and complete the process in six months. About violations of the peace agreement, the government came out with an equally long list of violations by the Maoist party.[7] The mediators expressed their readiness to appeal to the Maoist party to exercise restraint from their side. The chances of peace, of course, depend on both sides observing restraint. In Andhra Pradesh during the peace talks both the sides – Maoists and Government – observed remarkable restraint and there was no loss of human life for about ten months. That it did not last is a different story. The Rajashekhara Reddy government derailed the process for its own reasons.

Having witnessed the way the Rajashekhara Reddy government went back on the peace agreement and the way Home Minister Chidambaram broke the word he gave to Swami Agnivesh, the way Maoist leader Azad who engaged in finalising the process of peace talks was killed, and the way the agreement in Odisha has been treated, I fear the peace initiative does not seem hold much promise at this point of time. Yet the historical possibility of such an experiment persists.

Kidnap as a method of resistance has its own multiple facets which require a separate and detailed analysis. This kidnap was able to initiate a debate on Maoists' concerns and their approach to the development model. The media in the country has been debating and propagating their methods more and not their politics. The state in the process of containing or countering the movement is becoming increasingly repressive and lawless in its behaviour. It is this lawlessness of the state that make the people not to totally disapprove methods like kidnap. In this particular case the officer like Vineel Krishna, unlike many other insensitive corrupt bureaucrats, are more pro-tribals. There is an impressive goodwill for him among the tribals. An old tribal woman in a media coverage observed that: 'the previous collector should have been kidnapped and not this collector'. This may be symbolic but significant. A responsive and law-abiding culture in dealing with deprivation of the tribals on the part of the state would have had more far-reaching positive impact than responding to such contingencies. The Maoist party should also rethink on this method as it cripples the sympathetic civil servants to work for the people and the police force starts occupying the space legitimately belonging to the civil bureaucracy.[8] This has the danger of causing further brutalisation of the state.

A critical look at the entire kidnap episode and the issues that came up for negotiation unfolds more the nature of the model of development, a model which is unequalising and uprooting. Most of the issues raised by the Maoists emanate from the very model of development which cannot be negotiated nor altered through a kidnap. The model, undoubtedly, pushed the tribals into a vicious circle, where the way out is not clear. No lasting peace will come to these areas as long as the essence of those struggles and their opposition to the imperialist-driven model of development is not fully acknowledged and met with a shift in paradigm. Kidnaps and negotiating peace will remain transitory moves in transformative politics. The potential of such interventions in handling complexities and contradictions involved in the confrontationist counterproductive development model is yet to be fully explored.

## Notes

1 The mediators got an impression that the Odisha government was taking the decisions under pressure from Central Home Ministry.
2 Now the Odisha High Court has given a reasonably favourable judgement ordering the Odisha government to pay a compensation of Rs. 0.35 million to the victims. The Odisha government hopefully will abide by the judgement.
3 Seetanna's wife filed a habeas corpus petition which the court did not admit. The fact of the matter seemed to be that Seetanna was picked up by BSF, ever since his whereabouts are not known. In all possibility he might have been killed.

4 For instance, the government after some pressure called Prof. Radha Mohan and Sudhakar Patnaik and completed the formality of a meeting; neither was the government willing to give them the details about the tribals in prisons nor allow them any access to the prisons or prisoners. When they insisted, they said that such visits do not form a part of the agreement.
5 This included an incident of the killing of Lalitkumar Dehuri who was under police custody at the time of mediation. His detention along with four other persons was brought to the notice of the home secretary who did not pay serious attention to the issue. The life of this young man could not be saved.
6 In fact, the idea of peace talks has been in the air as the central home minister at least vaguely mentioned here and there about it. The Maoists party seems to be favourably inclined for peace tasks in West Bengal after the recent elections. There was such an initiative at All India level by the democratic-minded and peace-loving individuals drawn from different walks of national life. The prospect of peace talks at the national level is evasive but awaited.
7 A list of Maoist violations given by the Odisha government.
8 Vineel Krishna has already been shifted from Malankigiri district.

## Reference

Padel, Felix and Samarendra Das. 2010. *Out of this Earth*. Hyderabad: Orient Blackswan.

# 7

# TRIBAL RIGHTS AND BIG CAPITAL

## Critical reflections on the growing dichotomy and role of corporate media

*Sudhir Pattnaik*[1]

### Blunders in history burdening tribal identity

History does give us an account of what has happened: good, bad and the blunders. Many say history is full of blunders: some are buried and some live beyond history to appear in any contemporary time again and again, which of course depends on a number of factors that fuel them to revive, and only a few of them get challenged by the ones who can't afford to bear the burden any more. One such blunder which lives and relives through different phases of history as a burden is the definition of tribes, their identities and the design for their future which has been imposed on them. The way tribes and their identities have been defined in history has been quite troublesome for the tribes, as mostly those definitions have worked as an undeclared constitution for designing the future of the tribal societies, their life and their well-being in modern-day democracies. But any scientific and neutral analysis of history would reveal many other unexplored realities. They will tell us that tribal identity has been a victim of such a blunder in history which continues even today as a burden for them and the rulers refuse to lift that burden. The tribals on the other hand refuse to bear the burden any further and they challenge it in various forms, as a result of which we now see a number of anti-displacement struggles, movements for restorations of lands and rights-based resistances across the country wherever the tribal communities have been living in harmony with nature. The state which is gradually withdrawing from democracy under pressure from international finance capital who have an eye on resources in tribal regions is helping the blunder deepen further, which as a result is adding more onto the burden. The media instead of playing any proactive role for the burdened tribals is in fact proving again and again that it is an agent of the capital, and therefore, can't be expected to play even a neutral role.

I would like to begin by saying that tribal identities and tribal rights are going through a period of serious crisis today, often giving rise to conflicting assertions and confusing interpretations. It is also adding on to the complexity of the crisis, often creating an impression at times that they are very new in nature and, therefore, may have been impacted by liberal economic reforms. No one can belittle the impact of reforms on the primitive population of this country particularly in such places where nature has gifted them with plenty of resources. And also there is no denying the fact that reforms do help in widening all gaps in the society – physical, political, economic and intellectual, and therefore, impact of reforms is inevitable in a society with glaring inequalities. Though the tribal communities have remained more or less as autonomous entities but the mainstreaming approach has indeed broken their immunity to external influence and different kinds of inequalities also have appeared in their mutual relationships and also in the relationship with the external non-tribal world. One can see brilliant examples of this when one visits mining- and industrialisation-affected tribal areas. Over and above all other factors, it is the natural resources located close to tribal communities which are creating a new situation. These resources in tribal regions which have been so responsibly guarded by the tribal communities for generations did play a crucial role in the long past in inviting colonisers to exploit their potential to meet the demands/growing demands of industry in Europe and America. With developments in technology and science, the diverse use of these resources from agriculture to minerals got more focused and paved ways for precise interventions promising both capital and technology a fertile ground to grow. Now rapid changes in the economy of the globe again turned the focus more on these resources because of the potential they have in offering unlimited profits with relatively limited investments and with almost zero accountability towards the people who have been living on and around those resources. This coincides also with a fearsome reality that the precious resources of earth are getting exhausted, which further accelerates the pace of competition to grab them. On the other hand, the more natural resources one finds in a region these days while offering good possibility for the investors for maximising profit that an investment could provide for does create more fear in the minds of the natives that their land, water, forest, habitat, culture and peace could be devastated and destabilised in no time. The history of the modern state is indeed a history of war for control and appropriations of invaluable, non-sustainable and extremely limited resources which have been in the safe hands of tribal societies. The tribal communities in the past and present have been the losers and the mainstream society can't be considered as gainers. The problem is that the mainstream society does not have the time to reflect on what they themselves are losing now or their future generations will be losing later. The situation might continue despite resistances and challenges to the hegemony of the ruling class as resources in tribal regions have acquired more value in a highly competitive market, operated by finance capital.

There are two conflicting broad worldviews influencing the tribal predicament. These worldviews are also engaged in a war with each other which does play a role in leading or misleading the onlookers to take either this side or that side. The rich resource base in tribal regions does provide the context for such a war. These resources in the understanding of the tribals and Dalits are land, water and forest which sustain not only humans but all life forms on earth. For them natural resources mean those elements of nature without which it would not have been possible to see life on earth. The job of any generation of humans fundamentally is that they protect them at any cost. But this worldview on natural resources is not recognised and respected by the civilised world. For the civilised, the intelligentsia, the elites and the upward-looking middle class land, water and forest are not resources; rather they hide resources such as iron ore, coal, bauxite etc. within or beneath them. Land, water and forests at the most can play a supplementary role in reaching out to these resources and in processing the hidden resources to fetch good value for some from a growing market. According to this dominant worldview to which most of us subscribe, one has to find ways and means of reaching out to those resources and make use of them to advance human civilisation further. From accommodating small capital to that of providing legitimacy for the invasion of big capital in an area where people are alien to capital itself gathers momentum. Money continues to be an unknown subject for most of the tribal areas and they don't hesitate to admit their ignorance of money and capital. It is important to examine the history of capital making inroads in to tribal societies which has created inequalities which were missing in tribal communities. But before addressing some of those issues created by entry of small capital in different forms in the tribal region, a new situation was created by allowing big capital to enter in to the area without any control and regulation. In a classless society a design was drawn to create a class by using money, though for the majority money still remains an alien subject.

I may cite here my first-hand experience with an anti-displacement tribal leader who was addressing a press conference in Delhi in February 1997. The reporters asked him if he would still oppose even if the amount of compensation is increased five times compared to the package now offered. His answer was simple, 'You have given a handful of papers and you are now proposing to give a basket full of papers but papers are papers. What will our people do with those papers? Your men will come and collect them in different pretexts'. Kashipur is known to be an area for two things: a fertile valley where organic rice is being grown by the tribals – a practice that has been going on for centuries and a forest cover where non-timber forest produces are collected by the Kondha and Jhodia tribes for their livelihood. One hectare of good forest gives Siali leaves, Mahua flowers, Sal seeds; Hill Brooms enough for adjoining villages to sustain their economy. In 1996 alone tribal women of Kashipur had given a royalty of Rs. 2,000-plus to the state per each tonne of Hill Brooms they had collected from the forest. The trade on Non-Timber Forest Produces was then organised by Ama Sangthan of tribal women in Mandibisi Gram Panchayat of Kashipur block. But the dominant worldview on tribes and their development refuses to recognise this truth. For them the invisible bauxites beneath the surface carry more value, even though per one tonne of bauxite the state would get a royalty of only 32 rupees that time. Just compare Rs. 32 per tonne of bauxite, an exhaustible resource, and Rs. 2000 per tonne of Hill Brooms from a sustainable resource. Tribes all over the state have been demanding rights over forest resources. Understanding tribal identities is fundamental to that of understanding tribal rights. It is important as well as enlightening to understand what they themselves think about their own identity.

## How they redefine their identity

Tribes in different parts of the Indian state have been revolting against the domination of a few over them and against any kind of imposition of alien culture in the name of modernity over them. But the most important of them have been against colonisation of their resources and forcing them to abandon their ecological abode or habitation as the state has to progress and they are seen as the barriers. Chakara Bisoi and Birsa Munda have been the most-known names in Odisha history. But the modern and contemporary history also gives us some bright examples. It is important to recall what they say about their own identity.

## Maharaja Majhi

A major anti-displacement struggle was going on in Kashipur area of Rayagada district against a consortium of alumina companies which initially started with the Tatas, Norsk Hydro and Alcan. The project included an alumina plant and mining of Baphlamali with 173 million tonnes of bauxite. The resistance started when three tribal leaders of Kucheipadar village who were part of government departments started organising the resistance while in service after a local NGO briefed them about the forthcoming project.

They were Maharaja Majhi (a village postmaster), Laxman Majhi (a school teacher) and Krushna Santa (an employee of the irrigation department). The tribals lost three of their members in a police firing on December 16, 2000. In an interview to the author, Maharaja Majhi had the following words to offer in 1996. According to Maharaja, 'Baphlamali is our identity. It gives us hundreds of perennial streams to irrigate our land and makes it rich and fertile. Kashipur today is the birth place of rice in the world because of this mountain. You can't separate us from Baphlamali and ask us to give a definition of our identity'. They strongly believed if the identity of Baphlamali is lost, they will also be lost. The history of betrayal of tribals does not allow us to dismiss this fear.

## Dabur Kalundia

Dabur Kalundia belongs to a village called Baligotha in the newly constructed Kalinganagar Tehsil and Police station. Dabur was happy with his land in a not-so-known area of Sukinda region of undivided Cuttack and now Jajpur district. The dream of having the second steel plant drove Biju Pattnaik in to the region. Soon it came to be known as Kalinganagar. His village, Baligotha, is now surrounded from all sides by 12 steel and sponge iron factories. On 2 January 2006, he lost 14 members of his tribe who were opposing land acquisition by the Tatas. Later on 3 people died because of attacks by private militia. A dozen more died because they did not get proper medical care when they were in critical emergency situations. The whole area had been turned in to an open house prison. Dabur is among the top leaders of the Vistapan Virodhi Jan Manch, which was spearheading the movement against the Tata Steel Plant.

Dabur says,

> we are the originals. Mother Nature loves us because we love her and live with her. We stand for her. She gives us the identity. It is our fundamental duty to defend her when she is under attack. What rights you are talking about? We don't demand any right to live at the cost of others. We just want to be left to ourselves to be left to live with mother earth. Please don't touch her and allow us to live with her. You may not have to give us anything as right.

## Mukta Jhodia

The date was 30 January 2001. There was a huge rally of tribals in Kashipur town. They had travelled a 10 km distance from Maikanch to the Kashipur Tehsil headquarters to protest against the killing of their brothers while they were protesting against the alumina plant. The ex-speaker of Lok Sabha, Sri Rabi Ray, was to address them. Suddenly one woman appeared on the dais and took over the microphone. She introduced herself as Mukta Jhodia. Her questions were fundamental. 'Who is the government to invade our territory? Did the government create the mountains, the hills, the forests, the rivers, the land and the streams? How could they take them away from us? We are not the king. But we have been protecting them from the time of our forefathers. Who is government to destroy them?'

From Goanasika in Kenojhar of north Odisha to Gandhamardhan in western Odisha, one may come across thousands of such definitions which are original and close to the heart of tribals. Nowhere would one come across an example where a tribal believing in nature would accept any definition of his or her identity keeping nature or any life form related to nature away from him. The question which often comes to mind is how to assess the real impact of these views on economy, ecology, life and livelihood of the people. This is something we are unable to do properly in an era of media-driven democracy which coincides with the state shying away from its responsibility for people and also from nature that is holding life and livelihood. This is also the time one sees how independent research and analysis is declining at an alarming rate.

## Ecological collective versus ethnic collective and the rights regime

The concept of rights was alien to tribals who never considered themselves less than their own masters. They were not only their own masters, their livelihood systems depended entirely on ecological resources which they by nature conserved and thus worked as their natural custodians. This role of natural custodians having the commitment to nature and future generations has never been understood properly in the past by the so-called mainstream society and it is equally missing even today. The major reason for unrest and conflict comes from a lack of understanding them as natural custodians and treating them as natural hindrances to reach out to resources having promises for capital to grow and grow without bound. The ownership over resources was collective. And they did not recognise any authority over and above them. Till the time the colonisers developed a branch of discipline to study them mostly from their own perspective, they lived as ecological collectives, but soon they were seen as anthropological entities or ethnic collectives. The anthropological researcher treated the tribes as beings who looked to be human but completely lacked the knowledge about other human beings. Gradually the logic of mainstreaming them and bringing them close to the civilised world started gaining ground. Two approaches have broadly worked in most places. One approach did not care about their existence and knowingly or unknowingly tried to eliminate them and capture the resources around them (the history of European invasion in tribal American continents stands as a cruel testimony). Another approach attempted to liberate them as part of a new awakening or new enlightenment and bring them to the mainstream of the civilised world. (The white men's burden extended to tribal societies and later on was faithfully practiced by internal colonisers.) Mainstreaming the tribal was self-interpreted as a noble and pure work but that never allowed any kind of questioning till some kind of resistance surfaced and started questioning the mainstreaming approach. Because of a number of historical reasons, the concept of rights was constructed, which again is seen by many as an act to keep a balance between the worlds the tribes have hailed from over centuries and the world the civilised society is proposing for them. Everything was put in to a development framework and the state was given an undeclared mandate to deliver development within that framework. It was never adequately discussed or debated over the limitation that exclusion could be an inbuilt device in such a paternalistic and patronising developmental framework.

## The history of continuity

The tribal identity does not seem to be changing radically immaterial of the progress achieved globally and nationally in the areas of economic growth and growth-oriented development. This is not withstanding the number of remarkable conventions and agreements arrived at the United Nations among member countries on Indigenous people. Some of the countries like India have not even ratified certain conventions. Often one may think that it is more of continuity and less of change in any positive sense of the term. Now this identity seems to be disappearing with the physical extinction of the tribe. From the period of pre-colonial autonomous tribal lands and the period of colonisation and resistance to it, during which one comes across pre-Independence Government of India acts and special acts for agency areas to the post-colonial independent state and the discomforts or deprivation it brought along for them; from the era of protective discrimination promoted by the Constitution to the new economic policy regime which helped in perpetuating deprivation, each period in history has witnessed evolution of tribal identities and related conceptualisation of tribal rights in different forms. One may take a view on the tribal development subplans and special projects targeting tribes and primitive tribes. The state has always tried to define and redefine tribal identities by offering or by recognising one or the other rights, the latest being Forest Rights Act, necessarily not because of new enlightenment it receives in its understanding of the tribal predicament but perhaps because the quantitative size of the tribal population in the country continues to be a prominent factor in electoral politics.

## Big capital and the media

Interestingly at a time when one after another rights of tribals have been recognised by the Indian state, the tribal areas also have witnessed an unprecedented flow of foreign direct investment capable of derailing rights or launching assaults on rights of tribals. This has created a peculiar situation in which tribes discover a new image of the state, which in actual practice prefers to defend the foreign direct investment or big capital and ignores its constitutional responsibility of upholding or protecting rights of tribals when they confront one another. This also helps in creating a new political situation wherein political forces agreeing on development, foreign direct investment or interventions by big capital forming an undeclared coalition against which the helpless tribals have to raise their voice. The withering away of the welfare state is not questioned anywhere. The media which has almost become a part of big capital and has turned news sharing into an industrial activity that demands a very clear role for capital or big capital is also playing a partisan role to protect capital and its interest. In 2011, the total advertisement revenue generated by the Indian media was about rupees 300,000 million. As Livemint (2018) reports in its web edition of 14 February 2018, advertisement expenditure in India is going to reach more than Rs. 6,930 million in 2018, which would be 13 per cent higher than that of 2017. Anyone can get this figure by using Google search. It has by now become clear that the corporate media in India will never speak against its corporate masters. Therefore, truth will be sacrificed. This is happening at a time when successive committees and reports commissioned by the government are admitting in clear terms that tribal communities (the most prominent among them being the Planning Commission Expert Group Report on Development Challenges in Extremist Affected Areas led by Debu Bandopadhaya in 2008) have become victims of historical injustice, apathy and indifference, non-implementation of schemes and violation of rights. They now have started asserting themselves in various ways, non-violent and not so non-violent. The assertion for their rights is also being very conveniently interpreted by a pro-capital aggressive media with the single most objective of facilitating entry of private capital in to resource-rich regions of tribal India often at the cost of tribal rights. Therefore, the dichotomy between rights offered and rights realised by tribal communities is widening at a rate never calculated before. In an era of globalisation, localisation of news by media is also killing an issue. This is happening mostly in resource-rich regions where tribal communities have been living. Every regional newspaper today is trying out a subregional edition targeting advertisement revenues from mining and mineral-based industries. Issues of national importance get marginalised when they at the most focus it in their subregional editions. The rest of the state does not get a chance to know about it; therefore, an issue is effectively stopped from travelling beyond a locality. It is interesting to watch that at a time when resources controlling the media are getting globalised, the focus of media on crucial issues is getting localised. One would also come across dailies and news channels being launched by miners or with the absolute patronage of miners, micro-finance organisations and real estate developers. Land is the prime target of all these actors. Since the national media is grabbing most advertisement revenues, this is leading to an unholy competition between the national media and the regional media in one hand while on the other it does also lead to collaboration and co-option giving the national media an upper hand to dictate editorial framework which ultimately helps the corporate interest better served at the cost of issues affecting the common men in general and tribal and Dalit communities in particular.

Now the way the Indian state is turning itself into a security-centric state from that of a democratic state, the media in all probability would work as public relations units of the concerned agencies of the state. A security state will grow by injecting a fear in the mind of the people that their security is at stake because of some stated and some unstated reasons, thus, they must trust the state to provide security to them at some cost which they should not mind. Manufactured stories, misinterpreted or exaggerated events and manipulated facts are circulated in media to spread fear and to enable the state to suspend democratic processes to ensure security. But what ultimately gets protected is the interest of state as believed by the ruling class, which could not be separated from the interest of the finance capital in a reforms regime. The Green Hunt operations in tribal areas and the proposed National Counter Terrorism Centre in the light of the National Counterterrorism Centre of the USA could be taken as examples to understand this phenomenon. The predicament the tribal communities are facing across the country in terms of access to resources in which they have to confront a war imposed on them by alien forces, the Indian state because of its nature and association with finance capital would do very little to help the tribal societies deal with that predicament. The nature and composition of corporate media would never help them defend the tribes in distress as it would turn them against their own masters.

At the end, it could be concluded with a disappointing note that the media in tribal areas reflect a dehumanised and highly insensitive approach. They don't consider tribal communities as human beings who have equal rights to live a dignified life. There was a time when media was confined to print media only. The approach of media to any issue in tribal areas was based on the assumption that they were all ignorant and anything they did was viewed from the perspective of the enlightened souls whose mission was to drive out ignorance and illiteracy. This was very close to the dominant worldview on tribes which worked for mainstreaming them. Now tribes are viewed as people sitting over resources with primitive lifestyles and preventing finance capital from making use of it for maximising profit. This desire and the attached design are kept hidden in a sugar-coated capsule called development. Media works just to advance this approach and to locate a rationale for it. But it would be wrong to assume that the scenario offers no hope. The non-corporate media is growing everywhere and in different forms to keep the hope alive. It is time for researchers to focus on them and see how they have been echoing the voices and concerns to protect the tribal identities which are not simply ethnic but are based more on ecology and economics. What we require today is a mind which is willing to unlearn certain things and learn afresh from the wisdom of tribes without romanticising their exclusive culture and culture-based lifestyles.

## Note

1 The author has written this chapter based on a number of editorial pieces and articles written by him, which have been published in the reputed Odia fortnightly news magazine, *Samadrusti*. He also gratefully acknowledges the writings of many others published in the same journal. The magazine can be found online at www.samadrusti.com.

## Reference

Livemint. 2018. *Ad Spending in India to Grow at 13% in 2018: GroupM Report*. 14 February. https://www.livemint.com/Consumer/C2O1o18C8UF12L1HRxBM5L/Ad-spending-in-India-to-grow-at-13-in-2018-GroupM-report.html?utm_source=scroll&utm_medium=referral&utm_campaign=scroll (accessed on 16 July 2018).

# Part II

# UNTOUCHABILITY, ATROCITIES AND MARGINALISATION
An unspoken empirical veracity

# 8

# UNDERSTANDING ADIVASI DISPOSSESSION FROM THEIR LAND AND RESOURCES IN TERMS OF 'INVESTMENT-INDUCED DISPLACEMENT'

*Felix Padel*

At least 20 million Adivasis and 10 million Dalits have been displaced by dams, mines, factories and other 'development projects' since Independence. For the vast majority, this has caused a drastic drop in their standard of living. Instead of the fruits of development they were promised, they have ended up further excluded and marginalised. People already displaced, as well as communities resisting displacement right now all over the country, therefore strongly dispute whether such projects should be termed 'development' at all. What is not in question is that financial investment in 'development projects' is a prime cause of displacement, which fits with the analysis of many in Adivasi communities that 'we are being flooded out by money'.

Replacing the term 'Development-Induced Displacement' with 'Investment-Induced Displacement' we see more clearly the processes at work: basically, the investment is aimed at taking over land and resources from those who have always lived on the land, with a view to making financial profits – often very large profits, nearly all made very far from the original site of resource-extraction. Most of the people dispossessed have lived in a symbiotic relationship with these resources over centuries, based on principles of long-term sustainability. Adivasis displaced by a dam, factory or mine find not only that almost nothing they were promised materialises, but also that they have lost immeasurably in terms of food security and the former richness of their social life and natural environment, giving rise to an anger and disillusion that is very evident, for instance, in Subrat Kumar Sahu's documentary '*DAM-aged*' (Sahu 2010) about people displaced by the Upper Indravati Reservoir (southwest Odisha).

In unravelling the processes of exploitation and dispossession at work, the *Unbroken History of Broken Promises* (Sharma 2010) needs laying bare, along with the ideology that drives this investment with an overall promise of improving 'the greater common good'. One part of the ideology justifying the land-grabs involves perpetuating negative stereotypes about Adivasis and their culture, seeing these as 'primitive' and 'backward', when Adivasi cultures are highly developed in terms of knowledge systems (Padel 1999) of nature, skills of cultivation, channelling water, making houses and a peaceful web of social relationships.

The causes of poverty need laying bare too: basically a system of exploitation skewed against Indigenous cultivators that amounts to *structural violence*. India has numerous excellent laws designed to protect Adivasi rights, from the insistence in Schedules V & VI of the Constitution against the alienation of tribal land, to the PESA Act, Forest Rights Act, NREGA, among many others. Implementation has often been very poor, however: notoriously so of PESA, which offered, and still offers, means towards a real Panchayat Raj of decentralised decision-making.

When Adivasis and Dalits can approach the courts, and expect equality before the law, even when perpetrators are members of powerful corporations or government servants, then we can speak of real development. Until then, many 'development projects' are rapidly increasing the inequality, injustice and marginalisation of communities who have safeguarded the country's ecosystems over countless generations.

## Escalating dispossession and Indigenous movements

India has developed some of the strongest laws of any country to protect the rights of its Indigenous and poorer citizens, and to protect the environment. The Fifth and Sixth Schedules of the Constitution, reinforced by state-level acts against the alienation of Adivasi lands such as OSATIP, 1956, in Odisha (Orissa Scheduled Areas Transfer of Immovable Property Regulation, 1956), and the Environment Protection Act, 1980, have been supplemented over the last 15 years by PESA, the FRA, NREGA and RTI. Yet implementation overall remains very poor. While community activists trying to protect their basic rights meet frequent intimidation and enmeshment in false cases, the country's richest businessmen and their companies in effect buy clearance for projects that are currently displacing tens of thousands of poor people, in 'slum redevelopment' drives in cities, as well as in 'development projects' in the remote countryside.

Adivasis' dispossession from their land is often termed 'Development-Induced Displacement'. Although those displaced often say strongly that for them displacement projects cannot be called 'development', their voices are too little heard. What is undeniable is that the main force causing their dispossession is investment – the power of money, often seen as an obvious benefit to poor areas, yet in practice, as Adivasis often express this, 'Flooding us out with Money' (Padel and Das 2010: 148, 372). In the words of Bhagaban Majhi, a leader of the Kashipur movement against the Utkal alumina project since the early 1990s, and a Kond Adivasi:

> We have sought an explanation from the Government about people who have been displaced in the name of development: how many have been properly rehabilitated? You have not provided them with jobs; you have not rehabilitated them at all. How can you again displace more people? Where will you relocate them and what jobs will you give them? . . . . We are tribal farmers. We are earthworms. Like fish that die when taken out of water, a cultivator dies when his land is taken away from him. So we won't leave our land. We want permanent development.[1]

The main cause of poverty in tribal areas is as simple to comprehend as it is hard to unravel: a system of endemic exploitation. A key cog in this system, as has long been recognised (e.g. in Gopinath Mohanty's novels such as *Poroja*, 1945) is moneylending at compound interest rates aimed at acquiring Adivasi lands. This process of dispossession has continued, despite constitutional and state-level legislation designed to prevent it. For example, the main aims of the *Adivasi Mulya Adivasi Sangha* in Narayanpatna area of south Odisha were reclaiming illegally alienated lands, and closing illegal liquor shops. After Maoists publicly supported this campaign, the full force of state repression descended against it, starting with a contrived firing at Narayanpatna police station on 20 November 2009. The fact remains, this movement was basically an attempt to assert the rule of law by implementing fundamental Adivasi rights.[2]

The system of endemic exploitation has been vastly compounded since the year 2000 by the invasion of mining and construction companies, whose entry is invariably accompanied by timber mafia, illegal liquor shops, prostitution and high levels of corruption. The forces driving the dispossession and alienating tribal people today need to be understood as emanating from the world's financial centres under the banner of neo-liberal market fundamentalism. In many ways, neo-liberal economics represents the most dangerous fundamentalism of all time (Padel 2010b). Investment in resource-rich areas is aimed at making maximum profit out of them, without any knowledge or concern for devastating impacts on communities and ecosystems: a loot is taking place of India's unrenewable resources (see e.g. CSE 2008: *Rich Lands, Poor People*).

'Sustainable Development' and 'Corporate Social Responsibility' are regularly used as a mask, presenting a picture of benefits completely at variance with grassroots situations.

> CSR was, is and always will be about avoiding regulation, covering up the damage corporations cause to society and the environment and maintaining public co-operation with the corporate dominated system.
> (Fauset 2006: 2)

A *Reality Gap* therefore exists between models of development and ground realities, with top-down structures imposing 'missionary' attitudes, as if outsiders know what's best for Adivasi communities, and there was 'nothing there' before they came. This reality gap is especially evident in the 'Resettlement and Rehabilitation' process: what is meant to happen bears hardly any relationship to realities unfolding on the ground (Padel and Das 2008, 2011).

The rule of law is seriously undermined whenever communities' voices in Public Hearings are misreported. Time and again, communities express fundamental opposition to projects – often in the face of dire police repression – only to find that the very fact that a Public Hearing was held is represented by district authorities as communities giving their 'assent'! Companies such as Vedanta and Tata advertise their benefits through PR campaigns and CSR projects. Defining 'Sustainable Development' afresh in 2005, the UN World Summit placed economy first and environment third, defining the three 'interdependent and mutually reinforcing pillars' of SD as 'economic development, social development and environmental protection'. Logically, environmental sustainability should take precedence, as it is the basis of life on earth. If we fail to correct this fault in priorities, and fail to limit consumption of resources in time, then sooner rather than later, we're dead.

Society should come next, for without people, economy and market do not exist. Economic models tend to operate without defining society. 'The market' is an abstraction, denoting a highly complex financial system. People and their experience are absent. Without a concept of social structure, economists have no means to understand systemically how money affects people, and how certain groups use money to control and exploit others. Surely the economy and the market should be serving people in society, rather than the other way around?

The tribal cultures being dispossessed are precisely the kinds of society most highly evolved in the art of living sustainably, who developed the art of living from resource-rich nature without damaging it over centuries. Yet from Left as well as Right, tribal cultures are still often seen as 'backward' and 'underdeveloped', without understanding that they are highly developed, not just in knowledge of the forest and cultivation, but in the principle of sharing – the other end of the spectrum from the value placed by neo-liberal economics on competition! – and many other features, such as a legal system geared towards reconciliation rather than a primitive mentality of winners and losers.

When Lado Sikoka, a Dongria Kond confronting Vedanta's plans to mine Niyamgiri, says at a Public Hearing '*Niyamgiri is not a pile of money standing there – it's our Maa-Baap, who has nurtured us!*'[3] this idea of minerals as sources of life contradicts mainstream, materialist ideas that minerals on top of mountains are just 'resources lying unutilised' – ideas fuelled by investment from a nexus of the world's most powerful financial institutions.

The basic threat in this and countless areas is the *Resource Curse* – the logic which plunges resource-rich regions into Ecocide and Cultural Genocide – the opposite of promised prosperity – and which often spills over into resource wars. The Maoist-'Green Hunt' conflict needs to be understood as essentially a resource war. Maoism is a 'false flag', in the sense that both sides are materialist and believe in mining – no-one imposed industrialisation more ruthlessly than Mao, in his Great Leap Forward in 1958. A policy of rapidly increasing steel production is essentially Maoist! Both sides believe in violence and sacrifice of lives and cultures to achieve their aims, imposing their will through top-down structures.

In this context the recent announcement of 300 million for each Maoist-affected district as an incentive promoting 'development' to offset the appeal of Maoists is dangerous for many reasons: it reinforces top-down structures, threatens to intensify the dispossession and cultural genocide, and the idea of giving money for conflict-status adds fuel to the flames.[4]

To bring peace back to tribal areas demands real development: to start with, justice for all, based on principles of Truth and Reconciliation. Adivasi voices and perceptions need to be listened to carefully. Non-violent movements against ruthlessly imposed industrialisation represent a progressive force of the kind that we may all need if our species is to be saved from self-destruction.

These movements nearly always unite Adivasis, Dalits and other non-tribal groups. The anti-Posco movement is by small-scale farmers and fishermen, and has links to the Pauri Bhuiya Adivasis around Kandhadhara mountain in north Odisha. Farmers who protected their lands at Singur and Nandigram were predominantly Dalits. Movements against nuclear plants at Jaitapur and Kudankulam are joined by all sections of society. Big dams and mining/metal factory projects are overwhelmingly in tribal areas, so movements against these are mainly Adivasi movements. The Kalinganagar movement, which after six years still meets repression, took a name applicable to many: *Bisthapan Birodhi Jan Manch* – People's Platform Against Displacement.[5]

Northeast India, excluded from mainstream consciousness by geography as well as media marginalisation, now witnesses an escalation of movements against displacing projects, especially big dams, with 200 protestors against the Lower Subansiri dam, blocking the highway towards Arunachal and the dam site, arrested on Christmas night 2011. Protestors against the Lower Siang dam, after its planned output was raised secretly to 2,700MW, were fired on by tear gas and lathi-charged by CRPF at Pongging on 26 May 2010, injuring scores, four people severely, in an unprecedented upsurge of violence in Arunachal.[6]

The Arunachal dams seem to be motivated by loans/advance payments from private power and construction companies in what has been likened to a 'MoU virus', which means that construction has already started on at least 67 dams.[7] Protests have also multiplied, with the three Public Hearings necessary for granting clearance for Lower Siang dam indefinitely postponed in October 2011 due to 'public disturbance', referring to opposition by almost the whole of the Adi tribe, whose lands would be severely impacted by this dam. The Demwe dam, in Lohit district, was also put on hold in November 2011, by the National Wildlife Board, pending assessments of the dam's impact on the unique Kamlang sanctuary.[8]

Dams are seen as the key to Arunachal's prosperity, and there's no question that, for people at the top, huge sums are coming in from contracts. But nowhere, perhaps, is there a starker contrast between market forces offering quick financial incentives and sources of life at stake. 'Hydro-dollars' from the new projects are estimated to augment the state budget considerably – calculations that almost certainly fail to take into account the numerous loans taken on for infrastructure. The real motivating force seems to be down-payments – estimated at over Rs.1,500 million during 2005–2007, when the MoU signing spree began (Dutta 2008).

The Arunachal dams are justified on the grounds that they will bring 'development' to backward areas, far below the national average in roads and infrastructure. This highlights the concept spread through the World Bank and similar institutions of development as a single set path to be rigidly imposed. The concept of 'development' as it has come to be defined by mainstream discourse and apex financial institutions developed out of *social evolutionism*, the theory elaborated by Herbert Spencer, Marx and others out of Darwin's vision of biological evolution: that societies evolve in set stages from a 'primitive', tribal stage, to feudalism, to capitalism and (if one is a Marxist) to advanced socialism. While Darwin highlighted species evolving through multiple different paths, social evolutionism imagines – and when it becomes policy, imposes – a single, uniform path.

The usual stereotypes about tribal cultures stress 'primitiveness', 'backwardness' and 'underdevelopment'. But as Gustavo Esteva puts this, in *The Development Dictionary* (1992), the day that President Truman took office as President of the United States, on 20 January 1949, he inaugurated the concept of 'underdevelopment' as a blueprint for the spread America's development paradigm: 'On that day, 2 billion people became underdeveloped. . . . [The concept] took on an unsuspected colonizing virulence' (Esteva 1992: 7) – among those on the Left as well as Right. In India, Tribal Development plans promote this model in a standardised, top-down format, riddled with corruption (Sainath 1996). Paradoxically, mainstream models of development often bulldoze into oblivion tribal people's traditional economies and systems of cultivation developed over centuries of living in the midst of natural resources, drawing from them without depleting them. Too often, 'development projects' involve a privatisation, takeover and radical depletion of these resources.

Adivasis and Dalits are generally recognised as India's two most discriminated and excluded groups. In some ways their position in the overall social structure is very different though, and this difference is what has been exploited by those who instigated e.g. the Kandhamal violence in Odisha in 2008–09. In general, if Dalits were those forced into servitude by the dominant castes, Adivasis were those who resisted domination most radically, by retreating to the least accessible regions. They thus preserved distinct languages, cultures and knowledge systems (Padel 1998, 1999). One aspect of Adivasi cultures is that they preserve a close connection between the other linguistic derivatives of Latin *cultus* – a system of cultivation and a religious cult of the forces of nature. This is not to revert to 'primitive romanticism', saying that everything about tribal societies is good. But in many ways, these cultures are examples of what Marx and Engels called 'primitive communism', and as such, the antithesis of capitalism. It's not surprising therefore if Indigenous movements are at the cutting edge of opposing takeovers by capital investment in India.

What they are fighting at one level is not just dispossession from their land, but also *Cultural Genocide* and an annihilation of Adivasi identity (Tudu 2011; Padel and Das 2008; Padel 2011a), and also, in many cases *Ecocide* – the destruction of ecosystems that they always lived in harmony with (Higgins 2010).

## Investment from a financial system based on debt

Questioning investment is not done. Everyone wants more money, and the conventional attitude to large social problems is to throw money at them, without necessarily looking too closely at the top-down structures the money flows through. In the case of many 'development projects', it is apparent that the more money poured into an area, the worse its poverty gets. Focusing on the aspect of displacement this becomes blindingly obvious. The funds that go into building a dam cause mass displacement – in the case of mega-dams such as Rihand, Hirakud, Sardar Sarovar or Polavaram, the number of people displaced by one reservoir can be around 0.2 million.

The damage to communities and ecosystems is spoken about widely, even if this is often ineffective in stopping destructive projects. But the damage is also economic. What is less spoken about is that the financial cost of a dam – which often rises to five or ten times the original estimate – includes massive loans: 70 per cent is allowed, and seems to be a regular ratio. The nexus of government agencies, power companies, construction companies and financial institutions that combine to build a dam is often extremely complex, but whatever the loan-giving and loan-taking agencies, the upshot is to saddle the river water with a burden of debt.[9]

Debt is an instrument of power and control through *leverage*. Detailed studies of World Bank patterns of lending show that in effect there has been an undeclared policy of getting one 'developing' country after another into unrepayable debt, and when the Balance of Payment crisis hits, the country is forced through *conditionalities* placed on further loans that the government has invariably become dependent on to open up to penetration by foreign companies and banks, which means an increasing takeover of resources and assets.[10]

Development projects are implemented in the name of reducing poverty. The irony is that these projects nearly always make the poor poorer, and that many Adivasi communities who have not suffered displacement, do not see themselves as poor at all. In a letter to the Chief Minister of Madhya Pradesh, appealing against displacement by the Sardar Sarovar dam, an Adivasi in Madhya Pradesh wrote:

> You take us to be poor, but we're not. We live in harmony and co-operation with each other. . . . We get good crops from Mother Earth. . . . Clouds give us water. . . . We produce many kinds of grains with our own efforts, and we don't need money. We use seeds produced by us. . . . In the spirit of Laha (communal labour) we produce a house in just one day. . . . You people live in separate houses. You don't bother about the joy or suffering of each other. But we live on the support of our kith and kin. . . . How does such fellow-feeling prevail in our villages? For we help each other. We enjoy equal standing. We've been born in our village. Our Nara (umbilical cord) is buried here.
>
> (Mahariya 2001)

'Moneylender Colonialism' is essentially the reason why Odisha was India's most indebted state: it had received most loans from the World Bank and other agencies, financing dam, coal and other projects in order to create an infrastructure for the mining industry, playing on the state's poverty, but using this debt as leverage to open it up to foreign corporations, starting with a privatisation of electricity (Padel and Das 2010: 455–95).

World Bank loans are rarely brought into the political discourse in Indian elections. Organisations outside India continue to campaign for third world debts to be cancelled, but none of India's main political parties make this an issue. Why not? As soon as a party is elected to form a government, it becomes the recipient of loans as a basic part of government income, so dependency is built into the system, with policy directives basically handed down from the IMF and in line with US Treasury Department interests. The governments of 'developed countries' are caught in a similar system of spiralling debt themselves, with the US and UK notorious examples. In India, this debt-based investment is based on *Sacrificing People* (Padel 2010a), especially Adivasi the communities living in resource-rich regions.

World Bank loans to India started with the Damodar dams. By 1962 India was the world's most heavily indebted country. During 1964–76 India got $1.5 billion in 11 fast-disbursing Balance of Payment loans for industrial imports, deferring a Balance of Payment crisis through loans funding rapid industrialisation. By 1990 India's foreign debt had risen to $83.7 billion, and a Balance of Payment crisis loomed. With Narsimha Rao elected in May 1991, Manmohan Singh as Finance Minister swiftly put the New Economic Policy in place, and by 1992, the crisis was over, thanks to a massive injection of new fast-disbursing World Bank loans, given on condition of extensive IMF-dictated liberalising reforms, enshrined in the New Economic Policy, 1991.

In 2010, from a $3 billion average disbursement, the annual World Bank loans to India rose to $11 billion. This is the context of a new $1.5 billion loan agreed in January 2011 for expanding 24,000 km of roads, out of a total $40 billion of loans taken by the GoI from various sources to expand a total 747,000 km of roads.[11]

This new burden of debt, taken on for a new kind of 'modern' road network, should be seen as essentially dictated through economists in the IMF and World Bank on the rationale of driving growth through an 'export-driven economy'. This is why, throughout India, the roads being massively widened, with ancient trees cut and a lot of property encroached on, are sign-posted to ports more than to cities. This reveals the real intention behind these loans – to facilitate a rapid extraction of resources, in the name of a high growth rate. The loans are coming in fast, and state administrations are giving this work top priority, with no protests allowed to hold up the work, which is why several people were killed near Noida in UP in August 2010 and May 2011, where the Yamuna Expressway is taking fertile land from farmers, buying it for far too little. Land speculation and the housing market are at the root of India's Black Economy (Kumar 1999).

Debt works in the same way at macro- and micro-levels. The pattern of village moneylenders obtaining Adivasi lands through compound interest has been frequently recorded. The modern version of indebtedness to seed companies and microcredit agencies forcing small farmers off the land and often into suicide is now well recorded too.[12] At the international level, this is the same pattern as the World Bank forcing countries which WB loans have sunk into unrepayable debt to open up and yield their assets to foreign investment. Since the New Economic Order, and new legislation such as the SEZ Act (2005) – all apparently engineered from the IMF, WB and parallel institutions – the pace of takeovers escalates.

This is the substance of the 'bad economics' outlined by Josef Stiglitz in *Globalisation and its Discontents* (2002). Bad economics applies standard formulas without regard for effects on people and the ecosystems they live in, or even on a country's overall economy. In one case after another (such as Turkey, Mexico, Argentina and SE Asian 'tiger economies'), countries in crisis that follow IMF prescriptions end up compounding the crisis – and their debt burden. 'Moneylender Colonialism' sums up the power structure and systemic exploitation at work here. In other words, today's power structure is based on debt. Getting countries and people into debt, and using that as leverage to extract whatever the controlling financial interests desire, is a key technique of prevailing power structures.

The problem goes deeper still. Crises of ecocide and resource wars in many parts of the world, and governments' inability to make the emissions cuts necessary to check global warming, have their origin in a financial system based on debt. For one thing, a large part of the population of almost every country now lives in debt, to mortgage companies, banks and other entities. The subprime mortgage crisis in America that led to the crash in September–October 2008 was caused by a deregulation of derivatives trading that spread 'toxic debts', facilitated by Alan Greenspan (as Chairman of the Federal Reserve 1987–2006), Lawrence Summers (US Treasury Secretary 1999–2001 and for many years a key decision-maker in the World Bank), Henry Paulson and Timothy Geithner (Treasury Secretaries since 2006), top economists running Goldman Sachs and other leading investment banks, as well as academic economists who got large fees for writing articles supporting policies that inflated the debt-bubble, such as the massive investment in Iceland's banks that precipitated its crash (Ferguson 2010).

Finance was increasingly deregulated under Reagan and Greenspan, allowing derivatives trading in debt instruments to multiply rapidly. Paper money gave way to electronic money during the years 1980–2000, allowing 'hot money' to move across national boundaries at the click of a mouse. Edward Herman drew attention to the dangers of deregulation of finance, and derivatives trading when the market was emerging during the 1990s:

> The world's financial institutions have moved from one area of high risk and speculative investment to another in their search for fat profit margins, and they have vast holdings of risky debt. The enormous development of the derivatives market in the past decade is the latest new product yet to be tested in a crisis where such instruments might require selling in a falling market.
>
> (Herman 1995: 17)

A key dimension of this expansion of finance is in funding for mining, metal and energy projects. Since 2000, loans to extractive industry projects arranged in London and the US have multiplied by at least ten times. Speculation in metals trading, through 'reputable' mainstream banks as well as hedge funds and private equity funds registered in tax havens but mostly run from the world's top capitals, plays a key role in this finance (Nostromo 2011).

The prototype of an investment bubble using debt as a basis for speculation goes back to the South Sea Company, formed in 1711 in London to capitalise on the slave trade, and to finance Britain's national debt, inflated after a war with Spain. The company took on half the national debt – about £30 million – share prices went up and up, till the bubble burst, and many investors, big and small, were ruined, as happened again during the Bengal Bubble, when London-based investment in newly conquered Bengal caused the 1770 famine (Robins 2006). In many ways, the East India Company let loose in 1760s Bengal was a prototype of the corporate takeovers taking place all over India now, fuelled by foreign investment and speculation.

Economist Amit Bhaduri shows how today's emphasis on economic growth and a high GDP serves the interests of big corporations and those running the WB/IMF cartel,

> *while the ground reality steadily worsens. For the sake of higher growth, the poor in growing numbers will be left out in the cold, undernourished, unskilled and illiterate, totally defenceless against the ruthless logic of a global market dominated by large corporate interests.*

> *This is not merely an iniquitous process. High growth brought about in this manner does not simply ignore the question of income distribution, its reality is far worse. It threatens the poor with a kind of brutal violence in the name of development, a sort of 'developmental terrorism', violence perpetrated on the poor in the name of development by the state primarily in the interests of a corporate aristocracy, approved by the IMF and the World Bank, and a self-serving political class. . . . A massive land grab by large corporations is going on in various guises.*
>
> ('Growing Wasteland', in Bhaduri 2010: 42)

The Wall Street Crash in 1929 and the 2008 crash have many similar features with the 18th-century bubbles, starting with irresponsible encouragement of speculation by those running the financial system, whether from London or the Federal Reserve, Goldman Sachs and the US Treasury Department in the US. But the 2008 crash was caused specifically by using people's homes as a commodity for speculation in America; an American investment promoting the aluminium industry in Iceland was at the root of that country's bubble.

Behind the companies, the banks. To understand 'the outrageous debt which Third World countries have actually paid many times over, but which, due to interest, is now larger than ever before', Michael Rowbotham's *Grip of Death* exposes the theory behind bank loans as 'a complete and utter delusion' (1998). This is the system used to force economic growth onto resource-rich regions, geared towards extracting their resources, dispossessing their original inhabitants and destroying ecosystems in the process. Mining and metal production have been progressively outsourced to 'developing' countries, and as resources get scarcer, a frenzy of investment pours into India.

Industrial projects are often promoted with the offer of new employment, while the reality is a systematic undermining of labourers' rights and security due to the informalisation of labour through subcontracting, with highly skilled Adivasi cultivators classified as 'unskilled labour', often not paid for work or forced to give bribes even for the lowest level of jobs (Kalshian 2007). India's rapid, enforced integration into the global market vastly increases the exploitation of labour. Pressures on employers to increase *labour productivity* to become more competitive in the world market result in savage reductions of the workforce together with a decrease in wages.

> A high growth in GDP (around 7–8 percent for India in recent years) but a low growth in employment (slightly over 1 percent) necessarily implies that most of the GDP growth is accounted for by a growth in labour productivity (about 5–6 percent), and not by an expansion in employment. Jobless growth in both China and India is driven mostly by relatively high growth in labour productivity rather than in employment.
> (Bhaduri 2009: 104)

If economists and bankers have failed to find any way of checking the spiralling national debt and unemployment in Britain, America and other rich countries, it's not surprising if India and other 'developing countries' have not even begun to free themselves from their debt burdens. At least it is becoming clearer now that bankers' profits are based on a sleight of hand that dispossesses and impoverishes the poorer populations of the poorer countries, while devastating these countries' ecosystems. Isn't it clear that new loans – much sought-after by politicians as soon as their party is elected to form a government but escalating the burden of debt – create the leverage whereby key policy decisions are in effect being controlled through IMF/WB decision-makers?

The vast bank bailout which temporarily ended the credit crash in 2008 in the US and UK revealed the extent of the bubble, of what is increasingly being recognised as *phantom money* – money that does not exist, having no basis in existing currency (Korten 2009: 67). Nouriel Roubini, one of the few economists who predicted the 2008 melt-down, calls in *Crisis Economics* for far-reaching reforms of the financial system, along with economic theory, if the increasingly destructive swings between booms and busts are to be regulated (Roubini and Mihn 2010). Meanwhile, people on the streets are calling for fundamental reform of the system of finance along with the economic theory driving the system or used to legitimise it. Between 17 September and 29 October 2011, the 'Occupy Wall Street' movement and its offshoots have spread from New York and San Francisco to 'occupied zones' in at least 2,000 cities worldwide.[13]

## Indigenous voices, alternative perspectives and integrated action plans

In the words of women and men in a village to be affected by the Upper Indravati dams, who spoke to a WB consultant, who, unusually, recorded what they said:

You are a woman and we are women. . . . You are a literate person from a big country. You understand these things are happening to us. So please, as a woman, help us. . . . The human society living in America must know what is going on in another human society living in India. And they are responsible because we're all humans, living on earth. They can't escape, you know. If I starve, you also bear a responsibility.[14]

But have World Bank officials ever taken responsibility for communities who suffer because of their loans? Just as WB loans enmesh countries into unrepayable debt burdens that are used as leverage to force them to open up their resources and assets, so the 70 per cent of loan finance with which most dams are built mortgage the water in the country's rivers, in effect privatising it and removing it from access to the communities that have always depended on these rivers for drinking, washing and irrigation. In effect, the system of debt-based investment promoted by the World Bank has been steadily *Mortgaging the Earth* (Rich 1994).

While Jairam Ramesh was Environment Minister (May 2009–July 2011), the rate of clearances for projects actually increased, though at least he, and reports he commissioned, drew widespread attention to the shameful pattern of manipulated Environment Impact Assessments and Public Hearings that transgress the Law. His article in *EPW* (October 2011) focuses on the split between 'two cultures' that rarely listen to each other – business on one side, and environmental and social activists on one side, who are generally much more articulate if much less powerful than capital, not least because of ways they have been pitted against each other, when the essence of people's movements is an *Environmentalism of the Poor* (Martinez-Alier 2002).

In the noise of *Manufacturing Consent* (Chomsky and Herman 1999), the raw voices of people who have been or are being displaced often get drowned out. Adivasis' point of view is something too little heard. Since colonial times, tribal people and their interests have been over-defined and objectified by non-tribals, operating with a multitude of vested interests. This emerged in mid-2011 in a debate initiated by Gladson Dungdung over a Peace Award by the Gandhi Foundation, misleadingly advertised as 'to the Adivasis of India' when it was actually intended for Binayak Sen and Bulu Imam.[15]

Adivasis have been at the receiving end of unremitting violence and racism, with non-tribals tending to try and define who they are as well as taking credit for Adivasi movements, from colonial times to the extreme violence unleashed on communities in Operation Green Hunt right now.

> 'Operation Green Hunt' was launched with the clear intention to create fear, insecurity and livelihood crisis in the villages so that the villages would leave the vicinity. Consequently, the government can hand over the Adivasis land to the corporate shark comfortably. The Jharkhand government has allotted iron-ore to 19 steel companies including Mittal, Jindal, Tata, Atro-Steel and Torian in Saranda Forest. Therefore, of course, they want to clear the land.[16]

Of course, Adivasis speak with a multitude of voices, according to people's perceptions and place in the overall social structure that is becoming increasingly polarised: pro-mining-company, anti-company, Maoist or MLA; each strand amplified by media that's joint-owned with mining interests, polarising the population into often-antagonistic camps.

In this context, the Central Government's Integrated Action Plan, as a counteroffensive to the Maoist threat by a two-pronged strategy of Development and Security Offensive, appears to have seriously lost its way (Mahapatra 2011). In its earlier stages, the plan was to link funds for Maoist-affected Districts with progress in implementing the PESA Act, in order to bring real, decentralised democracy to the tribal areas, since a key study (Dandekar and Choudhury 2010) had shown how non-implementation of PESA was a main cause of the growth of Maoist insurgency in tribal areas.[17] In particular, research highlighted the need for Panchayats in Scheduled Areas to have the right of Free Prior Informed Consent to veto projects that contravened local wishes and the right to ban illegal liquor shops. Raising the Maoist-affected Districts from 60 to 98, and offering 30 crore for each, virtually guarantees an intensification of the top-down models that have dispossessed and alienated a large segment of the Adivasi population.

This is especially so, since, as E.N. Rammohan, a former director general of the BSF, pointed out after the killing of 76 jawans in Dantewada district in April 2010, there is no proper leadership of jawans to keep them from committing atrocities:

> our forces can go beserk. They will say we've lost 76 people and they will just shoot anyone, they'll kill everybody, even innocent people, unless there is a very strong leadership to

keep them in control. And I am afraid that leadership does not exist. This is something the government must understand.
(Chaudhury 2010)

In this context, the scheme of recruiting Adivasi youths as Special Police Officers (SPOs) is a recipe for civil war, since it pits Adivasis against Adivasis recruited by Maoists. It was recognised as such by the Supreme Court judgement banning SPOs of 5 July 2011, which was amended under pressure in November through a 'clarification' that this only applies to Chhattisgarh – when the Chhattisgarh SPO model has already been copied in other Maoist-affected states, and in practice is expanding in Chhattisgarh too, despite the SC ban.[18] A vicious pattern of left-wing extremists versus politician/police-supported militias in large areas of Central India is coming to resemble entrenched civil wars in Columbia and other countries (Wilkinson 2011).

All too often the police force, who are meant to serve the people, act on behalf of mining, construction and power companies. This became clear for example in Odisha on 16 December 2009, when the chief minister visited Kalinganagar for the first time since the police firing on 2 January 2006, to open a new police station paid for by the steel companies, for which he publicly thanked them, since when there have been mass deployment of police in the area, with associated repression, to facilitate the construction of Tata's factory on tribal land (*Samadrusti* 2012).

Among solutions offered to India's agrarian crisis are Panchayat Raj style decentralisation (considered under PESA), and the kind of land reforms that were intended after Independence, but sidelined through the Green Revolution and policy inputs from the Ford Foundation and USAID. Prabhat Patnaik also recommends a de-linking from global capital, in order to avoid the pernicious takeovers and manipulation from foreign finance (2011: 131–2). The global 'Occupy' movement against the power of the banks could benefit greatly by learning about India's Indigenous movements against enforced industrialisation; while these movements, to be more effective, may need to study their enemy in terms of how international finance works, links between mining and armaments, and vibrant alternative models of economics.[19]

On a small-scale, examples of different models of development are numerous and diverse in India. There is no lack of alternatives (Pattnayak 2000). Literally hundreds of examples are available from the Indian context and many other regions on earth. The question is, can we transform the role of money and debt, from a domination-oriented power structure based on competition and exploitation into a system based on sharing the earth's natural wealth? Can we, as a global species, develop beyond the paradigm of growth bubbles based on debt and the motivating ideology of self-interest?

Neoclassical economics traces its roots back to 18th-century 'Age of Enlightenment' philosophers, such Locke, Hume and Adam Smith, who made self-interest the key to economic behaviour. Could it be that these eminent thinkers performed a profound disservice to human thinking, and to humans' role as guardian of the earth we live from, by elevating selfishness and acquisitiveness to such a central role? People from tribal cultures often perceive this particularly clearly, from traditions that grounds spirituality and morality firmly in nature.

A tribe sees itself as a kin-group, tracing descent from common ancestors, and emphasising kinship with other life forms. Adivasi culture offers a view of the inter-relatedness of life forms that mainstream society urgently needs to re-learn. A World People's Conference on climate change at Cochabamba, Bolivia, in April 2011, adopted a Universal Declaration of the Rights of Mother Earth, that has been introduced at the UN:

> *We, the peoples and nations of Earth: considering that we are all part of Mother Earth, an indivisible, living community of interrelated and interdependent beings with a common destiny; gratefully acknowledging that Mother Earth is the source of life, nourishment and learning and provides everything we need to live well;*
>
> *recognizing that the capitalist system and all forms of depredation, exploitation, abuse and contamination have caused great destruction, degradation and disruption of Mother Earth, putting life as we know it today at risk through phenomena such as climate change;*
>
> *convinced that in an interdependent living community it is not possible to recognize the rights of only human beings without causing an imbalance within Mother Earth;*
>
> *affirming that to guarantee human rights it is necessary to recognize and defend the rights of Mother Earth and all beings in her and that there are existing cultures, practices and laws that do so;*
>
> *conscious of the urgency of taking decisive, collective action to transform structures and systems that cause climate change and other threats to Mother Earth;*
>
> *proclaim this Universal Declaration of the Rights of Mother Earth.*[20]

The PESA Act offered a blueprint for bringing democracy to the tribal regions. What is needed to bring peace back to the region above all is Justice, and Rule of Law.[21] The case of Soni Sori has become a symbol of the blatant miscarriage of justice meted out to thousands of Adivasis.[22] When false cases, unjust imprisonment and torture imposed on Adivasis and Dalits who try and speak out against gross injustice comes to an end, and people become truly equal before the Law, this will signal the end of marginalisation and a starting point for real development.

## Notes

1. Bhagaban Majhi, for the Kashipur movement in Odisha, in Das and Das (2005), quoted in Padel and Das (2007: 31).
2. 'Civil groups slam state for atrocities', *Times of India*,12 November 2009; and 'Mass acquittals hint at "fake" Narayanpatna police station attack', *Times of India*, 28 December 2011.
3. *Samadrusti*, at www.youtube.com/watch?v=ipHmVee_uXw&feature=related, showing Lado speaking at the Belamba Public Hearing, Lanjigarh, Kalahandi District, on 25 April 2009.
4. 'More districts included in "Red Belt"', *DNA*, 9 December 2011, at www.dnaindia.com/india/report_more-districts-included-in-red-belt_1623320; *Mahapatra*, December 2011.
5. www.amnesty.org/en/library/asset/ASA20/001/2007/en/943b2e72-d3c4-11dd-8743-d305bea2b2c7/asa200012007en.html; and *Samadrusti*, January 2012.
6. 'Stalemate over Lower Siang Project continues', *The Arunachal Times*, 30 May 2011, at www.arunachaltimes.com/may%2031.html; 'Assam's dam crisis', *Down to Earth*, 15 October 2010; and Neeraj Vagholikar and Partha J. Das. 2010. *Damming Northeast India: Juggernaut of Hydropower Projects Threatens the Social and Environmental Security of the Region*. Guwahati: Kalpavriksh, Aaranyak and Action Aid India. Also www.deccanchronicle.com/channels/nation/others/police-forcibly-evicts-protesters-704
7. www.downtoearth.org.in/content/mou-virus-hits-arunachal-pradesh
8. www.arunachaltimes.com/oct11%2024.html; 'Adi tribe fears Arunachal dam will extinct its community', *Deccan Herald*, 2 December 2011; www.downtoearth.org.in/content/demwe-hydroelectric-project-put-hold
9. On dam finance: Bosshard (2002) on Maheshwar dam; www.outlookindia.com/article.aspx?217326; www.indianexpress.com/storyOld.php?storyId=21935
10. Naomi Klein (2007), Padel and Das (2010: chapter 17).
11. Mukesh Jagota and Abhrajit Gangopadhyay. 14 January 2011. 'World Bank pledges nearly $2 billion to India', *Wall Street Journal*.
12. Interview with P. Sainath and Vandana Shiva, at www.growswitch.com/blog/2011/07/the-death-toll-of-indias-hidden-climate-change-catastrophe/
13. On the Occupy Wall Street movement, see the movement's online journal, *The Occupied Wall Street Journal*, at www.occupiedmedia.org/ and 'How

to liberate America from Wall Street rule' (Korten/New Economy Working Group, July 2011), activist-oriented online sequel to Korten (2009).
14. Padel and Das (2010: 455, quoting Caufield 1998: 226–7).
15. Gladson Dungdung (October 2011b).
16. Gladson Dungdung (August 2011a).
17. 'Govt may tweak conflicting laws', *Hindustan Times*, 8 November 2010. The Dandekar and Choudhury chapter of the Central Government–commissioned report on PESA was at first banned by the Ministry of Panchayti Raj, but later released: Paranjoy Guha Thakurta and Ayaskant Das, *Current*, 28 June–4 July, at http://news.fmota.com/wp-content/uploads/2010/06/EYES-WIDE-SHUT-MINISTRY-CENSORS-OWN-REPORTTHAT-BLAMES-GOVT-FOR-MAOIST-PROBLEM.pdf
18. 'SPOs ban will apply only to Chhattisgarh: Court', *The Hindu*, 18 November 2011, at www.thehindu.com/news/national/article2639134.ece
19. Among relevant works are: Susan Feiner (1999), Lietaer (2001), Fauset (2006), Naomi Klein (2007), Greco (2009), Korten (2009, 2011), Nostromo (2011), Padel (2008, January 2011b), Feinstein (2011) and Charles Ferguson's documentary *Inside Job* (2010).
20. April, 2010, at http://climateandcapitalism.com/?p=2268
21. Padel (July 2010b).
22. 'Court anguished at Soni Sori's medical report', *The Hindu*, 3 December 2011; Javed Iqbal. January 2010. 'Witness to "fake encounter" detained by police', *The New Indian Express*.

# References

Bhaduri, Amit. 2009. *The Face You Were Afraid to See: Essays on the Indian Economy*. New Delhi: Penguin.

Bhaduri, Amit. 2010. *Essays in the Reconstruction of Political Economy*. New Delhi: Aakar Books.

Bosshard, Peter. 2002. *Power Finance: Financial Institutions in India's Power Sector*. New Delhi: South Asia Network on Dams, Rivers and People, Urgewald, and International Rivers Network. www.sandrp.in/hydropower/Power_Finance.pdf

Caufield, Catherine. 1998 [1996]. *The World Bank and the Poverty of Nations*. London: Pan.

Centre for Science and Environment. 2008. *Rich Lands, Poor People: Is 'Sustainable' Mining Possible?* New Delhi: Centre for Science and Environment.

Chaudhury, Shoma. 2010. 'Bringing on the Army Against the Naxals Will Be a Disaster', interview with E. N. Rammohan, former DG of BSF, *Tehelka*, 7(23), 12 June. www.tehelka.com/story_main45.asp?filename=Ne120610bringing_on.asp

Chomsky, Noam and Edward S. Herman. 1999. *Manufacturing Consent*. New York: Pantheon.

Dandekar, Ajay and Chitrangada Choudhury. 2010. *PESA, Left-Wing Extremism and Governance: Concerns and Challenges in India's Tribal Districts*.

New Delhi: GoI, commissioned by the Ministry of Panchayati Raj. www.downtoearth.org.in/dte/userfiles/images/PESAchapter.pdf

Das, Amarendra and Samarendra Das. 2005. *Matiro Poko, Company Loko* (Earth Worm, Company Man, in Odia With English Subtitles & Commentary, about Movements Against Mining in Odisha). sdasorisa@gmail.com

Dungdung, Gladson. 2011a. 'Killing, Denial and Manipulation', *Jharkhand Mirror*, 30 August. http://gandhifoundation.org/2011/09/16/killing-denial-and-manipulation-by-gladson-dungdung/

Dungdung, Gladson. 2011b. 'Which Adivasi? What India?', tehelka.com, 22 October. https://jharkhandmirror.wordpress.com/2011/10/22/which-adivasi-what-india/(accessed on 17 July 2018).Dutta, Arnab. 2008. 'Reservoir of Dams', *Down to Earth*,15 May. https://www.downtoearth.org.in/coverage/reservoir-of-dams-4538 (accessed on 17 July 2018).

Esteva, Gustavo. 1992. 'Development', in Wolfgang Sachs (ed.), *The Development Dictionary: A Guide to Knowledge as Power*. London: Zed, 6–25.

Fauset, Claire. 2006. *What's Wrong With Corporate Social Responsibility? Corporate Watch CSR Report*. Oxford: Corporate Watch.

Feiner, Susan. 1999. 'A Portrait of *Homo Economicus* as a Young Man', Essay no. 9 in Martha Woodmansee and Mark Osteen (eds.), *The New Economic Criticism: Studies at the Intersection of Literature and Economics*. London: Routledge.

Feinstein, Andrew. 2011. *Shadow World: Inside the Global Arms Trade*. London: Farrar, Straus & Giroux.

Ferguson, Charles. 2010. *Inside Job* (About the Economic Crisis of 2008). New York: Sony Pictures.

Greco, Thomas. 2009. *The End of Money and the Future of Civilization*. Green Press Initiative.

Herman, Edward S. 1995. *Triumph of the Market: Essays on Economics, Politics and the Media*. Boston: South End Press.

Higgins, Polly. 2010. *Eradicating Ecocide: Laws and Governance to Prevent the Destruction of our Planet*. London: Shepheard-Walwyn.

Iqbal, Javed. 2010. 'Witness to "Fake Encounter" Detained by Police', *The New Indian Express*, 3 January.

Jagota, Mukesh and Abhrajit Gangopadhyay. 2011. 'World Bank Pledges Nearly $2 Billion to India', *Wall Street Journal*, 14 January. http://online.wsj.com/article/SB10001424052748703959104576081543105440036.html

Kalshian, Rakesh (ed.). 2007. *Caterpillar and the Mahua Flower: Tremors in India's Mining Fields*. New Delhi: Panos.

Klein, Naomi. 2007. *The Shock Doctrine: The Rise of Disaster Capitalism*. New York: Metropolitan.

Korten, David. 2009. *Agenda for a New Economy: From Phantom Wealth to Real Wealth*. San Francisco: Berrett-Koehler.

Korten, David and New Economy Working Group. 2011. *How to Liberate America From Wall Street Rule*. http://neweconomyworkinggroup.org/report/how-liberate-america-wall-street-rule

Kumar, Arun. 1999. *The Black Economy in India*. London and New Delhi: Penguin.

Lietaer, Bernard. 2001. *The Future of Money: Creating New Wealth, Work, and a Wiser World*. New Falls: Century.

Mahapatra, Richard. 2011. 'Only Plans, No Integration', *Down to Earth*, 31 December. www.downtoearth.org.in/content/only-plans-no-integration

Mahariya, Baba. 2001. 'Development at Whose Cost? An Adivasi on Dislocation and Displacement', in K. C. Yadav (ed.), *Beyond Mud Walls: Indian Social Realities*. New Delhi: Hope India.

Martinez-Alier, Joan. 2002. *The Environmentalism of the Poor: A Study of Ecological Conflicts and Valuation*. Cheltenham: Edward Elgar.

Mohanty, Gopinath. 1987 [1945]. *Paraja* (Translated From Odia by Bikram K. Das). London: Faber & Faber.

Nostromo Research. 2011. *From Money to Metals: Tracking Global Mining Deals*. London: Nostromo, and Germany: Heinrich-Böll-Stiftung. Updated repeatedly http://moneytometal.org/index.php/From_Money_to_Metals

Padel, Felix. 1998. 'Forest Knowledge: Tribal People, Their Environment and the Structure of Power', in Richard Grove, Vinita Damodaran and Satpal Sangwan (eds.), *Nature and the Orient: The Environmental History of South and Southeast Asia*. New Delhi: Oxford University Press.

Padel, Felix. 1999. 'The Silence of the Forest', *Index on Censorship*, 28(4): Special issue on Tribes, 86–90. London: Routledge.

Padel, Felix. 2008. 'Mining as a Fuel for War', *The Broken Rifle*, Issue no. 77: 1, War Resisters International, February. www.wri-irg.org/node/3576

Padel, Felix. 2010a. *Sacrificing People: Invasions of a Tribal Landscape*. New Delhi: Orient Blackswan.

Padel, Felix. 2010b. 'Searching for Peace and Justice in Eastern Central India', *Gandhi Foundation*, 12 July. http://gandhifoundation.org/2010/07/12/searching-for-justice-and-peace-in-eastern-central-india-by-felix-padel/

Padel, Felix. 2011a. 'Mining Projects and Cultural Genocide: Colonial Roots of Present Conflicts', in Biswamoy Pati (ed.), *Adivasis in Colonial India: Survival, Resistance and Negotiation*. New Delhi: Orient Blackswan, 316–37.

Padel, Felix. 2011b. 'The Most Dangerous Fundamentalism', *The New Indian Express*, 10 January. http://expressbuzz.com/opinion/op-ed/the-most-dangerous-fundamentalism/238252.html

Padel, Felix and Samarendra Das. 2007. 'Agya, What Do You Mean by Development?', in Rakesh Kalshian (ed.), *Caterpillar and the Mahua Flower: Tremors in India's Mining Fields*. New Delhi: Panos, 24–46.

Padel, Felix and Samarendra Das. 2008. 'Cultural Genocide: The Real Impact of Development-Induced Displacement', in H. M. Mathur (ed.), *India Social Development Report 2008. Development and Displacement*. New Delhi: Oxford University Press, 103–15.

Padel, Felix and Samarendra Das. 2010. *Out of This Earth: East India Adivasis and the Aluminium Cartel*. New Delhi: Orient Blackswan.

Padel, Felix and Samarendra Das. 2011. 'Resettlement Realities: The Gulf Between Policy and Practice', in H.M. Mathur (ed.), *Resettling Displaced People*. New Delhi: Council for Social Research & Routledge, 143–80.
Patnaik, Prabhat. 2011. 'A Marxist Perspective on the World Economy', in V. Athreya *et al*. (eds.), *Marx's Capital: An Introductory Reader*. New Delhi: Leftword, 120–33.
Pattnayak, Kishen. 2000. *Bikalpaheen Nahi Hai Duniya*. New Delhi: Rajkamal.
Ramesh, Jairam. 2010. 'The Two Cultures Revisited: The Environmental Development Debate in India', *Economic and Political Weekly*, 14(42), 16 October.
Rich, Bruce. 1994. *Mortgaging the Earth: The World Bank, Environmental Impoverishment and the Crisis of Development*. London: Earthscan.
Robins, Nick. 2006. *The Corporation that Changed the World: How the East India Company Shaped the Modern Multinational*. London: Pluto.
Roubini, Nouriel and Stephen Mihn. 2010. *Crisis Economics: A Crash Course in the Future of Finance*. New York: Penguin.
Rowbotham, Michael. 1998. *Grip of Death: A Study of Modern Money, Debt Slavery and Destructive Economics*. Charlbury: Jon Carpenter.
Sahu, Subrat Kumar. 2010. *DAM-aged* (Documentary in Odia With English Subtitles and Commentary, about the Upper Indravati Dams & Reservoir, Odisha). subrat69@gmail.com
Sainath, Palagummi. 1996. *Everybody Likes a Good Drought: Stories From India's Poorest Districts*. London and New Delhi: Penguin.
Samadrusti. 2012. *Waiting for Justice: A Brief Timeline of the Anti-Displacement Movement of Kalinganagar*, January. www.youtube.com/watch?v=1nwFbeX8JWc&feature=youtu.be&mid=56
Sharma, Brahma Dutt. 2010. *Unbroken History of Broken Promises: Indian State and Tribal People*. New Delhi: Freedom Press.
Stiglitz, Josef. 2002. *Globalization and Its Discontents*. London: Penguin.
*The Hindu*. 2011. *Court Anguished at Soni Sori's Medical Report*, 3 December. https://www.thehindu.com/news/national/court-anguished-at-soni-soris-medical-report/article2681984.ece (accessed on 17 July 2018).
Tudu, Joy. 2011. 'Adivasis', *Adivasi Solidarity and Networking*. http://adivasisinindia.wordpress.com/#comment-660
Vagholikar, Neeraj and Partha J. Das. 2010. *Damming Northeast India: Juggernaut of hydropower Projects Threatens the Social and Environmental Security of the Region*. Guwahati: Kalpavriksh, Aaranyak and Action Aid India, November. www.conflicts.indiawaterportal.org/sites/conflicts.indiawaterportal.org/files/Damming%20Northeast%20India,%20Single%20page%20format.pdf
Wilkinson, Daniel. 2011. 'Death and Drugs in Columbia', *New York Review of Books*, 23 June. www.nybooks.com/articles/archives/2011/jun/23/death-and-drugs-colombia/?pagination=false

# 9
# LIVELIHOODS OF ADIVASIS IN INDIA
## Continuing marginalisation

*G. Muralidhar*

India is home to more than 60 million Adivasis (Scheduled Tribes – STs, tribal people, also known as Indigenous people), spread out the entire country. About half of them live in pockets in the hills and forests with them as majority and the remaining half live in the plains, both rural and urban. Most STs in urban areas have settled in mainstream livelihoods like any non-tribal, barring a few traditional craftsmen. The STs in rural plains pursue mixed livelihoods, predominantly dependent on agriculture, wage labour and small artisanal activities around forest products. The STs in the hills and forests have livelihoods built around forests and other natural resources. The discussion here is focused on these STs in the hills and forests and their livelihoods.

Forest is the life line for millions of tribal people. It is so intertwined in every aspect of their lives that tribal people and forest are inseparable. Whether as deities whom they revere and celebrate, their music and instruments, the way their houses are built or the way they go about with their livelihoods, all vibrates with the spirit of life echoed in the forest.

Most of them have some land. They pursue sustainable and subsistence farming. They protect forests and biodiversity. They access non-timber forest produce including medicinal herbs for their local use and sale in the local markets. There are efforts to 'tap' the biodiversity for the mainstream. However, they are not able to realise even 25 per cent of the consumer rupee. Here and there, livestock-dependent livelihoods are also pursued. There are a few who still persist with hunter-gatherer living.

Critically, resource-rich tribal people are living a life of subsistence and hand-to-mouth existence. They are caught in the 'trap' of moneylender-trader. As they exist in the margins of the mainstream, with social and cultural diversity and geographic remoteness, most mainstream resources elude them or come with extremely unfair terms. These include financial inclusion/formal credit, infrastructure, appropriate technology, information and knowledge, aggregated demand and supply, appropriate institutional architectures, local value-addition, access to consumer market and linkages.

True, there are multiple tribes and all of them do not go about their lives and livelihoods identically. True, their lives and livelihoods have been impacted by the mainstream policies, processes and influences. Consumption habits and food habits are changing. Trading-in and therefore, wage employment, commercial farming and seasonal migration are increasing. Literacy is increasing and the new generation is seeking alternative livelihoods outside and locally. Unemployment is increasing with changing landscape and pressures on land, water and forests. A new self-employed class is emerging within their ranks.

Along with Integrated Tribal Development Agencies/Projects, Tribal Corporations and Tribal Welfare Departments, National Rural Livelihoods Mission is unveiling special efforts to evolve and support perspective plans at the state level to augment and enhance the livelihoods of the STs comprehensively and significantly.

## Livelihoods of Adivasis in India

Referred to as Scheduled Tribes in the Constitution, 700 tribal communities constitute more than 8 per cent of India's population (more than 100 million) and are spread across the country. The majority of them live in and around hills/hill slopes and forests and exclusive habitations, the remaining people live in the plains – urban, suburban and plain rural areas.[1] Major tribes include Andamanese, Bodos, Bhils, Chakma, Chenchu, Dhodia Tribes of Gujarat, Gonds, Koya, Khasis, Aboriginal people of Lakshadweep, Kurichiya, Kurumbar, Tripuris, Mizos, Mundaris, Nagas, Nicobarese, Oraon, Santhals, Todas, Maldharis of Gujarat, Cholanaikkan, Warli, Kisan Tribe, Dongria Kondh, Bonda, Kutia Kondh, Bishapus A'Mishapus etc.

## Profile of tribal communities

STs (8 per cent of India) live on 15 per cent of Indian area spanning various geo-climatic terrains – forests, hills, coastal areas and plains. The largest concentration (about 70 per cent of Indian STs) lives in the hilly areas of Central India (Madhya Pradesh, Orissa and, to a lesser extent, Andhra Pradesh); in this belt, which is bounded by the Narmada River to the north and the Godavari River to the southeast, tribal peoples occupy the slopes of the region's mountains. Another concentration lives in a belt along the Himalayas stretching through Jammu and Kashmir, Himachal Pradesh and Uttar Pradesh in the west, to Assam, Meghalaya, Tripura, Arunachal Pradesh, Mizoram, Manipur and Nagaland in the northeast. Other STs, the Santals, live in Bihar and West Bengal. There are smaller numbers of tribal people in Karnataka, Tamil Nadu and Kerala, in western India in Gujarat and Rajasthan and in the union territories of Lakshadweep and the Andaman and Nicobar Islands. It may be noted that some states like Mizoram, Nagaland, etc. are entirely (almost 90 per cent) tribal. Also, there are regions within the state, districts, subdistrict areas, and clusters with mostly tribal population; 187 out of 645 districts in the country are considered as tribal districts.

Tribal communities live in relative isolation of the mainstream. They live a simple life in harmony with their environment. They use low-level technologies and sustain natural resources. They have evolved their own distinct myriad ways of living, cultures, languages and religions. Their economy is predominantly subsistence and/or low-value economy. Given this situation, in order to protect the social, cultural and land rights of the tribal communities in Scheduled Areas, special provisions, policies and regulations are available in Scheduled Areas. These include prohibition of transfer of tribal land to non-tribals and restricted moneylending business.

Further, their indicators of 'development' are low – low nutrition, high mortality rates, low literacy etc. STs are amongst the poorest in the country. While most of them are considered vulnerable, half of the STs are considered below poverty line. Overall Literacy (47 per cent) and Female literacy (34 per cent) are way below the national averages. Infant mortality rate at 36 is way above the national average of 18. Thus the disparities between the tribal and non-tribal sections of the population cut across various development indicators. However, Gross Enrolment amongst STs, as in other communities, has been increasing over the years. Their education levels are going up and mainstream employment is increasing, albeit slowly. Interestingly, sex ratio among ST communities (977 females for every 1,000 males) is more favourable than the national average.

It is to be noted here that tribal communities in the country are at different stages of development – both across the tribes and within each tribe. Some of them pulled themselves into mainstream ways and lead lives and pursue livelihoods no different from that of non-tribals. At the same time, there are some who have been pushed out (migrated) into mainstream ways and are struggling to cope with them. There are also certain communities, within STs, characterised by a stagnant or dwindling population, low literacy and hunter-gatherer subsistence. Seventy-five such communities, referred to as 'primitive tribal groups' (PTGs), have been identified and found to be more backward and left out of the mainstream than other ST communities. Certain tribal communities dwell in plain areas and pursue mixed livelihoods but predominantly practice agriculture. Some tribal communities such as the Lambadas of AP, unlike a typical tribal community, are at the forefront of development within the tribal communities and pursue livelihoods around farming and livestock and wage labour. Within all tribal communities, there are intra-community differences. All the members are not at the same level. Some are resource-rich and some are otherwise. Still, a significant proportion of STs are still dependent on forests for their livelihoods.

## Livelihoods framework

In this context, this chapter discusses the trends (not going too much into the numbers) in livelihoods of the tribal communities with the help of the livelihoods framework. The livelihoods framework helps in understanding the elements (dimensions, capitals and contexts, with their interrelationships) and complexity of portfolio of livelihoods of a household/community and the support systems/ecosystem required for these livelihoods to be pursued/practiced. The livelihoods framework, when applied to a context, identifies gaps and opportunities and indicates scope for further interventions.

Livelihoods have four characteristics: income, expenditure (money, time and energy), employment and risk.

- A household earns income in various forms and through various means. Usually, the income of the household depends on the set of knowledge-skills-resources it has. Further, the income of the household need not necessarily be in the form of wages, it can come in the form of produce/goods and services as well that may meet the needs of the household and/or could be converted into monetary income.
- A household has to spend on basic needs such as food, clothing, shelter and water as well as other needs as education, health,

transport and entertainment. Some expenses, such as marriages and organising other social gatherings, though not recurring are considered while analysing the expenditure of a household. Like income, expenditure also is not always in monetary terms. The payment to meet the expenditure can be through the produce/goods and services. Further, time and energy are also spent.
- Employment refers to the time or number of days a household is engaged in some activity or the other in the portfolio of livelihoods of the household. The employment depends upon its skill-set, resources available and the ecological and environmental context.
- Risks are the vulnerabilities the household has to face in pursuit of its livelihoods. Risks are present in every livelihood activity but the degrees of risk vary. These vulnerabilities are accentuated by the environment, technological, financial contexts of the household. The impact of the risks on the household depends on the risk-mitigating strategies adopted by the household. For instance, even a minor illness can send a poor household into disarray as it lacks access to qualitative healthcare. Further, the local ecological context and lack of health insurance augments the impact of the illness on the household.

All livelihoods interventions aim to increase income, decrease expenditure, increase employment and decrease risks. In the framework, these characteristics are known as four arrows by virtue of the desired direction they are to move in.

Livelihoods of a household depend on resources or capitals which can be broadly classified into six categories – natural, physical, social, human, financial and spiritual.

- Natural capital refers to natural resources available to the household to carry about a particular livelihood. This would include land, water, forest, air, etc.
- Physical capital comprises man-made physical structures such as roads, buildings and also machines and appliances that aid humans in their work.
- Social capital entails the support one receives due to kinship/relationship with other individuals and institutions in society.
- Human capital essentially consists of the skills, knowledge, abilities and aptitude possessed by a person.
- Financial capital enables a household to obtain goods and also aids production (investment). There are two components of financial

capital – stock (the amount of financial capital available with the household at any given point of time) and flow (the financial capital the household earns).
- Lastly, spiritual capital refers to the quest present in the household to seek better living conditions. This drive is essential for the other capitals to be tapped fully.

The livelihoods a household pursues are influenced by the availability and accessibility to these capitals, the variety of capitals at its disposal and also its ability to tap these capitals to its advantage.

Further, these capitals as well as the households exist in a context that affects the availability, accessibility and use of the capitals. The context allows certain activities and prohibits certain activities despite the presence of required capitals. Though the context is a unified whole, for the purpose of analysis, the context is understood in four interrelated spheres – Environmental and Ecological Context, Techno-economic, Distribution and Investment and Expenditure Contexts.

- The environmental and ecological context refers to the larger environmental and social context the household exists in.
- The techno-economic context is the technical know-how available with the household to tap the capitals effectively.
- The distribution pattern of resources, infrastructure, wealth, knowledge, etc. in a society also affects the livelihood choices of a household.
- The investment and expenditure patterns of the household affect its livelihoods. Investment in production, health, food, education, insurance, employment is relevant in this context. The investment may not yield immediate results but may aid the households in pursuing or sustaining its livelihoods in the long run.

When livelihoods are thus understood, it is easier to identify the grey areas in the livelihoods being pursued by the household and plan interventions accordingly. These, then, could be consolidated upwards for making policy decisions and interventions on one hand and launching major programmes.

## Understanding major Adivasi livelihoods

Adivasi Livelihoods, or Livelihoods of STs, when analysed using the livelihoods framework, reveal how the social, economic and political injustices meted out to them have adversely and irreversibly abetted the collapse of their traditional livelihoods and economy. According to the 2001 Census, 81 per cent of STs are engaged in the primary sector – this includes Non-timber Forest Produce (NTFP) collection, agriculture, livestock rearing, daily wage labour, etc. In fact, NTFP collection is significant in the portfolio of livelihoods for nearly 70 per cent of the tribal population in the country. Considerable number of STs also feed themselves through seasonal migration.

Thus, the Adivasi livelihoods triumvirate is NTFP, farming (agriculture, horticulture and livestock and agriculture wage labour), and migration. Mahatma Gandhi National Rural Employment Guarantee Act (MGNREGA) is also providing some employment to the STs. Only a tiny proportion of STs are outside of these four livelihoods spheres. These include petty business, artisanal activities and service.

> *A primary study (carried out by us two years ago) in 15 tribal villages across five states reveals that the tribal villages remain remote and important service institutions like school, health centre, veterinary sub-centre, anganwadi etc., are not in the accessible distance to the people in 50 per cent of the villages.*
>
> *Major sources of income of the select families include NTFP Collection, Wage Labour, Agriculture and Livestock rearing, MGNREGA and other activities in that order. However, about 30 per cent of the days in a year on which they are not able to do any work.*
>
> *Men and women share responsibility in livelihoods activity. However, women work at least three to four hours more in a day when compared to men.*
>
> *More than 50 per cent the expenditure has been on food and liquor.*

### NTFP collection

It is revealing to note that the 187 tribal-dominated districts have 60 per cent of India's forest cover (India has a forest cover of 23.28 per cent which is about 77 million hectares and the six major types of forests identified in India are moist tropical, dry tropical, subtropical, mountain temperate, alpine and subalpine). The entire forests (read:

forest areas) in the country have been classified into reserved forests (considered to be the most valuable as far as conserving forest and wildlife are concerned and more than half of the total forest area has been classified as reserved forests); protected forests (protected only to a certain degree and the government has property rights over it); and village forests (partly owned by the government and partly by people who inhabit these lands). The STs living near the forests have rights on the usufruct in all the forests.

The relationship between tribes and the forest transcends the economic sphere. Tribal communities have intertwined every aspect of their lives with the forest. Their houses are built of the locally available timber, the tools and implements they use are made from locally available raw material, and so are their music instruments. It is commonly acknowledged that tribal religions are a form of 'animism' distinct from other 'mainstream' religions. STs consider nature and its resources as their deities and their customs and rituals invoke elements of nature. The reverence tribal people render to nature is rooted in their belief that their lives and sustenance is dependent upon these elements.

Forests are unique ecosystems that host a multitude of products and services. Products include timber, herbs, nuts, seeds, fruits, flowers, etc. They also provide raw material such as twigs, roots leaves, etc. which are value-added to make products such as ropes, plates, brooms, etc. As for services, forests play a crucial role in regulating and preserving ecological systems. Forests have served as an abode of wealth for different communities – hunter-gatherers, NTFP collectors, shifting cultivators and modern timber-based industries.

For STs, they offer life support. They meet their basic needs (food, fodder, fuel-wood, healing ailments, shelter etc.,) to a large extent. In addition, they provide income to them through the sale of NTFP (there are about 3,000 species of plants in Indian forests which provide NTFP), on which they have traditional rights. Traditionally, most of the NTFP collected was consumed by the collectors themselves. Over time, with the rise of modern economy, the collectors have also started to sell their produce in the nearest *shandies* (local markets) and use the money so generated to fulfil other needs by buying from the market. However, the income generated by collecting NTFPs is not directly proportionate to the labour spent and the risks involved in procuring them. Not even a quarter of the consumer rupee finally reaches the tribal collector. In spite of uncertainties and risks, poor gatherers resort to NTFP collection in the absence of better remunerative opportunities, to meet their food, fodder and medical needs or as a seasonal and emergency activity.

It appears that the most disadvantageous factor for the STs is their lack of awareness of the market that NTFP actually has. Their ignorance is exploited by middlemen and industries that pay meagre sums for the labour and toil that the tribal people put into the procurement of the NTFP. The possibility of exploitation is further accentuated by the absence of a transparent, state-supported procurement system in most states barring Andhra Pradesh. Furthermore, the collectors are also unaware of the forms in which these products are marketable. Some of this exploitation could be partly attributed to the manner in which tribal people conduct business. It should be borne in mind that these are a people who have only recently done away with the barter system. Their business sense is dominated by necessity rather than profit. They generally sell only so much produce as is required for them to sustain themselves.

Yet another disadvantage to the collectors is that they lack access to the machinery/equipment required to do the value-addition to the NTFP to make it marketable. Most of the value-addition to the NTFP is done in factories and large production centres. Introduction of simple, manageable value-addition units in the local areas could go a long way in reducing the intermediaries between the collectors and the consumers. The introduction of such value-addition techniques to the tribal people should not disintegrate existing sustainable methods of collection. The market-awareness of the STs should not result in them fully exploiting the entire forest at one go. Instead, the traditional practice of taking only how much is necessary must be retained. Efforts towards enhancing the livelihoods of trials should combine the best of modern technology with the sustainable ways of traditional methods.

It is also important to know that the quality lost at the beginning may not be regained later. Therefore, the sustainable harvesting of NTFP with care and quality consciousness produces NTFP that lasts longer and the core properties of the product remaining intact. Since the consumer pays for the quality and core properties, the collector would realise better returns on the NTFP. For instance, quality *gum karaya* collection has ensured increases in returns by five to six times (500–600 per cent) to the collectors.

A vast repository of knowledge regarding the uses of the NTFP rests with tribal people. Many NTFP products have medicinal properties. Tribal communities have recognised their properties and have used these products to treat ailments for centuries together. Some NTFP products are used as raw material in modern production industries. A case in point is the use of gum karaya by pharmaceutical companies as edible adhesive in the composition of tablets and capsules. Cleaning nuts are used as an alternative to alum. The nuts are used to clarify water and further research has also revealed that they have the properties to dispose heavy metallic waste.

Ownership, Natural Regeneration, Sustainable harvesting, Local Value-addition, Aggregation, Moving up the value-chain directly, or through institutions and partnerships are the key elements of way forward in NTFP.

*Farming*

While there are some hunter-gatherers amongst them, agriculture is a major occupation among tribal communities, after NTFP collection. Most STs own small tracts of land on which they pursue sustainable and subsistence farming. Tribal communities cultivate crops that the soil and land in the area support, i.e. the crops they cultivate are not different from what non-tribal farmers cultivate in the area. Major crops cultivated by the STs include paddy, millets, maize, tubers, etc. Horticulture (cashew, etc.) is also not uncommon. Tribal farming practices are thought to be sustainable methods that make best use of local resources and preserve the local ecology.

> *There are still some tribal families/communities that are persisting with shifting cultivation or 'slash and burn cultivation' (known as podu and jhum – in different parts of the country). This practice entails cutting down trees in a certain part of the forest, cultivating crops on the land and then burning the tract after harvest. The land is left fallow for a while (five to 10 years), allowing it to recover or recoup. Shifting cultivation practices have come under criticism and are even restricted by the Forest Policy of 1956. Critics believe that the practice contributes to massive deforestation resulting in disturbing the local ecological system. However, there are contrarian studies to show the sustainable nature of this practice that also leads to protection of the local ecology. In any case, given the pressure on the forests and land, and the restrictions, the shifting cultivation has declined significantly.*

> *For example, in January 2011, the FAO recognised the Koraput farming systems traditionally practiced by tribes in Orissa as a Globally Important Heritage System (GIAHS). The FAO stated that the farming system has helped in preserving numerous rice, millet, pulse varieties, medicinal plants and also the local ecological system. While recognising the significant contribution of the Koraput farming system in preserving the local ecology, the FAO has also sought to bring attention to the preservation of the farming system itself.*

The Koraput case is not the only such practice employed by tribes in the country. These practices are fast reaching the brink of extinction, yielding to modern agriculture practices. In the wake of a market-driven economy, agriculture has been rapidly commercialised. Tribal farmers who traditionally cultivated crops only for consumption have been compelled to shift to cultivate cash crops for survival. The introduction of Public Distribution Systems (PDS) that does not cater to the staple diet (based on local minor millets and pulses) of the STs has resulted in their food habits undergoing major changes and has contributed critically in changing the cropping patterns of STs.

As part of farming system, the STs have also pursued rearing livestock for farming. Gradually, milch animals have come in. Apart from hunting animals from the wild, they have been rearing small livestock (sheep, goats etc.,) and birds for consumption and for local market.

The labour-sharing mechanisms that exist among local STs to meet their peaks in demand for labour for farming are giving way to wage labour. Aggregated lands with a few STs and non-tribals taking over lands seek wage labour. There are cases of buying the standing agriculture crops and horticulture crops in advance at very low rates and the tribal owners of the crops become the labour in their own land.

Sustainable organic farming (agriculture, horticulture, watershed management, medicinal herbs/plants cultivation, fisheries, kitchen gardens) for food security coupled with high-value product farming for market, local value-addition, aggregation and market linkages with institutions and partnerships are the elements of the way forward.

## Seasonal migration and MGNREGA

With declining forest cover, not-so-good returns for NTFP and seasonality in NTFP, large sections of tribal communities look for new livelihoods outside the traditional sectors as well as their traditional environment. Many STs, mostly without their families, migrate for work as wage labour in other areas (away from their home), in agriculture, in construction, in road work etc. Since the launch and implementation of MNREGA, STs have been taking up work under the scheme and the seasonal migration has seen some decline.

It is revealing that STs constitute about 25 per cent of the total MGNREGA workforce. It appears that many a tribal household, more than any other social group in the country, is looking towards MGNREGA as a livelihoods activity and is participating in the scheme. The danger here is that they are giving up their traditional livelihood(s) and become dependent on casual wage labour for sustenance. It is likely that they lose their skills, knowledge and maybe their traditional rights in the process. Their resources may be alienated and their access to commons may be denied. Also, the association of certain tribes with certain occupations may start to deteriorate leading to an erosion of the unique identity of tribal community.

## Livelihoods for market

Through interaction with non-tribals, markets and education, the tribal communities have started to include new elements in their existing four livelihoods spheres and/or add new livelihoods activities. Dairying, Goatery, Poultry and Fisheries for market are growing in tribal areas. However, lack of established markets for their produce in local areas and proper support systems, including marketing mechanisms, is hampering their growth as viable livelihoods activities.

Tribal people also make handicrafts from locally available raw material (like bamboo). Traditionally, these handicrafts were used as implements or decorative items but efforts are being made to market these handicrafts. Presently, these products have a huge market in urban centres in India and internationally. Yet, as is the case with other tribal livelihoods, STs engaged in this activity too face market exclusion and are not able to realise a good proportion of consumer rupee.

## Resource alienation

Resources, for STs pursuing their livelihoods, are fast being eroded or captured by non-tribals. Land is a major bone of contention between tribal population and non-tribals.

Most STs own land or have access to land. Only 21 per cent of STs are landless. The average landholding among STs is 1.14 acres but land alienation is reducing per capita land of the STs. Land alienation of STs is made easier with lack of clarity on land rights among the community. For the STs, the lands they reside on are theirs and are unaware of the legal procedures to be undertaken to ensure that the land remains under their custody. Manipulation of land records, *benami* transactions, leasing or mortgage, marital alliances with tribal women, adoption of tribal families by non-tribals are all rampant methods of encroaching the land of STs.

It is estimated that as many as 375,000 cases involving 850,000 acres of land are awaiting verdict. Besides land-grabbing done by private parties, large infrastructure projects have also been responsible for infringing on land rights of STs resulting in their displacement. Loss of land and resources is a big loss for STs.

The repercussions of physical displacement are dire and far-reaching. Not only are the communities left landless, they lose their familiar ecosystem (culture, neighbours, commons, familiarity etc.) and resources to carry out their traditional occupation(s). This breakdown in their livelihoods leads to food insecurity, disintegration of the established social fabric, etc. The psychological impact that displacement has on the victims can never be compensated in monetary/physical terms. Many can never come to terms with the impact of being totally uprooted from their ecological contexts.

The Forest Rights Act, 2006 attempted to address the issue of ownership and the rights of forest dwellers over forestland. The act seeks to undo the 'historic injustice' meted out to the tribal population in the country by allowing them rights over the lands they reside on or currently practice agriculture on and letting them collect NTFP without any hassles from the local administration. Further, STs dwelling in the forest are to be given legal documents recognising their right over the land they dwell on. Even before the Forest Rights Act, efforts were made to ensure that tribal peoples administered the use of resources in the local area through Joint Forest Management (JFM) initiatives. JFM entailed the formation of a Forest Protection Committee (Vana Samrakshana Samiti – VSS) at the village level. The VSS protects the forest from depletion and destruction and in turn VSS gets the right on the NTFP and a share in income from the sale of timber from the forest.

It appears that the financial and economic contexts are extremely disadvantageous to tribal people. To start with, many of them reside in remote and less accessible areas that do not have the required infrastructure. True, efforts have been taken to make these areas accessible through roadways, railways and telecommunications. Yet, this effort has resulted in the unprecedented entry of non-tribals into tribal areas, pushing the tribal communities up into further remote areas.

When it comes to access to financial resources such as loans, bank accounts, savings, insurance and remittances, it is the lowest in the country for tribal people. Added to this is the fact that most STs do not possess proper, government-recognised legal documents essential to open bank accounts, to take loans etc. The lack of will from formal financial institutions to cater to tribal people in general and the poor in particular is denying these communities access to much-needed credit. To worsen the situation, local moneylenders fill the vacuum left in the wake of absence of formal financial institutions. The moneylenders are often exploitative and charge high rates of interest and keep no record of transactions. Moneylenders often take away whatever little assets the STs own when the latter are unable to repay their debts. Moneylender–trader nexus ensures that the STs pay higher prices for their purchases and do not get due prices for their produce, apart from the high interest rates and consequent benami resource alienation in due course. All this is happening even with 'stringent' moneylending regulation. Further, financial exclusion of the tribal people also prevents them from having a sound insurance system essential to mitigate risks and unprecedented situations.

Even the self-help movement sweeping the country is taking its time to catch up pace in tribal areas.

In essence, STs are in the process of losing the advantage of rich endowment of natural capital and spiritual capital which they had on one hand, and they are yet to catch up to the levels of physical, human, institutional and financial capital that is required for a decent living. Building on the commons, collectivisation and savings-led financial capital are the key elements of the way forward.

### *Livelihoods continuum*

As discussed earlier, all the tribal communities are not at the same footing and all the households within a tribal community are not at the same level and each of their livelihoods portfolios is unique and variegated. The livelihoods of the STs are in a continuum. Some STs have shifted entirely from their traditional ways of life and have assimilated into the mainstream like any other non-tribal. Such members of the community are usually those who have had access to primary and higher education. Some others still persist in the hunting-gathering way of life. Some sections continue pursuing their traditional livelihoods along with other, non-traditional ones. But the general trend is that the tribal communities are moving away from their traditional ways of life and are fast taking to the juggernaut of being mainstreamed, although the terms are unfair to them. There is a new, rising class of self-employed service providers and entrepreneurs among the tribal people. Of course, there are some job holders too amongst the STs now. Younger generations in tribal communities who have had access to some school education are reluctant to take up traditional livelihoods and resort to wage labour, agriculture labour and migration, the only available alternatives.

## Eroding tribal identity

Further, the increased literacy among tribal people has resulted in the transformation of tribal culture and social fabric. With government-aided education being in the official language of the state or in Hindi and not the mother tongue of the student, STs are fast losing their lingual identity. Of course, it may seem daunting to ensure that students are taught in their respective mother tongues (304 recognised tribal languages are spoken among the tribes), but education in an alien language is not the only onslaught on tribal identity. The reach of telecommunications and mass media too has had lasting impact on tribal identity. Mainstream cinema, music, culture is eroding the traditions of tribal people.

Eroding tribal identity combined with the tribal people not oriented psychologically and culturally to fight injustices that are being meted out to them is coming in the way of self-reliant and sustainable tribal livelihoods. It is sad to note we do not hear tribal voices speaking for their rights, justice and equity. This space is mostly occupied by the people from outside the community. Building responsive and sensitive community leadership in large numbers at various levels from within the communities is the key element in the way forward.

## Special provisions to tribal communities

Under the circumstances, taking into account the vulnerabilities of the tribal population, the Constitution has made several social, economic and political provisions (enabling and empowering) to aid the advancement of tribal communities and ensure that they are at a level-playing field with other communities in the country. The issue is how conducive an environment the state and the non-tribal population of the country have created for the tribal communities to pursue their culture, livelihoods and traditional systems economy, polity and society.

For instance, the Fundamental Right to Freedom provides for pursuing any livelihood one deems fit. This right does not seem to exist for many a tribal. STs are being pushed out of their traditional livelihoods and ecological milieu to pursue less dignified livelihoods, either in their existing habitat or away from their habitat. It is becoming clear that tribal people are not able to get over resource alienation and loss of their traditional livelihoods and move into new contexts and livelihoods smoothly.

Since the Fifth Five Year Plan, the Tribal Sub Plan (TSP, for areas with more than 50 per cent tribal population) for development of the area and the communities in the area, consolidated at state and national level, is being prepared based on the resources and funds. In a state, the funds for TSP are allocated in proportion to the population of STs in the state. The TSP is being implemented by District/sub-district Integrated Tribal Development Projects/Agencies (ITDPs/ITDAs). The Project Officer, ITDP/ITDA is a single-line administrator (all the departments in the area are responsible to the Project Officer and work in consultation and close coordination with the Project Officer).

The National Commission for Schedule Tribes is a statutory body set up in 1992. The commission's function is to look into the protection of the safeguards of the STs and report regularly to the president of India on the progress in their implementation. Similarly, the National Scheduled Tribes Financial Development Corporation (NSTFDC) was set up under the auspices of the Ministry of Tribal Affairs. The mandate of the NSTFDC includes identifying and supporting economic activities of tribal communities in the form of providing financial resources of upgrading existing skills and technology used by the tribal people. Tribal Cooperative Marketing Developing Federation (TRIFED) was set up by Government of India to market and ensure better prices for the produce of the STs. In each state, there is a Tribal Development Cooperative Corporation (TDCC) to help the tribal NTFP collectors to realise higher returns.

For example, one of the TDCC, Girijan Cooperative Corporation (GCC) of Andhra Pradesh (a federation of 45 primary cooperatives), provides support to tribal people engaged in the collection of NTFP at their doorstep and links them with potential markets. The GCC provides necessary financial and technical support to help the NTFP collectors carry out their occupation without being exploited by middlemen and small traders. GCC also supplies daily requirements to the tribal families. GCC with its Rs. 100 crore annual turnover has been able to reach out to 4 million tribal families in the state.

### National Rural Livelihoods Mission

The recently launched National Rural Livelihoods Mission (NRLM), the largest poverty reduction programme in the world, to support 10 crore poor families across the country with an outlay of about Rs. 200,000 crore [i.e. 2,000 billion] over 15 years, has specific focus on developing the perspective plans for Scheduled Tribes in each state to improve their livelihoods significantly so that they have a decent portfolio of livelihoods. Mobilising the tribal poor into self-help institutions around savings, credit and insurance, livelihoods collectives, social collectives, community-managed sustainable agriculture, health and nutrition etc., are the key elements in these perspective plans.

Further, NRLM works closely with other major flagship programmes/guarantees including MGNREGS, NRHM, Food Security (in the pipeline), RTE so that the NRLM-supported institutional structures create demand on the programmes to deliver for the STs.

Of the 187 tribal dominant districts, more than 60 of them are considered sensitive and a special support – Integrated Action Plan (IAP) – is made operational. The government is deploying three high-end young professionals – Prime Minister's Rural Development Fellows – in each district directly with District Administration, to help in implementing IAP.

## Conclusion

Tribal communities are living in distress poverty despite rich natural resource, social resource and spiritual resource endowment. Their major livelihoods spheres – mostly around forests – include NTFP, farming, seasonal migration and MGNREGA. The proportion of the consumer rupee realised for their produce is extremely meagre. On the whole, they are subject to resource alienation (forests, commons and lands), financial exclusion and market exclusion. Their identity and cultural capitals are eroding, and there is an increased disruption in their social fabric. Thus, the STs are losing what they have (resource endowment) and are not getting on par with what the mainstream could access in return or otherwise. That is the big irony. Change in the traditional diet, through Public Distribution System which is not tailored to the local tribal needs and preferences, has brought about a slow deterioration of health and nutrition among tribal people. Tribal health systems are 'fading' out. In the absence of access to quality healthcare, their health risks have multiplied.

Often we realise that we are getting back to the lifestyle and methods of STs as we pursue sustainable living. Tribal ways of living need to be appreciated and may have to be adopted if we are keen about addressing the various crises in our livelihoods domain – environment/climate, biodiversity, water, food, energy, health etc. When the crunch comes, we know that what matters the most is life – air, water, food, clothes, shelter and entertainment. All else does not matter. Therefore, we need to find ways to globalise time-tested tribal ways of living (with minor modifications, if warranted), instead of trying to pull them into exploding mainstream ways of living. Adivasis may be the original inhabitants of this land and need to have their ecosystem intact (better still, improved) so that they lead a life of dignity, contentment and peace, by pursuing their sustainable portfolios of livelihoods to meet their basic life needs directly or through realisation of a higher proportion of consumer rupee, commensurate with the real value of the products and services. Increased social, financial and institutional inclusion and support and reduced/reversed resource alienation would accelerate their prosperity for themselves, their next generations and for all of us.

## Note

1 The discussion hereafter in this chapter is limited to the livelihoods of the tribes living in and around hills/hill slopes, forests and exclusive habitations.

# 10

# ADIVASIS WATER EXCHANGE AND CASTE-BASED WATER LORDS

A case of groundwater market in a village of Gujarat, India[1]

*Farhat Naz*[2]

Water has been acknowledged as an instrument for representing power and is the source of collaboration, conflict and determines geopolitical boundaries around the world (Mosse 1999; Ioris 2007; Wade 1987; Wittfogel 1957). Water is also not homogenous, as it comprises multiple forms, materialities and temporalities, which intersect with material and informal social relations to produce distinct hydro-social arrangements across space and time (Bear and Bull 2011; Budds 2009; Linton 2010). At the macro- or micro-level, water politics tends to involve a range of interaction patterns in water management, including negotiations, struggle, and also less explicit and longer-term disputes and controversies (Mollinga 2008). Therefore, the social power relations in a given society intersect with the material, social and symbolic dimensions of water to shape access and configure water arrangement amongst different social groups (Loftus 2009; Swyngedouw 2005). It has also been widely acknowledged that water's cultural meanings in a given society engages, influences and shapes histories, subjectivities, management and governance around water (Bakker 2003; Strang 2004; Loftus 2007; Sultana 2009).

Globally and locally, inequities are socially embedded and ecologically shaped (Naz 2015) and water in particular is power, and water-related arrangements and developments have to be understood as drenched with uneven and complex socio-natural power relations that affect the lives and opportunities of the people (Budds and Sultana 2013). Thus, through water, the dominant groups make an efforts to take control over local water resources by rationalising the water control by standardising and externalising the local perception, rights and rituals, in line with domain interest (Boelens 2014). Water, being a 'natural' resource with economic value, correspondingly has dominant symbolic, cultural and religious meanings attached to it and its usage is highly differentiated within a local and caste context (Mehta 2005, 2007).[3] Taking this as the starting point – in Mathnaa, a village in northeastern Gujarat, which is the case study of this chapter, access to water is determined by caste and the caste-based social hierarchy is determined locally through notions of purity and pollution within the larger realm of Hinduism, and is used in local culture to determine and reinforce inequitable access to, control over and distribution of water and its usage rights (Naz 2014).[4] The upper-caste status of Mathnaa's 'water lords' allows them to wield influence over Adivasi and Dalits as well as control the groundwater market.[5]

My work follows the recent scholarship of political ecology, water studies and social exclusion; I approach the Mathnaa's groundwater market through a political ecology lens. A political ecology framework relates nature to political economy and links local processes with larger social structures and macro-economic processes (Blaikie 1985; Blaikie and Brookfield 1987; Bryant 1998; Moore 1993; Peet and Watts 1996). Social exclusion is a process by which certain groups are systematically disadvantaged because they are discriminated against on the basis of their ethnicity, race, religion, sexual orientation, caste, descent, gender, age, disability, HIV status, migrant status or where they live (Khan 2015). Hence, social exclusion involves denial of rights and opportunities which the privileged group enjoys, and it is a process of keeping a social group outside the power centres and resources. Therefore, social exclusion is a powerful form of discrimination and culminates in a system of domination and subjugation. This chapter explores how power produces water reality, knowledge and truth claims, and how power is expressed within multiple micro-realities, even producing the ways in which truth is made true (Foucault 1980). However, the structure of power, at the local level, tends to be embodied in class, caste, ethnicity, gender and/or religion (Ahmed and Zwarteveen 2012).

The fieldwork for this study is based on my longitudinal primary research between 2008–09 and 2012–14, in the Mathnaa village located in the state of Gujarat, India. It started when I decided to live in the village as a participant observer with my fellow respondents in order to observe and comprehend the everyday processes, interactions and life events of actors in the village for a period of 10 months in 2008–09 and going back to visit again for two to three weeks in July 2012, December 2013 and December 2014 subsequently. The technique of living with people in order to learn about them and their lives is the core of classical anthropological data collection (Jerstada 2014). With social interactions, observations and interviews as the method, the researcher becomes a part of the research process.

I chose Mathnaa to do my fieldwork, as the village had a good mix of Hindu castes and tribes. The research methodology used for the analysis presented in this chapter can be categorised as ethnographic, as case study methods were adopted (Yin 2003). The research methodology was composed of a mix of participatory rural appraisal (PRA) tools, key informants interviews, focus group discussions, direct observation, thick description and household survey. According to Long (1992: 38), 'social sciences have always been characterised by a multiplicity of paradigms', so no method or technique can be fool proof and totally reliable. For the present inquiry, multiple research methods and techniques (both qualitative and quantitative methods) were used in order to collect the data in triangulated format, which would leave less scope for error.

I surveyed 50 farmers in the villages who were engaged in groundwater markets as either water-sellers or buyers. Then, over my next several visits spanning from the period of 2008–14, I followed up on these surveys with repeated in-depth interviews, and conducted in total 121 semi-structured interviews and 16 focus group discussions, to get a broad understanding of the water issues in the village, groundwater market, gender, tribe and caste relations. Apart from this I conducted a household survey, which covered 200 households, to generate quantitative evidence of the characteristics of rural households in terms of caste and tribe ratio, kinship lineage, gender control and access to natural resources and level and scope of knowledge about the watershed project.

The chapter is divided into two parts; in the first part, I elaborate on water scarcity in Gujarat, a region that had insignificant efforts in developing irrigation in colonial and post-colonial times. I next discuss the groundwater in India, and in Gujarat specifically. The second part is a case study of Mathnaa, Gujarat, where I undertook ethnographic fieldwork in 2008–09 and in 2012–14. In this part, I illustrate the social fabric of Mathnaa community and how social exclusion is practiced through the notions of caste purity and pollution by its upper-caste members against Adivasis and Dalits in the groundwater market, in order to maintain the hegemony as 'water lords'.

## Water scarcity and the politics of the making of a market

Gujarat is situated on the western side of India; it came into existence as a separate state on 1 May 1960, when it was carved out of the bilingual state of Bombay (Government of Gujarat 2009). It derives its name from Gujara (or, the land of the Gujjars who ruled the area during the 8th and 9th centuries) and the settlers in Gujarat were the Gujjars who happened to be an ethnic group of India, Pakistan and Afghanistan, although their origins remain uncertain and the name of the tribe was 'Sanskritised' to 'Gurjara' (Government of Gujarat 2009). Gujarat covers 5.96 per cent of India's landmass, having a population of 60.3 million (Government of Gujarat 2013). Gujarat districts have been divided into four agrarian socio-ecologies. These four regions differ from each other socio-economically, culturally, hydrologically, geologically and institutionally, and this division helps one understand how various regions of Gujarat interplay (Naz 2014). Gujarat only has 2.28 per cent of India's freshwater reserves, which are further constrained by imbalances in intra-state distribution (Gupta 2012). The northern part of the state is dry and arid, whereas in the southern region moist weather predominates, owing to the region's proximity to the Arabian Sea and Gulf of Cambay. Tropical monsoons dominate and provide violent but erratic amounts of rainfall from June/July to September/October, receiving less than approximately 40 inches annually (Naz 2015). Moreover, 78 per cent of Gujarat is subject to erratic monsoons and suffers from large-scale soil erosion, reducing land productivity over the years (Hardiman 2007; Rani 2004). Around 61 per cent of the geographical area of Gujarat is under cultivation, of which 64 per cent is un-irrigated (Government of Gujarat 2010). In addition, about twice every five years the state experiences drought conditions. With the exception of Narmada, Tapi, Mahi and Purna in southern Gujarat, the rivers are seasonal and dry outside the monsoons (Rani 2004). After becoming a state in 1960, successive Gujarat governments have devoted significant budgetary resources for the construction of major and medium canal irrigation projects. This led to changes in the ecology of the estuaries of the rivers in Gujarat, due to the construction of multiple irrigation dams (Singh 2000). Out of all the irrigation dams in Gujarat, the most controversial has been the Narmada Valley Development Project (NVDP), a multipurpose river valley development scheme, with a planned construction of 30 large dams, 135 medium and 3,000 small dams on the Narmada River (Parasuraman *et al.* 2010).[6] Like any large river valley development project, the NVDP has led to large-scale submergence of land and displacement of thousands of tribal and peasant communities for whom this land provided habitat, livelihood and life world (Naz 2015).[7]

In most of northern Gujarat, Saurashtra and Kutch, there are no perennial rivers of much importance, and irrigation has either been dependent on wells or channels taken from the reservoirs formed by small-scale dams or embankments (Singh 2000). Moreover, highly uneven patterns of groundwater exploitation has resulted in salinity ingress, which has resulted in the deterioration of the quality of water pertaining to excessive salinity and excessive fluoride in the water in the different regions of Gujarat (Hirway 2000). The agriculture of the region has relied on the ability to harvest water during the dry months of the year, and over the last 30 years this ability has come under increasing threat. The foremost source of irrigation in Gujarat (71 per cent) comes from open wells and electrically operated borewells, with an additional 14 per cent canal irrigation and 15 per cent from other sources (Government of Gujarat 2010). Between 1971 and 2001, the use of diesel pumps in irrigation increased by up to 56 per cent and the use of electric pumps by 585 per cent (Shah *et al.* 2008). Indeed, groundwater development in Gujarat has taken off with such speed that it has left behind state intervention in terms of canals; this has significantly affected groundwater resources in the state (see table 10.1).

*Table 10.1* Net area irrigated by source in Gujarat (area in '00 hectares)

| Year | Govt. canals (including Panchayat canals) | Tubewells and other wells |
| --- | --- | --- |
| 1970–1 | 2358 | 10831 |
| 1980–1 | 3668 | 15884 |
| 1990–1 | 4731 | 19301 |
| 2000–1 | 3476 | 24347 |
| 2001–2 | 3824 | 25901 |
| 2002–3 | 3804 | 26373 |
| 2003–4 | 5997 | 27364 |
| 2004–5 | 6762 | 27764 |

Source: Directorate of Agriculture (2009).

Extraction of groundwater from wells in many areas of Gujarat has surpassed natural replenishment in the subsoil, leading to an alarming fall in the water table (Rani 2004). Due to hard rock conditions, the recharge rate is only 5 per cent to 10 per cent in more than half of the total geographical area (Rani 2004). In 2009, 31 blocks (subdistrict revenue divisions) in Gujarat were declared 'overexploited', 12 as 'dark' (critical) and 69 as 'grey' (semi-critical) (Government of India 2009).[8]

In spite of all this, well irrigation in Gujarat remains critical and groundwater forms the backbone of the Gujarat agriculture economy since colonial times. During colonial times, no canal irrigation projects were undertaken in Gujarat. In the 1930s about 78 per cent of the irrigated area of British Gujarat was irrigated by wells and only 10 per cent by canals (Desai 1948). The colonial government found the cost of building irrigation infrastructure prohibitively high, leaving agriculture at the mercy of the rain and groundwater irrigation. In regions like central and southern Gujarat, which were more prosperous, village elites from leading castes had complete ownership of the wells. This is termed 'community control', but in actuality it benefitted only a small clutch of elite villagers (Hardiman 1998, 2007).

Therefore, access to groundwater since colonial times has given rise to new forms of social organisation and these forms are shaped by and in turn shape social and economic aspects within an agrarian set-up. Thus it becomes necessary to give importance to the implication of dependence on groundwater and the struggle to maintain access to it; in order to understand the social-cultural-economic and political change in a rural society of India. In Gujarat the sale of groundwater through markets has been a common phenomenon to have access to water irrespective of landownership and has led to the creation of water lords.

Groundwater institutions, which we find today in India, were developing in the early years of the 19th century, for example the jointly owned wells in the 19th century (Islam 1997) operated like the tubewell companies of north Gujarat (Shah and Bhattacharya 1993) and Punjab (Tiwary 2010). Groundwater is an important source of irrigation in India and as result, water markets have developed in many parts of the country (Shah 1993). Groundwater markets that exist in India are informal, where transactions between water-sellers and water-buyers are carried out without any legal sanction or regulation. The markets are localised, as water vending is made to fellow villagers and the market is unregulated, as the government does not exercise any direct authority on the functioning of the market (Shah 1993; Foster and Sekhri 2008).[9] The water in the groundwater markets is transported from the seller's well to the buyer's field by lined or unlined field channels or underground pipe networks (Foster and Sekhri 2008). The payments for the water transactions are in cash or kind, and different types of contracts like output sharing, labours contracts and input-output sharing have emerged (Shah 1993). Therefore, the groundwater markets in India – most of which are monopolies (Anderson 2005; Sekhri 2012) – have emerged across rural India in the past few decades and have become a critical water source for irrigation (see Aggarwal 1999; Dubash 2002; Janakarajan 1993, 1994; Mukherji 2007; Naz 2014, 2015; Pant 1992; Prakash 2005; Shah and Ballabh 1997; Tiwary 2010; Wood 1995).

Out of theses, the groundwater market in Gujarat has been widely studied, often cited and is considered to be the most organised and developed. The most pioneering work on Gujarat groundwater market has been of Shah (1993) who first brought to notice the existence of groundwater markets in Gujarat and stated that markets in groundwater in Gujarat are competitive, efficient and individualised and have economic rationality, but his work overlooks the issue of caste, tribe and community in the analysis. Tubewell partnerships are formed around caste affiliations between landholders belonging to the same caste; as so often happens in rural India, the plots are contiguous with the same caste and ethnic backgrounds (Naz 2014).[10] Tubewell partnerships are formed around caste affiliations, and often 'caste is the bond that binds the partners together', leaving Adivasi, lower castes and other disadvantaged and socially excluded groups from entering the market (Naz 2014). Tubewell partnerships involved huge expenditures, which are often beyond the reach of the small and marginal famers who mainly belong to the Adivasi and Dalit community (Naz 2014).[11] The inability of Adivasis and Dalits to form tubewell partnerships on a large-scale removes them from the groundwater market (Dubash 2002).

Private ownership and unchecked extractions in northern Gujarat have led to competitive well deepening and capital investment in groundwater pumping equipment is high, which frequently results in the control of groundwater by wealthy farmers (Dubash 2002; Prakash 2005). In the Banaskantha and Mehsana districts of Gujarat 'tubewell companies' have emerged, which operate like joint companies. These ventures result from adjoining farmers' pooling capital and sharing water based on investment, as individually installed tubewells incur extensive investment (Shah and Bhattacharya 1993). The question of inequity in accessing groundwater is very important, as investments in groundwater pumping equipment are often lopsided and disparate, which often results in the ownership of groundwater assets lying in the hands of wealthy farmers and leads to the creation of 'water lords', who are often from the dominant community, which comprises the upper caste (Bhatia 1992; Dubash 2002; Hardiman 2007; Prakash 2005; Mukherji 2006).

## Mathnaa's social fabric around its water

Research for this study was conducted in a small village called Mathnaa, located in Sabarkantha district, in northeast Gujarat. Mathnaa is a rainfed village, with a total area of 503 hectares and has no irrigation facility from the government. The climate of Mathnaa is semi-arid and the topography is mountainous and rough; the soil is sandy in character. Average temperatures rise to 45.5 °C in summer and fall to 7.7 °C in winter. It is predominantly an agricultural village, where primarily two crops are sown – *kharif* and *rabi*.[12] Due to erratic rainfall and water scarcity, it is not possible to plant major crops during the summer months, except fodder or seasonal vegetables for subsistence. The village is divided along caste, tribe, gender and wealth and has a population of 1,150, with Hindus predominating and Adivasi also constitute a significant proportion of the inhabitants. Caste determines living space and frames social interaction over water. The village has several clusters of settlements along the lines of caste or *was* (residential abodes in the Gujarati language). There are eight *Jadeja* (*Rajputs*) households, and they occupy the highest status in Mathnaa. These households consider themselves superior to other castes, trace their origin back to Sambha, son of Lord Krishna, and believed to have ruled Sabarkantha and driven away tribes to the forest (Mukherjee 2003). Rajput clans include the *Jadeja, Solanki, Parmar, Chauhan*, etc., but it is claimed that in the local Rajput caste hierarchy, Jadeja Rajputs occupies the highest position. The households legally own around 113 hectares of land, but also control encroachments on village *gauchar* (pasture) apart from that.

Next in the hierarchy are *Thakores*, constituting 100 households. Thakores claim descent from the Rajputs; they also claim to be *Kshatriyas* and are an agriculture caste. In Mathnaa, these 100 households own 137 hectares of land. There are also 56 *Dungri Garasia* households, who are Adivasis, an Indigenous population. Dungri Garasia, literally meaning *jagirdars* or *inamdars* of the hilly areas (Gazetteer of India 1974). 'Dungri' means hills and 'Garasia' means grass. People who have cleared the forests and prepared it for cultivation are the Dungri Garasia. They migrated from the Mewar region of Rajasthan three centuries ago. They live on their fields/farms with agriculture and land their main sources of livelihood. The Dungri Garasia tribe is patrilineal in character. In total, 122 hectares of land is owned by Adivasi households.

At the bottom of the caste hierarchy are 36 Dalit households. Formerly known as *Harijans* or 'Untouchables' – 'untouchability' having formally been abolished in India – they are still discriminated against informally. There is also an intra-Dalit hierarchy, and those living in Mathnaa come from the group of *chamars*. While their original occupation was skinning the hides of dead animals, in Mathnaa they practice agriculture. Dalits do not have any control of Mathnaa's common lands and live on the periphery of the village. Nor are they allowed to fetch water from the village common wells during times of scarcity, even in summers. Water, unlike earth, is a standard by which we can measure how deeply the essence of caste has penetrated and perverted social relations (Guru 2009).

Caste and tribe not only determines the living space in Mathnaa but also landholdings, access and bases for social interaction in terms of water. In Mathnaa access to land is based on inheritance, caste and claims grounded in local history. Although with the land reforms introduced in 1960 and the Gujarat Agricultural Lands Ceiling Act, enforced in 1961, provided ceilings for existing landholding and for the future acquisition of land. As a result, it provided some relief to marginalised communities like the Adivasis and the Dalits in the form of land redistribution. However, realistically though, Jadejas and Thakores own more than 250 hectares of land in Mathnaa and 69 per cent of the large farmers come from the Jadejas and Thakores factions (Naz 2015).[13] Hence, the majority of small and marginal farmers comprise Adivasis and Dalits in Mathnaa (Naz 2014). Hitherto, the main source of irrigation in Mathnaa was open dug wells, operated by a diesel or electric motor. There were about approximately 50 open dug wells 60–70 feet deep before 1999 but all have dried up since.

The agents of change in Mathnaa have been the Jadejas, since the late 1980s – it was in the late 1980s that the Jadeja farmers sourced a diesel engine and installed it next to the well and were able to irrigate, whereas others were dependent only on rain. With the introduction of motor technology, others also made an effort to have installed electric/

diesel engine motors in the open dug wells. In the words of Jethusingh Jadeja, whose father was the first person in Mathnaa to use a motor for an open well:

> My father introduced the engines to everyone in Mathnaa in the late 1980s. Many in Mathnaa had open dug wells but were not using any motor on them, due to lack of information about such motors and also because diesel was expensive. The majority of people in Mathnaa practiced only rainfed agriculture. Later with rural electrification, which came at a subsidised rate, people got motors; also water was found in abundance at short depths below the surface. Electricity was cheap and people could afford it, although the electricity supply was not regular.
> (Interview with author, 15 October 2008)

In the year 2000, it was again members of the Jadeja community who introduced the borewell technology in Mathnaa. In the words of Daljeetsingh Jadeja and Gambhirsingh Jadeja:

> It was me who introduced this borewell technology in Mathnaa. It is an expensive technology but it bears fruit as it goes deep, up to 200–250 feet, to fetch water for longer periods, even in the summer. I had gone to Himatnagar to buy spare parts for my dug well electric motor, and then the agent of the local borewell company told me about this incredible borewell technology and how it was far better than the normal motor used in the dug well. I immediately decided to have this on my field.
> My family brought this technology to Mathnaa, similarly, as my uncle Jethusingh had introduced the electric motor, for the open dug well operation in the late 1980s. Once we got the borewells installed, others also slowly started getting the borewells on their fields. When they saw the borewell water pumping capacity, many others were encouraged to have one of their own.
> (Interviews with author, 20 November 2008)

The number of borewells in Mathnaa increased subsequently with different caste groups' ownership, and by 2013 there were about 24 borewells as deep as 200–250 feet (Jadejas 4, Thakore 11, Dalits 2, and Adivasi 7). Borewells are collectively owned by a group of relatives in Mathnaa, who are often the wealthiest amongst their own caste or tribe groups. However, unlike the 'tubewell companies' found in Banaskantha and Mehsana district of northern Gujarat, the farmers in Mathnaa have small and fragmented landholdings, which lead them to undertake kinship-based ownership of smaller bore and tubewells. The reason for switching to other means, as explained by few farmers:

> With the water level going down, due to borewells on nearby farms, my well was becoming dry with each passing year. Deepening of my dug well costs more and it was not very fruitful decision. Therefore, installing a borewell was considered wise, although it involved a huge expenditure, hence I decided to own a borewell collectively with my brothers. Borewell go deeper and does not go dry in the summer. Furthermore, the rate at which water was sold has changed. Now the majority of the people's wells have dried up. Few people in Mathnaa have borewells and buying water is turning out to be expensive due to the new electricity scheme. Moreover, the rains have not been very good for the past few years, so the viable option is to own a borewell collectively.
> (Field notes of the author, 2008)

In the village, well ownership goes hand in hand with landownership, as wells are bored on private land, hence no one can stop the construction of these private borewell/tubewells.[14] There are 22 government-owned handpumps under the village Panchayat (elected council) supervision located in each caste quarters of Mathnaa. Out of these, only nine were in working conditions in 2015, which led to drinking water scarcity. In summers, most of the handpumps go dry as they are not very deep, and water level is very low during the summer season. Different caste members do not fetch water from the handpumps installed in the other caste or Adivasi was, due to the stigma, attached to purity and pollution of water in the caste context. Caste inequality has also not spared the handpumps of Adivasi either and the access to water in handpumps is clearly marked by the caste dynamics and social exclusion practice against the Adivasi, involving the pollution and purity concept of caste hierarchies. Irrigation is a resource of 'unusual social power', as stated by Hunt and Hunt (1976), as those who have the access to water and who own the borewells are indeed the wealthiest and most powerful actors in Mathnaa (Naz 2014).

## Mathnaa's groundwater market: the rules of the game and the power hegemony of the caste water lords

Till 2000, Mathnaa did not have a widespread water market, because irrigation was done through open dug wells run on electric motors and rainfed agriculture was practiced extensively. Three crucial factors led to the emergence of the groundwater market: 1) borewell technology was introduced in the village in the year 2000, and it extracted more water, as it went very deep compared to open dug wells; 2) the majority of the dug wells had dried, no longer meeting the growing agricultural water demand; and 3) check dams were constructed near the borewells as part of the watershed project (Naz 2014).[15] These factors acted as incentives in the development of groundwater and the groundwater market in Mathnaa.

Most of the players i.e. the water-sellers in the groundwater market are from the upper-caste community, as they were the first to get access to the borewell technology which is capital intensive, as they had the economic resource to own borewells. There was no standardised price for water prior to 2005; instead; the price was determinedby the caste affiliation of buyers and sellers ranging initially from Indian rupees (INR) 15 to 25 per hour of water supplied (in terms of quantity) for irrigation.[16] After 2005, the price of water accelerated (see table 10.2).[17] Nevertheless now a uniform water price for irrigation is prevalent, irrespective of the caste and tribal affiliations of the borewell owners. This is a result of the newly introduced *Jyotirgram* Scheme (JGS), as a result of which electricity is no longer available at a low flat rate (Naz 2014).[18] In retort, Mathnaa's water lords increased prices. About

*Table 10.2* Increase in water price over the course of ten years

| Years | Price of water per hour in INR |
| --- | --- |
| 2005–06 | 50 |
| 2006–07 | 50 |
| 2007–08 | 50 |
| 2008–09 | 65–75 |
| 2009–10 | 65–75 |
| 2010–11 | 90 |
| 2011–12 | 90 |
| 2012–13 | 100 |
| 2013–14 | 100 |

Source: Author's field data.

80 per cent of water-buyers and 64 per cent of water-sellers noted that prices had increased in the informal groundwater market due to the Jyotirgram Scheme (Naz 2014). Although all of them agreed that electricity supply had improved impressively, they blamed the JGS for the increase in water prices since 2005 onwards.

Water is sold on two bases: firstly, for cash on an hourly provision of water, and, secondly for a one-third share of the crop or '*trijo bhag panino*', meaning a third part of the crop is to be given away for water, in lieu of cash. As the result of increase in water prices, the Adivasis and the Dalits have turned into sharecroppers and are often participating in off-farm activities such as working as daily labourers or casual labour on construction sites in nearby towns.

The upper-castes borewell owners often operated on capitalist principles when they are selling water to their subordinates, and in the process reinforce caste domination and social inequality. But with the passage of time some Adivasi and Dalits have tried to break the hegemony of the upper-caste borewell owners by participating in the groundwater market as water-sellers. By doing this they have tried to challenge the superiority of the upper-caste well owners and this has not gone down well with the upper-caste water lords of the groundwater market.

As caste and Hindu religious–based traditions lay down clear rules and regulations about purity and pollution regarding 'whose' water can be drunk and 'whose' should be avoided, this is being used by the upper-caste water lords to keep a check and exclude as far as possible the Adivasi water-sellers from the groundwater market operating in Mathnaa. In Hinduism and village cosmology, water is considered pure and consecrated because of it possessing cleansing and purifying qualities. Therefore, for example the higher caste abstains from buying drinking water from the Adivasi or lower caste; thus Thakores do not buy drinking water from Adivasis or Dalits water-sellers, as their water is considered polluted and deemed unfit to be placed in pots next to the idols of gods and goddesses, as practiced in other households. For drinking water, there are very strict rules, which are religiously practiced and endorsed by all the residents of Mathnaa. The residents of Mathnaa have elaborated this point.

> Water has a very strong place in the village life, as Mathnaa has water scarcity. Earthen pots containing drinking water are kept near the idols of the local deity in each household. Thus, we cannot buy drinking water from the *Adivasis* or *Dalits*, as it will put us in *paap* (sin) and we will get impure. We have to

follow the religious and caste rules, so there is there no question of us buying (drinking) water from Adivasi or 'untouchable' borewell owners. But we will certainly buy it for irrigation.
(Interview with author, 11 January 2009)

For irrigation purposes, farmers, irrespective of caste and tribe affiliation, buy water from the borewell owner adjacent to their field, as according to them water for irrigation does not have the concept of being pure or impure. Thus, water is sold and purchased freely.

There is no problem in taking water from the borewells which are owned by the adivasis or dalits, as water for irrigation is purified when it mixes with the soil, so the question of getting polluted or impure by taking water from the adivasi or lower caste does not arise.
(Interview with author, 22 December 2008)

Thus, the purpose for which water will be used and not the source (borewell) is given due importance and is the deciding factor for the villagers when buying water in relation to caste purity and pollution.[19] Though, water which is an everyday, commonplace, utilitarian and mundane aspect of life in its profane sense, acquires a sacred meaning when kept next to religious portraits, conjuring principles of devotion, respect, mystery, esteem and honour (Durkheim 1965). In order to keep a check on the Adivasis and Dalits borewell owners, the water lords use the concept of Durkheim's sacred and profane within the large realm of pollution and purity, in the context of Hinduism and caste rules, to practice social exclusion. Although the Adivasis have been able to break the upper-caste water lords hegemony in the groundwater market by participating as water-sellers, it is limited to the extent that resident of Mathnaa buy water from them only for irrigation purposes and not for drinking water. Hence they have been not able to break away from the untouchability aspect attached to them in the context of water when it boils down to the drinking purpose. Thus social exclusion is practiced against them in the context of water, which is a contested natural resource in Mathnaa.

## Conclusion

Mathnaa's world is rooted deeply, religiously and cosmologically in terms of water-related practices; its upper-caste water lords take their cue from Manu's repressive code and use water for creating a perpetual divisions and social exclusion.[20] The bias of the repressive law of Manu is exploited by the upper-caste water lords to prevent the Adivasis and lower caste from actively participating in the groundwater market; and by doing this, the water lords use the social barriers of caste within a larger realm of sacredness and profanity to limit the possibility of water exchange and maintain their hegemony in the groundwater market of Mathnaa. As a result, water is used as a metaphor to assert these social differences and maintain the control of water resources (Naz 2015). Thus, the caste-based social hierarchy is determined locally through notions of purity and pollution, which are used in the local culture to determine and reinforce inequitable access to, control over and distribution of water and its usage rights (Naz 2014). The groundwater market in Mathnaa is dependent on social structure, social norms and practices deeply embedded in caste in its interplay with irrigation and drinking water developed at the village level.

## Notes

1 An earlier version of this chapter was presented at the Adivasi Rights and Processes of Exclusion in India conference, held at the Central University of Hyderabad in February 2012. A version of 'Adivasis Water Exchange and Caste Based Water Lords: A Case of Groundwater Market in a Village in Gujarat' by Farhat Naz was previously published in *The Socio-cultural Context of Water: A Case Study of Gujarat* (New Delhi: Orient Blackswan Pvt. Ltd., 2014).
2 The author acknowledges the comments received by the participants of the conference and also wishes to thank German Academic Exchange Service (Deutscher Akademischer Austasch Dienst, or DAAD), German Ministry for Education and Research (Bundes ministerium für Bildung und Forschung, or BMBF), the German Society for International Cooperation, Deutsche Gesellschaft Internationale Zusammenarbeit, or GIZ for the generous grants for this research.
3 Caste is a pan-Indian phenomenon and is based on social inequality and in principle all castes within a locality can be ranked within a single hierarchy. Castes are endogamous and segmentary, as all castes are divided into subcaste (Beteille 1971; Srinivas 1989). The social hierarchy of the caste system in Hindu society allegedly originated from the four-fold class system (Das 1982; Fuller 2003; Murray 1994). The word 'caste' is sometimes used to translate varna denoting the four 'classes' of the Hindu society with the Brahmins, the priestly class; Kshatriyas, the warrior class; Vaishya, the merchant class; Sudras, the service class; and finally, the untouchables (also known as Harijans, Dalits or the Scheduled Caste, their official designation) are the bottom and are outside the four-class system and object of

extreme stigmatisation. The Rig-Veda hymn 'the Purusha Sukta' describes how from the Purusha (primeval man) body the four varnas originated, i.e. from his mouth came the Brahmins, his arms the Kshatriyas, his thighs the Vaishya and from his feet the Sudras (Fuller 2003).

4  I chose pseudonyms for the village and participants for the sake of anonymity, as per the participants' wishes.

5  Adivasi literally means 'original/earliest settler'. This term is used to designate the Indigenous people of India who are officially known as 'Scheduled Tribes' (ST) and who make up around 8 per cent of the Indian population. Scheduled Tribes are lists of marginalised Indigenous (tribal) people, comprising different ethnic subgroups. In this chapter, I use the word 'Adivasi' instead of their tribe name, as the term 'Adivasi' is widely used in the village to address them.

6  At 815 miles in length, the Narmada is the longest river in central Asia, the fifth-longest river in south Asia, and the longest Indian river flowing in Central India. Various organisations and individuals, including Narmada Bachao Andolan (NBA) meaning 'Save the Narmada Movement' led by Medha Patkar, have criticised the construction of the dam and through the movement of NBA made attempts to publicise the ecological disaster and the plight of the poor in the region.

7  For details on this see Baviskar's sociological work (2004) work on the tribals living in the Narmada valley, where she examines the *Andolan* (agitation or campaign) politics and how the Adivasis were incorporated into a larger, more diverse movement against the Sardar Sarovar Project. She further elaborates the issues of development, tribal reality and relationship of the tribals with nature and the question of representation.

8  The Central Ground Water Board (CGWB) categorises the groundwater blocks according to the decline in water level and the stage of groundwater use (the latter is the annual groundwater draft expressed as a percentage of net annual groundwater availability): (1) semi-critical or grey (stage > 70 per cent and < 100 per cent: significant long-term decline in pre- or post-monsoonal water level); (2) critical or dark (stage > 90 per cent and < 100 per cent: significant long-term decline in both pre- and post-monsoonal water level); and overexploited (stage > 100 per cent: significant long-term decline in pre- or post-monsoonal water level or both).

9  Groundwater appears as an open access good of which anybody can extract as much as they want from the ground below, since there is no social authority that defines and enforces the rights of individuals or a group to use open access resources (Naz 2015). Therefore, each resource user ignores the consequences of his behaviour on others (Bromley 1992). However, the open access nature of groundwater is restricted due to the fact that landowners are able to gain access only if they have the means to invest in the necessary infrastructure required for the extraction of water. Subsequently, in reality, groundwater open access is a 'restricted' or 'skewed' open access regime.

10  For more detail, see the work of Dubash (2002), Hardiman (2007), Prakash (2005) and Sekhri (2012).

11  Small farmers are those whose landholding is between one to two hectares, and marginal farmers are those who own land less than one hectare.

12 *Kharif*, or rainfed, crops are sown in June and July and are harvested in September–October. In Mathnaa, they consist of maize, millet, pulses, castor and cotton. *Rabi*, or irrigated, crops are sown in October–November and harvested in February–March. Rabi crops grown in Mathnaa are wheat, mustard, gram, potatoes and turmeric.
13 Larger farmers are those whose landholdings are two hectares and above.
14 Gujarat was the first Indian state to pass groundwater legislation in the year 1976 to deal with the regulation and licensing of tubewell construction and to control the use of groundwater. But its implementation proved to be very difficult as the regulation was usually bypassed.
15 Check dams are low cemented or earthen barriers made to capture monsoon run-off in empty streambeds, creating a series of small reservoirs, which percolate to nearby wells and recharge the groundwater aquifers. Check dams were constructed as a part of the activity of the watershed development project in Mathnaa under the Integrated Wastelands Development Programme (IWDP) in 1999 by a local NGO, under the Common Guidelines of 1994. For more detail see Naz (2014).
16 One Indian rupees is equal to 0.015 USD. Therefore 15 INR = 0.25 USD and 25 INR = 0.37 USD respectively.
17 50 INR = 0.75 USD, 65 INR = 0.97 USD, 75 INR = 1.12 USD, 90 INR = 1.35, 100 INR = 1.50 USD and 110 INR = 1.65 USD respectively.
18 Under the *Jyotirgram* (Lighted Village) Scheme (JGS), a separate electricity supply is provided to domestic and agriculture-related activities in villages. The scheme was initially launched as a pilot project in eight districts of Gujarat, but by November 2004 it was extended to the entire state, assuring a 24-hour supply for domestic use and 8 hours for agriculture. This has helped in curtailing the overexploitation of groundwater pumping through illegal means and is described by the government of Gujarat as a win-win solution (Shah *et al.* 2008).
19 In the sample survey of 25 water-buyers, consisting of different caste groups, it was unambiguously stated that they will buy drinking water only from their own caste or a caste higher than their own but for irrigation they can buy from any caste or Adivasi group.
20 *Manusmriti* (The Laws of Manu) is the foundation of Hindu religious law and social conduct written by Manu and is popularly known as the Manu code.

# References

Aggarwal, Rimjhim. 1999. *Risk Sharing and Transaction Costs in Groundwater Contracts: Evidence From Rural India*. College Park: University of Maryland.

Ahmed, Sara and Margreet Zwarteveen. 2012. 'Gender and Water in South Asia: Revisiting Perspectives, Policies and Practices', in Margreet Zwarteveen, Sara Ahmed and Suman Rimal Gautam (eds.), *Diverting the Flow: Gender Equity and Water in South Asia*. New Delhi: Zubaan, 3–30.

Anderson, Siwan. 2005. *Caste as an Impediment to Trade*. Vancouver: University of British Columbia, Mimeo.

Bakker, Karen. 2003. *An Uncooperative Commodity: Privatizing Water in England and Wales*. Oxford: Oxford University Press.

Baviskar, Amita. 2004. *In the Belly of the River: Tribal Conflicts Over Development in the Narmada Valley*. New Delhi: Oxford University Press.

Bear, Christopher and Jacob Bull. 2011. 'Water Matters: Agency, Flows and Frictions', *Environment and Planning A*, 43: 2261–6.

Beteille, Andre. 1971. *Caste, Class and Power: Changing Patterns of Stratification in a Tanjore Village*. Berkeley: University of California Press.

Bhatia, Bela. 1992. 'Lush Fields and Parched Throats: Political Economy of Groundwater in Gujarat', *Economic and Political Weekly*, 27(51 and 52): A142–A70.

Blaikie, Piers. 1985. *The Political Economy of Soil Erosion in Developing Countries*. New York: Longman.

Blaikie, Piers and Harold Brookfield. 1987. *Land Degradation and Society*. New York: Methuen Press.

Boelens, Rutgerd. 2014. 'Cultural Politics and the Hydrosocial Cycle: Water, Power and Identity in the Andean Highlands', *Geoforum*, 57: 234–47.

Bromley, Daniel W. (ed.). 1992. *Making the Commons Work: Theory, Practice and Policy*. San Francisco: ICS Press.

Bryant, Raymond L. 1998. 'Power, Knowledge and Political Ecology in the Third World: A Review', *Progress in Physical Geography*, 22(1): 79–94.

Budds, Jessica. 2009. 'Contested H2O: Science, Policy and Politics in Water Resources Management in Chile', *Geoforum*, 40: 418–30.

Budds, Jessica and Farhana Sultana. 2013. 'Guest Editorial', *Environment and Planning D: Society and Space*, 31: 275–9.

Das, Veena. 1982. *Structure and Cognition: Aspects of Hindu Caste and Ritual*. New Delhi: Oxford India Paperback.

Desai, Maganial Bhagwanji. 1948. *The Rural Economy of Gujarat*. Bombay: Oxford University Press.

Directorate of Agriculture. 2009. *Statistical Abstract of Gujarat State*. Gandhinagar: Government of Gujarat.

Dubash, Navroz Kersi. 2002. *Tubewell Capitalism: Groundwater Development and Agrarian Change in Gujarat*. New Delhi: Oxford University Press.

Durkheim, Emile. 1965. *The Elementary Forms of the Religious Life*. Glencoe: Free Press.

Foster, Andrew and Sheetal Sekhri. 2008. *Water Markets, Local Networks and Aquifer Depletion*. Working Paper, Department of Economics, University of Virginia, USA.

Foucault, Michel. 1980. *Power/Knowledge: Selected Interviews and Other Writings, 1972–1977*. London: Harvester Wheatsheaf.

Fuller, Christopher J. 2003. 'Caste', in Veena Das (ed.), *The Oxford India Companion to Sociology and Social Anthropology*. New Delhi: Oxford University Press, 477–501.

Gazetteer of India. 1974. *Gujarat State, Sabarkantha District*. Ahmedabad: Government of India.

Government of Gujarat. 2009. *Gujarat Official State Portal*.www.gujaratindia. com (accessed on 25 September 2010).

Government of Gujarat. 2010. *Executive Summary: Final State Agriculture Plan (SAP): Gujarat*. Agriculture and Co-operation Department, Government of Gujarat. http://agri.gujarat.gov.in/informations/sap_final.pdf (accessed on 23 September 2010).

Government of Gujarat. 2013. *Socio-Economic Review 2012–2013 Gujarat State*. Gandhinagar: Directorate of Economics and Statistics Government of Gujarat. http://financedepartment.gujarat.gov.in/budget13_14_pdf/34_ Socio_Economic_Review_English.pdf (accessed on 20 May 2014).

Government of India. 2009. *Groundwater Scenario of Gujarat*. New Delhi: Central Ground Water Board, Ministry of Water Resources, Government of India. http://cgwb.gov.in/gw_profiles/st_Gujarat.htm (accessed on 15 June 2010).

Gupta, Rajiv Kumar. 2012. 'The Role of Water Technology in Development: A Case Study of Gujarat, India', in Reza Ardakanian and Dirk Jaegar (eds.), *Water and the Green Economy: Capacity Development Aspects*. Bonn: UN-Water Decade Programme on Capacity Development (UNW-DPC), 115–27.

Guru, Gopal. 2009. 'Archaeology of Untouchability', *Economic and Political Weekly*, XLIV(37): 49–56.

Hardiman, David. 1998. 'Well Irrigation in Gujarat: Systems of Use, Hierarchies of Control', *Economic and Political Weekly*, 33(25): 1533–44.

Hardiman, David. 2007. 'The Politics of Water Scarcity in Gujarat', in Amita Baviskar (ed.), *Waterscapes: The Cultural Politics of a Natural Resource*. New Delhi: Permanent Black, 40–64.

Hirway, Indira. 2000. 'Dynamics of Development in Gujarat: Some Issues', *Economic and Political Weekly*, 35(35–36): 3106–20.

Hunt, Robert and Eva Hunt. 1976. 'Canal Irrigation and Local Social Organization', *Current Anthropology*, 17(3): 389–410.

Ioris, Antonio A. R. 2007. 'The Troubled Waters of Brazil: Nature Commodification and Social Exclusion', *Capitalism Nature Socialism*, 18(1): 28–50.

Islam, M. Mufakharul. 1997. *Irrigation Agriculture and the Raj, Punjab, 1887–1947*. New Delhi: Manohar Books.

Janakarajan, S. 1993. 'Triadic Exchange Relations: An Illustration From South India', *Institute of Development Studies Bulletin*, 24(3): 75–82.

Janakarajan, S. 1994. 'Trading in Groundwater: A Source of Power and Accumulation', in Marcus Moench (ed.), *Selling Water: Conceptual and Policy Debates Over Groundwater Markets in India*. Ahmedabad: VIKSAT, 47–58.

Jerstada, Held. 2014. 'Damp Bodies and Smoky Firewood: Material Weather and Livelihood in Rural Himachal Pradesh', *Forum for Development Studies*, 41(3): 399–414.

Khan, Seema, Fraser Emilie Combaz and Erika McAslan. 2015. *Social Exclusion: Topic Guide*, Revised edition. Birmingham: GSDRC, University of Birmingham. www.gsdrc.org/wp-content/uploads/2015/08/SocialExclusion.pdf (accessed on 3 December 2015)

Linton, Jamie. 2010. *What Is Water? The History of a Modern Abstraction.* Vancouver: University of British Columbia Press.
Loftus, Alex. 2007. 'Working the Socio-Natural Relations of the Urban Waterscape in South Africa', *International Journal of Urban and Regional Research,* 31: 41–59.
Loftus, Alex. 2009. 'Rethinking Political Ecologies of Water', *Third World Quarterly,* 30: 953–68.
Long, Norman. 1992. 'From Paradigm Lost to Paradigm Regained? The Case of an Actor-oriented Sociology of Development', in Norman Long and Anne Long (eds.), *Battlefields of Knowledge: The Interlocking of Theory and Practice in Social Research and Development.* London: Routledge, 16–46.
Mehta, Lyla. 2005. *The Politics and Poetics of Water: The Naturalisation of Scarcity of Western India.* New Delhi: Orient Longman.
Mehta, Lyla. 2007. 'Whose Scarcity? Whose Property?: The Case of Water in Western India', *Land Use Policy,* 24: 654–63.
Mollinga, Peter Paul. 2008. 'Water, Politics and Development: Framing a Political Sociology of Water Resources Management', *Water Alternatives,* 1(1): 7–23.
Moore, Donald. 1993. 'Contesting Terrain in Zimbabwe's Eastern Highlands: Political Ecology, Ethnography, and Peasant Resource Struggles', *Economics Geography,* 69(4): 380–401.
Mosse, David. 1999. 'Colonial and Temporary Ideologies of Community Management: The Case of Tank Irrigation Development in South India', *Modern Asian Studies,* 33(2): 303–38.
Mukherjee, Aditi. 2003. 'Jadeja', in Kumar Suresh Singh (ed.), *People of India: Gujarat, Anthropological Survey of India,* Volume XXII, Part 1. Mumbai: Popular Prakashan, 519–23.
Mukherji, Aditi. 2006. 'Political Ecology of Groundwater: The Contrasting Case of Water-Abundant West Bengal and Water-Scarce Gujarat, India', *Hydrogeology Journal,* 14: 392–406.
Mukherji, Aditi. 2007. *Political Economy of Groundwater Markets in West Bengal, India: Evolution, Extent and Impacts.* PhD Thesis, University of Cambridge.
Murray, Milner Jr. 1994. *Status and Sacredness: A General Theory of Status Relations and an Analysis of Indian Culture.* New York: Oxford University Press.
Naz, Farhat. 2014. *The Socio-Cultural Context of Water: Study of a Gujarat Village.* New Delhi: Orient Blackswan.
Naz, Farhat. 2015. 'Water, Water Lords, and Caste: A Village Study From Gujarat, India', *Capitalism, Nature Socialism,* 26(3): 89–101.
Pant, Niranjan. 1992. *New Trends in Indian Irrigation: Commercialization of Groundwater.* New Delhi: Ashish Publishing.
Parasuraman, S., Himanshu Upadhyaya and Gomathy Balasubramanian. 2010. 'Sardar Sarovar Project: The War of Attribution', *Economic and Political Weekly,* XLV(5): 39–48.

Peet, Richard and Michael Watts (eds.). 1996. *Liberation Ecologies: Environment, Development, Social Movements*. New York: Routledge.

Prakash, Anjal. 2005. *The Dark Zone: Groundwater Irrigation and Water Scarcity in Gujarat*. New Delhi: Orient Longman.

Rani, Uma. 2004. 'Core Issues in the Economy and Society of Gujarat', in Ruedi Baumgartner and Rudolf Hogger (eds.), *Search of Sustainable Livelihood Systems: Managing Resources and Change*. New Delhi: Sage Publications, 81–93.

Sekhri, Sheetal. 2012. 'Caste-Based Clustering of Land Parcels in Two Villages in Uttar Pradesh', *Economic and Political Weekly*, XLVII(26 and 27): 106–9.

Shah, Tushaar. 1993. *Groundwater Markets and Irrigation Development: Political Economy and Practical Policy*. Mumbai: Oxford University Press.

Shah, Tushaar and Vishwa Ballabh. 1997. 'Water Markets in North Bihar: Six Villages Studies in Muzaffarpur District', *Economic and Political Weekly*, XXXII(52): A183–A190.

Shah, Tushaar, Sonal Bhatt, R. K. Shah and Jayesh Talati. 2008. 'Groundwater Governance Through Electricity Supply Management: Assessing an Innovative Intervention in Gujarat, Western India', *Agricultural Water Management*, 95(11): 1233–42.

Shah, Tushaar and Saumindra Bhattacharya. 1993. 'Farmers Organizations for Lift Irrigation: Irrigation Companies and Tubewell Cooperatives of Gujarat', *Network Paper 26*. London: Overseas Development Institute.

Singh, H. S. 2000. *Mangroves in Gujarat: Current Status and Strategy for Conservation*. Gandhinagar: Gujarat Ecological Education and Research (GEER) Foundation.

Srinivas, M. N. 1989. *The Cohesive Role of Sanskritization and Other Essays*. New Delhi: Oxford University Press.

Strang, Veronica. 2004. *The Meaning of Water*. Oxford and New York: Berg/Bloomsbury.

Sultana, Farhana. 2009. 'Community and Participation in Water Resources Management: Gendering and Nurturing Development Debates From Bangladesh', *Transactions of the Institute of British Geographers*, 34(3): 346–63.

Swyngedouw, Erik. 2005. 'Dispossessing H2O: The Contested Terrain of Water Privatization', *Capitalism Nature Socialism*, 16(1): 81–98.

Tiwary, Rakesh. 2010. 'Social Organization of Shared Well Irrigation in Punjab', *Economic and Political Weekly*, XLV(26 and 27): 208–19.

Wade, Robert. 1987. *Village Republics: Economic Conditions for Collective Action in South India*. Cambridge: Cambridge University Press.

Wittfogel, Karl August. 1957. *Oriental Despotism: From Comparative Study of Total Power*. New Haven: Yale University Press.

Wood, Geoff D. 1995. *Private Provision After Public Neglect: Opting Out With Pumpsets in North Bihar*. Bath: Centre for Development Studies, University of Bath.

Yin, Robert K. 2003.*Case Study Research: Design and Methods*. New Delhi: Sage Publications.

# 11
# ATROCITIES AGAINST ADIVASIS
## The implicit dimension of social exclusion

### G.C. Pal

Historically, the Adivasis, well known as Scheduled Tribes or Tribals, have been the victims of exclusion and marginalisation in India. The Constitution shows the exclusive concern to see that the human rights situation of Adivasi communities is improved, justice and equality in all its facets are secured to them, and they are mainstreamed into the nation's development processes. Within the constitutional framework of 'equal treatment and social justice', special social enactments have come to force from time to time to combat large-scale human right violations against them. The Protection of Civil Rights (PCR) Act, 1976 (Government of India 1976) is laid down to enforce civil rights of Adivasis. The Scheduled Castes and Scheduled Tribes (Prevention of Atrocities) Act, 1989 (Government of India 1989) is enacted to protect them from atrocities on the ground of discrimination and exploitation and denial of social, economic and democratic rights. The Prevention of Atrocities (PoA) Act delineates specific offences against Adivasis and Scheduled Castes (Dalits) as 'atrocities' and prescribes stringent penalties to counter these offences. The basic conditions for taking cognisance of offences under the act is that the offender should not be a member of Adivasi and Dalit communities and the offences so committed should be made with prior knowledge of the ethnicity or caste background of the victims. The objectives of the two acts clearly emphasise the intention of the state government to deliver justice to both Adivasi and Dalit communities to enable them to live in society with dignity. The Scheduled Castes and Scheduled Tribes (Prevention of Atrocities) Act Rules, 1995 (Government of India 1995) provide guidelines to the state in terms of specific administrative mechanisms to enforce the act effectively, vigorously monitor the situation of atrocities taking place against Adivasis and Dalits, and ensure social safeguards and support measures to the victims of atrocities. However, despite the implementation of the PoA Act over 25 years, atrocities against the Adivasis and Dalits have been continuing unabated in several spheres of society.

Although a large section of Adivasis and Dalits have been subjected to atrocities, the problems of Adivasis remain unique for various reasons. A large section of Adivasis live in Scheduled Areas and their level of social and economic interaction with the dominant mainstream society is much less than that of the Dalits. The underlying causes of various forms of oppressive and exploitive behaviours against Adivasis therefore remain qualitatively different. While the factor of 'untouchability', by and large, governs everyday interactions of the Dalits in mainstream society, and they are expected to live under the caste-based rules, the confinement of the Adivasis in remote areas makes them subjected to various forms of disadvantages, exploitations, abuses, violence and deprivation. Their isolated living pattern and unwariness very often make them prey to different forms of human rights abuses. As their socio-economic life, to a larger extent, is governed by multiple authorities within the local governance structure, they have to face many restrictions under laws. A large proportion of them therefore have to live with the lowest security of life and livelihood, keeping them at the lowest level of society and economy (Krishnan 2009). The Asian Centre of Human Rights recognises that Adivasis are among the most exploited communities in the country. According to Gill *et al.* (2015), they have been victims of social exclusion not simply because of the geographical isolation, but recent dispossession of their traditional habitation and rights to resources and erosion of their autonomy because of other development interventions. The nexus between different departments of the state administration largely become responsible for their human rights violations (Saravanan 2010). In many of the cases, non-Dalit and non-Adivasi perpetrators also align with the enforcing agencies to underperform the laws (Pal and Lal 2010). Further, it has been recognised that the changing nature of atrocities often marginalises the law. Several of the offences such as ostracisation or social boycotting, forced migration, custodial death, displacement, denial of basic rights to livelihood etc., which are highly true for the Adivasis, are not adequately addressed under the various clauses of the PoA Act. The Report Card of National Coalition for Strengthening SCs and STs (Prevention of Atrocities) Act (2010) recognises that misinterpretations of clauses of the PoA Act sometimes defeat prosecution, leading to denial of justice to victims of atrocities.

Thus, the limitations in the laws to deal with various forms of atrocities against Adivasis and lack of proper implementation invite serious attention of the state and human rights organisations, as it involves lager consequences on the life conditions of Adivasis.

Notwithstanding the fact that Adivasis are vulnerable to different forms of atrocities, the issues related to atrocities against Dalits have been a dominant factor in the discourse of human rights violations and social exclusion. The atrocities against Adivasis, on the other hand, have been more implicit, very often kept stubbornly in place and get less percolated to mainstream society. As a result, it has not drawn much attention of social science researchers. There are several critical issues that need to be understood in the context of atrocities against Adivasis within the existing social and legal contexts. What have been the magnitude and patterns of atrocities against Adivasis? Who are the actors normally commit these atrocities? In what ways the nature and patterns of atrocities against Adivasis are different from that of against Dalits? What have been the responses of the state machinery towards atrocities against Adivasis? How atrocities affect Adivasis regarding enjoyment of their fundamental human rights. This chapter draws on evidence from the official data on atrocities against Scheduled Tribes compiled by the National Crime Record Bureau (NCRB) to reflect on the overall patterns of atrocities against Adivasis, although the data has limitations in terms of poor reflection of actual magnitude of atrocities. Besides, it uses media reports, fact-finding reports of non-governmental organisations, official documents and limited literature to build up an understanding of the nature, causes and potential trend of atrocities against Adivasis. Based on insights from the analysis of the both macro- and micro-level data, the chapter sheds light on emerging critical issues that would have implications for the protection of human rights of Adivasis.

## Patterns of atrocities against Adivasis: an analysis at macro-level

Despite the strong enforcement of various social policies and special measures for the protection of rights of Adivasis, incidence of cognisable crimes registered against them continues to increase in recent years (figure 11.1). According to the NCRB data, a total of about 88,000 crimes were registered against the Adivasis in India during the period 2001–14, with an annual average of about 6,000 cases. Although the number of registered cases showed an increasing trend from 2011 onwards, it went up drastically in 2014. The number of

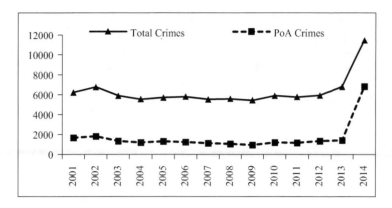

*Figure 11.1* The trend of registered cases of the total and PoA crimes against Adivasis, 2001–14

Source: Crimes in India, National Crime Record Bureau, Ministry of Home Affairs, Government of India.

cases registered in 2014 was 11,451 as against 6,793 in 2013, 5,922 in 2012 and 5,756 in 2011. A similar trend was observed for the registered PoA crimes against Adivasis, offences considered as atrocities. The number of cases registered under the PoA Act rose to 6,826 in 2014 from 1,390 cases in 2013, 1,311 cases in 2012 and 1,154 cases in 2011. The proportion of registered PoA crimes to the total crimes against Adivasis during 2001–14, on an average, was about 22 per cent. However, the figures on PoA crimes might not be reflecting on the actual magnitude of atrocities against Adivasis if we consider protests of Adivasis against such repressive acts, experiential accounts of human right activists, and reported cases in various media on a day-to-day basis. Many of the crimes against Adivasis committed by state officials and other powerful members in the society, as a matter of fact, are either non-registered at all or registered under the law other than the PoA Act.

Although noticeable change has not been observed in the number of registered PoA crimes between 2001 and 2010, the steady increase from 2011 and sudden upsurge in the year 2014 may be attributed to the special efforts of many civil society organisations who have been active in the tribal belt to raise awareness among Adivasis about various laws, and also help them to register the cases. A nation-wide demand for amendments in the PoA Act in the wake of several heinous atrocities committed against both the Adivasis and Dalits in recent times drew the attention of the government not only to take a serious note of such human rights violations, but also to bring key amendments in the Act in 2015. As a result, new offences have been added to the list of atrocities, with a shift in focus towards greater protection for Adivasis and also women from these two marginalised communities.

### Forms of atrocities

Various forms of crime are classified under different special laws. Major crimes registered under the Indian Penal Code include murder, rape, kidnapping and abduction, arson, physical hurt and other economic crimes such as dacoity, robbery and burglary. The incidence of these crimes against Adivasis has, however, not been uniform. According to the NCRB data, among various forms of crimes against Adivasis, the incidence of grievous physical hurt constituted the highest proportion followed by rape and murder. During the period 2001–14, on an average, 739 cases of physical assault, 644 cases of rape and 149 cases of murder were registered annually. But, the number of registered rape cases increased to 1,159 in 2014 from 847 in 2013. Similarly, there was a significant increase in the number of registered murder cases showing an increase from 122 cases in 2013 to 247 cases in 2014. While the number of registered cases of physical assault decreased considerably during the same period, it slightly increased in the case of kidnapping and abduction, arson and other economic crimes such as dacoity and robbery. The overall trend of crimes against Adivasis indicated that registered cases of rape and kidnapping and abduction increased over the years, but no such noticeable changes were there in other forms of crimes. The number of registered rape cases against Adivasis during 2001–14 was higher than the registered cases of murder, kidnapping and abduction, dacoity and robbery and arson put together. There were over 9,000 registered rape cases against Adivasi women over 14 years. The data, thus, indicated that Adivasi women are highly vulnerable to such atrocity.

### Regional variations in atrocities against Adivasis

The concentration of the Adivasi population widely varies across states. The central belt of India consisting of Madhya Pradesh, Maharashtra, Chhattisgarh, Jharkhand, Orissa, Gujarat and Rajasthan together account for more than two-thirds of the total Adivasi population in the country. Other major states in the central belt with moderately large Adivasi populations are Andhra Pradesh, West Bengal and Karnataka. All the northeastern states are predominantly populated by Adivasis. It may be mentioned that although substantial proportion of Adivasis lived in the northeastern part of the country, they faced lower incidence of crimes, perhaps living in a more 'unified' culture. The macro-level analysis therefore is confined to some selected states in the central belt, keeping in view the proportion of Adivasi population and registered cases of crimes against them in these states. Figure 11.2 presents data on crimes against Adivasis for nine major states with a higher percentage share of registered crimes.

The data indicated that states like Madhya Pradesh and Rajasthan, on an average, contributed about 45 per cent crimes to the total crimes against Adivasis in India annually during 2005–14. Other states which had a substantial proportion of crimes are Odisha, Andhra Pradesh and Chhattisgarh. Thus, in terms of actual number of registered crimes, these five states remained at the top of the country's crime map for Adivasis. About three-fourth of total crimes against Adivasis were registered in these five states. Other states like Karnataka, Maharashtra and Jharkhand with higher concentration of Adivasis also witnessed higher incidence of crimes.

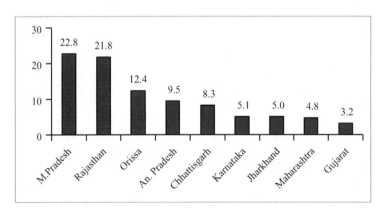

*Figure 11.2* States with percentage contribution of registered crimes to all India crimes against Adivasis

Source: Government of India (2005–14).

Note:
(1) Figures indicates annual average during 2005–2014.
(2) The figure for Andhra Pradesh in 2014 includes figure of undivided state of Andhra Pradesh though it was divided into two states in 2014.

The percentage share of crimes against Adivasis in different states to all India crimes showed slight increase for Rajasthan, Andhra Pradesh, Chhattisgarh, Karnataka and Maharashtra, whereas it slightly decreased for Madhya Pradesh, Jharkhand, Orissa and Gujarat. The proportion of registered PoA crimes to total crimes against Adivasis revealed a higher percentage of PoA crimes against Adivasis in Karnataka, Andhra Pradesh, Jharkhand, Orissa and Rajasthan.

The rate of registered crimes against Adivasis in the states (i.e. incidents of crime per 1 lakh tribal population) showed that in 2014, a distinctively higher rate of registered crimes against Adivasis was in Rajasthan. It also showed a significant increase in recent years. Other states which had a higher rate of crimes than that of the national rate were Madhya Pradesh, Odisha, Andhra Pradesh and Karnataka. The trend of rate of crimes indicated that states like Andhra Pradesh, Jharkhand, Madhya Pradesh, Maharashtra, Orissa, Rajasthan and West Bengal showed an increasing trend over the period from 2005 to 2014. A relatively higher increase in the rate of crimes was noticed in states like Madhya Pradesh, Orissa and Rajasthan.

The percentage share of the PoA crimes to total crimes against Adivasis over the years revealed interesting findings. The year 2014 witnessed a distinct pattern than the earlier years (table 11.1). It showed a significantly higher percentage share in the majority of states than previous years. In the states like Bihar, Maharashtra and Gujarat, almost

*Table 11.1* State-wise percentage share of the PoA crimes to the total crimes over the years

| States | 2005 | 2010 | 2011 | 2012 | 2013 | 2014 |
| --- | --- | --- | --- | --- | --- | --- |
| Andhra Pradesh | 38.1 | 27.9 | 28.9 | 19.1 | 18.8 | 60.4 |
| Bihar | 72.0 | 46.5 | 73.2 | 99.2 | 74.7 | 100.0 |
| Chhattisgarh | 18.7 | 26.0 | 0.3 | 0.0 | 0.0 | 65.9 |
| Gujarat | 30.8 | 21.9 | 15.0 | 29.4 | 25.9 | 97.4 |
| Jharkhand | 31.5 | 32.1 | 33.7 | 46.3 | 49.2 | 93.1 |
| Karnataka | 52.8 | 57.1 | 56.8 | 43.9 | 56.6 | 81.5 |
| Madhya Pradesh | 15.6 | 0.3 | 0.1 | 0.0 | 0.0 | 69.2 |
| Maharashtra | 23.2 | 18.8 | 19.0 | 17.2 | 10.8 | 100.0 |
| Orissa | 33.9 | 60.3 | 83.9 | 84.2 | 64.9 | 42.3 |
| Rajasthan | 10.5 | 2.0 | 1.6 | 2.3 | 1.5 | 42.5 |
| West Bengal | 25.0 | 44.7 | 46.3 | 5.5 | 21.3 | 75.9 |

Source: Crimes in India, National Crime Record Bureau, Ministry of Home Affairs, Government of India.

all the crimes against Adivasis were registered under the PoA Act. It might be noted that at all India level while less than 30 per cent of cases got registered under the PoA Act in the last decade, it increased to more than 50 per cent in 2014. In Madhya Pradesh, no crimes were recorded under the PoA Act between 2010 and 2013, but in 2014, the share of registered PoA crimes were 69 per cent. Except Odisha, which had a declining trend in PoA crimes against Adivasis in recent times, the share of the PoA crimes in other states increased significantly.

Although the official data revealed wide variations in the number of registered crimes across states, it would be noted that these state-wise variations on registered crimes against Adivasis might not reflect upon the prevalence of crimes only, rather the efficiency of the administrative system in a few states in ensuring registration of a higher number of cases. Further, proactiveness of civil society organisations and Adivasis organisations in the states might have played a significant role in registering more cases.

## Disposal of atrocities against Adivasis: access to justice

Notwithstanding the fact that there has been poor registration of atrocities against Adivasis, and there are specific Rules under the PoA Act for the speedy disposal of cases, still many cases of atrocities remain pending for investigation and court trials. The disposal of overall crimes against Adivasis by police revealed that on an average about 22 per cent of registered cases remained pending for investigation at the end of each year during 2001–14 (figure 11.3). The average annual pendency rate for PoA crimes during the corresponding period was found to be higher. The average annual chargesheet rate by police was 94 per cent during the same period. The data, thus, revealed that on an average about 6 per cent of the total registered cases were not chargesheeted by police in each year during 2001–14. It might be mentioned here that the chargesheet rates for crimes such as kidnapping and abduction, dacoity and robbery, and murder were found to be relatively lower than other forms of crimes. This might be due to the time taken for collecting evidence as these crimes normally take place under concealment.

The disposal of cases by courts was different from that by police. The data revealed that during 2001–14, the yearly pendency rate was considerably high but the conviction rate was quite low. Despite special provisions of special courts and prosecutors under the PoA Act Rule 1995 for speedy trial of atrocities, during 2001–14, on an

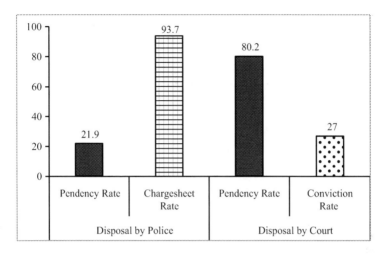

*Figure 11.3* Disposal of crimes committed against Adivasis by Police and Courts

Source: Crimes in India, National Crime Record Bureau, Ministry of Home Affairs, Government of India.

Note: Figures indicate annual average percentage over the period 2001–2014.

average, about 80 per cent of total crimes against Adivasis remained pending for trials at the end of each year. The pendency rate for the PoA crimes was found to be slightly higher. Further, the pendency rates for crimes such as arson, murder and kidnapping and abduction were relatively higher than other forms of crime. However, the matter of concern is that on an average, about 27 per cent of total crimes against Adivasis were resulted in conviction yearly. The conviction rate for the PoA crimes was even about 4 per cent lower than that of total crimes. The conviction rate for various crimes revealed that it was considerably lower for rape and arson. However, Krishnan (2009), based on the analysis of the Annual Reports on the PoA Act for the years 1999 to 2003, reported that convictions were secured in only 11 to 13 per cent of the cases that were trialled in courts.

The trend in the disposal of crimes against Adivasis indicated that the pendency rates at police stations for overall crimes slightly increased from 2001 to 2013 (figure 11.4). But there was no significant change in the pendency rate in the courts. The chargesheet rate showed considerable decrease in 2014 from previous years. On the other hand, the

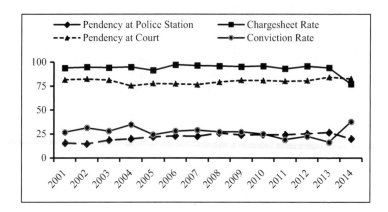

*Figure 11.4* Trend in the disposal of crimes against Adivasis by the Police and Courts, 2001–14

Source: Crimes in India, National Crime Record Bureau, Ministry of Home Affairs, Government of India.

conviction rates which were declining after 2009 showed a significant increase in 2014.

State-wise variations in the disposal of cases against Adivasis by police showed that the states like Jharkhand, Andhra Pradesh and Orissa had consistently higher percentage of pending cases for investigation at the end of the year. On the other hand, Madhya Pradesh, Chhattisgarh, Rajasthan, Karnataka and Maharashtra witnessed relatively lower percentage of pending cases. The chargesheet rate by police over the years was found higher in majority states. The disposal of cases by courts in different states showed that like the pendency rate in police stations, Jharkhand and Orissa had a higher pendency rates in courts at the end of year than the national pendency rate, besides other states like Gujarat, Karnataka and Maharashtra. State-wise variations in conviction rates indicated that in Gujarat, Karnataka, Maharashtra and Andhra Pradesh it was significantly lower over the years. On the other hand, the states like Chhattisgarh, Jharkhand, Madhya Pradesh and Rajasthan had relatively higher conviction rates. Evidence suggests that the factors such as lack of awareness among victims about laws, difficulty in access to state machinery, complexities in administrative processes etc. slow down the processes of investigation and court trials. The lower conviction rate across states reflect a dismal picture in the functioning of the criminal justice system in the states, which is also believed to be one of the reasons for perpetuating crimes against Adivasis.

## Atrocities against Adivasis: an analysis at micro-level

The official data on atrocities against Adivasis do not reflect on the actual magnitude of atrocities due to non-registration or under-registration of many cases of atrocities. Under the disguise of many forest-related laws, Adivasis remain vulnerable to exploitations, abuses and repressions. Many of them are subjected to structured violence of different kinds perpetuated by the state officials like forest department officials, police personnel and civil administration officials; often in cohort with the local political leaders, timber mafia, moneylenders, contractors and other influential persons in society. An attempt is made in this section to highlight some patterns of atrocities against Adivasis, the role of various state actors in these atrocities and other critical issues based on evidence drawn from over 100 individual cases of atrocities against Adivasis collected from media reports and fact-finding documents of non-governmental organisations pertaining to the period from 2008 to 2010. The results clearly indicated that structural atrocities by state forest officials, police, paramilitary forces, armed opposition groups were prominent. Unlike atrocities against Dalits where the main perpetrators are dominant caste groups, in case of atrocities against Adivasis, the main perpetrators were police officials and special security forces, constituting about 40 per cent of the total perpetrators. Forest officials were involved in about 10 per cent of cases of atrocities against Adivasis whereas officials from other departments were involved in another 4 per cent of cases. While in about 20 per cent of cases, the perpetrators were members from the dominant caste groups, in another 5 per cent of cases both dominant caste members and police personnel were offenders. Furthermore, in 6 per cent of cases, the perpetrators constituted leaders/activists. Notably, in 14 per cent of cases, Adivasis were victims of the actions of Maoists/Naxalites, and militant outfits particularly in northeastern states.

In the name of laws, the common forms of atrocities that the state officials commit against Adivasis include killings/murder, arbitrary arrests, illegal detentions, torture, custodial and extrajudicial killings, destruction of properties, rape and other acts of awful cruelty. Of the total cases, one-fourth were associated with killing or murder, whereas 20 per cent were rape and gang rape cases, 13 per cent with humiliation and insult, 11 per cent with physical assault and torture, and 7 per cent each with sexual exploitation and kidnapping and abduction. In about 40 per cent of the cases, there were individual victims and in another 17 per cent of cases there were two victims. Notably, in about one-third of cases, the number of victims was found to be more than ten persons, of which, in the majority of cases, it was either a group of Adivasis families or members of a whole Adivasi community.

An examination of the contexts of atrocities against Adivasis revealed that about one-third of the cases were linked to police excesses under an 'atmosphere of suspicion and intimidation' (branding/suspecting as Naxals/Maoists or their sympathisers/supporters during anti-Maoists operations, encounters between police and Maoists etc.). In about 27 per cent of cases, atrocities were committed on protests by Adivasis against illegal acts of officials or non-fulfilment of demands on development issues or demand for release of arrested/jailed Adivasis and forced eviction from forestland. In 9 per cent of cases, Adivasis were suspected on petty issues (e.g. theft, use forest resources, as activists etc.). Among other cases, 11 per cent were linked to sexual exploitation/outraging modesty, 5 per cent to 'going against wishes of dominant caste' and 11 per cent to repressive behaviours by Maoists and others relating to revenge taking, non-payment of loan, discriminations, pointless harassments etc. Thus, more than three-fourth of the cases were linked to the oppressive behaviours of different state officials.

There is numerous evidence of violations pertaining to different rights of Adivasis by different actors. Some of the cases of atrocities against Adivasis perpetuated by different state actors in the name of law as well as non-Dalits/Adivasis during 2008–10 are presented in the following sections to understand the causal dynamics and other interrelated issues pertaining to atrocities against Adivasis.

## *Repression under laws*

In recent years, one of the major concerns has been the state violence against Adivasis. Krishna Iyer (2010) views that 'even the judiciary and executive treat Adivasis as the fourth world within the third world', signifying how the rule of law in the state blinks at them and Adivasis, as a micro-community, remain victims of social deprivation. In terms of perpetrators, when it comes to committing direct atrocities against Adivasi communities, forest officials and civil administration are involved in many cases of atrocities under the rule of state law. They are involved in illegal acts in the name of implementation of 'forest law and order'. They use their official power under the law in the area to prevent Adivasis from asserting their rights to forest resources. Atrocities that they perpetrate against Adivasis include arrest for accessing minor forest produce, eviction from their forest lands, and forcing to migrate with constant torture and threaten. Officials are also involved in supplying false information or evidence to police officials, causing them to act against Adivasis. They also pass false information to protect other non-Adivasi perpetrators. Adivasis are often suspected to be smugglers of forest products with an outside nexus. Sometimes, official control over traditional life resources of Adivasi communities make Adivasis feel helpless, and they have fear of retaliatory acts from them. There are many instances where the laws are misused to impose violence on Adivasis. A few cases in point are illustrated, as follows:

> On 11 January 2008, a team from forest department swooped in on two villages in Burhanpur district, Madhya Pradesh, to evict the Adivasis from land occupied by them for almost 30 years. Adivasis faced the destruction of their houses and looting of their property. Instead of punitive action against the forest department personnel responsible for inciting violence and terrorising the hapless Adivasis, in the name of carrying out inquiry, the officials got scot free. Angry Adivasis protest against such atrocities.
> 
> (*The Hindu* 2008a)
>
> In two villages in Harda district, Madhya Pradesh, land titles were issued to some of the residents with no proper process. When other residents complained against arbitrary practices, they were prevented from cultivating plots that they had been operating for a number of years. Such actions by forest departments were aimed at establishing that the plots have not been under cultivation by the villagers and thus deny residents to obtain an ownership to their lands. In the process, there had been intimidations, registration of false cases, repeated attacks, detention and arrests of residents in the two villages, leading to continued violence. This was confirmed by the fact-finding team who found the flawed implementation of the Forest Rights Act, 2006 and repeated atrocities on Adivasis by officials of the State forest department in the district.
>
> (*Central Chronicle* 2009)

In Tamil Nadu, more than 1500 Adivasis from several villages living generation after generation on the hill, took out massive rally and staged a demonstration before the district authority demanding adequate protection to the life and property. They expressed grave concern over the persistent threat from forest officials on the hill.

*(The Hindu* 2010a)

## Terrorisation by police and security forces

Another powerful force who violates Adivasis' right to security of life through perpetuation of atrocities against them is the police and special task forces where they are in operation in Adivasis areas. The perpetrators are being part of the law and order machinery; they easily inflict a sense of helplessness. According to the Government of India (2004), in areas affected by insurgency and Naxalite activities, the Adivasis face dual violence – from dominant caste (caste-Hindu) landlords, who often have private militias and from the state. The two operate with a certain degree of nexus but with different motivations. The Report also points that the police and security agencies in the name of maintaining public order while carrying out combing operations to check the growth of insurgency tend to unleash violence on residents of Adivasi villages. The police machinery often resorts to various machinations to inflict violence directly besides playing a role in shielding other dominant caste accused. The common strategies used against Adivasis are illegal detention, arbitrary arrests, torture, custodial killing and extrajudicial killings. There are also instances where Adivasis directly face excesses and violence of police and security forces. Often Adivasis with no faults are caught between security forces and militant groups. A few illustrations of gross human right violations against Adivasis by policy/security force are as follows:

The residents of 19 Adivasis villages in Manipur protested against the killings by police and security forces, what the latter term as 'encounter killings'. The Adivasis demanded to bring an end to the actions of the security forces who bring people out of village and kill them in custody.

*(The Telegraph* 2008)

In North Cachar Hills district of Southern Assam, at least 40 houses belonging to one Adivasi group was burnt down by unidentified militants, leaving about 160 Adivasis homeless. The Security Personnel had taken away the licensed guns of affected villagers. The miscreants took advantage of the situation. One week earlier, at least five Adivasis were killed and 10 injured by separatist militants who set ablaze an entire village in this trouble-torn district. With the incidences, many continued to flee from this Hill district and took shelter in another district of an adjacent state.

(*Kangla Online* 2009)

Hundreds of Adivasis families caught in the crossfire between security forces and Maoists in the vast forest terrain of Dantewada district of Chhattisgarh. Many deserted their homes in anticipation of an intensified conflict after the Maoists massacred 75 Central Reserve Police Force (CRPF) troopers and one policeman. With the anticipation that CRPF might attack their villages and other areas of forest where the troopers had a night stay before being killed by Maoists, a fear ran deep in the minds of these Adivasis and they fled away.

(*Deccan Herald* 2010)

In Koraput district of Orissa, 17 Adivasis were detained for questioning after an exchange of crossfire between Maoists and Security Forces. Adivasis were picked up as a part of a joint operation conducted by the police of Orissa and Andhra Pradesh along the inter-state boarder and held in custody for three days. They were also brutally assaulted in custody, interrogated on the movement of Maoists companies.

(*The Hindu* 2010b)

*Atrocities against Adivasi girls and women: soft targets*

The women from minority communities always remain targets of violence and atrocities, as a strategy by perpetrators to subjugate the communities (Pal 2014, 2016). Large-scale violations of Adivasi women's rights can be evidenced by the significant increase in the incidence of registered rape cases against Adivasi women over the years. Gender atrocities against Adivasi women normally takes place in the form of physical assault, sexual abuse and exploitation and sexual harassment. A study by Aloysius and Mangubhai (2003) revealed that these offences are mainly committed by non-Adivasis, forest officials, revenue officials, police, estate/farm owners, moneylenders and security forces. Further, the study revealed that the main perpetrators of physical assault against Adivasi women were forest officials whereas other non-Adivasis were perpetrators of sexual exploitation and sexual harassment. State officials and police look for opportunities to visit houses under some pretexts, particularly when the male members remain out of village. Adivasi women sometimes have to bear the brunt of state officials' actions when the latter are in search of their husbands on several false accusations. However, many cases of gender atrocities are not reported, and even where reported, they are not registered by the police. The main reason for this non-reporting is fear of retaliation by non-Adivasis, fear of losing their jobs or wages, poverty entailing dependence on forest officials or market traders to secure their livelihood, or feelings of shame especially in cases of sexual exploitation.

Given the higher vulnerability of Adivasi women to broad-ranging of gender atrocities on the one hand, and indifferent attitude of the 'law and order' machinery, on the other, the sense of insecurities among Adivasi communities always get heightened. Some cases of such atrocities are presented here to understand the vulnerability of Adivasis girls and women to different forms of atrocities at the hands of the law enforcement personnel, the armed opposition groups, local leadership and dominant caste villagers among others.

> A 10 year-old tribal girl was raped by a cop in a remote village of Giridih district in Jharkhand =while the cops were in the village for an anti-Maoist operation. The incidence took place when the girl had gone to collect firewood along with her six-year-old brother. While a group of three policemen were involved in the incidence, two of them kept her brother in their custody and one policeman took the girl to the nearby jungle. When the girl did not return home after several hours, the mother of the girls with other neighbours traced the girls in jungle and found the girl unconscious. The three cops gave Rs. 500 to her younger brother not to disclose the incident. The accused was later arrested and suspended following a complaint by the victim's family.
>
> (*Times of India* 2008a)

> Two Adivasi teenaged girls were gang-raped by four special police officers in Dantewada district of Chhattisgarh. The victims allegedly were whisked away from the huts when they were living in with parents, and were taken into the

forests and raped. While villagers could catch hold one of the accused, three others who were in possession of weapons fled the place after the incident. Under the Adivasi Mahasabha, a road blockade was organised to lodge a protest at local police station seeking action against the accused. However, instead of taking immediate action against the accused, police forces were deployed in the town to control the tribal protests.

*(The Hindu* 2008b)

In Damoh district of Madhya Pradesh, a 15 year old girl was burnt to death by a policeman's son when she resisted his rape attempt. The victim was alone at her house when the son of a constable forcibly entered and tried to rape her. When the girl opposed, the accused allegedly poured kerosene over her and set her afire making the victim succumbed to burn injuries.

*(The Hindu* 2010c)

Despite the fact that majority of Adivasi population stay away from mainstream society, girls and women form Adivasi communities remain vulnerable to atrocities committed by dominant caste members and local leaders. Due to the social power and close association with local administration and police, the perpetuators sometimes escape after committing atrocities due to the police inaction even after being informed about such atrocities. Some of the incidents are as follows:

An Adivasi girl was gang-raped in front of her family in Theni district, Tamil Nadu by a group of three upper caste people. The accused dragged the girl into a nearby mango groove and a three member gang raped her. When her parents tried to intervene, the accused brandished weapons and threatened to kill them. When the victim's parents approached the police station, a woman constable discouraged them from pursuing the case. The family of victim fled the village and stayed with a relative in a nearby village. However, police registered a case against the accused after about one month of the incidence when the victim gathered courage to register a complaint and informed about the incidence to a human rights organisation to take up the issue. On the other hand, the police constable entrusted with the petition enquiry along with others advised parents of victims, not to antagonise caste-Hindus (dominant castes) in the area. However, with the intervention of a local

> human rights organisation, a special team led by a higher police official investigated the case and booked the accused under the PoA Act.
>
> (*The Hindu* 2008c)

> In another case, cops inaction against molestation led a 13 year old Adivasi girl committed suicide. The victim in her suicide note charged the police refusing to take action against the accused who tried to outrage her modesty. The local police and Tehsildar who conducted an enquiry into girl's complaint declared as false case. It was allegedly reported that this investigating officials following oral complaints from the girl tried to sort out the issue amicably. However, based on the official committee report on girl's charges, no case was registered. Being upset with police decision, the girl committed suicide by jumping into the village well.
>
> (*Times of India* 2008b)

### *Power and dominance by local leaders/village council*

Local leadership mainly in the hands of dominant caste groups plays a pivotal role in perpetuating atrocities against Adivasi girls and women. These atrocities are taken as strategies to keep Adivasis caught up in a culture of fear, silence and submission so that they are prevented from asserting or voicing their rights which would go against their vested interests and in turn would help them to hold on to their authority. The power and dominance by local leadership can be understood from some cases of atrocities against Adivasi women, as follows:

> On 28 May 2008, two tribal women (identified as two sisters), one being a minor, were raped by two persons. The victims alleged that the local village heads conducted an inquiry and offered Rs. 2,000 to them as compensation for the act and advised them to settle the issue. The accused were not punished. The police filed cases against the accused following the help of a non-governmental organisation.
>
> (*The Hindu* 2008d)

> In Sirohi district of Rajasthan, an Adivasi woman was seriously injured after being tortured allegedly at the order of the Village Panchayat (village council) which found the victim

guilty of being a 'witch'. She was summoned to the Village Panchayat court on the charge of killing two persons by her witchcraft. The Village Panchayat allegedly directed the victim to undergo an 'Agnipareeksha' (trial by fire) test by dipping her hands twice in a vessel filled with boiling oil to retrieve a silver coin to prove her innocence. If she could retrieve the coin, her innocence would be proved, otherwise she would be held guilty. When she refused to undergo the test, she was allegedly beaten up with hot iron rods.

(ACHR 2009: 169)

A 19 year old Adivasi teacher was held captive, raped and burnt allegedly by a local leader in Jhabua district of Madhya Pradesh. The leader held her captive for two days during which he raped and set her on fire.

(*Times of India* 2010)

Many times, Adivasis face atrocities while demanding for their rights. They are not only denied their rights but also made to suffer through various oppressive behaviours. One such case in point was seen where:

Six persons from non-Adivasi communities in Madhya Pradesh, including the husband of a female village 'sarpanch' were arrested for allegedly forcing two Adivasis to consume human excreta in full public view for demanding job cards under the MNREGS. The victims while approached the husband of village sarpanch who handles all her official affairs and sought their job cards under the scheme, infuriated by their demand, the sarpanch's husband and his other five associates forced them to consume human excreta in front of the villagers.

(*Indian Express* 2008)

To sum, Adivasis are made to suffer from human rights violations in two ways – denial of civil rights and atrocities. In both the situations, Adivasis have to suffer physically and mentally. But the increased number of atrocities by law enforcement personnel makes them to live under constant fear and sometimes forces them to migrate from their traditional territory. But 'According to the Asian Indigenous and Tribal Peoples Network's Report (2009), more than four lakh Adivasis have been displaced due to extremists' activities by Maoists in various parts of India. These displaced Adivasis have been living miserable lives without basic amenities . . . and livelihood opportunities' (*Hindustan Times* 2009).

## Atrocities against Adivasis and Dalits: a comparative perspective

Although the Adivasis face many problems similar to that of the Dalits, the nature, magnitude and causes of atrocities against these marginalised groups vary. The officially registered data suggests that Adivasis are subjected to atrocities but not to the same extent as Dalits. As evident, atrocities against Dalits are about five to six times larger in number than those against the Adivasis, although the population of Dalits is only about twice as large as that of the Adivasis. However, it should be noted that the proportion of different forms of atrocities against these groups and the main perpetrators are different. Adivasis are more prone to arson, destruction of property and rape as compared to Dalits. The registered cases of various forms of atrocities against Dalits and Adivasis revealed that the proportion of these atrocities against Dalits was about two times higher than Adivasis, whereas other atrocities were higher by more than four times.

While atrocities against Dalits are regularly reported from almost every part of the country over the years, there has been a significant increase of atrocities against Adivasis in recent years, where the Naxalite movement is especially active (National Commission for Scheduled Tribes 2010). Although women of both Dalits and Adivasi communities face denial of justice on the ground of gender, unlike Dalit women who face atrocities largely of dominant castes, Adivasi women face atrocities at the hands of the law enforcement personnel, the armed opposition groups and village Panchayats due to their isolated living conditions.

So far as the causes of atrocities against the two groups are concerned, Dalits are vulnerable to atrocities mainly due to the 'traditional caste practices' coupled with economic dependence on other social groups. They are largely being a part of the Indian hierarchical mainstream society and face the dominance of caste-Hindu in an attempt to rise against the social oppression. On the other hand, Adivasis remain vulnerable to exploitations and abuses under the disguise of many forest-related laws. The intersection and flawed implementation of the Forest Rights Act (2006) and the PoA Act make the Adivasis more vulnerable to exploitation. Although atrocities against the Adivasis are included in the list of offences under the PoA Act, many of the offences are not directly addressed under the provisions. Subramanian (2009) argues that although the development process has contributed significantly to the increasing atrocities against both Dalits and Adivasis, for Dalits, it is the socio-economic mobility of the community that breaks the power relations between communities whereas for Adivasis, it is the state development process that distorts the livelihood of Adivasis, and any resistance leads to atrocities committed by official agencies colluded with powerful members of society. Many of the atrocities against Adivasis, thus, arose from the development process itself. A study by National Commission for Scheduled Castes and Scheduled Tribes (Government of India 1990) revealed that many atrocities against Adivasis were related to land. The predatory expansion of non-Adivasis into Adivasi areas and the dispossession of Adivasis through fraud, debt and other means was a continual source of violence and atrocities against Adivasis. Similarly, the Ministry of Rural Development (Government of India 2009) points that interfering with Adivasis rights over land has been the important factor of atrocities against them.

With the implementation of the Forest Right Act atrocities very often are submerged with the influence of administration mechanisms. While the role of the dominant caste in committing atrocities against Dalits is widely recognised, Adivasis in their territories are subjected to atrocities not in the hand of this dominant social group but of police and other officials when they protect their age-old traditional rights and resources. However, often they face this type of atrocities at the behest of non-Adivasi influential persons like traders, estate owner etc., who under the government rules try to own the resources occupied by Adivasis. As atrocities in police action is not covered by the PoA Act, 1989, the non-Adivasi members escape from any legal action against them. In many cases, Adivasis, because of lack of awareness of the legislations such as the Forest Rights Act and the PoA Act, are not able to take advantage of the laws. Lack of access to administration and community support due to their unorganised living pattern also put them into a position of helplessness in the face of exploitation. Moreover, as in the case of Dalits, the human rights movement is very weak among Adivasis to make the administration to be responsive. Incidences of atrocities against Dalits, by and large, take place in the mainstream society, easily draw attention of the media, public and administration, hence remains in the limelight. But atrocities against Adivasis do not find due space in the media domain. Although many cases of atrocities against Adivasis are documented by non-governmental organisations in the tribal belt, the information remains confined to knowledge of local administration and becomes a neglected agenda of human rights violations.

## Conclusion

Analysis of atrocities against Adivasis from both macro and micro perspectives suggest that atrocities of different natures have been an integral feature of Adivasis life. They are more vulnerable to exploitations and specific forms of atrocities. Due to the geographical isolation and lack of constant sources of livelihood, their socio-economic lives, to a larger extent, are governed by multiple administrative authorities. As a majority of Adivasis follow their traditional lifestyles, the lack of awareness of legislations, specifically about the Forest Rights Act and the PoA Act, make them vulnerable to face the excesses of officials in the local governance such as forest officials, policemen, revenue officials, and other officials at the local level administration. In many cases of atrocities, the members of the law enforcement agencies themselves are being the offenders. Adivasis are not in a strong position to take advantages of protective legislations meant for the fulfilment of their rights. They have to depend upon the mercy of local officials to use the forest resources, hence, any assertive behaviours are treated as offences under law.

From the perspective of legal safeguards, the PoA Act which attempts to curb the atrocities against Dalits and Adivasis through various clauses has not been equally meaningful for these two groups. Unlike Dalits, in many cases of atrocities faced by Adivasis, the members of government security forces and other state administrative officials have been the biggest abusers of their rights and privileges. Many offences committed by these state actors are not directly addressed in various sections of the PoA Act. Based on the views of a large number of social activists who have taken up tribal issues from within the communities as well as from outside, Mahaprashasta (2009) points that 'the PoA Act which has attempted to include the exploitation of the Scheduled Tribes in its list of "atrocities", does not actually address the specifics and the unique dimensions of the problems faced by these communities'. It is argued that the act needs to be amended in order to address the issues of Adivasis specifically. While reviewing the implementation of the PoA Act and other related issues, National Commission for Scheduled Tribes (2010) suggests that there is a need of specific provisions under the PoA for Adivasis as these groups very often do not face atrocities for the reasons similar to Dalits. Notwithstanding limitations in the existing law, state government has a constitutional duty to protect Adivasis communities from exploitation and social injustice. The major obstacles to implementation of laws have been the primary enforcers of the legislations. The state being an actor by itself or in collusion with non-state actors has failed to a large extent to fulfil its responsibility in protecting rights of Adivasis. This asks for addressing the structural roots of atrocities and strengthening institutional mechanisms aimed at addressing issues of atrocities against Adivasis. Given the large-scale rights violations against Adivasis, it is significant to monitor the situation of implementation of existing law vis-à-vis protection of human rights of Adivasis vigorously.

The exploitations and harassments faced by Adivasis very often do not get well manifested in different forms of crimes. Despite the numerous forms of atrocities being inflicted on Adivasis by various actors both at societal and state levels, a majority of cases are not registered because they are prevented by powerful perpetrator groups. Atrocities faced by Adivasis therefore remain highly implicit. Considering that several rights violations interplay to influence the livelihood and security of life of Adivasis, and perpetrators of violation of rights are mainly 'actors with power', these restrict the 'access to justice' for many victims of atrocities. Efforts of Adivasis to gain justice following atrocities are further suppressed by the indifferent attitudes and negligence of state machinery. All these create social conditions which perpetuate the cycle of violations of rights of Adivasis.

# References

ACHR. 2009. *Indian Human Rights Report, 2009*. New Delhi: Asian Centre for Human Rights (ACHR).

Aloysius, I. S. J. and J. Mangubhai. 2003. *Adivasis Speak Out: Atrocities Against Adivasis in Tamil Nadu*. Bangalore: Books for Change.

Asian Indigenous and Tribal Peoples Network. 2009. *The State of India's Indigenous and Tribal Peoples*. New Delhi: Asian Indigenous and Tribal Peoples Network.

*Central Chronicle*. 2009. 'Atrocities on Tribals in Harda: Fact-Finding Team', 10 September.

*Deccan Herald*. 2010. 'Chhattisgarh Tribes Caught in Crossfire', 13 April.

Gill, K., R. Bhattacharya and S. Bhattacharya. 2015. *The Political Economy of Capitalism, Development and Resistance: The State and Adivasis of India*. New Delhi: Oxfam India.

Government of India. 1976. *The Protection of Civil Rights (PCR) Act. 1976. Act No. BC.12013/2/76-SCT-V, Dated 15 September*. New Delhi: Ministry of Social Welfare and Empowerment.

Government of India. 1989. *The Scheduled Castes and Scheduled Tribes (Prevention of Atrocities) Act. 1989. Act No.33, Dated 11 September*. New Delhi: Ministry of Social Welfare and Empowerment.

Government of India. 1990. *Atrocities Against Scheduled Castes and Scheduled Tribes: Causes and Remedies*. New Delhi: National Commission for Scheduled Castes and Scheduled Tribes.

Government of India. 1995. *The Scheduled Castes and Scheduled Tribes (Prevention of Atrocities) Act Rules. 1995.G.S.R 316E, Dated 31 March*. New Delhi: Ministry of Social Welfare and Empowerment.

Government of India. 2004. *Report on Trafficking in Women and Children in India 2002–3*. New Delhi: National Human Rights Commission.

Government of India. 2005–14. *Crimes in India*. New Delhi: National Crime Record Bureau (NCRB).

Government of India. 2009. *Annual Report, 2007–08*. New Delhi: Ministry of Rural Development.

*Hindustan Times*. 2009. 'Maoists Activities Displaced 4 Lakh Tribals: Report', 25 May.

*Indian Express*. 2008. 'Tribals Forced to Eat Excreta for "Demanding Job Card"', 29 January.

*Kangla Online*. 2009. 'Forty Houses of Tribals Torched in Southern Assam', 10 June.

Krishna Iyer, V. R. 2010. 'Atrocities on Adivasis', *Outlook*, 26 August: 1–4.

Krishnan, P. S. 2009. 'Walls in Minds', *Frontline*, 26(24): 25–8.

Mahaprashasta, A. A. 2009. 'High and Dry', *Frontline*, 26(24): 22–4.

National Coalition for Strengthening SCs and STs (Prevention of Atrocities) Act. 2010. *Report Card: 20 Years Scheduled Castes and Scheduled Tribes (Prevention of Atrocities) Act*. New Delhi: National Campaign for Dalit Human Rights.

National Commission for Scheduled Tribes. 2010. *Minutes of the Meeting of National Commission for Scheduled Tribes with Senior Officials of Chhattisgarh Government to Review the Implementation of SCs and STs (PoA) Act and Other Related Issues*, 23 April. Raipur: Chhattisgarh.

Pal, G. C. 2014. 'Access to Justice: Social Ostracism Obstructs Efforts By Dalits for Equal Rights', *Journal of Social Inclusion Studies*, 1(1): 122–34.

Pal, G. C. 2016. 'Caste-Gender Intersectionality, Atrocities and Social Dominance', Paper presented in the *National Conference on Examining Intersections: Caste/Gender Narratives in India*, 8–10 February. Kolkata: Institute of Development Studies.

Pal, G. C. and L. D. Lal. 2010. *Mapping Caste Atrocities Against Dalits: A Status Report*. Project Report. New Delhi: Indian Institute of Dalit Studies.

Saravanan, V. 2010. 'Subalterns vs. State Institution: Politician, State, Forest, Law and Atrocities on Tribals in Tamil Nadu, 1990–2000', *International Journal of Human Rights*, 16 August: 1744–53.

Subramanian, K. S. 2009. *Political Violence and the Police in India*. New Delhi: Sage Publications.

*The Hindu*. 2008a. 'Angry Tribals Protest Against Atrocities', 22 January.

*The Hindu*. 2008b. 'Gang Rape: Tribals Stage Road Blockade', 17 June.

*The Hindu*. 2008c. 'Police File Case of Rape of Tribal Girl in Theni District', 4 June.

*The Hindu*. 2008d. 'Case Against Two for Raping Women', 30 May.

*The Hindu*. 2010a. 'Protect Our Life: Tribals', 19 January.

*The Hindu*. 2010b. 'Adivasis Allege Torture in Anti-Naxal Operations', 18 May.

*The Hindu*. 2010c. 'Cop's Son Allegedly Sets Tribal Girl Afire for Resisting Rape', 22 March.

*The Telegraph*. 2008. 'Tribals of Sadar Hills Protest Against Violence', 17 November.

*Times of India*. 2008a. 'Constable Rapes 10-Year-Old, Tribals Protest', 26 January.

*Times of India*. 2008b. 'Cops Inaction Drives Tribal Girl to Suicide', 14 September.

*Times of India*. 2010. 'Tribal Teacher Held Captive, Raped, Burnt in Madhya Pradesh', 7 February.

# 12
# EXCLUSION AND PERSISTENCE OF POVERTY AMONG ADIVASIS IN INDIA
## A disaggregated analysis

*Amaresh Dubey*

The objective of this chapter is to document the level of living and poverty incidence among the Adivasis[1] at the aggregate level as well as at the level of districts in India. It is well documented that the well-being of social groups in India differs. Recent research has tried to quantify the disparities across population groups. As a population group, Scheduled Tribes (STs) are at the bottom on a range of development indicators including consumption and poverty, and disparities with other groups are reported to be worsening (de Haan and Dubey 2005; de Haan *et al.* 2009; GOI 2007; Newman and Thorat 2010; Desai and Dubey 2011). However, in a more recent study, Thorat and Dubey (2012)[2] show that though the Adivasis continue to be at the bottom of the development ladder with the highest level of poverty incidence during 2009–10, during 2004–05 to 2009–10, the pace of poverty reduction among *Adivasis has accelerated significantly*. This chapter further substantiates this point, but also brings in further disaggregation with respect to the STs highlighting the need for more context-specific understanding of deprivations.

The recent literature also suggests that certain population groups identifiable by their caste, religion and ethnicity have not been able to participate in the growth process (GoI 2006). The two main population groups identifiable from the data are the untouchables or *Scheduled Castes* (SCs) and the *STs*.[3] The SCs are the larger group of the two, accounting for nearly 17 per cent of the Indian population and their underdevelopment is attributed to social exclusion as a direct consequence of the Hindu social order. The other excluded group is the STs (also called *Adivasis* or Tribals), accounting for about 9 per cent of the Indian population, but have been excluded even from the detailed analysis that the SC has received in recent times. While some of the STs, if not all, have remained outside the purview of the rigid Hindu hierarchal social order, in terms of the welfare indicators, they are, on the average lower than even the SCs.

Though scattered over the geographical domain of India, there are regions where STs have moderate to very high concentration. It is argued that their exclusion is a consequence of geographical isolation as these groups inhabit areas that are not easily accessible. There are thousands of such groups scattered across the length and breadth of India with a diverse socio-cultural, ethnic and even economic organisation. In this chapter we focus on the deprivations among the Adivasis, especially in consumption and poverty. The analyses are reported at the aggregate as well as the disaggregated level across the districts with varying levels of ST population concentration.

The rest of the chapter is organised in the following fashion. In the next section, a brief description of the data used and distribution of ST population is discussed. This is followed by description of the level of living and poverty incidence among STs vis-à-vis other (OTH) population groups at aggregate level in section three. In section four, the analyses is extended to disaggregated level. In section five, the results of decomposition of change in poverty into growth and distribution is reported. Findings of the chapter and policy issues are summarised in section six.

## Data-related issues

Analyses in this chapter is based on the household level National Sample Survey Organisation (NSSO) data on consumption expenditure collected during the three most recent and comparable round of surveys, 50th, 61st and 66th. The reference periods are July 1993 to June 1994, July 2004 to June 2005 and July 2009 to June 2010. The households in these surveys are selected using a stratified sampling design. Therefore, weights or multipliers are an integral part of the data (GoI 1983).[4]

The quinquennial rounds of NSSO surveys cover almost the entire territory of India except some inaccessible areas that are less than 0.01 per cent of the Indian Territory and have an even lower proportion of population. In general, for geographical domains, NSS data does not permit analyses at a lower than NSS regional. And even at the

NSS region or for smaller states, it is often not possible to calculate poverty and other indicators by socio-religious groups. Keeping this limitation of the data in mind, we have looked at the concentration of Adivasi population across districts in India. Based on the share of ST population, we could divide the districts in six mutually exclusive groups as reported in table 12.1.

It is apparent from the table that 21 per cent of the districts (94 out of 453) in 1991 do not have a single ST household. Another 36 per cent of the districts have 5 per cent or less of ST population and only 51 districts (just over 12 per cent of the total districts) have 50 per cent or more ST population with only about 30 districts with 75 per cent or more ST population.[5] In this last category, most of the districts belong to northeastern states except Jhabua district in Madhya Pradesh that has about 86 per cent ST population and is located in the central part of India.

From the distribution of ST population across districts, it emerges that unlike the distribution of SCs among the districts in most of India, the ST population is concentrated only in a few, just about 50–60 districts (as per 1991 census districts). Also, unlike SCs who have no numerical majority in any of the districts, STs are in the majority in about 50 districts (as per 1991 census). One of the hypotheses in the recent literature points at the caste dominance[6] as one of the leading factors in determining the participation in growth. The varying degree of concentration of ST population among districts provides an opportunity to test this hypotheses in the case of STs.

*Sample size*

We are using household level consumption expenditure data to measure poverty and malnutrition at the disaggregated level. Given that

*Table 12.1* Distribution of population STs across districts (census)

| Pop share of STs | Distribution of dist (no.) | Per cent of districts |
|---|---|---|
| Nil | 94 | 20.8 |
| 0.1 to 5 | 165 | 36.4 |
| 5 to 10 | 44 | 9.7 |
| 10 to 20 | 52 | 11.5 |
| 20 to 50 | 47 | 10.4 |
| 50 to 75 | 21 | 4.6 |
| 75 to 100 | 30 | 6.6 |

Source: Tabulation by the author from Census of India, 1991 district data.

the households in NSSO surveys are selected through a stratified sampling design, the probability of the ST households being in the NSS sample in a large number of districts is very small as shown in table 12.1. Therefore, for an analysis of ST deprivations, we clubbed together the districts based on the share of population estimated from NSS unit level data.

Estimated population shares and sample sizes across social groups (comparable in 50th, 61st and 66th round) is reported in table 12.2. In column 1 of the table, numbers indicate ST population share, with 5 indicating 50 per cent or more ST population in the district. It is to be noted that districts in category five are scattered across India. However, a closer scrutiny suggests location-wise two very distinct groups emerge, districts located among the states in the northeastern region and districts located in the so-called major states.

Though there are a few recent studies that estimate the district level consumption and poverty incidence (Bhandari and Dubey 2009; Chaudhuri and Gupta 2009), there are some words of caution here. First, districts in India have been undergoing constant reorganisation. As a result, the number of districts and the geographical domain of a large number of districts in the data during the three quinquennial rounds of surveys is vastly different. Moreover, given the NSSO sampling strategy, there are many districts where sample sizes are too small (e.g. there are 64 districts in the 61st round survey that have a total of less than 100 households selected for the survey which was depleted even further during the 66th round). In order to have comparable geographical areas with adequate sample size for calculation of the statistic of interest, therefore, we have resorted to combining contiguous districts. There are about 43 'districts'[7] (created by merging out of a total of 127 districts) for which the results are reported in this chapter.

### Measures of deprivation

For the measurement of poverty, there are two indispensable requirements, welfare profile of the population and poverty norm. In this chapter household consumption expenditure data, arguably the best suited for measuring level of living and poverty, collected by the NSSO is used. The other requirement, a suitable poverty norm, is contentious. Several aspects of the poverty norm – its specification, spatial variation, adjustment for temporal change and spatial variation in prices – have been hotly debated (Dubey and Palmer-Jones 2005a; 2005b; 2005c).[8] Keeping clear of these issues, the poverty norm used by the Planning Commission, Government of India for calculating poverty incidence for 1993–94 and 2004–05 is used. For 2009–10, the 2004–05 Planning Commission PLs have been updated using appropriate price indexes as recommended in GoI (1993).[9]

We have converted the nominal PCTEs at constant (1993–94) prices. The price deflator that we used to convert the household expenditure at constant prices is the implicit price deflator derived from the state-wise poverty line for two sectors separately. This is equivalent to deriving a deflator using state and sector-wise CPIs. The value of deflator is defined as

$$Def_t = \frac{PL_t}{PL_{1993-94}}$$

In this chapter the incidence of poverty in the two sectors and among different social groups is captured using only one measure, Head Count Ratio (HCR).[10]

In addition to measurement of consumption expenditure and poverty incidence, we report summary measure of inequality, Gini coefficient. Further, in recent times, researchers have decomposed changes in incidence of poverty attributable to growth and distribution components. In this chapter we report the result of this exercise for the period 1993–94 and 2004–05.

## Consumption and poverty incidence: the macro picture

It has been pointed out above that there are several studies in recent times that report poverty incidence and level of living by socio-religious groups. In one of the most recent chapters, Thorat and Dubey (2012) report that though Adivasis continue to have the highest level of poverty incidence in 2009–10, the rate of expenditure growth and poverty reduction has been quite different over different time periods (see appendix tables 12.9 and 12.10). While during the 1980s, the rate of consumption expenditure growth and poverty reduction has been higher, the 1990s appear to have been worst as far as STs are concerned. However, during 2004–05 to 2009–10, the consumption expenditure growth and reduction in poverty among the STs accelerated significantly (tables 12.1 and 12.2).

However, the story at the disaggregated level has been quite different (de Haan et al 2009). In table 12.2, the mean per capita consumption

*Table 12.2* Sample size by population distribution of STs

| Share ST pop | ST | SC | OTH | Total |
|---|---|---|---|---|
| | | 66th round | | |
| 0 | na | 2,942 | 11,685 | 14,631 |
| 1 | 936 | 7,888 | 36,827 | 45,647 |
| 2 | 639 | 1,860 | 7,780 | 10,279 |
| 3 | 4,034 | 3,268 | 12,882 | 20,184 |
| 4 | 1,697 | 311 | 1,441 | 3,449 |
| 5 | 5,844 | 119 | 685 | 6,648 |
| Total | 13,150 | 16,388 | 71,300 | 1,00,838 |
| | | 61st round | | |
| 0 | na | 2,088 | 8,450 | 10,538 |
| 1 | 900 | 10,682 | 45,001 | 56,583 |
| 2 | 1,159 | 2,658 | 12,376 | 16,193 |
| 3 | 1,930 | 2,428 | 10,547 | 14,905 |
| 4 | 7,805 | 254 | 2,275 | 10,334 |
| 5 | 4,616 | 1,951 | 8,356 | 14,923 |
| Total | 16,410 | 20,061 | 87,005 | 1,23,476 |
| | | 50th round | | |
| 0 | na | 2,313 | 9,595 | 12,045 |
| 1 | 1,689 | 9,651 | 44,700 | 55,954 |
| 2 | 859 | 2,135 | 10,957 | 13,956 |
| 3 | 1,904 | 2,233 | 9,139 | 13,283 |
| 4 | 5,375 | 180 | 1,879 | 7,440 |
| 5 | 3,634 | 1,792 | 7,284 | 12,716 |
| Total | 13,461 | 18,304 | 83,554 | 115,394 |

Source: Author's tabulation using NSS CES unit record data, respective rounds.

expenditure for STs, SCs and OTH groups is reported for the 50th, 61st and 66th rounds for six group of districts as discussed above.

The first panel in table 12.3 shows the hierarchy in mean consumption expenditure reported above. Mean consumption of STs as a group in 2009–10 was less than 74 per cent of the OTH group comprising non-SC and non-ST population. The disparity has increased markedly between 1993–94 and 2004–05 first before improving in 2009–10. Compared to STs, SCs in 2009–10 were marginally better off at about 77 per cent of mean consumption of OTH.

But the disparities between ST and OTH is remarkably different in different parts of the country. In group five, where STs have a

*Table 12.3* Mean consumption and inequality

| Share ST pop | ST | SC | OTH | All | ST%OTH | Gini |
|---|---|---|---|---|---|---|
| | | | 66th Round (2009–10) | | | |
| 0 | na | 295 | 394 | 370 | na | 0.318 |
| 1 | 468 | 343 | 507 | 472 | 99.2 | 0.383 |
| 2 | 382 | 326 | 476 | 439 | 87.0 | 0.391 |
| 3 | 283 | 319 | 435 | 380 | 74.5 | 0.355 |
| 4 | 259 | 307 | 401 | 311 | 83.3 | 0.351 |
| 5 | 358 | 269 | 397 | 360 | 99.4 | 0.276 |
| Total | 315 | 326 | 469 | 426 | 73.9 | 0.371 |
| | | | 61st round (2004–05) | | | |
| 0 | na | 287 | 384 | 362 | na | 0.335 |
| 1 | 317 | 303 | 437 | 406 | 72.5 | 0.360 |
| 2 | 263 | 286 | 390 | 358 | 67.4 | 0.321 |
| 3 | 264 | 303 | 379 | 346 | 69.7 | 0.327 |
| 4 | 224 | 296 | 414 | 330 | 54.1 | 0.376 |
| 5 | 423 | 352 | 354 | 390 | 119.5 | 0.242 |
| Total | 265 | 298 | 416 | 379 | 63.7 | 0.351 |
| | | | 50th round (1993–94) | | | |
| 0 | Na | 244 | 336 | 316 | na | 0.307 |
| 1 | 274 | 265 | 367 | 344 | 74.7 | 0.340 |
| 2 | 261 | 244 | 337 | 314 | 77.4 | 0.316 |
| 3 | 227 | 252 | 320 | 290 | 70.9 | 0.286 |
| 4 | 228 | 266 | 371 | 306 | 61.5 | 0.329 |
| 5 | 337 | 275 | 279 | 304 | 120.8 | 0.237 |
| Total | 247 | 258 | 353 | 325 | 70.0 | 0.326 |

Source: Author's calculation from NSSO CES unit record data, respective rounds.

Note: Mean consumption refers to mean per capita consumption expenditure at constant (1993–94) prices. Inequality has been calculated on real mean consumption expenditure.

numerical majority, the mean consumption of STs is about the same as that of OTH group 2009–10. The largest disparity is found in group three where share of STs in total population is significant but still in minority, their mean consumption is by far the lowest at over 74 per cent of that of the OTH group. In areas where STs form a smaller minority (groups one and two), STs are marginally better off than the average for STs, but well below that of the group OTH in the same areas. The main message that emerges from this table is that during 2004–10, the relative distance between STs and OTH has narrowed.

If the population dominance[11] argument is used to scrutinise these results, then until a group has majority in the population, its participation in the income earning and growth is severely hindered. The calculations reported in table 12.3 suggest that there is substance in the dominance hypothesis. The other interesting result is the level of inequality as captured by the Gini coefficient. The distribution is most equitable where STs are the dominant group and it is the most unequal where there is substantial but less than majority ST presence (group one, two and three in table 12.3).

Table 12.4 reports the average annual change in the consumption expenditure over the three rounds. The average annual change among the STs has been less than half of what has been among the OTH group during 1993–2005. However, during 2004–10, there is a remarkable increase in the growth of consumption expenditure, the rate has increased to 3.8 per cent per annum compared to only 0.7 per cent in the earlier period. The most significant message from table 12.4 is the large deceleration in the growth of consumption expenditure in group 5 districts where the STs are in majority, more than 50 per cent

*Table 12.4* Average annual change in mean per capita consumption

| Share ST pop | ST | SC | OTH | ALL |
|---|---|---|---|---|
| | | 2004–05 to 2009–10 | | |
| 0 | Na | 0.6 | 0.5 | 0.4 |
| 1 | 9.5 | 2.6 | 3.2 | 3.3 |
| 2 | 9.0 | 2.8 | 4.4 | 4.5 |
| 3 | 1.4 | 1.1 | 3.0 | 2.0 |
| 4 | 3.1 | 0.7 | −0.6 | −1.2 |
| 5 | −3.1 | −4.7 | 2.4 | −1.5 |
| Total | 3.8 | 1.9 | 2.5 | 2.5 |
| | | 1993–94 to 2004–05 | | |
| 0 | Na | 1.6 | 1.3 | 1.3 |
| 1 | 1.4 | 1.3 | 1.7 | 1.6 |
| 2 | 0.1 | 1.6 | 1.4 | 1.3 |
| 3 | 1.5 | 1.8 | 1.7 | 1.8 |
| 4 | −0.2 | 1.0 | 1.1 | 0.7 |
| 5 | 2.3 | 2.5 | 2.4 | 2.6 |
| Total | 0.7 | 1.4 | 1.6 | 1.5 |

Source: As in table 12.3.

*Table 12.5* Poverty incidence during 1993–94, 2004–05 and 2009–10 (in per cent)

| Share of STs in Pop | 1993–94 ST | OTH | ALL | 2004–05 ST | OTH | ALL | 2009–10 ST | OTH | ALL |
|---|---|---|---|---|---|---|---|---|---|
| 0 | na | 32.2 | 36.7 | na | 26.0 | 29.5 | na | 25.0 | 28.3 |
| 1 | 46.0 | 29.9 | 33.9 | 32.8 | 21.1 | 24.6 | 24.5 | 15.2 | 18.3 |
| 2 | 47.6 | 30.4 | 35.3 | 40.6 | 21.5 | 26.8 | 33.7 | 20.4 | 22.6 |
| 3 | 54.1 | 33.4 | 39.9 | 39.5 | 25.1 | 29.3 | 25.0 | 18.0 | 20.9 |
| 4 | 53.4 | 29.0 | 40.2 | 56.5 | 28.0 | 40.5 | 39.9 | 25.3 | 31.9 |
| 5 | 25.3 | 42.3 | 34.8 | 7.5 | 19.9 | 13.0 | 30.0 | 18.2 | 27.0 |
| Total | 49.7 | 30.7 | 35.8 | 43.8 | 22.8 | 27.6 | 32.5 | 17.7 | 21.6 |

Source: As in table 12.3.

in the total population. On the other hand, in the districts which have a really minority ST population, overall growth in consumption in the second period has been remarkably high.

In table 12.5, poverty incidence (head count ratio) is reported at three time-points. Going by the disparities in mean consumption and inequality, HCRs mirror similar pattern and inter-group difference. In 2009–10, the ST-OTH difference in HCR is about 10 per cent points at the aggregate level. In 1993–94, the gap was 14 per cent points that worsened in 2004–05 to 16 per cent points.

Going by the share of ST population among the districts, for less than majority population of STs in the districts, the poverty ratios have been higher with the largest gap (over 28 per cent points) between the two groups for the districts which have less than majority ST population and are located in the so-called major states in 2004–05. But in 2009–10, there is a change in the ordering. First, in the districts that have more than 50 per cent of ST population, HCR increased dramatically, from under 8 per cent in 2004–05 to 30 per cent in 2009–10. Secondly, all other groups of districts experienced significant reduction in poverty incidence during 2009–10.

While the temporal change in poverty incidence in the 61st round over the 50th round has been consistent with changes in the mean consumption expenditure and inequality, the change in 2009–10 over 2004–05 is worrisome. The key message from the table is that the disparities in poverty incidence between STs and OTH have declined during 2009–10 compared to 2004–05. This is driven largely by the increase of poverty incidence in the groups one to four districts.

## Consumption and poverty: districts

As pointed out earlier, there are only 43 districts for which the district level calculations are reported. These 43 districts have been created from a total 126 districts that account for over 21 per cent of total districts in India. These 126 districts (43 after merging contiguous districts) account for over 12 per cent of total population but have 54 per cent of total ST population. Thus, the calculations in this section cover about 12 per cent of total population and over 54 per cent of ST population of India.

In table 12.6, the mean per capita consumption expenditure is reported for STs and OTH for the 50th and 61st rounds. There seven districts in which mean consumption of STs either at par or higher than OTH. Compared to these, there six districts with substantial ST population that have highest ST-OTH disparities.

There are some very interesting observations that are emerging from this table. Firstly, the location of the districts is quite distinct. Most of the districts where ST-OTH gap is favouring STs are located in the northeastern region. These are smaller states that fall under VI Schedule or the dominant tribal population among the districts makes them fall under the V Schedule. One of the specific provisions of the VI Schedule states is incidence of direct taxes where the Indigenous population is exempted from paying individual direct taxes. Secondly, the districts with largest ST-OTH gap in mean consumption are located in major states, Gujarat, Madhya Pradesh, Maharashtra, Orissa and Rajasthan. Thirdly, out of the major states which have the largest ST-OTH consumption differences, Gujarat, Maharashtra and Rajasthan have benefited the most from the recent episode of liberalisation and economic growth. Clearly, the participation of STs in growth is not happening even in the fastest-growing states, and in the slow-growing states like Orissa whatever little growth there is also is unevenly distributed.

The differences in consumption could persist between population groups for some more time even if different groups get an equitable share from the surging economic growth. Table 12.6, though, suggests otherwise. In these six districts (with highest ST-OTH consumption gap), the ST-OTH gap has increased during 1993–94 and 2004–05. The annual average change in mean real consumption expenditure over the two time-points suggests that the largest increase in APCTE (over 10 per cent per annum) is recorded among the OTH groups in the six districts that have largest ST-OTH mean APCTE difference. Compared to this, the annual average increase in the real mean

Table 12.6 Mean consumption and disparities in consumption

| State-dist | State | 1993–94 (in Rs) ST | OTH | 2004–05 ST | OTH | ST-OTH50 (%) | ST-OTH61 (%) | AAC-ST (%) | AAC-OTH (%) |
|---|---|---|---|---|---|---|---|---|---|
| 301 | APR | 302 | 664 | 465 | 598 | 45.5 | 77.8 | 4.9 | 2.6 |
| 302 | APR | 378 | 591 | 547 | 479 | 64.0 | 114.2 | 4.1 | -1.1 |
| 303 | APR | 251 | 318 | 362 | 374 | 78.9 | 96.8 | 4.0 | 0.3 |
| 401 | ASS | 260 | 232 | 326 | 277 | 112.1 | 117.7 | 2.3 | -1.4 |
| 403 | ASS | 257 | 266 | 358 | 362 | 96.6 | 98.9 | 3.6 | 0.1 |
| 406 | ASS | 252 | 309 | 371 | 409 | 81.6 | 90.7 | 4.3 | 0.9 |
| 410 | ASS | 259 | 326 | 270 | 359 | 79.4 | 75.2 | 0.4 | 3.0 |
| 518 | JHA | 220 | 287 | 219 | 284 | 76.7 | 77.1 | 0.0 | 2.7 |
| 523 | JHA | 274 | 390 | 222 | 257 | 70.3 | 86.4 | -1.7 | 1.4 |
| 524 | JHA | 279 | 445 | 289 | 390 | 62.7 | 74.1 | 0.3 | 3.2 |
| 707 | GUJ | 229 | 311 | 237 | 450 | 73.6 | 52.7 | 0.3 | 8.2 |
| 713 | GUJ | 322 | 416 | 312 | 630 | 77.4 | 49.5 | -0.3 | 9.3 |
| 714 | GUJ | 279 | 472 | 357 | 644 | 59.1 | 55.4 | 2.5 | 7.3 |
| 1306 | MPR | 201 | 344 | 196 | 321 | 58.4 | 61.1 | -0.2 | 5.8 |
| 1309 | MPR | 224 | 424 | 234 | 579 | 52.8 | 40.4 | 0.4 | 13.4 |
| 1313 | MPR | 205 | 315 | 207 | 326 | 65.1 | 63.5 | 0.1 | 5.2 |
| 1314 | MPR | 207 | 452 | 173 | 230 | 45.8 | 75.2 | -1.5 | 3.0 |
| 1315 | CHH | 205 | 261 | 204 | 297 | 78.5 | 68.7 | 0.0 | 4.1 |
| 1316 | CHH | 227 | 299 | 283 | 327 | 75.9 | 86.5 | 2.2 | 1.4 |
| 1317 | CHH | 213 | 301 | 240 | 267 | 70.8 | 89.9 | 1.2 | 1.0 |
| 1318 | CHH | 197 | 300 | 178 | 355 | 65.7 | 50.1 | -0.9 | 9.0 |
| 1402 | MAH | 309 | 635 | 249 | 632 | 48.7 | 39.4 | -1.8 | 14.0 |
| 1405 | MAH | 180 | 283 | 188 | 344 | 63.6 | 54.7 | 0.4 | 7.5 |
| 1501 | MAN | 295 | 405 | 327 | 325 | 72.8 | 100.6 | 1.0 | -0.1 |

| | | | | | | | | |
|---|---|---|---|---|---|---|---|---|
| 1601 | MEG | 396 | 527 | 450 | 706 | 75.1 | 63.7 | 1.2 | 5.2 |
| 1602 | MEG | 351 | 377 | 390 | 437 | 93.1 | 89.2 | 1.0 | 1.1 |
| 1701 | MIZ | 442 | 698 | 603 | 601 | 63.3 | 100.3 | 3.3 | 0.0 |
| 1702 | MIZ | 431 | 404 | 487 | 406 | 106.7 | 120.0 | 1.2 | -1.5 |
| 1801 | NAG | 499 | 499 | 778 | 618 | 100.0 | 125.9 | 5.1 | -1.9 |
| 1802 | NAG | 426 | 505 | 618 | 1060 | 84.4 | 58.3 | 4.1 | 6.5 |
| 1901 | ORI | 218 | 287 | 170 | 258 | 76.0 | 65.9 | -2.0 | 4.7 |
| 1902 | ORI | 185 | 343 | 187 | 426 | 53.9 | 43.9 | 0.1 | 11.6 |
| 1903 | ORI | 193 | 317 | 218 | 344 | 60.9 | 63.4 | 1.2 | 5.3 |
| 1907 | ORI | 169 | 218 | 168 | 225 | 77.5 | 74.7 | -0.1 | 3.1 |
| 1908 | ORI | 168 | 326 | 143 | 355 | 51.5 | 40.3 | -1.4 | 13.5 |
| 2110 | RAJ | 378 | 365 | 255 | 445 | 103.6 | 57.3 | -3.0 | 6.8 |
| 2111 | RAJ | 237 | 427 | 227 | 454 | 55.5 | 50.0 | -0.4 | 9.1 |
| 2201 | SIK | 285 | 298 | 340 | 357 | 95.6 | 95.2 | 1.8 | 0.5 |
| 2202 | SIK | 356 | 345 | 556 | 531 | 103.2 | 104.7 | 5.1 | -0.4 |
| 2401 | TRI | 316 | 404 | 321 | 430 | 78.2 | 74.7 | 0.1 | 3.1 |
| 2402 | TRI | 300 | 368 | 248 | 310 | 81.5 | 80.0 | -1.6 | 2.3 |
| 2901 | DAD | 214 | 594 | 287 | 779 | 36.0 | 36.8 | 3.1 | 15.6 |
| 3201 | LAD | 523 | 556 | 727 | 861 | 94.1 | 84.4 | 3.5 | 1.7 |

Source: As in table 12.3.

Note: AAC: Average Annual Change in Mean Per Capita Consumption.

See appendix table 12.9 for name and composition of districts.

consumption among the STs in the districts that have favourable gap (ST-OTH) in mean consumption has experienced the highest growth though substantially lower than the OTH group in the districts that have largest ST-OTH gap. In fact, there is perceptible decline in the mean consumption of OTH groups that have a dominant ST population group and are located in the northeastern region.

The patterns observed in the mean consumption expenditure and changes therein are reflected in the incidence of poverty reported in table 12.7. Given that districts located in the northeastern region have experienced significant growth in mean consumption and the ST-OTH difference favouring STs in these districts, the level of poverty in these districts is substantially lower compared to the districts with a sizeable ST population but located in major states. For example, among 16 districts that have less than 10 per cent HCR, all are located in the northeast with three districts reporting no poverty at all.

On the other hand, the highest incidence of poverty (over 84 per cent) is recorded in Koraput district located in Orissa. In fact out of seven districts that have more than 70 per cent incidence of poverty, four districts are in Orissa, two in Chhattisgarh and one in Madhya Pradesh. An additional 10 districts have poverty incidence in the range of 50–70 per cent located in Chhattisgarh, Gujarat, Jharkhand, Madhya Pradesh, Maharashtra, Orissa and Rajasthan.

There are two other important issues that emerge from this table. One, there is substantial ST-OTH disparity in poverty incidence too (as observed earlier in mean real consumption). Secondly, there is some kind of inertia in the poverty incidence, as the high level of poverty incidence in some of the districts continues to be there despite the impressive economic growth experience that the Indian economy has had over the last 20 years.

The district level analyses from the 66th round is not included in the discussion but given the dramatic deceleration in growth of MPCE and increase in poverty, the poverty levels in the districts in category five could have increased or remained stagnant.

## Has growth been helpful in reducing poverty?

In the last two sections we have shown that the poverty incidence did decline but this decline has been different for both STs and Others across districts with varying levels of ST population. It has also been noted that in districts falling in group one and five (the ST population share is either very small or over 50 per cent), the reduction in poverty

*Table 12.7* Incidence of poverty (in per cent)

| State | State dist code | 61st HCR ST | 61st HCR OTH | 50th HCR ST | 50th HCR OTH |
|---|---|---|---|---|---|
| APR | 301 | 7.4 | 0.6 | 36.3 | 8.5 |
| APR | 302 | 5.0 | 10.5 | 44.0 | 1.6 |
| APR | 303 | 22.2 | 14.2 | 52.1 | 30.7 |
| ASS | 401 | 15.3 | 40.4 | 6.8 | 65.2 |
| ASS | 403 | 4.5 | 6.5 | 32.1 | 37.8 |
| ASS | 406 | 8.4 | 8.2 | 37.7 | 21.2 |
| ASS | 410 | 25.5 | 2.2 | 44.8 | 23.3 |
| JHA | 518 | 64.6 | 46.7 | 55.9 | 44.1 |
| JHA | 523 | 59.0 | 59.2 | 45.7 | 25.4 |
| JHA | 524 | 29.3 | 13.2 | 38.2 | 15.9 |
| GUJ | 707 | 52.9 | 15.2 | 48.3 | 25.5 |
| GUJ | 713 | 29.1 | 5.9 | 5.3 | 17.3 |
| GUJ | 714 | 14.9 | 5.6 | 22.5 | 18.4 |
| MPR | 1306 | 73.1 | 30.2 | 58.3 | 22.7 |
| MPR | 1309 | 50.6 | 20.3 | 53.4 | 29.9 |
| MPR | 1313 | 57.8 | 35.6 | 69.1 | 36.0 |
| CHH | 1314 | 78.5 | 48.7 | 46.2 | 42.9 |
| CHH | 1315 | 51.9 | 43.5 | 55.9 | 46.3 |
| CHH | 1316 | 40.6 | 26.6 | 57.6 | 42.3 |
| CHH | 1317 | 34.7 | 29.1 | 40.8 | 19.2 |
| CHH | 1318 | 72.0 | 46.7 | 62.4 | 46.4 |
| MAH | 1402 | 60.2 | 15.9 | 16.1 | 7.6 |
| MAH | 1405 | 62.8 | 26.4 | 70.5 | 31.7 |
| MAN | 1501 | 7.0 | 5.2 | 26.5 | 0.0 |
| MEG | 1601 | 3.3 | 0.0 | 4.8 | 2.8 |
| MEG | 1602 | 3.6 | 0.0 | 35.0 | 41.9 |
| MIZ | 1701 | 0.0 | 0.0 | 3.4 | 0.0 |
| MIZ | 1702 | 3.7 | 0.0 | 6.2 | 0.0 |
| NAG | 1801 | 0.0 | 0.0 | 1.2 | 0.0 |
| NAG | 1802 | 0.0 | 0.0 | 2.3 | 0.0 |
| ORI | 1901 | 79.9 | 55.2 | 49.7 | 33.5 |
| ORI | 1902 | 70.5 | 15.3 | 72.7 | 30.9 |
| ORI | 1903 | 63.3 | 33.7 | 67.4 | 21.4 |
| ORI | 1907 | 79.1 | 63.6 | 75.7 | 57.0 |
| ORI | 1908 | 84.7 | 43.9 | 78.1 | 47.7 |
| RAJ | 2110 | 34.1 | 14.1 | 53.2 | 20.4 |
| RAJ | 2111 | 51.1 | 7.3 | 54.0 | 16.9 |
| SIK | 2201 | 20.7 | 19.6 | 30.3 | 29.7 |
| SIK | 2202 | 6.3 | 8.3 | 37.7 | 24.0 |
| TRI | 2401 | 32.6 | 15.1 | 29.2 | 11.4 |
| TRI | 2402 | 44.7 | 36.0 | 43.3 | 21.6 |
| DAD | 2901 | 44.3 | 5.2 | 58.5 | 6.6 |
| LAD | 3201 | 6.3 | 0.0 | 9.3 | 0.0 |

Source: As in table 12.3.

has been substantial. It is conceivable that growth has not been uniform across geographical domains (as proxied by differences in the increase in real mean per capita expenditure in tables 12.3 and 12.7), consequently relative contribution of growth in reducing poverty may be different across districts. But since several redistributive policies have been in place including affirmative action for STs and SCs to make growth more equitable, it would be interesting to see how these policies have been faring as far as reduction in poverty is concerned. In this section we have decomposed the relative contribution of growth and redistribution policies in reducing poverty in districts. Once again the exercise has been done only for ST and Others clubbed into five groups based on share of ST population.[12]

Change in poverty ratio can be broadly attributed to change in per capita expenditure and change in relative size distribution.[13] The mean effect is defined as change in poverty due to change in real mean per capita expenditure (PCTE) while keeping relative size distribution at base year. Similarly, the distribution effect can be defined as a change in poverty measurement due to the change in relative size distribution while keeping MPCE constant at base year. Recall that the districts have been divided into six groups based on population share of STs. The decomposition exercise has been carried out for the group of districts one to five. As shown in table 12.5, among STs the poverty incidence has declined in all groups except group five.

The results of the decomposition exercise are reported in table 12.8. Column two of the table shows the observed decline in poverty incidence ($\Delta H$) for STs and Others for districts groups one to five. Column 3 shows the reduction in hypothetical HCR. It is interpreted as the change in the HCR because of the change in PCTE (growth effect) provided the distribution of expenditure is held at base year (1993–94 in this case) level. Column 4 shows what would have happened to HCR if mean PCTE is held constant at base year level but distribution is changed to terminal year level (2004–05 in this case).

As can be seen from column 3, for STs, decline in HCR because of the change in mean PCTE (growth effect is not uniform, when share of STs in the population is very small they have benefited from both growth as well redistribution (actual decline in HCR, $\Delta H$, is algebraic sum of columns 3 and 4)). In group two districts, had the relative distribution been constant, the HCR for STs would have marginally increased. The small decline in HCR for this group, therefore comes from redistribution effect. In group three districts, the distribution

*Table 12.8* Decomposition of change in head count ratio

| Share of ST Population | ΔH (actual) | Mean Effect (calculated) | Redistribution Effect (calculated) |
|---|---|---|---|
| 1 | 2 | 3 | 4 |
| STs | | | |
| 1 | −18.89 | −13.64 | −5.25 |
| 2 | −4.06 | 0.29 | −4.35 |
| 3 | −12.29 | −15.13 | 2.85 |
| 4 | 3.73 | 5.11 | −1.39 |
| 5 | −13.21 | −15.40 | 2.19 |
| Others | | | |
| 1 | −13.65 | −24.11 | 10.46 |
| 2 | −14.01 | −19.71 | 5.70 |
| 3 | −11.57 | −27.24 | 15.67 |
| 4 | −6.62 | −13.91 | 7.29 |
| 5 | −16.87 | −30.69 | 13.82 |

Source: As in table 12.4.

Note: Share ST population refers to share of ST populations in total population in group of districts defined in table 12.1.

deteriorated though marginally. But in group districts, because of the marginal decline in PCTE, HCR could have increased by over 5 per cent points. But with the marginal contribution from redistribution, the increase is relatively lower. Thus, in general 'growth has not been good' for STs where the ST populations is substantial but not dominant. Similarly, for Others, the growth would have been good (the decline in poverty should been far higher than actually observed), but it has been offset by an increase in inequality.[14]

The decomposition at the disaggregated level for STs and OTH is not yet available for 2004–10 but Thorat and Dubey (2012) report that in the rural areas, the growth has contributed to substantial reduction in the poverty incidence. However, in the urban areas, a large part of the reduction of poverty incidence has been offset due to an increase in inequality among the STs.

## Conclusion and policy issues

In this chapter levels and changes of mean consumption expenditure and poverty incidence is reported at three time-points, 1993–94,

2004–05 and 2009–10 for STs at the aggregate as well as at the district level. The focus of the analysis is the level and change in consumption and poverty incidence among STs and the disparities in these two indicators between STs and other population groups (OTH).

The findings of the chapter reaffirms the persistence of disparities in mean consumption and poverty incidence between STs and OTHs. At macro-levels, the worrying factor is the stagnant ST-OTH disparities on both the indicators. Average annual change in mean consumption of STs has been substantially lower than the growth experienced by the OTH group during 1990s, which is fostering the disparities. However, the recent data show that the STs have benefited from growth.

The proportion of STs who have benefited during this period could be smaller as they are located in the areas that do not have a majority ST population. Though detailed sectoral growth data is not available at the district level, location of these districts (where STs are the dominant population group) in Schedule V and VI areas seems to have helped in the first period. In most of these Scheduled Areas, the service sector led growth has benefited the STs. This is further corroborated when we looked at the role of growth in reduction of poverty. The decomposition exercise carried out suggests that, in general, STs have not benefited either from growth or redistribution during the first period but during the second period they have.

The deprivation levels of STs residing in major states and with less than a majority ST population appear to be the most vulnerable groups among all STs. The incidence of poverty in excess of 50 per cent among the districts with substantial ST populations and located in the states that are recognised as the most investor-friendly and have been fastest-growing, Gujarat and Maharashtra, suggests non-participation of STs in the current episode of economic growth. The analysis also indicates that that some of these districts do not fall in economically stagnating regions and the benefits of growth are concentrating among the majority OTH and fostering inequality.

## Notes

1 Although the term 'ST' is used here to denote, implicitly, a single population group, in reality there are more than 4,000 distinct tribes spread over the length and breadth of the country defined in the Indian Constitution. Each one of these tribes is different from the others in their socio-cultural, linguistic and religious characteristics.
2 See table 12.9 in the appendix.

3 The terms 'Scheduled Caste' and 'Scheduled Tribe' are of relatively recent origin and include caste and tribes notified by the Government of India. The third deprived group identified on the basis of religion is Muslims (GoI 2007).
4 Weights or multipliers provide the number of households each one of the surveyed households represent in the data. For details on NSS sampling design and other related issues, see GoI (1983, 1994 and 2004). See also Gangopadhyay et al. (1997) and Dubey and Gangopadhyay (1998).
5 Since the 1991 census, there has been a reorganisation of districts, taking the total number of districts in India to well over 600. With the reorganisation of the districts in several states, the number of districts with substantial ST population has increased.
6 Share of different social groups in a district varies. However, if a particular group has over 50 per cent share in population, it could be considered to be in majority.
7 Although there are more districts that have over 50 per cent ST population, for comparability of geographical areas and reliability of estimates, these districts have been merged to create fewer comparable geographical domains that are being referred here as districts.
8 See GoI (1979, 1993), Dubey and Gangopadhyay (1998), Deaton and Tarozzi (1999), Deaton and Dreze (2002) for details on these issues.
9 A new set of urban and rural PLs have been proposed by the Expert Group (GoI 2009). But the suitability of these PLs is still being debated. Moreover, choice of a particular poverty norm does not make any qualitative difference in the measurement of poverty across population groups (Dubey and Gangopadhyay 1998).
10 There are several other indices that are prescribed in the literature, e.g. Poverty Gap Index (PGI), Foster Greer and Thorbecke (FGT) Index, Sen Index etc. We have used HCR as our objective is to highlight the disparities across social groups. Moreover, at least first two indices, PGI and FGT, show a similar variation and trend.
11 Given the socio-religious distribution of the Indian population, a population group – social or religious – could be defined as a dominant group if the share of the social or religious group in the population is more than 50 per cent. For example in a large number of districts in northeastern states, the share of STs in the total population is often more than 50 per cent, thus making STs the dominant group.
12 The districts where there are no STs have been left out of this analysis.
13 In recent times, a number of researchers have tried to decompose the relative contribution of growth and redistribution in reduction of poverty. See for example Kakwani and Subbarao (1990), Jain and Tendulkar (1990), Datt and Ravallion (1992) and Kakwani (2000). We have used Kakwani (2000) methodology to decompose the change in poverty incidence in this chapter. The details of the methodological issues are discussed in Dubey and Tiwari (2010).
14 In all the calculations in this chapter, we have used NSS CES data, which for reasons well known, shows lower level as well as change in inequality. Both levels and change in household-income-based inequality measures are substantially higher.

# References

Bhandari, Laveesh and Amaresh Dubey. 2009. *District Level Poverty Estimates in 2004–05*. New Delhi: Indicus Analytics, Mimeo.

Chaudhuri, S. and Nivedita Gupta. 2009. 'Level of Living and Poverty Patterns: A District-wise Analysis for India', *Economic and Political Weekly*, 44(9): 94–110.

Datt, Gaurav and Martin Ravallion. 1992. 'Growth and Redistribution Component of Changes in Poverty Measures: A Decomposition With Application to Brazil and India in 1980s', *Journal of Development Economics*, 38(2): 275–95.

Deaton, A. and J. Dreze. 2002. 'Poverty and Inequality in India: A Re-Examination', *Economic and Political Weekly*, 37(36): 3729–48.

Deaton, A. and A. Tarozzi. 1999. *Prices and Poverty in India*. Princeton: Mimeo.

De Haan, A. and A. Dubey, 2005. 'Orissa: Poverty, Disparities, or the Development of Under-Development?' (with Arjan de Haan), *Economic and Political Weekly*, 40 (18): 2321–29.

De Haan, A., A. Dubey and G. Sabharwal. 2009. 'Between Emergency Responses and Rights-based Approaches: Addressing Poverty and Undernutrition in Eastern India', *IDS Bulletin*, 40(4): 39–44.

Desai, S. and A. Dubey. 2011. 'Caste in 21st Century India: Competing Narrative', *Economic and Political Weekly*, 46(11): 40–49.

Dubey, A. 2003. 'Quantitative Analysis of Social Group Disparities in India', Paper submitted to the *Department for International Development*, New Delhi: British High Commission, June.

Dubey, A. and S. Gangopadhyay. 1998. *Counting the Poor: Where Are the Poor in India?* Sarvekshana, Analytical Report, No. 1, February.

Dubey, A. and R. W. Palmer-Jones. 2005a. 'Poverty Counts in India During 1983: New Poverty Counts and Robust Poverty Comparisons', *Artha Vijnana*, 47(3–4): 287–328.

Dubey, A. and R. W. Palmer-Jones. 2005b. 'Prices, Price Indexes and Poverty Counts in India During 1980s and 1990s: Calculation of UVCPIs', *Artha Vijnana*, 47(3–4): 259–86.

Dubey, A. and R. W. Palmer-Jones. 2005c. 'Prices, Price Indexes and Poverty Counts in India During 1980s and 1990s: From CPIs to Poverty Lines?', *Artha Vijnana*, 47(3–4): 259–86.

Dubey, A. and S. Tiwari. 2010. *Decomposing Poverty Into Growth and Redistribution Components*. New Delhi: JNU, CSRD, Mimeo.

Gangopadhyay, S., L. R. Jain and A. Dubey. 1997. *Poverty Measures and Socioeconomic Characteristics: 1987–88 and 1993–94*. Report submitted to the CSO. New Delhi: Department of Statistics, Government of India.

Government of India. 1979. *Report of the Task Force on Projections of Minimum Needs and Effective Consumption Demand*. New Delhi: Planning Commission, Perspective Planning Division, January.

Government of India. 1983. *Instructions to Field Staff: 38th Round (1983)*, Calcutta: National Sample Survey Organisation, Survey Design Research Division.

Government of India. 1993. *Report of the Expert Group on Estimation of Proportion and Number of Poor*. New Delhi: Planning Commission, Perspective Planning Division, July.

Government of India. 1994. *Note on Sample Design and Estimation Procedure: 50th Round (July 1993–June 1994)*. New Delhi: National Sample Survey Organisation, Survey Design Research Division, March.

Government of India. 2004. *Note on Sample Design and Estimation Procedure: 61st Round (July 2004–June 2005)*. New Delhi: National Sample Survey Organisation, Survey Design Research Division, March.

Government of India. 2006. *Towards Faster and More Inclusive Growth: An Approach to the 11 Five Year Plan*. New Delhi: Planning Commission, December.

Government of India. 2007. *The National Tribal Policy (Draft)*. New Delhi: Ministry of Tribal Affairs.

Government of India. 2009. *Report of the Expert Group to Review the Methodology for Estimation of Poverty*. New Delhi: Planning Commission.

Jain, L. and S. Tendulkar. 1990. 'The Role of Growth and Distribution in the Observed Change in Head-Count-Ration Measure of Poverty: A Decomposition Exercise for India', *Indian Economic Review*, 25(2): 165–205.

Kakwani, N. and Subbarao K. 1990. 'Rural Poverty and Its Alleviation in India', *Economic and Political Weekly*, 25(13): A2–A16.

Kakwani, N. 2000. 'On Measuring Growth and Inequality Components of Poverty With Application to Thailand', *Journal of Quantitative Economics*, 16(1): 67–79.

Newman, K. S. and S. K. Thorat. 2010. *Blocked by Caste: Economic Discrimination in Modern India*. New Delhi: Oxford University Press.

Rajaraman, I., O. P. Bohra and V. Renganathan. 1996. 'Augmentation of Panchayat Resources', *Economic and Political Weekly*, 31(18): 1071–83.

Thorat, S. K. and Amaresh Dubey. 2012. 'Has Growth Been Socially Inclusive During 1993-94-2009-10?', *Economic and Political Weekly*, 47(10): 43–54.

# APPENDIX

Table 12.9 HCR and by socio-religious groups and sector (in per cent)

| SRGs | 1983 Rural | 1983 Urban | 1983 Total | 1993–94 Rural | 1993–94 Urban | 1993–94 Total | 2004–05 Rural | 2004–05 Urban | 2004–05 Total | 2009–10 Rural | 2009–10 Urban | 2009–10 Total |
|---|---|---|---|---|---|---|---|---|---|---|---|---|
| ALL | 46.5 | 42.2 | 45.6 | 36.9 | 32.8 | 35.9 | 28.0 | 25.8 | 27.5 | 21.9 | 20.8 | 21.6 |
| ST | 63.9 | 55.3 | 63.3 | 50.2 | 42.9 | 49.6 | 44.7 | 34.2 | 43.8 | 33.0 | 28.6 | 32.5 |
| SC | 59.0 | 55.8 | 58.4 | 48.3 | 49.7 | 48.6 | 37.1 | 40.9 | 37.9 | 29.6 | 32.8 | 30.3 |
| OTHERS | 40.8 | 39.8 | 40.5 | 31.2 | 29.6 | 30.7 | 22.7 | 22.6 | 22.7 | 17.5 | 18.2 | 17.7 |
| Hindus | 47.0 | 40.3 | 45.6 | 36.5 | 30.6 | 35.1 | 28.0 | 23.6 | 26.9 | 22.7 | 18.8 | 21.7 |
| Muslims | 51.2 | 57.2 | 53.1 | 45.0 | 47.7 | 45.9 | 33.0 | 40.6 | 35.5 | 20.5 | 34.3 | 25.1 |
| ORM | 30.2 | 29.3 | 29.9 | 27.1 | 22.4 | 25.7 | 18.2 | 13.7 | 16.9 | 11.7 | 11.2 | 11.5 |

Source: Thorat and Dubey (2012).

Table 12.10 Annualised growth of MPCE by socio-religious groups and sector (in per cent)

| SRGs | Rural | | | Urban | | | Total | | |
|---|---|---|---|---|---|---|---|---|---|
| | 1983 to 1993–94 | 1993–94 to 2004–05 | 2004–05 to 2009–10 | 1983 to 1993–94 | 1993–94 to 2004–05 | 2004–05 to 2009–10 | 1983 to 1993–94 | 1993–94 to 2004–05 | 2004–05 to 2009–10 |
| ALL | 0.9 | 1.3 | 1.7 | 1.4 | 1.9 | 3.0 | 1.2 | 1.5 | 2.5 |
| ST | 1.9 | 0.5 | 3.0 | 1.5 | 1.8 | 5.0 | 2.0 | 0.6 | 3.7 |
| SC | 1.0 | 1.3 | 1.6 | 0.9 | 1.4 | 2.5 | 1.0 | 1.4 | 1.9 |
| Others | 0.8 | 1.4 | 1.7 | 1.5 | 2.0 | 3.0 | 1.3 | 1.6 | 2.6 |
| Hindus | 1.0 | 1.2 | 1.5 | 1.4 | 1.9 | 3.0 | 1.3 | 1.5 | 2.3 |
| Muslims | 0.8 | 1.7 | 1.8 | 1.3 | 1.5 | 3.0 | 1.1 | 1.5 | 2.3 |
| ORM | −0.1 | 2.2 | 4.4 | 1.6 | 2.2 | 2.5 | 0.6 | 2.2 | 4.0 |

Source: Thorat and Dubey (2012).

Table 12.11 State and districts

| State | State district code | Districts | Merged with districts in col 3 | Sample ST | Sample Total |
|---|---|---|---|---|---|
| Arunachal Pradesh | 301 | Tawang | West Kameng, East Kameng, Papum Pare, Lower Subansari, Upper Subansari | 604 | 827 |
| Arunachal Pradesh | 302 | West Siang | East Siang, Dibang Valley, Upper Siang | 406 | 600 |
| Arunachal Pradesh | 303 | Lohit | Changlang, Tirap | 311 | 616 |
| Assam | 401 | Dhubri | Kokrajhar, Bongaigaon | 115 | 530 |
| Assam | 403 | Nalbari | Darrang | 122 | 420 |
| Assam | 406 | Lakhimpur | Dhemaji, Jorhat | 123 | 420 |
| Assam | 410 | Karbi anglong | North Cachar Hills | 172 | 240 |
| Jharkahnd | 518 | Deoghar | Dhanbad, Bokaro | 147 | 600 |
| Jharkahnd | 523 | Ranchi |  | 282 | 280 |
| Jharkahnd | 524 | Purbi singhbhum |  | 127 | 240 |
| Gujarat | 707 | Sabarkantha | Gandhinagar, Panchmahals, Dohad | 149 | 597 |
| Gujarat | 713 | Surat |  | 101 | 438 |
| Gujarat | 714 | Valsad | The Dangs, Navasari | 148 | 280 |
| Madhya Pradesh | 1306 | Satna | Rewa, Shahdol, Sidhi, Umaria | 164 | 720 |
| Madhya Pradesh | 1309 | Jhabua | Dhar, Indore | 256 | 517 |
| Madhya Pradesh | 1313 | Narsimhapur | Chhindwara, Seoni | 109 | 400 |
| Madhya Pradesh | 1314 | Mandla | Balaghat, Dindori | 112 | 360 |
| Chhattisgarh | 1315 | Surguja | Koriya | 166 | 320 |
| Chhattisgarh | 1316 | Bilaspur | Korba, Jahangir-Champa, Kawardha | 117 | 757 |
| Chhattisgarh | 1317 | Raigarh | Jashpur | 115 | 280 |

| | | | | |
|---|---|---|---|---|
| Chhattisgarh | 1318 | Rajnandgaon | Durg, Bastar, Kanker, Dantewada | 300 | 879 |
| Maharashtra | 1402 | Thane | | 128 | 946 |
| Maharashtra | 1405 | Dhule | Nandurbar | 125 | 320 |
| Manipur | 1501 | Senapati | Tamenglong, Churachanpur, Chandel, Ukhrul | 1144 | 1,217 |
| Meghalaya | 1601 | East Khasi Hills | Jaintia Hills, Ri-Bhoi | 661 | 720 |
| Meghalaya | 1602 | West Khasi Hills | East Garo Hills, West Garo Hills, South Garo Hills | 739 | 876 |
| Mizoram | 1701 | Aizawl | Mamit, Kolasib, Serchip | 1095 | 1,113 |
| Mizoram | 1702 | Lunglei | Chhimtuipui, Lawngtlai, Saiha | 775 | 799 |
| Nagaland | 1801 | Kohima | Dimapur | 373 | 440 |
| Nagaland | 1802 | Phek | Zunheboto, Wokha, Mokokchung, Tuensang, Mon | 828 | 840 |
| Orissa | 1901 | Sambalpur | Balangir, Baragarh, Jharsuguda, Debgarh, Sonapur | 140 | 757 |
| Orissa | 1902 | Sundargarh | Kendujhar | 211 | 440 |
| Orissa | 1903 | Mayurbhanj | | 111 | 240 |
| Orissa | 1907 | Phulabani | Kalahandi, Baudh, Nuapada | 128 | 460 |
| Orissa | 1908 | Koraput | Raygada, Nabarangapur, Malkangiri | 279 | 540 |
| Rajasthan | 2110 | Udaipur | Rajsamund | 108 | 360 |
| Rajasthan | 2111 | Dungarpur | Chittaurgarh, Banswara | 165 | 439 |
| Sikkim | 2201 | North District | South District, West District | 286 | 640 |
| Sikkim | 2202 | East District | | 153 | 480 |
| Tripura | 2401 | West Tripura | | 263 | 1,120 |
| Tripura | 2402 | North Tripura | South Tripura, Dhalai | 229 | 1,200 |
| DAD | 2901 | Dadra and Nagar Haveli | | 150 | 240 |
| Lakshadweep | 3201 | Lakshadweep | | 184 | 199 |

Source: Thorat and Dubey (2012).

# Part III

# INCLUSIVE POLICIES
## Myth or reality

# 13

# AN UNBROKEN HISTORY OF BROKEN PROMISES
## Exploration from a tribal perspective

*Pradip Prabhu*[1]

The starting point of this critical review is that the history, of the dealings of the post-colonial Indian state with the tribal people, is inextricably linked to the independent nation's failure to recognise the incessant uprisings of the tribal people against the colonial state as freedom movements.[2] Tribal India was in ferment right from the beginning of the East India Company's forays into the tribal tracts. Already in 1778, Tilka Mahji led the fierce resistance of the Pahariya people and fought the illegal entry of the sepoys of the East India Company into their forested homelands in the Mal-Pahariya Region. Tilka Mahji paid with his life for the nascent struggle for freedom, grossly misinterpreted as a mere act of insubordination. Political arrangements, which recognised tribal 'nations' co-existing with established states and empires prior to the colonial period, were due to the absence of dominant commercial interests in their forested tribal homelands. In retrospect, subsequent uprisings in the tribal areas were triggered, almost totally, by intrusion into their territories and attempts at domination by the colonial powers and their minions.

The consolidation of colonial rule in India was virtually co-temporaneous with forest denudation both in the British Isles and its earlier colonies, making capture of India's rich forests an important goal of colonial conquest. But intrusions into their forests were stoutly resisted by the tribal people, ensuring that conquest with a strong military thrust into resistance areas including the remote forested regions remained the goal of the colonial rulers till 1887. In a calculated exercise, tribal areas were opened up to civil and military officials, timber contractors and traders under the guise of 'good governance'. While people living in erstwhile feudal states adjusted to colonial rule following surrender of their erstwhile livelihood, as it meant no more than a shift in loyalty from one ruler to another or erstwhile rulers functioning under the supervision of the new rulers. But the same did not prevail in the tribal homelands as the imposition of the colonial rule was viewed as an act of subjugation. Therefore 'confrontation' continued as the quintessence of the situation in tribal areas after the rise of the 'colonial state' as a formal political and administrative authority. Widespread discontent led to the first Ho uprising of 1820, which was quelled only to re-emerge in 1821. The Oraons rebelled in 1820, 1832, 1890. The Kols organised an insurrection in 1831–32 which was directed mainly against government officers and private moneylenders. A more stirring source of inspiration for future struggles was the Santhal uprising of 1854–57 led by Kanu and Sidhu, two brothers in their mid-20s (Bannerjee 1984: 15–16).

While the uprisings were brutally suppressed by the military might of the colonial powers, legislative measures aimed at addressing tribal protest were simultaneously put in place. As early as 1773 the Houses of Parliament, admitting the reality of long disturbed tracts and a virtually uncontrolled empire, passed a Regulating Act making the company responsible for governing these territories and appointed Warren Hastings as Governor General of Bengal with supervisory authority over Madras and Bombay Presidencies (Hibbert 1980: 18). Hastings introduced a cultural policy advocating an informed mode of governance, grounded in liberal political thought. Its political implications were spelt out in the Queen's Proclamation of 1858, consisting of two complementary components of colonial strategy for governing the tribal homelands: regulate protest and conflict and practice cultural non-interference (Savyasaachi 1998: 9).

But though theoretically the political rulers in Great Britain postulated cultural non-interference; its representatives displayed hardcore opposition to the cultural and politico-legal institutions of the tribal people as they challenged colonial domination and commercial exploitation of natural resources. Additionally 'opposition' continued as a significant intervention against the Forest Department, who 'in the name of "scientific management" sought to eliminate the "wasteful practice of shifting cultivation" and evict tribals from their homelands by creating "Reserved" forests' (Report of the Bombay Forest Commission 1887: 132). These measures severely threatened the social and cultural certitude of tribal communities, rooted in their way of life with the forest at the centre (Prabhu and Shiraz 2013: 8) and with physical and cultural survival under threat as a result of the restrictions, 'the Rampa leaders found adherents . . . and soon five thousand square miles were affected by the rebellion' (Haimendorf 1992: 36–7).

Each rebellion against colonial rule, of which close to a hundred have been unearthed by subaltern historians,[3] calls for a critical distinction in the historical narrative of freedom movements in regions where citizen subjects quickly adjusted to the transfer of power from various ruling dynasties to the new colonial rulers and the uprisings in the tribal homelands. The important questions are: what were the distinctive ground realities in the tribal tracts which made them consistently reject and continuously rebel against colonial rule? Were the rebellions of the tribal people in colonial India similar to the rebellions of other Indigenous people against colonial domination in other parts of the globe?

A careful examination of fragments of history, oral traditions, narratives and socio-political systems leads to a tentative answer – that the tribal people in India, as did other Indigenous peoples across the globe, considered themselves in their homelands as 'first nations'.[4] Tribal confrontations with the colonisers, interchangeably termed as 'uprisings', 'rebellions', 'insurrections', were actually an attempt to overthrow the yoke of colonial rule while re-affirming their own politico-legal systems and institutions of governance. Whatever be the level of 'primitivity' that mainstream scholars assign to their political formations, the 'tribal first nations' were constituted by a 'people' who adhered to sui generis participatory democratic 'governance systems' developed by them within their 'homelands' from distant times which were de facto recognised and respected by other neighbouring rulers. Therefore the numerous 'tribal nations' principally identified the incursion of the British as an attempt at conquest of their 'nation' and therefore fought the 'capture' of their territories, the imposition of the alien system of colonial governance on their traditional institutions and obliteration of their citizenship of their nations, as was the situation in most other first nations across the globe.

Modern scholarship would admit that tribal communities developed technologically, philosophically, ideologically and socio-politically, following a trajectory vastly different from the caste-stratified Indian people. The tribal societal construct is grounded on the respect for the 'other', including nature, which in turn is sustained by ecological lifestyles and cultures. While distortions have emerged, resulting from an imposed modernity, tribals developed and still subscribe to relatively egalitarian, inclusive societal self-governing systems which still survive in several regions. Tribal communities evolved sophisticated mechanisms of internal solidarity to provide for the dis-advantaged and dis-privileged; their investment in nature was to address need and not promote greed; practices of community administration are not adversarial and seek to restore harmony; community positions are offices of service and not power; silence is not submission but deference when relating to the other. Their ethical standards are rooted in not taking advantage of another's disadvantage (weakness) and trust is based on respect for the other. Their choices have been based on conviviality with all life forms; consuming forest food, generally associated with poverty, is actually enjoying nature's nutritional security. Ecological lifeways can be erroneously associated with poverty and backwardness.

An important feature that needs recognition is that the matrix of philosophical premises around human being and becoming, ethical standards and ethos, living cultures and functional relations are organic parts of an evolved civilisation, observed with a great degree of similarity in most tribes. The 'backwardness' being imposed on 'advanced' tribal consciousness is a construct of the elites espousing a modernity advocated by capitalism. The ruling elites seek the integration of the tribal in their mainstream on their terms, which has remained an important feature of a global history of external and internal colonisation over the past four centuries. Hence we view backwardness as an essential construct of colonisation, both external and internal.

Admittedly, a distinctive eco-socio-political environment prevailed in the tribal tracts. Ironically, isolation from mainstream Indian society provided the matrix for tribal society to evolve an independent civilisational construct, distinctive political organisation of society and standards of human behaviour in a continuous dialectico-dialogical interface with their natural and social environment. These patterns of collective survival persisted for centuries and survive to a degree in the 'excluded areas of the northeast', where colonial hegemonic expansion, constrained by resistance and combined with inaccessible terrain, ensured traditional tribal/Indigenous lifeways and human–nature relationships to survive. Land was viewed not as a commodity but the basis of survival, citizenship, historical mooring, political organisation and symbolic significance. Nature ensured a sense of identity and rootedness because of its durability and permanence and a deep sense of the supernatural, spiritual and ancestral attachment, so much that the entire eco-socio-politico-cultural life revolved around land to which they belonged (Longkumer 2014: 23–4).

Orality also played an important role in the eco-socio-politico-cultural construct of the tribe and contributed to the development of its philosophical foundations, metaphysical reasoning, ethical standards and critical thought. The relational frame was founded on mutual affirmation of the other and the collectivity, an example of which is the philosophical narrative of the Warli people; *Kahankar & Ahankar* (Prabhu and Bulsara 2014: 2–7). Two major inferences can be drawn from the narrative in the present. The first inference is the 'word is dynamic and infused power' and respected as a 'word of honour'. Orality also evolved into the principle of mutual 'affirmation' as the core of societal formation and engagement, built on affirmation of the other rather than assertion of the self as the basis of civility. It was manifest in internal solidarity which remained a central feature of their collective existence. Orality affirmed and reproduced conviviality, inclusive of all life forms and the interdependence of human and nature at the core of their social ecology.

Resistance to an alien state was also built into their consciousness. A thought-provoking illustration is the rite of passage of initiation a new born into the community through the chanting of the *suin* (midwife). The ceremony, performed for every new born child, reiterates and reinforces the four tenets of tribal Warli consciousness. The first two tenets affirm dictates are associated to conviviality with nature. They begin with *wagha, nadgala bihijas nako* – don't fear the tiger and the bear, live with them as part of your 'extended family'. The second tenet is *vizlaval tar paljas nako* – don't run away from lightning and thunder, align your life with the forces of nature. The third tenet is the principle of internal solidarity *dari koni aala tar bhukha ghaljosh nako* – never send anyone who comes to your door hungry; and fourth tenet is the principle of self-governance, *sarkarchya payrya chadjas nako* – don't remain in awe of the state, govern yourselves and deal with the state on equal terms. The *suin* then continues with other tenets of tribal life. Tribal consciousness traverses multiple conceptual terrains, political, historical, social, sacred, emotional and existential. Most importantly their homeland territory is referred to as '*des*' (nation or country) (Sharma 2010: 28) the site of belonging as a people, within whose boundaries the community manages its affairs according to their customs and whose boundaries have been defended with their lives.

Forced to address the continuous uprisings emerging across the tribal homelands, the British introduced two administrative arrangements to diffuse conflict and prevent its spread. Inaccessible areas predominantly inhabited by 'un-reconciled tribal populations' were kept, under notional military control but without a civilian administration, as non-regulated areas while accessible territories had a civilian administration provided by the Regulation Act 1834, based on the experience of the 1820s in the Aran Hills in North East India (Singh 1982: ix). As early as 1874, the British administration promulgated the Scheduled Districts Act to administer the tribal tracts, enabling the government to notify laws appropriate for enforcement in the Scheduled Districts (Mehta 1991: 77–8). The Government of India Act, 1919, allowed the Governor General in Council to declare any territory in British India to be a 'Backward Tract' where a law could apply only if the Governor General so directed. By defining the role of Governor to be a 'cultural administrator', colonial historians sought to deny the rationality of nationality behind tribal resistance and revolt. In line with their 'cultural imperialism' revolts were labelled as 'backward looking' and 'un-progressive', 'blind hitting out' of a people enslaved by a 'primordial' or 'superstitious consciousness' (Hardiman 1992: 2).

The practices of the colonial administration were formalised in the Government of India Act 1935 and the Government of India (Excluded and Partially Excluded Areas) Order 1936, which classified the tribal areas of the relatively inaccessible northeast as 'wholly excluded areas' and the more accessible and thickly forested Central Indian tracts as 'partly excluded' (Agency) areas. By excluding these areas and keeping administration to a minimum, the British unwittingly ensured that the tribal people retained their traditional self-governing institutions. Ironically Government of India continued the same policy after Independence though earlier the nationalists saw the administrative arrangements as a device to retain British control over selected areas (Haimendorf 1992: 39). The resistance did not stop; the tribals rose in revolt, were suppressed with brute force and occasionally handled through special arrangements, like the Wilkinson Rules, which recognised the autonomous Munda-Manki system of governance in the Kolhan region of Jharkhand (Prabhu 1998: 232).

On 13 December 1946, Jawaharlal Nehru moved the Objectives Resolution in the Constituent Assembly of India, which proclaimed that the soon-to-be-free nation would be an 'Independent Sovereign Republic'. Its Constitution would guarantee citizens 'justice, social, economic and political; equality of status; of opportunity, and before the law; freedom of thought, expression, belief, faith, worship, vocation, association and action, subject to law and public morality'. The resolution went on to say that 'adequate safeguards shall be provided for minorities, backward and tribal areas, and depressed and other backward classes'. In moving the resolution, Nehru invoked the spirit of Gandhi and the 'great past of India', as also modern precedents as the French, American and Russian Revolutions. The debate on the Objectives Resolution went on for a week. Among the speakers were Purushuttomdas Tandon, a conservative Hindu; Shyama Prasad Mukherjee, a right-wing Hindu; Scheduled Caste leader B.R. Ambedkar; liberal lawyer M.R. Jayakar; socialist M.R. Masani; woman activist Hansa Mehta and communist Somnath Lahiri. After all these stalwarts had their say, a tribal leader and former hockey player Jaipal Singh rose to speak.

'As a jungli, as an Adibasi', said Jaipal,

> I am not expected to understand the legal intricacies of the Resolution. But my common sense tells me that every one of us should march on that road to freedom and fight together. Sir, if there is any group of Indian people that has been shabbily treated it is my people. They have been disgracefully treated, neglected for the last 6,000 years. The history of the Indus Valley civilisation, a child of which I am, shows quite clearly that – most of you here are intruders as far as I am concerned. It is the newcomers who have driven away my people from the Indus Valley to the jungle fastness. . . . The whole history of my people is one of continuous exploitation and dispossession by the non-aboriginals of India punctuated by rebellions and disorder, and yet I take Pandit Jawahar Lal Nehru at his word. I take you all at your word that now we are going to start a new chapter, a new chapter of independent India where there is equality of opportunity, where no one would be neglected.
>
> (Guha 2016: 105)

Freedom from colonial rule did bring new hopes and aspirations as the cause of the tribal people was accepted as a national task with a clear constitutional commitment. But for the tribal people, the history of dishonouring the promises made to the valiant fighters for freedom had just begun.

During British rule, as one would have expected from any colonising power, an administrative perspective existed which considered the homelands of tribals fighting for freedom as 'unregulated and inhabited by un-reconciled tribes'. It would be presumed that the initial colonial definition of the regions of tribal revolt to be subsequently revised to 'backward tracts inhabited by savages' and later redefined to 'excluded and partially excluded areas' inhabited by primitive people. The tribal people felt betrayed with the post-Independence nomenclature of 'scheduled areas inhabited by backward scheduled tribes' which was a continuation of the same colonial definition of the tribals. It is no surprise that Jaipal Singh, a tribal member of the Constituent Assembly, began to seriously question the 'hope' that the independent nation held out to the tribal people, who by no stretch of imagination were 'backward'.

The betrayal of tribal aspirations in the new independent nation began with the refusal to recognise the tribal uprisings as attempts to free their 'des' by overthrowing colonial rule. Sadly while laying the foundations of democratic India, the Constitutional Fathers neither examined the logic of 'excluded/partially excluded area' arrangements during colonial rule. Nor did the leaders of Independent India make a serious attempt to ascertain why the tribal people fiercely resisted British conquest and what the tribals sought from an Independent India. Continuing to adhere to the colonial view that the tribal people were primitive and backward, the Constitution sought to deal with problems of social justice without examining issues of cultural difference. The provisions for the tribal people, evolved in the debates, followed the parameters of the liberal political tradition adopted by the British rulers. The hundreds of tribal uprisings and the blood of thousands of valiant fighters from the forest lay in vain.

The failure to reject the colonial thought matrix of 'excluded/partially excluded area' was clearly reflected in Article 244, even though the Constitution created a special niche for the tribal areas, the Fifth Schedule was claimed a 'Constitution within the Constitution'; financial requirements for welfare and administration were made a 'charge on the Consolidated Fund of India' and the executive power of the Union extended to giving of directions concerning administration and welfare of Scheduled Tribes. The lack of serious anthropological discussion and debate leading to an informed perspective impacted the process to define 'tribes' and understand 'ethnicity'. To make things worse, tribal communities were perfunctorily classified as Scheduled Tribes with no conscious efforts made to ascertain tribal expectations. Centuries of continuous tribal struggles for freedom from British rule were not even examined, let alone understood. It was a sad day in the history of the tribal people of Independent India when the term

# AN UNBROKEN HISTORY OF BROKEN PROMISES

'Scheduled Tribe' was clearly viewed by the nation builders as an intermediate stage of 'backwardness' prior to the absorption of the primitive savages into the 'civilised mainstream'. Tribal aspirations for self-governance were perfunctorily subsumed under the task of nation building with the definitive goal of 'assimilation' of 'backward tribes' into the national mainstream.

The backward appellation suited the ruling elites as it provided a convenient way to follow a strategy no different from the ones which were imposed on the tribal people of the first nations, where the process of development began with 'residential schools' to de-school and alienate the children of the Indigenous 'red indians' of their language, history, culture, traditions and knowledge and subsequently colonise their minds, alienate them from their 'un-civilised past' and then prompt them to follow the 'teachings' of the coloniser. Sadly this practice continues in the present educational practice of the 'ashram schools'.

The dice was cast, when the prolonged tribal freedom struggle of 20 decades was subsumed as an anecdotal footnote of history when defining the agenda of nation building itself. It is not clear whether it was an error of history or a deliberate strategy to splinter organically linked tribal homelands so as to pre-empt a tribal upsurges like those of the colonial period. To pre-empt a Bhil leader of the stature of 'Tantya Bhil' or a 'Khajya Naik', terrors for the colonial rulers till their summary execution by hanging; the homelands of the Bhils were split four ways in Rajasthan, Madhya Pradesh, Gujarat and Maharashtra; with the Bhils of Rajasthan speaking Rajasthani, those of Madhya Pradesh speaking Hindi, Bhils of Gujarat speaking Guajarati and the Bhils of Maharashtra speaking Marathi. None of the later generations of the erstwhile Bhil community would be able to communicate with each other. Like the homelands of the Bhils, the ancestral homelands of the Gonds in the central Indian tracts, often referred to as Gondwana, was distributed in four states, Chhattisgarh, Madhya Pradesh, Maharashtra and Andhra, with the Gonds of Chhattisgarh speaking Chhattisgarhi, Gonds of Madhya Pradesh speaking Hindi, those of Maharashtra speaking Marathi, Gonds of Adilabad speaking Telugu. The suppression of the Gondi language as a medium of education soon after independence effectively eliminated any possibility of regrouping of one of the nation's largest tribal communities. It was no different with the Jharkhand tribal communities. Their homelands were also split in four parts. One part of tribal Bihar was merged with Bengal and spoke Bengali, another part was remained erstwhile Bihar, a third part was merged with Madhya Pradesh and spoke Hindi, the fourth part was merged with Orissa and spoke Oriya. It was a repeat of the Tower of Babel as the different sections of a tribal community were not able to communicate with each other and were effectively fragmented, never to rise up again.

In 1958 in his Foreword to the second edition of *A Philosophy for NEFA* by Verrier Elwin, the Prime Minister, Jawaharlal Nehru, articulated a set of premises of development in his Panchsheel Policy for the tribal people, a classical manifestation of Gandhi-Nehru socialist humanism influenced by Verrier Elvin. Recognition and respect for difference and diversity of culture, affirmation of rights, enhancement of the quality of life and the dignity of the people as important development indices were at variance with what was the stated or presumed though unstated agenda of mainstreaming and development. 'Panchsheel' presented an alternative development paradigm enshrined in five fundamental principles: (1) People should develop along the lines of their own genius and we should avoid imposing anything on them. We should try to encourage in every way their own traditional arts and culture. (2) Tribal rights in land and forests should be respected. (3) We should try to train and build up a team of their own people to do work of administration and development. Some technical personnel from outside will, no doubt be needed, especially in the beginning. But we should avoid introducing too many outsiders into tribal territory. (4) We should not over-administer these areas or over-whelm them with multiplicity of schemes. We should rather work through, and not in rivalry to, their own social and cultural institutions. (5) We should judge results, not by statistics or the amount of money spent, but by the quality of human character that is evolved.[5]

The Panchsheel Policy best reflected a model of tribal emancipation and advancement, which would ensure development with dignity for the tribal people (Bhowmik 1985: 11). The approach to tribal development after Independence consisted of adopting a middle path between the extremes of complete insulation and free play of market forces in the tribal homelands, as differentiated from the 'leave alone policy' of the British rulers. Nehru believed that the national leaders 'cannot allow matters to drift in the tribal areas'. At the same time 'we should avoid over-administration in these areas. It is between these two extreme positions that we have to function' and desired that development space be ensured for the tribal people to develop along the lines of their own genius. Concern was shown for the cultural heritage of the tribal people, which would infuse into the development process. This would mean development would be routed and modified to ground realities through their own social and cultural institutions and not overwhelmed and displaced by the maze of modern, formal, economic institutions. Thereby the strengths of tribal societies would be the foundation on which would be built the edifice of development.

Administrative policy repeated at nauseam 'the tribesmen come first, last, and all the time' but this approach was meant for public consumption only and operationally the tribals were the losers. Take the examples of roads. Linking of tribal areas with the plains was considered a strategy to break historical tribal isolation, provide the easy exposure to interact with the men of the plains. But the tribals gained nothing of the speculated road benefits. Roads made the entry of traders into the tribal villages easy. All they did was to enhance consumerism. Entry of non-tribals also shattered the health of the tribals. Robbed of whatever little forest fruit and produce they had enjoyed, all they received from the traders who temporarily resided in the tribal villages was serious venereal diseases. Islands of wealth, largely composed of the urban and rural elites, were surrounded by a sea of poverty and misery, peopled by the Scheduled Castes and Scheduled Tribe population (Doshi 1997: 18). Power attracted privilege and development was the bonus for the privileged few at the cost of the marginalised. Although the results of the first four Five Year Plans highlighted the failure of the dominant growth-driven agenda to restore security and dignity to the marginalised, the growth-driven approach continued[6] with what was called greater emphasis, or by hindsight lip service to the advancement of the weaker and poorer sections of society.

Following the dismal results of four plan periods a new strategy for tribal development was launched during the Fifth Five Year Plan. Areas of tribal concentration were identified for larger investments and more focused efforts, with the goal of bridging the yawning gap between the rich and poor and resolving growing tribal and non-tribal economic disparities, but the intended goal was to bring the tribals into the national mainstream.[7] The Tribal Sub Plan was conceived as a plan within the plan and envisaged pooling of all available fiscal and personnel resources in an integrated effort. In states with substantial tribal concentration, units comprising a few CD Blocks were selected, called Integrated Tribal Development Projects (ITDPs) and made the focal point in planning and implementation of what came to be known as the Tribal Sub Plan (TSP). But it was not merely the proverbial slip between planning and implementation, but the logic of the development process unleashed on the tribal people which laid low the high hope of the plan; the efforts to mainstream them divested them of their survival resources, placed them at the bottom of the heap and at the margins of the capitalist economy as ecological refugees.[8]

The Sixth Plan document on the approach to tribal development described the state of affairs without mincing words: 'In the name of tribal developments we have spent a lot of money during the last several Plans, but, notwithstanding Constitutional safeguards for the tribals, accounting at the end of the last period showed that actual benefits trickling down to the tribals have not been consistent with the promise we have made . . . 75 per cent of the total benefits have not reached that tribals'.[9] Notwithstanding lofty premises, the sixth plan did no better and the evaluation of its achievements noted that achievements were found wanting in eight out of the nine indicators namely: i) the TSP was merely an agglomeration of state plans, ii) with little or no consultation of tribal beneficiaries, iii) arithmetical considerations in family-oriented programmes defeated efforts at poverty alleviation, iv) defective integration in administration of ITDP with other same level development programmes, v) totally ineffective implementation of protective measures particularly relating to exploitation, vi) unscientific territorial and population coverage of the programme, vii) failure to enhance inputs of appropriate technology and viii) inconsequential monitoring and evaluation. The state of affairs revealed only marginal gains and that too with small sections[10] in widely dispersed locales. The TSP had failed to live up to expectations (Doshi 1997: 18). Once more a betrayal of the chance of a better life.

A radical review and reformulation of the TSP calling for depth and consistency of the thinking behind the approach and the system of implementation was called for. But notwithstanding repeated reports of ineffective and defective implementation which in effect undermined the goals of the Tribal Sub Plan, no serious thought or change took place in the subsequent plans. The observations during the current Tenth Five Year Plan are as revealing of the malaise in tribal development as the observations, without mincing words, indict the development executive at the central and the state. The ITDPs/ITDAs have by and large become defunct. It is an accepted fact that the TSP, in the form it is being implemented now, is not a success and the failure of the TSP can be attributed to the fact that seriousness in the implementation of the TSP concept was always lacking both at the central and state level. TSP allocations were not pursued seriously in letter and spirit and there were no concerted efforts to ensure that such resources benefited the target groups.

The report also observed that there was no enforcing mechanism to watch that allocations were actually spent on STs and not just reported notionally. It noted with alarm that most ministries merely make some notional allocations towards TSP every year. ITDPs/ITDAs, many a time, did not even get these funds from the state governments in time. The report highlighted the unpleasant fact that state governments have often not been willing to make a claim for central funds because of their own disinclination to bring in their own share with respect to centrally sponsored schemes, where cost sharing between the central government and the states is necessary. The report goes further to point out the reprehensible acts of some states to defraud the centre, on several occasions, by not contributing their own funds after availing central funds in spite of an agreement to contribute their own share.[11]

Tribal peoples' dreams of development appear to have been subverted. They believed the process of development of Independent India, in the main, would be freedom from exploitation, restoration of their homelands and community survival resources appropriated from them under the colonial law of res nullius, emancipation from the colonial categories of poor, backward and primitive, affirmation of their communitarian culture of internal solidarity and co-operation, strengthening of their traditions of interdependence with nature, assertion of their freedom and creativity; a development which would build on their strengths, both individual and communitarian, that would recognise their rights and restore their dignity. It was not to be.[12]

On the contrary development became a process of expanding liberties and license for the elites to appropriate their survival resources. Development led to the creation of elites, who mediated the presence of both the development bureaucracy and the outsider and leveraged their influence to syphon off both their survival resources, like land and resources earmarked for tribal development, increasing stratification, differentiation and fragmentation of their relatively egalitarian and solidarity-based societies, inculcation of tendencies of dependence and subservience to elites within and without their society, destruction of their communitarian strength based on a culture of independence and dignity.

In addition, the juggernaut of development displaced them by the millions, reducing them to ecological refugees, victims of a strategy of growth which forced them to pay the price for development while others reaped the fruits.[13] A price which called for the surrender of their past, present and future and rendered them mute witnesses to a hegemonic development paradigm they could not understand, let alone negotiate.[14] It would not be an exaggeration to conclude that the developmental paradigm, systematically put in place as the core of the agenda of nation building, has been without doubt the most significant cause for the erosion and disintegration of the tribal way of life.

It would be too facile an explanation to limit the blame for the present situation on widespread corruption, place the onus for poor performance on lower functionaries, and reduce the dismal situation to an implementation failure. While these factors have played a role, the roots for the failure of development, as the process of expanding freedoms, lie in a failure to understand the tribal world, the overt dilution of the vision for tribal people[15] and their place in nation building and the unchallenged imposition of the dominant development paradigm, which has effectively subverted the goals of tribal development.[16]

The reflections of Jawaharlal Nehru to say a decade after he presented his concept of Panchsheel for the advancement of the tribal communities remain as applicable to the present situation as ever:

> I am alarmed when I see – not only in this country but in other great countries too – how anxious people are to shape others according to their own image or likeness, and to impose on them their particular way to living. We are welcome to our way of living, but why impose it on others? . . . I am not at all sure which is the better way of living, the tribal or own. In some respects I am quite certain theirs is better. Therefore, it is grossly presumptuous on our part to approach them with an air of superiority, to tell them how to behave or what to do and what not to do. There is no point in trying to make of them a second-rate copy of ourselves.
>
> (Shashi 1990: 24)

Mainstream administrative thinking refused to recognise that tribal resistance was grounded in the right to their survival resources, land, forests, culture and self-governing institutions. As a result, the history of near to seven decades of 'planned development' sadly indicate that internal colonialism replaced British rule, which viewed tribal homelands as a resource base to fuel India's march towards development, with little thought to the inevitable devastation of the tribal people. The widely pervasive powers of governors were never used and failed to protect the entitlements of the tribal people despite constitutional provisions and guarantees. Continuing the colonial practice of divide and rule, compact areas of tribal majority are divided in different administrative units rendering the tribal people a minority in each unit, errors in scheduling tribal majority areas in 1954 remain uncorrected, tribal areas in West Bengal, Karnataka, Tamilnadu and Kerala remained unscheduled. Colonial legislations like the Indian Forest Act, the Land Acquisition Act continued to ravage tribal homelands while the administration remained foreign in spirit and deed and the system made criminals of those who followed their age-old traditions (Sharma 1998b: 8).

Reports of Commissions on Tribal Questions, the Scheduled Areas and Scheduled Tribes Commissions, the Sheila Ao and the Debar Commission collect dust even while valuable cultures and languages are suppressed, traditional councils superseded, self-governing institutions disrupted by state-sponsored Panchayats and development patronage, tribal people forced to become part of the 'mainstream' in the name of development. This development, however, justified open loot of resource-rich tribal homelands, while dams, industries and mining have displaced more than 10 million tribals post-Independence. 'Public good' opened tribal homelands while the administration subserved the 'interests' of development as alienation of lands, displacement, bondage, disorganisation of their lives and destitution and starvation deaths were the 'gains' development had to offer (Prabhu 1992: 2528). The situation in tribal tracts can be equated to internal colonisation and the condition of the tribals, the destruction of their language, culture, history and ethos and spirituality borders on 'ethnocide' (Prabhu 1994: 480).

On the one hand, by not providing them with decent education and healthcare, the Government of India has dishonoured its constitutional guarantee to provide the tribals equal opportunities for social and economic development. On the other hand, the policies of the government have more *actively* dispossessed very many tribals of their traditional means of life and livelihood. For the tribals of the mainland live amidst India's best forests, alongside many of its fastest-flowing rivers, and on top of its richest mineral resources. Once, this closeness to nature's bounty provided them the means for subsistence and survival. However, as the pace of economic and industrial development picked up after Independence, the tribals have increasingly had to make way for commercial forestry, dams and mines. Often, the tribals are displaced because of the pressures and imperatives of what passes as 'development', sometimes, they are displaced because of the pressures and imperatives of development's equally modern other: namely, 'conservation'. Thus, apart from large dams and industrial townships, tribals have also been rendered homeless by national parks and sanctuaries.[17]

But with history as a mute witness, Panchsheel was seen as a minor aberration and diversion from the overarching logic of capital and given a quick burial. The goals of tribal development were subsumed under the logic of capitalistic growth and its attendant indices. The tribal people were to be sacrificed on the altar of development as the nation marched forward plan after plan, till experience of the first four Five Year Plans, demolished fond expectations of growth and economic advancement and forced the planners to sit up and take notice of the fact that the rise in the standard of living did not result in equituous distribution of the national income. A candid analysis of the plan period shows that the elites have been out for the selling of the tribals. Without understanding the tribal social structure and its socio-historical ups and downs, assumptions were formulated at total variance with the realities of their structure. Under the guise that tribals enjoyed some constitutional safeties and securities and protective discriminations, according to which priorities of development benefits have to be given to the tribals. Administrative policy repeated at nauseam 'the tribesmen come first, last, and all the time' but this approach was meant for public

How many tribals have lost their homes and lands as a result of conscious state policy? The estimates vary – they range from a few million to as many as 20 million. Even if we cannot come up with a precise, reliable number, to the question 'How many tribals have been involuntarily displaced by the policies of the government of India', the answer must be: 'Too many'. The sociologist Walter Fernandes estimates that about 40 per cent of all those displaced by government projects are of tribal origin. Since tribals constitute roughly 8 per cent of India's population, this means that a tribal is five times as likely as a non-tribal to be forced to sacrifice his home and hearth by the claims and demands of development and/or conservation (Fernandes 2006).

Already, by the 1960s, reports commissioned by the Government of India were demonstrating the utter failure of the state in providing a life of dignity and honour to its tribal citizens. Nor was this a generalised critique; rather, the specific problems faced by the tribals were identified – namely, callous and corrupt officials, the loss of land, indebtedness, restrictions on the use of the forest and large-scale displacement. The evidence offered in these (and other reports) should have called for a course correction, for the formation and implementation of policies that ensured that India's industrial and economic development was not to be at the cost of its tribal citizens (GoI 1961).

Much of the poverty and degradation they saw, said the committee, was the fault of us, the 'civilised' people. We have driven [the tribals] into the hills because we wanted their land and now we blame them for cultivating it in the only way we left to them. We have robbed them of their arts by sending them the cheap and tawdry products of a commercial economy. We have even taken away their food by stopping their hunting or by introducing new taboos which deprive them of the valuable protein elements in meat and fish. We sell them spirits which are far more injurious than the home-made beers and wines which are nourishing and familiar to them, and use the proceeds to uplift them with ideals. We look down on them and rob them of their self-confidence, and take away their freedom by laws which they do not understand.[18]

In the central Indian tribal tracts, the British were continuously confronted by tribal uprisings and as they were unable to curb the repeated uprisings by force or machination, they set in motion administrative changes to erode the tribal capacity to revolt. Central to their agenda was the abolition of community ownership of land and alienation from the forest, which was recognised as central to sustain community cohesion and internal solidarity. The colonial rulers rightly assessed the criticality of loss of land and forest in the life and psyche of the tribal people which could never be under-estimated (Prabhu 2007). Hence the colonial government segregated tribal homelands depending on administration's ability to quell revolts. The central Indian tracts, where quick military intervention was possible and state presence could be kept low by using the feudal and comprador bourgeoisie to facilitate population control and resource-extraction for the rulers, were declared 'partially excluded', while the hilly tribal tracts beyond the Brahmaputra were declared 'excluded' hence traditional systems survived.

The introduction of the alien concept of private property began with the permanent settlement of the British in 1793 and the establishment of the zamindari system which conferred control over vast territories; tribal territories were designated to feudal lords for the marginalised; the growth-driven approach continued with what was called greater emphasis, or by hindsight lip service to the advancement of the weaker and poorer sections of society. Sixty years have passed since Jaipal took Nehru and all the others at their word. What has been the fate of his people, the tribals, in this time? This chapter will argue that, in many ways, the tribals of peninsular India are the unacknowledged victims of six decades of democratic development. In this period they have continued to be exploited and dispossessed by the wider economy and polity. At the same time, the process of dispossession has been punctuated by rebellions and disorder. Their relative and oftentimes absolute deprivation is the more striking when compared with that of other disadvantaged groups revenue collection by the British (Bijoy 2007).

The seizure of tribal homelands and their conversion into government property as Reserved, Protected Forests, Grazing and Wastelands accompanied the process of re-ordering land relations, from community to state to individual, across tribal areas of Central India. One example are the tribal tracts, adjacent to Mumbai in Thane district, where 'by a simple notification, nearly 401,566 acres of community lands, not privately owned, belonging to the tribals and controlled . . . through their elders, were classified as wasteland and taken away overnight and merged into Government Forest land amounting to nearly 50 per cent of the forest area of the District' (GoB 1887). By 1850, the colonial administration had brutally suppressed the practice of collective jhum cultivation, forced them out of the forest and resettled them in more or less permanent habitations on the fringes of the forest (Prabhu 2007). Community life broken and resistance shattered, the tribals were pushed into debt bondage and serfdom with their land alienated to merchants, traders, timber and excise contractors.

Tribal ecologic-social systems came under greater threat post-Independence, as the entrenched comprador class facilitated the transfer of power from the colonial powers and consolidated themselves in political and economic systems. The Indigenous or tribal civilisations were categorised as 'backward hindus' and subsumed to facilitate 'building a modern nation-state', at immense cost to their distinct societies, cultures and governance systems. This was considered a necessary condition for the Indian state to facilitate extraction of the mineral and natural resources in the tribal homelands. The state refused to recognise the existence of a distinct tribal civilisation and the compulsions of democracy curbed repression of alternative civilisational aspirations, though protection of their unique lifeways was promised by the first prime minister in his Panchsheel for the tribal people. Hence we need to recognise the distinction between the premises of conservationist versus consumptionist civilisations and recognise the premises of human development of the tribals accordingly. Blindly adopting standards of consumptionist capitalistic civilisations as the normative order and comparing the present tribal conditions to the premises of the ruling elite will cause grave harm to the tribal people and the 'value' based lives that they live.

Almost all tribals without exception recognise that landlessness is the result of state surrender to land, mine and industry lobbies resulting in its indefensible failure to protect tribal land, a result of the lack of political will, complicit bureaucracy, dysfunctional governance, failure of the political elite, defenceless citizens, failure to uphold the law and Constitution, while meekly surrendering to a market-driven development paradigm of the dominant elites. This view is the basis of the Supreme Court's view in the Samatha Case, 'the purpose of the Fifth and Sixth Schedules to the Constitution is to prevent exploitation of truthful, inarticulate and innocent tribals and to empower them socially, educationally, economically and politically. . . . The Constitution intends that the land always should remain with the tribals'.[19] This position is in akin to International Conventions (ILO 107 and 169), which call on governments to 'respect the special importance for the cultural and spiritual values of the people's relationship with lands or territories, or both as applicable, which they occupy or otherwise use, in particular the collective aspect of their relationship'. About 45 per cent tribals are landless today (Sharma 2000).

Maoist supporters emphasise huge class and wealth disparities in Indian society, especially in rural areas and the worsening situation since the 1990s, fed by a total failure to implement either land reforms right from Independence, or decentralised democracy in Scheduled Areas envisaged in PESA. Maoist supporters criticise mainstream political parties for colluding with exploitative structures defeating land reforms. From a position of supporting big dams in Andhra Pradesh, Maoists have recently made strong statements against the spate of secret deals with mining companies and the trend of tribal displacement, though evidence shows protection money from mining companies is often a main source of Maoist funding and leaders have been reticent on their own policy regarding mining (Dandekar 2013).

Indeed, many feel the tribals pay the price for development and official estimates place the number of project-displaced tribal people at 60 million since Independence with not even a third properly resettled. Most of the displaced are now asset-less rural poor, marginal farmers, quarry workers and migrant labour. Around 80 per cent are tribals. Official statistics testify that tribals have been the worst off on all indicators of development. Already at the bottom of the development pyramid, being deprived of their land completely pauperises them, forcing many to move and live in subhuman conditions in the metros. The last two decades have also seen unprecedented agrarian distress, with more than two lakh farmers committing suicide, as per the National Crime Records Bureau, unparalleled events in Indian history (Shah 2015).

It is in this backdrop that we look at the palpable anger over forcible land acquisition. With 90 per cent of coal and more than 50 per cent of minerals, prospective dam sites and industrial enclaves mainly in tribal regions, tension over land loss grows, posing questions on our development strategy; the delicate fabric of Indian democracy is terribly frayed at the edges. In the remote tribal heartlands, the tribals feel a deep abiding sense of hurt, alienation and cynicism that they have allowed themselves to be helplessly drawn into a terrible vortex of violence and counter-violence, even when they know it will lead nowhere. There is no political will to protect tribal land to save the Indigenous/tribal communities in India. In the debates around the history and future of tribal communities, the role of the state, the role of mining and industrial development, private property and the landscape of legislation around tribal rights cannot but be on top of the agenda.[20]

Every promise was broken by the political thrust of nation building which totally excluded the genuine aspirations for self-governance of their homelands, and worse still reduced the core of their expectations as first nations to wishful thinking. Almost 50 years after Independence, seeing an opportunity to bring in the issue of tribal self-governance in the 73rd Amendment, Dr. B.D. Sharma, then Commissioner for Scheduled Castes and Scheduled Tribes, ensured that a special act was made for the Scheduled Areas. Hence on the 23 December 1996, when the president of India gave his assent to the Panchayats (Extension to the Scheduled Areas) Act, a new paradigm of governance was put into place, the praxis of administration was tempered in the crucible of tradition. A new chapter in the history of modern India was waiting to be written or re-written (Sharma 1998a: xiii). The authors of the new history would be the tribal people of India.

PESA was a qualitative leap forward for the 73rd Amendment. Gram Sabha (the village assembly) became part of the Constitution. Democratic decentralisation reached its logical conclusion in directly empowering the 'citizen' through 'participatory democracy'. PESA moved from 'development delivery' to 'empowerment'; from implementation to planning; from 'circumscribed involvement' to 'conscious participation'. PESA constructed tribal self-governance around six axes: i) affirmation that an organic self-governing community was a habitation, ii) people and not the state are competent to be seized with all matters concerning their day-to-day life, iii) common tribals acting through community could decide the path of their development, enjoin the Gram Panchayat to prepare and implement developmental projects, iv) communities have right to be consulted on acquisition of or access to land and land-based resources, v) community has the capability and competence to adjudicate on and act to end all exploitative relations including land alienation, moneylending, market relations and alcohol, iv) the powers of the Gram Sabha, whose powers could not be usurped by a superior body.

Notwithstanding PESA's constitutional status and the mandatory compliance required, states with Schedule V areas were reluctant to amend their PR laws to protect the powers of the ruling elites; cosmetic amendments were introduced to give a semblance of compliance under pressure; PR laws of all the states are not in conformity with the central act, vary in their application and at times are even contrary to PESA. As PESA provides the opportunity for government to move away from 'eminent domain' to constructive 'trusteeship', but state governments still enjoy the colonial legal frame. Infusion of participation and transparency would uproot corruption, nepotism and diminish contractor-driven development, but it lies shattered as state governments refuse to put rules in place. 'Public Interest' has undermined 'Peoples Survival'. Minimal rules in ensuring compliance, and despite safeguards put in place by PESA, rights of the villagers are being violated with impunity. When the villagers voice their opposition in the consultation process, the final authority remains with the DC to overrule the opposition, a power that emanates from the colonial concept of 'eminent domain'. What are observed are adversarial relations between the officials and the villagers, with the state considering the demands and protests of the villagers to be a nuisance and in some cases even anti-social. It is critical that the observations of the Supreme Court in 'Samata v/s State of Andhra Pradesh',[21] calling for a fundamental change in considering the tribals as shareholders rather than stake holders which could become the basis of resolution of this ticklish problem, are not even considered. Sadly most of the governments are ignorant of the observations of the Samata Judgement or follow them in the spirit in which they are formulated.

Land laws have failed to stop tribal land alienation following massive incursion of non-tribals into tribal areas. Estimates suggest that 48 per cent of the total land in Scheduled districts is in possession of non-tribals, while hundreds of thousands of cases are pending disposal for decades. PESA took a radical step of conferring the right of identifying 'tribal alienation' where it takes place and with whom it takes place and the responsibility to take action to remedy the wrong at the place where the land lies and in the interests of justice. Sadly no state has taken any concrete legal steps with the exception of Madhya Pradesh where the Land Revenue Code incorporates the provisions of the PESA

Our study showed that about 99 per cent of the members of the Gram Sabha and the elected representatives of PRIs and about 90 per cent of the official functionaries working at the village and block levels have said that they are not aware of PESA or the state conformity acts and their provisions. State governments have not made any specific efforts to educate the people about the provisions of the acts which aim at giving specific protection to the economic and political rights of tribal people in the Scheduled Areas and their traditional and cultural practices. Sad but true. There is blindness and feigned blindness, while the former calls for sympathy, the latter is nothing but criminal.

Where do we go from here is in the minds of tribal activists across the nation. 'Our life is one long struggle' has been on the lips of most activists of a myriad of tribal movements. Even while they seek to contend with the multiple betrayals and negations that have punctuated the interface of the Indian state with the tribal people, the movements seek to redefine their agendas in four directions, reaffirming of the tribal self, recapturing the control over resources, reclaiming political domain and redefining development. This nascent shift from resistance to resurgence, if taken to its logical conclusion, will be synonymous with ethno development. Broadly speaking ethno development is the practical manifestation of internal self-determination which is essentially in conformity with the constitutional provisions. Ethno implies respect for peoples, societies and cultures and their wishes and desires while development refers to a total phenomenon combining economics, politics and culture in an all-encompassing whole defined by the concerned people themselves. Ethno development then means control of the ethnic over its lands resources, social organisation and culture; it implies that the tribal ethnics have the right to freely negotiate with the state the kind of relationship they individually wish to have. In other words, it conveys that tribals will choose to confront the challenges posed by pseudo-modernity rooted in their traditional institutions and values. This is not a self-imposed isolation or political secession but redefining development and nation building on the basis of the legitimate aspirations of culturally distinct groups. Ethno development should not be confused with romantic tribalism and does not seek to keep tribals outside the matrix of change or take refuge in the supposedly unadulterated romanticised past. It recognises the history of repeated betrayals of the tribal peoples, but it affirms the tribal peoples' right to elaborate and change as a strategy of survival. While assimilation, integration and apartheid condemn the future of tribal peoples into a blind alley, ethno development pleads that they have the right to choose what to conserve and what to change, what to adopt and what to reject from other cultures, and all these in what pace and intensity in this fast-changing world.

Tribal movements have come a long way. Twenty-five decades of struggle is a treasure of experience few communities can boast of. The tribal ethos, the way of life, the logic of relationships between person/person and person/nature could provide answers to the questions the world is asking. Tribal societies, particularly those who have retained their systems of meaning and traditions of community solidarity, egalitarian relationships, basic honesty and internal integrity, even in the face of a continuous onslaught, may perhaps provide solutions to a troubled planet. Tribal movements as processes of discovering and articulating synergistic solutions can probably contribute in a large measure to the learners of tomorrow. I hope this chapter serves as a step in that journey.

## Notes

1 The title of this chapter has been specifically chosen in honour of Dr. B.D. Sharma, an IAS Officer who spent his entire career as a civil servant and, after a premature retirement from the Indian Administrative Service, his entire waking hours in the promotion and defence of the rights of the Indigenous/tribal people, beginning with an important assignment as the Vice-Chancellor or the strife-torn North Eastern Hill University, Shillong; which was established to cater to the academic aspirations of the tribal people of the North East, to turn around what could have deteriorated into an academic misadventure and to bring the University on an even keel. Dr. Sharma returned from NEHU to shoulder the responsibilities as the Commissioner for Scheduled Castes and Scheduled Tribes. In his new assignment, Dr. Sharma produced two path-breaking reports, which placed before the Central Government the critical issues confronting the tribal people in the nation, particularly emergent internal colonialism. After finishing his term, Dr. Sharma led the Bharat Jan Andolan and played an irreplaceable role in the Narmada Bachao Andolan. Dr. Sharma repeatedly referred to the history of the treatment of the tribal people by the state in post-colonial India as an 'Unbroken History of Broken Promises'. His last book also used the same title. As a close colleague of

Dr. Sharma and a member of the core committee of Bharat Jan Andolan, the author is using the same title as a mark of honour and respect for a person whose life was circumscribed by the struggle of tribal India against de facto disempowerment, alienation of their resources and destruction of their ethos and identity.

2  The arguments put forward in this chapter are the result of four decades of careful participant learning from a long history, both recorded and oral, of struggles of the tribal/Indigenous peoples across the nation and the rationale behind their incessant aspiration for freedom both during the rule of the colonial state and subsequently the post-colonial Indian state, albeit with different nuances. Though recorded history has been significantly deficient in its registry of post-colonial and post-Independence tribal uprisings, more recent efforts of scholars from the subaltern school have been able to unearth a large measure of historical anecdotes from the oral traditional knowledge of a large number of tribal communities.

3  Subaltern historians have unearthed a wealth of information of tribal resistance to the colonial intrusion into the homelands (*des*); listed below are a cross section of tribal uprisings that have been identified so far. The first 1778 – The revolt of the Pahariyain Bihar-Malpahariya Region; 1784–1785 – the Kolis of Maharashtra; 1789, 1794–1795, 1801 the Tamar of Chota Nagpur in present-day Jharkhand; 1795–1800 the Chuari Movement in Bihar; 1803, 1822, 1862, 1879, 1880 – the Koyasin Andhra Pradesh; 1807–1808, 1811, 1817, 1820 – the tribal revolts in Chotanagpur; 1809–1828, 1846, 1857–1858 – Bhils in Western India; 1818, 1831–1832 – Kols in Chotangpur; 1825, 1828, 1843, 1849, 1869 – Singphos in Assam; 1827, 1855 – Mishmis in Arunachal Pradesh; 1828 – tribals of Assam; 1829 Khasis of Assam; 1820, 1832, 1867, 1889 Mundas of Jharkhand; 822–1823 – Kherwar uprising in Jharkhand; 1834–1841, 1842, 1850, 1860, 1871–1872, 1892 the Lushais of Assam; 1835, 1872–1873 – Daflas of Assam; 1838, 1868 – Naiks of Gujarat; 1839–1843 – Khampti in Assam; 1842 – Gonds of Bastar in Chhattisgarh; 1850 – Kondhs in Orissa; 1854 – North Kachari hill people of Assam; 1855, 1869–1870 – Santhals in Jharkhand; 1858 – Naikdas in Gujarat; 1860–1862 Syntengs of Jaintia Hills of Meghalaya; 1861 – Phulaguri uprising in Assam; 1861 – Juangs in Orissa; 1867, 1883 – Sentinel Islanders in the Andaman Islands; 1868–1869 – Raigmels of Assam; 1879, 1932, 1963–1971 – Nagas of Nagaland; 1811 – Bastar tribal uprising; 1913, 1914, 1920, 1921 – Tana Bhagat rebellion in Bihar; 1941 Gond and Kolam revolt in Andhra Pradesh; 1942 – Koraput revolt in Orissa, 1942–1945 – revolts by Andaman Island tribes against Japanese occupation army; 1945–1950, 1956–1958 – Warli revolt of Maharashtra; 1966–71 – Mizo revolt in Mizoram; 1967–1971 – Naxalbari in West Bengal; 1967–1969 – Srikakulam Uprising; 1990–1998 – Adilabad Uprising; 2000 – Resistance of Bastar Gonds.

4  The term 'First Nations' is still being used by the Indigenous people of the American continents to distinguish their government systems, based on political construct of governance of citizens and their homelands as totally alien to the governance of the colonisers. For a clearer expose on the governance of land of the Indigenous tribes of North America, read the 'Letter of Chief Seattle to the Great Chief in Washington' in 1855.

5 'We cannot allow matters to drift in the tribal areas or just not take interest in them. In the world of today that is not possible or desirable. At the same time we should avoid over-administering these areas and, in particular, sending too many outsiders into tribal territory. It is between these two extreme positions that we have to function'. – Jawaharlal Nehru, New Delhi, 9 October 1958.

6 'In the first twenty five years of India's independence, despite massive inputs, only nominal benefits reached down to the tribal people. The tendency to ignore subtle tribal differences and underplay the diverse needs of different tribal groups allowed an unimaginative bureaucracy to work for the solution of what it saw as the tribal problem. Programs were not need based; unwanted reforms were foisted, a rigid and ham handed approach obscured development objectives and blocked the attainment of specified goals. Non tribals benefited more from the funds that were earmarked for the development of the tribes' (Dube in Sharma 1978: ii).

7 'A new strategy for the Fifth Five Year Plan period was development and reducing tribal non-tribal economic disparities . . . but the ultimate objective was to bring tribals to the national mainstream' (Singh and Bhandari 1980: 2013).

8 'Development implying higher consumption and a better quality of life, cannot per se be accepted as an unqualified goal of development, literature on economic development equating tribal society with poverty is neither sound, based on entirely different premises and has no relevance to the tribal scene . . . communities living in inaccessible regions, with plentiful natural resources, sufficient to meet their basic physical needs, cannot be termed as poor. Their needs are limited and resources plentiful. . . . Use of monetary norms to compute income and expenditure is irrelevant' (Sharma 2010: 4).

9 Approach to Tribal Development in the Sixth Plan: A Preliminary Perspective, Planning Commission, New Delhi.

10 'Consequences of development have gone against them, increased the chances of a few of newly emerged elites and non-tribals, largely high-caste Hindus. Government departments, voluntary agencies, nationalised banks, corporate sector, multinationals are all partly or largely party to the sabotage of the course of the tribal development. The sociologist or anthropologist are no exception' (Doshi 1987: 17).

11 Report of Standing Committee on Inter-Sectoral Issues Relating to Tribal Development, *Planning Commission*, 2005.

12 'An objective appraisal of different tribal areas would show that in our over-enthusiasm we have caused much greater harm to the tribes. We have not redressed their grievances, but have imposed our will on their affairs in such a manner that tribals are fast losing their confidence in the present order. Social workers sermonise in a manner that offend the tribals. Administrators of different denominations want to shape things according to their own reference. They achieve little and make the tribals apathetic to various programmes' (Das 1972: 193).

13 The essence of this sentiment is reflected in subaltern poetry and music. One classical example is the Bhil song *Deshbhakt Log Tomara, Tyag Amha ka Mangatha* which translates as 'You, who claim to be the patriots

of the nation, why do you continuously demand sacrifice of us' composed by Vahru Sonavne, a Bhil intellectual.
14 'Earlier tribals knew three types of officials; revenue collector, village chawkidar and forest guard. After the CD program the long arm of administration reached remote corners. Tribals could not comprehend the development-oriented administration. As CD program stressed targets and area development erstwhile exploiters and non-tribal middle class got all schemes and benefited from development projects meant for the tribal people. Block staff, mostly from non-tribal areas were corrupt. It was impossible for a tribal to get any grant, subsidy or loan without bribing venal officials. Development spread disaffection . . . everything sponsored by the bureaucracy was seen with distrust and suspicion, efforts to train the bureaucracy in tribal life and culture were ineffective, policies framed for economic betterment of the tribals were unrealistic, special projects failed due to bad administration and avoidable red-tape. Non-tribals cornered funds, government policies did not address economic or educational or employment issues' (Sachchidananda 1972: 173).
15 'The consequences of development have gone against them, have increased the life chances of a few of their newly emerged elites and non-tribals. Government departments, voluntary agencies, nationalised banks, corporate sector and multinationals – are all partly or largely party to the sabotage of the course of the tribal development. The sociologist and the anthropologist are no exception to this neglect or omission' (Doshi 1987: 17).
16 'As they possess constitutional privileges for their development, we sell most of our things in their name. Items of development, be it a school, dispensary, rail road, telephone, cooking gas and what not are all accounted as tribal development. . . . Those in the development market, understand little of the realities of the tribal society . . . our approach of tribal development has been misdirected, we have imposed values, structures and aspirations of the super-ordinate ruling elites on tribal society. In "alliance" with social scientists, intellectuals and corporate sector have provided an exaggerated dimension to the consumerisation of tribals barely living at the subsistence level' (Doshi 1987: 20).
17 Rangarajan and Shahabuddin (2006).
18 Government of India (1960).
19 Government of India (n.d.).
20 Chanchani (2007).
21 'Samata v/s State of Andhra Pradesh AIR 1997 SC 3297'.

# References

Bannerjee, Sumanta. 1984. *India's Simmering Revolution: The Naxalite Uprising*. New Delhi: Select Book Service Syndicate.
Bhowmik, K. L. 1985. 'Perspectives of Current Researches on Rural Development', in *Current Anthropological and Archaeological Perspectives, Volume VII: Rural Development*. New Delhi: Inter-India Publications.
Bijoy, C. R. 2007. 'Tribals of India, A History of Discrimination, Conflict and Resistance', in *This Is Our Homeland*. Bangalore: Equations.

Chanchani, Aditi. 2007. *This Is Our Homeland: A Collection of Essays on the Betrayal of Adivasi Rights in India*. Bangalore: Equations. https://www.equitabletourism.org/files/fileDocuments493_uid10.pdf (accessed on 13 July 2018).

Dandekar, A. 2013. *Why and Wither the Maoists*. New Delhi: NAC Note.

Das, Nityanand. 1972. 'The Tribal Situation in Orissa', in K. Singh Suresh (ed.), *The Tribal Situation in India*. Shimla: HAS.

Doshi, S. L. 1997. *Emerging Tribal Image*. Jaipur: Rawat Publications.

Dube, S. C. 2003. 'Foreword', in B. D. Sharma (Author), *Tribal Development: The Concept and the Frame*, pp. 9–10. New Delhi: Sahyog Pustak Kuteer Trust.

Fernandes, W. 2006. 'Development-Induced Displacement and Tribal Women', in Govind Chandra Rath (ed.), *Tribal Development in India: The Contemporary Debate*. New Delhi: Sage Publications.

Government of Bombay. 1887. *Report of the Bombay Forest Commission*. Bombay: Government Central Press.

Government of India. 1960. *Report of the Committee on Special Multipurpose Tribal Blocks*. New Delhi: Ministry of Home Affairs. http://dspace.gipe.ac.in/xmlui/handle/10973/26430 (accessed on 13 July 2018).

Government of India. 1961. *Report of the Scheduled Areas and Scheduled Tribes Committee*. New Delhi: Government of India.

Government of India.n.d. *Issues of Social Justice: Scheduled Castes, Scheduled Tribes and Other Backward Classes – An Unfinished National Agenda*. New Delhi: National Commission to Review the Working of the Constitution. http://www.humanrightsinitiative.org/publications/const/issues_of_social_justice_scst_obc.pdf (accessed on 13 July 2018).

Guha, Ramachandra. 2016. *Democrats and Dissenters*. London: Penguin.

Haimendorf Von Furrer, Christoph. 1992. *Tribal India: The Struggle for Survival*. New Delhi: Oxford University Press.

Hardiman, David (ed.). 1992. *Peasant Resistance in India 1858–1914*. New Delhi: Oxford University Press.

Hibbert, Christopher. 1980. *The Great Mutiny India 1857*. New Delhi: Penguin.

Longkumer, Lanusashi. 2014. 'Nagaland-Land Alienation, Dynamics of Colonialism, Security and Development', in *Status of Tribal/Indigenous Peoples Land Series-6*. New Delhi: Aakar Books.

Mehta, Piarey Lal. 1991. *Constitutional Protection to Scheduled Tribes in India: In Prospect and Retrospect*. New Delhi: H. K. Publishers and Distributors.

Prabhu, Pradip. 1992. 'Tribal Deaths in Thane District: The Other Side', *Economic and Political Weekly*, 27(47): 2527–30.

Prabhu, Pradip. 1994. *Sustainable Tribal Development*. Golden Jubilee Issue on Sustainable Development. New Delhi: Indian Institute of Public Administration.

Prabhu, Pradip. 1998. 'Tribal Movements: Resistance to Resurgence', in Desai Murli et al. (eds.), *Towards People Centered Development*. Mumbai: Tata Institute of Social Sciences.

Prabhu, Pradip. 2007. *Legally Looted and Cheated: Land Reforms and Tribals in Maharashtra*.

Prabhu, P. and S. Bulsara. 2014. *Wisdom From the Wilderness*. Baroda: Bhasha.
Prabhu, P. and B. Shiraz. 2013. *Wisdom From the Wilderness*. Baroda: Bhasha.
Rangarajan, M. and Ghazala Shahabuddin. 2006. 'Displacement and Relocation from Protected Areas: Towards a Historical and Biological Synthesis', *Conservation and Society*, 4(3): 359–78.
*Report of the Bombay Forest Commission*. 1887. Volumes 1–2. Government Central Press.
Sachchidananda. 1972. 'Tribal Situation in Bihar',in K. S. Singh (ed.), *Tribal Situation in India*. Shimla: HAS.
Savyasaachi. 1998. *Tribal Forest Dwellers and Self Rule*. New Delhi: Indian Social Institute.
Shah, M. 2015. 'Land Development and Democracy', *The Hindu*.
Sharma, Bhram Dev. 1998a. *Self Rule Laws: Madhya Pradesh*. New Delhi: Sahyog Pustak Kutir.
Sharma, Bhram Dev. 1998b. *The People Versus the System*. New Delhi: Sahyog Pustak Kutir.
Sharma, Bhram Dev. 2000. *The Fifth Schedule: Volumes I & II*. New Delhi: Sahyog Pustak Kutir.
Sharma, Bhram Dev. 2010. *Unbroken History of Broken Promises*. New Delhi: Freedom Press.
Shashi, S. S. 1990. *Nehru and the Tribals*. New Delhi: Concept.
Singh, B. and J. S. Bhandari (eds.). 1980. 'Dynamics of Development', in B. Singh and J. S. Bhandari (eds.), *The Tribal World and Its Transformation*. New Delhi: Concept Publishing Company.
Singh, K. S. (ed.). 1982. *Tribal Movements in India*. New Delhi: Manohar Books.
Verrier, Elwin. 1957. *A Philosophy for NEFA*. Comments by Jawaharlal Nehru (Prime Minister of India).

# 14
# LANGUAGE AND SCHOOLING OF ADIVASI CHILDREN IN INDIA
Issues relating to their right to education

*V. Srinivasa Rao*

It is an established fact that language is not merely a medium of communication; it constitutes culture and knowledge and is embedded in hierarchies of domination and power relations. Language is a key area of concern in the context of Adivasi education. Almost every Adivasi community has its own language or dialect. But their languages are not considered appropriate for instruction in school education as they do not have scripts, although it is constitutionally binding (Article 350 A) to teach in mother tongues at the primary stage of education to children. In line with the constitutional provisions on mother tongue education, the National Curriculum Frameworks of 2005 too has strongly emphasised that the mother tongue should be the medium of instruction at least up to the primary stage (GoI 2005).

In fact, the script is not a criterion as a language can be written in any script. It is important to note that the national language and official language of India, i.e. Hindi and English, have no script of their own. But they are taught as compulsory languages in schools as first and second languages. They are taught simply because they are languages of the dominant speaker community. Importantly, this results in poor performance and drop-out of Adivasi children from school due to the difference between the home language of the child and the medium of instruction followed at school. The lack of comprehension and participation in the classroom transactions causes the child to lose interest and finally being pushed out of school. This chapter examines how the Adivasis are being denied the right to education by imposition of an alien language on their children, particularly in the context of the recent Right to Education Act.

It is a universal fact that language plays a pivotal role in understanding and comprehension and cognitive development. If a child cannot make sense of the teacher's teaching, it becomes irrelevant and disastrous not just for the pupil but also for the teacher. In such circumstances the presence of the teacher becomes inconsequential in the classroom. This is more so in the context of a classroom where Adivasi children are in dominant numbers. An Adivasi child in the early years usually uses her home language to communicate her views, as she has yet not been exposed to the regional language. A child with this background certainly requires a teacher who could communicate in her home language. Therefore, when we speak about the relevance of a teacher to an Adivasi pupil, the teacher is expected to communicate with the child in the 'child's language' instead of the 'teacher's language'. This is imperative in the context of Adivasi education, particularly in a more diverse society like India where it is witnessed with multiple languages, cultures and regional disparities.

It is said that one of the important functions of education is to bring about social transformation in society. This is particularly so for the Adivasis who have remained relatively isolated from the surrounding society and have been predominately engaged in agriculture and related activities. It is through education that the Adivasis can have an exposure to the outside world with information on a range of matters relevant to life (Talesara 1994: 14). Emphasising the importance of education for Adivasis, Shah (1985: 1) observed that, 'learning is a prerequisite for social transformation in a welfare State. Education also opens up an avenue which enables them to enter the non-agricultural sector for earning the livelihood'. It has been observed that education makes life better for all and this includes the Adivasis. While describing the intrinsic relationship between Adivasi culture and success of their education, Sinha (1989: 23) brings in the inside-outside argument. According to him, the real difficulties of Adivasis' access to education can be encapsulated as:

> one existing inside and the other outside. Because of the traditional way of life and concept of magic oriented notions, the tribals have always resisted any reformation, education and trans-culturisation, purely on a feeling that any such importation of thought is a challenge to their existence. The outside difficulty is that on account of peculiar way of thinking of the tribals any organisation including the State have not

properly appreciated which is the right side first to tackle for the development.

The success of Adivasi education has been dependent upon both, the inside view which encompasses the Adivasi's traditional way of life, and the outside view which is represented by the external organisation including the state. This has resulted in raising specific questions regarding the educational programmes with reference to the Adivasis. Is it possible for the state to formulate education policy which embraces and balances the Adivasi traditional way of learning with the modern perspective of education? Is it really necessary to protect the Adivasi traditional way of learning in policy making? As an answer, Heredia (1995: 891) states that the development of the Adivasis does not lie in merely preserving their cultural autonomy but in making them 'participate in their own development where education will have a necessary and crucial role to play'.

Further, the issue of Adivasi education has also been discussed in relation to the question of providing equality and justice through access to formal schooling. It has been stated that to attain self-reliance and social development, the major task before the country is to expand the system of education at all levels, make education available to all and to remove various inequalities of different types (Premi 2000). In order to create equal opportunities by expanding education, particularly in a diverse society like India which has a significant population of Adivasi or Indigenous peoples, communicating in the 'child's language' in the classroom is certainly more appropriate. In order to understand the 'child's language', we need to understand their culture and community as a whole, in line with their home language.

## Language, culture and community

With a natural disposition towards the local dialect/language, an Adivasi child is generally unfamiliar with the state language used in the school. As a child, s/he has a very limited knowledge of the regional language. In some cases, Adivasi children face challenges to understand what exactly the teacher teaches in the classroom. This is because the cultural practice of speaking in their home language is a natural instinct and inbuilt in their culture. The community as a whole uses its Indigenous language to communicate. Language for the Adivasi community is not about power as is in the case of general society, but a method of understanding relationships; a relationship not only among the people in Adivasi society, but also the relationship between the Adivasi community and ecology. Ecology, in this case, means 'a study of the relationship between organisms and their environment' (Xaxa 2008: 101).

Therefore, without the home language, there is no Adivasi community, and without the Adivasi community, there is no ecology. In this context, the understanding of the relationship between culture and community in Adivasi society is an important aspect to presume their natural disposition towards the local dialect. As a matter of fact, this is evident from their close association with land, forest and water. Their particular ways and practices of living with these natural resource perpetuate the environment. It is in this background that the Adivasi community and its culture has an undisputed relationship with its home language. Thus, a sudden shift from the home language to the regional language becomes a 'burden of language' for an Adivasi child in the state-run schools. This 'burden of language' causes them to withdraw from the formal education system. They desire education purely in their mother tongue until they pick-up the regional language. This makes much relevance to achieve universalisation of elementary education. However, the reality in most government schools is different, which is not welcoming for the Adivasi child. This kind of environment in the class is contradictory to the objectives of the Right of Children to Free and Compulsory Education Act, 2009, which came into force on 1 April 2010. The implementation of this act has to ensure that education in the mother tongue is followed during the initial years of schooling of an Adivasi pupil.

## Mother tongue education

The Constitution of India in 1956 recognised the need for primary education in the mother tongue for linguistic minorities through Article 350A. Today, however, education continues to be imparted primarily in the 22 official Indian languages and English. The denial of schooling in their respective mother tongues to children of Adivasi communities assumes significance in the context of their poor response to formal education and high drop-out rates. Exclusion of Adivasi languages, particularly at the primary stage of their schooling, results in a slow rate of literacy among the Adivasi community. Still after 67 years of India's independence, Adivasi communities are far behind in terms of their schooling, education and literacy in comparison with other social groups including the Scheduled Castes. Exclusion of the home language of Adivasi pupils at the school further accelerates the already existing literacy disparities.

Unless and until the home language is encouraged in the school to bridge the 'backward and forward linkages' (Ramachandran 2003: 1–16), it would lead to further exclusion of Adivasis, which will have multifaceted consequences in a liberalised society like India. The existing literature on language and schooling of Adivasi children shows that most of Adivasi children drop-out at the primary stage of their schooling. While analysing the reasons for their poor response at the primary stage, scholars tend to point out that the absence of teaching in the mother tongue language is one of the main reasons besides the other economic and social aspects of schooling (Selvaraj 2011). The existing policy frameworks since 1960 have been emphasising the respect of the home language of Adivasi pupils in the classroom as a measure for their 'inclusion' in the larger society. Let us have a brief review of the existing policies that have dwelt upon the importance of mother tongue language for the Adivasi pupil.

## Policy concerns on Adivasi language

All major policy documents that dwell on education in Adivasi areas emphasise that in the early years of primary schooling, the medium of instruction for children should be their mother tongue. In the early 1960s, the Dhebar Commission highlighted the importance of language in the schooling of tribal children. It states that, 'it is experienced that tribal children pick-up lessons easily when taught through tribal dialects. It is felt that the tribal dialects should be developed and preserved' (as cited by Nambissan 1994: 2748 from GoI 1962). With specific reference to Adivasi communities, the Kothari Commission, 1964–66 (GoI 1978: 127) recommended that the 'medium of education in the first two years of the school should be the tribal language and books should be specially prepared in these languages (using the script of the regional language)'. A part of the National Policy on Education, 1986, the revised Programme of Action (POA 1992) recommends that 'children from tribal communities be taught through the mother tongue in the earlier stages in primary school' (GoI 1992: 10).

D.P. Pattanayak, former Director of the Central Institute of Indian Languages, states that unless a strategy for transition from the home language to school language is built into the elementary education of the Adivasi children, it is almost impossible to meet their learning needs (Pattanayak 1981: 90). He further states that 'unless special reading manuals are prepared keeping in view the difficulties of the tribal child he is bound to lag behind' (ibid.). While the importance of mother tongue as medium of education has often been emphasised, it is significant that no tribal language is included in the Eighth Schedule of the Constitution except for Manipuri in 1992 and Santhali in 2004. Referring to the education of minority language speaking children, Corson (1993: 88–9) emphasised that:

> It seems very important that the minority child's first language is given maximum attention up to the stage of middle schooling, so that skill in using it to manipulate abstractions develops and so that it can be used to perform the cognitive operations necessary for acquiring the second language. . . . For all these children intensive early exposure in school to the majority language, accompanied by school neglect of their first language, may result in low achievement in the majority language as well as a decline in mother tongue proficiency.

Singh and Nayak (1997: 16–17), while explaining the difference between school language and home language, strongly opined that:

> The school language of the tribal is invariably different from the home language. Even if he speaks a variety of the dominant language it is invariably different from the standard variety which is the language of the books. . . . It is no wonder that the child is taught to learn the textbook by heart. The tribal child being the first generation learner does not have a chance to use an elaborate code in diversified circumstances.

Existing research by academicians, ethnographic research of various non-governmental organisations and policy documents of the government all strongly hold the view that unless a strategy for transition from the home language to school language is built at the elementary education level of the Adivasi children, it will be near impossible to meet their learning needs. This has been the view of our civil society too since Independence. It has also been accorded in Article 350A in the Constitution that imparting education in the mother tongue at the primary level to all linguistic minorities should be the responsibility of the state. Irrespective of these strong convictions, the Eighth Schedule of 'languages' in the Indian Constitution did not include any Adivasi language/dialects till 1991.

## Eighth Schedule of 'Languages'

Scheduled Tribes who comprise 8.6 per cent of the total population of India, according to the 2011 census, speak around 400 mother tongues. The Eighth Schedule of the Constitution officially recognises 22 languages at present. Of these languages, 14 were included at the time when the Constitution was made. The Sindhi language was added through the 21st Amendment in 1967. Until 1991, no Adivasi language was included in the Eighth Schedule. It was only subsequently that the Adivasi language of Manipuri, along with Konkani and Nepali, was added to the list of official languages by the Constitution (71st Amendment) Act, in 1992. Thereafter, through the 100th Amendment Bodo, Dogri, Maithili and Santhali were added in 2004. Except for Manipuri, Bodo and Santhali, none of the other Adivasi languages being spoken are recognised by the Schedule. Even in the case of these languages, Manipuri was recognised due to political obligations, while Bodo and Santhali were recognised as a result of a long struggle and sustained movement for their recognition as official languages. In the context of the Eighth Schedule, one can say that the recognition of a language as an 'official language' has its own political and economic obligations rather than social accountability.

## Political economy of 'language'

The official Indian Census of 1991 reports 114 languages and 216 'mother tongues' spoken by more than 10,000 people. Since 1991, the Census has neglected the smaller language groups which in sum comprise about 566,000 speakers (Benedikter 2013: 12). In 1991 and 2001 the data of the Census on the mother tongue question were processed and regrouped in order to reach a consistent list of 'rationalised mother tongues'. The 1991 Census listed 1,576 'rationalised mother tongues', but these were subsequently regrouped into 114 languages. In 2001 the Census registered 114 languages. All states in India have linguistic minorities, and no state is monolingual with reference to its autochthonous population. In India, the question of mother tongue is often conflated with region, religion, profession, ethnicity, caste names and similar characteristics. A clear classification of languages, as distinct from dialects, from a linguistic point of view is still lacking (Bhattacharya 2002).

In contrast to the Census report on the number of languages existing in India, the *People's Linguistic Survey of India* (PLSI) carried out between 2010 and 2014 reports in its survey of Indian languages that there are over 780 living languages and 66 different scripts in India. While explaining the outcome, the Chief Editor of PLSI, G.N. Devy, revealed that there are many uncounted tribal languages which are spoken by less than 10,000 people (Singh 2013):

> As per the 2011 Census, there are about 122 languages spoken by more than 10,000 people. Of them 22 are the scheduled languages. Other than the 122 languages, the survey has come up with languages that are spoken by less than 10,000 people many from tribal areas, nomadic communities and from the interiors of north-eastern part of the country.

An official recognition, based on scientific criteria, of what exactly a language is, would avoid both political arbitrariness regarding the attribution of official recognition and rights, as well as a biased and subjective self-classification. The notion of 'majority language' as a criterion is only an unofficial criteria to recognise language as 'official language'.

Languages cannot be 'Scheduled' as official language merely on the grounds of sheer numbers of speakers based on their majority. According to the 2001 Census, only 29 languages have more than 1 million native speakers, 60 languages have more than 100,000 speakers and 122 languages have more than 10,000 native speakers. Languages with less than 10,000 speakers are not registered by the Indian Census. Some of the non-scheduled languages have 3, 4 or 5 million speakers which is more than some medium-sized European national languages. In 2001, the group speaking non-scheduled languages accounted for 3 per cent of the total population (around 30 million speakers).

Often linguistic minorities are denied rights when their languages are not recognised. Current politics in many countries tries to minimise the size and importance of minority languages, seeking to avoid any subsequent support. In India, due to the 2004 recognition, the number of speakers of Scheduled languages reached 97 per cent of India's total population. But what rights can these speakers derive from recognition under the Eighth Schedule? Languages of the Eighth Schedule are gaining greater importance due to their dominance in the field of education, mass media and examinations by the Public Service Commission for recruitment, and generally due to government policy to strictly implement their language policies.

The denial of recognition within the Eighth Schedule to several Non Scheduled languages, including some which have a large number of native speakers, appears rather arbitrary and conditioned largely by politics. There is no precise criteria for scheduling and the scheduling is certainly not based only on the number of speakers. Some languages with a large number of speakers still are not 'scheduled', the largest of these being Bhili/Bhilodi with 9.6 million native speakers (ranked 14th in the Schedule), Gondi with 2.7 million speakers (ranked 18th) and Khandesi with 2.1 million speakers (ranked 22nd). Only Santhali, with 6.5 million speakers (ranked 15th) in 2003, succeeded in being admitted to the Eighth Schedule as the first Adivasi language. On the other hand, two languages with fewer than 2 million native speakers have recently been included in the Eighth Schedule for largely political reasons: Manipuri/Meitei with 1.5 million speakers (ranked 25th) and Bodo with 1.4 million speakers (ranked 26th). For cultural and historical reasons, Sanskrit is on the official Schedule with only 14,000 people claiming it as their language.

How does recognition of merely 22 languages out of a total of 114 spoken Indian languages impinge upon equal opportunities for all Indian citizens? Indeed, it is difficult to find sufficient justification for the list of the Eighth Schedule as it is in force today (Bhattacharya 2002: 299). From the existing data of recognition of a few languages and exclusion of many is evidence of the fact that it is the languages of the dominant groups which figure in the Schedule. The manner in which the languages are scheduled and the subtraction of minority languages projects power relations and hegemony between the speaker communities. Two entire language families, the Sino-Tibetan and Austro-Asiatic family, are almost disregarded under the Eighth Schedule. A clear set of criteria has never been applied in according recognition to languages in India. In this case, however, Viswanatham (2001: 305) identifies one main reason, which exhibits the notion of dominance and power while recognising any language as an official language. According to him:

> That is, only languages with large number of speakers spread over and concentrated in large geographical areas, with cultivated and well developed literatures, having their own scripts, and publishing newspapers and magazines were included in the list.

What are the benefits of official language recognition within the Eighth Schedule? One example of such a useful nature of recognition is the potential for employment of the speakers of that language.

The conferment of official status leads to programmes which require speakers of the language to participate as teachers, literacy workers, translators and so on. The resulting jobs do not take people away from their communities. What happens when an Adivasi language gets scheduled? The speakers of the language can participate in employment as teachers, literacy workers, translators and would even be qualified to appear in Public Service Commission exams to take part in the Indian administration. Since most of the Adivasi languages (3 per cent of the total population) are not recognised, the youth of these communities are excluded from these opportunities.

The struggle of minority language speakers for the recognition of their languages under the Eighth Schedule of the Indian Constitution continues. Nevertheless, when languages are recognised, as in the recent cases of Nepali, Konkani and Manipuri, they are not recognised out of government benevolence, but as the result of appeals from actual and potential pressure groups. As the official policy of language recognition is so inherently biased, the inclusion of a language in the Eighth Schedule has depended largely on the ability of its speakers to influence the political process:

> Any plea for recognition is met with standard refrain that the administrative costs of implementing any such decision would be prohibitive and would ultimately set a trend wherein all the 1,652 mother tongues would have to be recognized. As a result there is forced bilingualism and there is a continuous threat of a language being wiped out due to sheer lack of usage. It is estimated that in India half of the tribal people have lost or shifted their mother tongues.
> (as cited by Benedikter 2013: 18 from Aggarwal 1995: 225)

If not the numerical strength of a language, then does its literary tradition contribute to recognition? If so, there are several Adivasi languages with rich literary traditions. These languages are still excluded from the Eighth Schedule such as Oraon, Bhili and Gondi. On the other hand, how would it be possible to produce and preserve literature if public support in language planning is denied? In this case these languages require substantial support not only from the civil society, but also the state. Inclusion of these languages in the Eighth Schedule makes much sense in terms of education development. Based on the diversification and exposure of Adivasis to the mainstream society in terms of home language and regional language, classification of Adivasis based on their language exposure would resolve the intensity of language burden of the class.

## Classification of Adivasis based on classroom language priority

The Adivasi community is not a homogeneous community. Their cultural diversity represents their heterogeneity. The character of heterogeneity is visible in their everyday life practices. For example, the practice of cultivation, learning systems, cultural values/practices, food habits and so on differs from one Adivasi community to another. Each Adivasi community has its own home language, some of them have a script and some only have the language in oral form. These languages of Adivasi community across India vary in number from 400 to 500. As a matter of fact, some Adivasi communities speak purely in their mother tongue and cannot understand the regional language; some maintain close ties with the regional language even though they have their own mother tongue because of their exposure to the outside society.

In some cases, certain Adivasi communities do not have home dialects, and as such the question of 'burden of language' does not arise. Therefore, in this diverse background, understanding the language requirements of Adivasi children in school cannot be on the same lines across communities. Since their languages function under diverse contexts, the following classification of Adivasi communities would help to address their language requirements in the school.

The first, in this classification, is the already mainstreamed Adivasi who can cope with the regional language, the second is the semi-mainstreamed Adivasi who can manage with the regional language and the third is the Adivasi who lives in remote areas and who are comfortable with their home language but find the regional language difficult. Mother tongue education should be especially prioritised for the third category of the Adivasi community which is comfortable with the home language and cannot cope-up with the regional language. This classification, along with addressing the needs in terms of their specific language requirements may minimise the difficulties of the state with regard to the language issue.

There are a couple of issues in Adivasi schooling which the state is bound to address. Among many, appointing teachers from the same community who can communicate in Adivasi language in the school, printing text books in their home language are important in order to ensure that they continue their schooling. In the context of Adivasi education, language is thus a 'need' and not 'power', and the functionality of its implementation would be very significant. In view of the implementation of the Right of Children to Free and Compulsory Education Act, 2009, the state is required to address the contradictory approaches, wherein on one hand the act says 'compulsory education to all children of the age of six to fourteen years' and on the other hand excludes the home languages of Adivasi pupils. In this context, understanding the relation between the home language, school language and right to education is an important aspect to ponder upon.

## Home language, school language and right to education

According to the Right of Children to Free and Compulsory Education Act, 2009, 'every child of the age of six to fourteen years shall have a right to free and compulsory education in neighbourhood schools till completion of elementary education'. Merely enacting laws in favour of people is not enough. Every act requires effective implementation. Unless a teacher teaches in the class using the home language of Adivasi pupils, the objective of right to education is bound to fail where Adivasi communities are concerned. The Right to Education Act should not become another 'paper tiger' as it is in the case of most of the laws in India. It is not sufficient to enact laws; the state should create a conducive environment to implement such laws for the benefit of its people. Therefore, imposing the school language on the Adivasi pupil, who is not exposed to it, at the early state of schooling, results in drop-out.

The official records of the Indian Census reveal that as the Adivasi children move to higher classes, their drop-out becomes higher. The number of children who enrol at class one seem to gradually withdraw from the school as they proceed to the next class. When enquired upon the reasons for their drop-out at the early schooling, the existing literature has found that the 'school language' imposed upon them makes them alien to their 'home language'. Therefore, as the policies recommend creating of an environment where an Adivasi child is taught in her/his home language in the initial years of schooling, it is an important strategy to retain them in school. Otherwise the purpose of Right to Education would be assumed as a dish prepared by the fox for the crane. Let us wish that the state does not become another 'fox'.

## References

Aggarwal, Kailash. 1995. 'Epilogue', in R. S. Gupta, Anvita Albi and Kailash S. Aggarval (eds.), *Language and the State*. New Delhi: Creative Books.
Benedikter, Thomas. 2013. *Minority Languages in India: An Appraisal of the Linguistic Rights of Minorities in India*. Kolkata: Institute for Minority Rights, European Academy.
Bhattacharya, S. S. 2002. 'Languages in India: Their Status and Function', in N. H. Itagi and S. K. Singh (eds.), *Linguistic Landscaping in India: With Particular Reference to the New States*. Mysore: Central Institute of Indian Languages (CIIL).
Corson, David. 1993. *Language, Minority Education and Gender: Linking Social Justice and Power*. Multilingual Matters Ltd.
Government of India. 1962. *Report of the Scheduled Areas and Scheduled Tribes Commission*, Volume 1. New Delhi: Government of India.
Government of India. 1978. *Report of the Education Commission 1964–66*. New Delhi: Education and National Development, Ministry of Education.
Government of India. 1992. *Programme of Action*. New Delhi: Government of India.
Government of India. 2005. *National Curriculum Framework 2005*. New Delhi: National Council of Educational Research and Training (NCERT).
Heredia, R. C. 1995. 'Tribal Education for Development: Need for a Liberative Pedagogy for Social Transformation', *Economic and Political Weekly*, 30(16), 22 April.
Nambissan, Geetha B. 1994. 'Language and Schooling of Tribal Children: Issues Related to Medium of Instruction', *Economic and Political Weekly*, 29(42): 2747–54.
Pattanayak, D. P. 1981. *Multilingualism and Mother-Tongue Education*. New Delhi: Oxford University Press.
Premi, K. K. 2000. 'Access, Equity and Equality in Education With Focus on Scheduled Castes, Scheduled Tribes and Girls', A paper presented at the *National Seminar on Implementation of Education Policy in India*, 11 March, National Institute of Educational Planning and Administration, New Delhi.
Ramachandran, Vimala. 2003. *Getting Children Back to School: Case Studies in Primary Education*. New Delhi: Sage Publications.
Selvaraj, J. D. 2011. 'Education in a Second Language: Struggles and Achievements of Betta Kurumbar Children', in G. N. Devy et al. (eds.), *Voice and Memory: Indigenous Imagination and Expression*. New Delhi: Orient Blackswan.
Shah, Ghanshyam. 1985. 'A Profile of Education Among the Scheduled Tribes in Gujarath', in Ghanshyam Shah et al. (eds.), *Tribal Education in Gujarath*. New Delhi: Ajanta Publications.
Singh, S. S. 2013. 'Language Survey Reveals Diversity', *The Hindu*, 22 July. www.thehindu.com/news/national/language-survey-reveals-diversity/article4938865.ece (accessed on 21 December 2016).

Singh, U. K. and A. K. Nayak. 1997. *Tribal Education*. New Delhi: Commonwealth Publishers.

Sinha, A. P. 1989. 'Tribal Development and National Integration', in Kanchan Roy (ed.), *Education and Health Problems in Tribal Development*. New Delhi: Concept Publishing Company.

Talesara, H. 1994. *Social Background of Tribal Girl Students*. New Delhi: Himanshu Publications.

Viswanatham, K. 2001. 'The Eighth Schedule and the Three Language Formula', in C. J. Daswani (ed.), *Language Education in Multilingual India*. New Delhi: UNESCO.

Xaxa, Virginius. 2008. *State, Society, and Tribes: Issues in Post-Colonial India*. New Delhi: Pearson Longman.

# 15
# DEVELOPMENTAL CHALLENGES OF NOMADIC AND DENOTIFIED TRIBES OF INDIA
With special reference to Andhra Pradesh

*Malli Gandhi*

I

The idea of labelling members of an entire tribe as criminal tribe or habitual offenders was indeed brutal. There are questions about how these communities live their lives, being stigmatised and branded as criminal, habitual and juvenile offenders. What makes a society label the entire section of people as a criminal tribe? What does such labelling mean even if there are grains of truth in it? We read, listen and meet people from many of these communities in our life. Our interaction with these communities makes us realise that a unique phenomenon of prejudices has been established against them. Societal prejudices to a great extent are responsible for the pathetic way of their living. The very label, *born criminals*, is the burden they carry throughout their life. It is evident from their life that such a burden moulds their future in certain ways of living. However, these communities make an interesting and revealing subject for study. Their present living standards and conditions hold lessons for contemporary society. It shows us the context in which the society has placed them.

They are depressed not because of their poverty, but the general outlook of what the public, society and institutions have about these communities. There is a sort of resignation, a sign of scorn, vengeance and uncertainty in their world. They are very enterprising and productive people. There are a few sections of these people who are settled as agriculturists, teachers, police constables, railway and postal department employees, and a few members of their youth completed their education up to graduate and post-graduate level. Removal of the societal prejudices on these communities and willingness of the society will ultimately liberate them from their stigma and tarnished historical past. However, what will change their present ways of living is an important consideration for all of us. Conditions of 196 denotified communities (59 communities in Andhra Pradesh) are rather disheartening. They are also living with great hope and aspirations.

## II

Denotified, nomadic and semi-nomadic people constitute a major segment of India's population. According to the latest population estimates they constitute 8 million of the total population. The criminal tribes of erstwhile British rule were denotified during the year 1952 and the Indian government officially declared them as denotified tribes. The nomadic and semi-nomadic tribes were shown as a separate category of people in the 1931 census reports. Growth rate of NT and DNT population is more when compared to the general population figures. They generally live on the outskirts of villages, settlements and *thandas*. Many of them do not have a fixed place of dwelling. Most of them are residents of urban and rural slums. Their colonies are not connected with roads, electricity, bore-wells, drinking water and sanitation. Youth among these communities were a totally neglected lot. The first five-year plan referred to 198 sections of the people as NT and DNTs numbering forty lakhs spread over most of the states in India.

Oral traditions inform us that some of the denotified communities had a glorious history going back to the time of Mahabharata, the Delhi Sultanate, the Satavahanas, Rashtrakutas, Bahamanis, Vijayanagara rulers, the Mughals and the Nizam and the British rulers. They were the chief transporters of goods and services throughout the Indian subcontinent. They were a highly independent and mobile community on a well-developed network of caravan trade. Destruction of their trade virtually led them to slavery under British colonial rule. Yerukulas were known as Koravas in Tamilnadu, Korachas in Karnataka and Kaikadis in Maharashtra. They had been major caravan merchants since the 10th century. Various sections of Indigenous society sought their services. Yerukalas were also as known by different names such as Karivepauk Yerukalas as they were involved in procurement and sale of *Karivepauk* (curry leaves). They also served as vegetable sellers, plantation workers, stone quarry workers, earth workers, baggage carriers, food grain transporters, basket-makers, rope weavers etc. Traditionally they had played a crucial role in the long distance trade. They carried food grains from surplus to deficit areas during famines. Merchants in their own right, they acted as caravans for other merchants and dealers as well. Establishment of the British colonial rule in India enforced new economic relations through legal control. Railways ruined and marginalised the Yerukula community. The innumerable fairs and *jataras* that had created a vibrant network of trade and commerce throughout the Indian subcontinent were declared by the British as backward and irrational. They were discouraged and suppressed. Reasons for such drastic action can be found in the European intellectual culture during the second half of the 19th century. In Europe the mental attitude was dominated by theories of social Darwinism, scientific racism and eugenics. These theories looked at the conquered non-Europeans in racial terms as biologically inferior. The same mind set was transmitted to colonies whereby the subject people were categorised by their racial futures. Accordingly, permanent characteristics were accorded to them based on their physical appearance.

Modernisation and development constitute a threat to the identity and human dignity of certain Indigenous people. There is no official policy of protection and promotion of nomadic, semi-nomadic and denotified tribes even after 65 years of our independence. In order to integrate these people there is an urgent need to restructure economic development and political participation. Structural violence has been inflicted on these marginalised sections of people for centuries together. They are subjected to indignity and humiliation. Cultural hegemony is subverting their very identity. Colonial government through their brutal laws made them crippled and powerless. They could have mobilised themselves to resist their domination, affirm their dignity and struggle for their share and place in the society. But, unfortunately these poorer sections of the society lead a nomadic, wandering life in order to eke out their livelihood. They were subjected to social prejudices, cultural hegemony, economic exploitation, oppression, political exclusion and marginalisation (Arnold 1979).

Yerukulas had always traded and provided their commissariat services freely to all parts including the state areas. But once they entered into contact with the British colonisers, they lost their independence. Their trading activities came under strict regulation. They were not allowed to trade with anyone other than the British. Any breach of contract was deemed criminal and severely punishable. The British destroyed unity among Yerukula camps and settlements by setting up police constabulary, *Karanams* and *Munusubs* (village chiefs) who emerged as intermediary controlling authorities directly reporting to their colonial superiors. Grain, salt and vegetables were the items which Yerukulas traded throughout the subcontinent. Whatever little internal trade that was left became subject to heavy customs duties and outright plunder by colonial officials. Customs and tax policies benefited the British at the expense of the local people. Structured and rigid colonial towns replaced the fluid mobile markets of pre-colonial times. These towns came to be dominated by Parsis, Jains, Baniyas, Komatis, Marwadis and Christians who ultimately marginalised the trading activities of Yerukulas. Railway lines constituted the final straw on their back. Yerukulas were thus forced to abandon their traditional occupations and take to cattle-raising and agrarian labour.

Condition of the nomadic, semi-nomadic and the denotified communities in India is vulnerable and pathetic. Today, many changes are taking place in their life. They are assimilated in the lowest strata of Indian society. They are displaced from their traditional forest lands. Development is completely alien to them. They did not understand and accept development because they did not receive any benefits from the constitutional provisions (Aiyappan 1948).

The colonial government considered the criminal law as one of the greatest gifts to India. There were innumerable examples of writings by colonial officials and writers that were simply reflective of the attitude of dominance. For them, the oriental systems of culture and governance are meant for correction, but not continuation. For example, in 1881 a colonial writer, Hunter (1881), stated that *a more secure, more prosperous India where roads, railways, bridges, canals, schools and hospitals had been built: famines tackled: thugi, dakaiti and the predatory castes suppressed: trade developed; barbaric social practices like widow burning and infanticide abolished.* With the establishment of British rule and consequent introduction of machine-made goods, Asiatic groups were deprived of patronage for their handicrafts and hand-made goods. Many of them were forced to take to petty crime to eke out their livelihood. By the early 19th century, petty offences of these groups became a serious law and order problem. To tackle it, the government enacted the Criminal Tribes Act 1871 under which they were notified as criminal tribes in each district on the recommendations of district superintendents of police. Movements and activities of CTs used to be under the surveillance of station house officers of the respective police station in which the notified criminal tribe used to live. As a result of restrictions on movements of the entire community, members of community became backward economically and educationally. Further, the entire community suffered social stigma of being labelled as CTs (Bhowmick 1963).

After the advent of independence, Government of India appointed CT enquiry committee under the chairmanship of Anantha Sayanam Ayyangar. The committee after studying the conditions of criminal tribes in the country recommended for the repeal of the act. Accordingly, the act was repealed and replaced with the Habitual Offenders Act 1952. The new act was state governments' legislation (Bhowmick 1975). With the repeal of the act, CTs were denotified with a view to undertake ameliorative measures for ex-criminal tribes. A list of denotified tribes was issued by the respective state governments. Thus, came into existence sate-wise lists of denotified tribes or *Vimukta Jatis*(Bhargava 1949). The list of the Denotified tribes of the erstwhile Madras State was issued in 1952. There were 66 entries in the list. These communities were related to Andhra Pradesh and Nizam provinces. Many of the communities were not included in any particular community or tribe. For example, the gang of hired assassins, Jatur mixed gang and Tenkela Ramanas were listed or notified as gangs. Some communities in the list belong to the same tribe. For example, Yerukulas, Urkorchas, Koravas, Korachars, Dabba Yerukulas, Nawabpeta Korachas, Veyal Pad Korachas etc. Some important communities listed as ex-criminal tribes in Andhra Pradesh are Doms, Rellis, Waddars, Paidis, Reddikas, Urali Goudars, Mutharachas, Tandari Mandalam, Kintali Kalingas, Boyas, Chakkalas, Dommaras, Dasaris, Jambuvandai, Jogis, Telaga Pamulas, Konda Doras, Mondi Vagulas, Monda Pottas, Mutharachas, Nakkalas, Pitchikaguntalas, Nirshikaris, Lambadis, Yerukulas and Yanadis. In the state of Telangana the Waddars, Dommaras and Kaikadis were notified as criminal tribes.

Koracha, Korava and Kaikadi are synonymous of the Yerukula. After repeal of the act and consequent de-notification some of the ex-criminal tribes were listed in the Scheduled Tribes' category. For example, Yerukulas, Yanadis, Sugalis and Nakkalas are placed under ST category. Some communities were listed in the category of Scheduled Castes. For example, Malas and Madigas are shown under SC category. Other communities were listed as socially and educationally backward classes. These sections of people have not received any attention of government for their development.

The Criminal Tribes Act of 1911 suppressed many predatory castes, itinerant communities and wandering tribes and stigmatised and stereotyped them as criminal tribes; 198 communities became victims of the act. It destroyed the life of nomadic and wandering communities.

The Criminal Tribes Act of 1871 was first executed in Bengal during the year 1876 and later extended to the whole of British India. In the Madras Presidency the Criminal Tribes Act was passed during the year 1911. In the beginning a few tribes were included in the fold of criminal tribes. Gradually many new communities were added. In India, the notion of the criminal tribes is based upon occupations and professions. The notion of hereditary principle of the criminality gained popularity during the 19th century.

## III

Reformation or rehabilitation of these sections of the people was sought through the policy of social engineering. Missionary organisations like American Baptist Telugu Mission, Canadian Mission and Salvation Army and other philanthropic agencies were often consulted and given the responsibility of rehabilitating backward Hindu communities. The Salvation Army called it criminocurology. Wandering communities were placed in separate settlements. The intention of legislation and settlements was not to punish and segregate people. But criminal tribes' acts worked as powerful instruments in colonial India to suppress poor people. Relationships between itinerant and sedentary communities are always problematic. There was mutual antagonism between the two. The treatment of colonial government towards Indian wandering communities was reflective of those methods adopted in England. The denotified tribes are branded, stigmatised, dishonoured and labelled as criminal tribes in colonial and post-colonial India. Rehabilitation and reformation programmes designed by the government did not fulfil their aspirations and desires. Their conditions are becoming worse day by day. Problems such as illiteracy, gender discrimination, underdevelopment, violation of basic human rights and criminalisation are haunting them in free India.

NT and DNT communities face a number of problems. It is necessary for them to keep moving from place to place repairing agricultural implements, contract works, petty business, *cooli* work, grazing cattle etc. in order to eke out their livelihood. They move seasonally in search of paid work in urban centres. They are found in almost all parts of India. Their daily income is very meagre. It is difficult for their children to attend the schools, colleges and universities because of their livelihood patterns and poor economic conditions. Above all, most of these communities face the problem of social stigma and identity crisis. In the growth of human life, youth plays an important position. It is marked by rapid physical and psychological changes, sexual maturity and a period of tension. Particularly the youth shape their future and understand their roles during this period. Every one passes through the same universal stages of development such as infancy, adolescence, adult hood and old age. But the amount of stress and strains DNT communities are passing through shed light on the internal churning that takes place within these communities over a period of time (Bhowmick 1963).

Government of India recognised the denotified communities as a group that needs special attention. The nation's urge for youth welfare is reflected in various plans and policies. Almost every five-year plan had emphasised on the development of these communities. Separate welfare schemes were planned for the development of these communities by the central and state governments as a part of their state sector programmes in the first five-year plan. In the second five-year plan the government sanctioned funds for their education and economic development. During the third five-year plan, a provision of 375 lakh was made for the purpose. Special steps were initiated in the fourth plan for a close study of the problems of these people. Economic, social and cultural aspects were taken into consideration. From the fifth five-year plan onwards no separate provisions were made either under centrally sponsored programmes or the state-sponsored programmes for their development. No arrangements are made for distribution of land, payment of wages, supply of seeds, fertilisers, pesticides, bank loans, house sites, rickshaws, cattle etc. for their economic development. Input supply programmes were not implemented to help agricultural communities among nomadic and denotified communities under economic support schemes (Devy 2005).

Welfare measures initiated for the development of NT-DNT communities bear a resemblance to the efforts at squeezing oil from sand. Development of the youth is a real challenge to democratic governments. The utterances of various governments are making much noise emanating from empty vessels. Policy formulation and its execution, most often, fall apart. There is a lot of injustice done to tribal youth in the distribution of surplus lands. Their repeated memoranda to revenue officials are of no avail. In the sphere of employment also NT-DNT youth are facing serious problems. Though the public advertisements earmark a number of vacancies for these people, they appear so with a clause saying that the posts would be filled by candidates of other castes in the absence of eligible tribal candidates. In such a situation the very policy of reservation loses its meaning and validity.

It is suggested that the government should take appropriate measures to overcome these problems. The elected representatives from tribal region should educate governments about the fundamental hardships of DNT tribal youth (Fuches 1975).

With the repeal of the amended Criminal Tribes Act of 1924, these tribes were freed in 1952 from the stigma of born criminality. Accordingly, restrictions to their movements were removed. They are treated on par with SC/ST and other backward communities. However, there are a large number of communities not included in the list of Scheduled Castes and Scheduled Tribes. In some states the same tribes are listed as Scheduled Castes, in some states as Scheduled Tribes and in some states as other backward classes. Due to various anomalies of caste and tribe development of the youth is seriously affected. It is to be noted that NT-DNTs are Scheduled Tribes in the erstwhile British period and therefore all the categories listed as criminal tribes should be provided the status of Scheduled Tribes in order to develop their youth. So far, central and state governments have not bestowed their full attention on development of youth among the NT and DNTs. Even today, some youths were under surveillance of police and are considered prospective threats to society. As a result DNT communities were segregated from the society. Youth among them are developing a hostile attitude towards government, police and people. They lose self-confidence and develop an attitude of resignation and distance themselves from their kith and kin. Youth consider that they are let down by society and, hence prefer to deceive it. Moreover, destitution and poverty are the great causes and curses to lower the status and dignity of individual, youth and community. Development programmes concerning the youth among NT-DNTs should either be entrusted to reputed educational institutions or apex youth development bodies like Rajiv Gandhi National Institute of Youth and Rural Development or private institutions like Tata Institute of Social Sciences or reputed social service organisations that can evince real interest in them.

Economic development should go hand in hand with social and cultural development. Development of NT and DNT youth largely depends on how far they are integrated into the society. Development with a human approach is urgently required. Economic development is continuous process. Youth of the DNTs may be exposed to social and cultural intercourse, which might indirectly help to achieve millennium development goals. With all the defects and inadequacies, youth development programmes initiated for the NT and DNTs are slowly yielding results because of the hopes for better future. Young members are found to be willing to take to regular and honourable occupations, professions and employment. Rural banks should be opened in the colonies of NT and DNTs for mobilising savings of youth. NT-DNT communities have suffered economic difficulties as well as social neglect for centuries. This made them hostile to the so-called neighbours. Their social status should be raised in order to wipe out the long cursed social negligence. As long as youth suffer from the stigma of criminality, they cannot enjoy their due share of the nation's growth. Aloofness from society, fear of domination and distance from family make them stubborn. They develop feelings of hatred and suspicion. Development of the youth among NTs and DNTs is an integral part of national development. Central and state governments are given equal responsibility to execute the constitutional guarantees given to Scheduled Tribes. At the state-level programmes designed for development of youth among NT-DNT suffer from frequent overlaps.

NT-DNT communities need to be protected from various kinds of atrocities. The Prevention of Atrocities Act of 2006 should be seriously implemented in order to safeguard youth. Special courts are the need of hour in order to tackle problems of youth. Bonded labour is a serious threat for development and child labour practice is very common among NTs and DNTs. Separate steps should be contemplated to arrest the malpractices of selling children and women to others. NGOs should come forward to tackle the problems of these sections of people. Tribal languages should be protected under Article 21 (1) and 350 (a) of the Constitution of India.

## IV

During the 19th and 20th centuries communication facilities, such as railways and roads, were carried through the hills and forests and the land hungry peasants of upper castes invaded the sparsely populated tribal regions of central and south India. Moneylenders, contractors and land-grabbing landlords encroached upon and the tribals were kept in perpetual indebtedness. Formerly, tribals depended upon forests for their living which were fast denuded by landholders and government. The non-tribals on the one hand and the forest laws framed by colonial administration made the tribals to migrate from place to place for their bare living from time to time. As Bhowmick (1963) put it *this economic and territorial displacement under a new setting affected very seriously the old patterns of economic life and upset the equilibrium of the whole society.* The most important so called ex-criminal tribes of North India are Bawaris, Bhantu, Kanjar, Nat, Kawal, Meena, Pakhiwars, Tagu, Sansiya and Lodhas. Likewise, Lambadis, Koravas, Dommaras, Waddars, Kallars etc. are important ex-criminal tribes of South India. In Eastern India, Lodhas and Kherias are generally known criminal tribes.[1]

The Criminal Tribes Act was passed by colonial government as early as 1871, arbitrarily and unjustly against some of the Aboriginal tribes, castes and even a section of Muslims of our country. This act was in place to control some turbulent and criminally proclaimed sections of population. By gradual modifications, this act was consolidated in the year 1924. Madras Presidency repealed the Criminal Tribes Act in 1947 and Bombay in 1949. The All India Criminal Tribes Enquiry Committee in 1949 evaluated the problems of criminal tribes and recommended for repealing the act. To check the criminal tendencies of these tribes, the British government started several settlements and entrusted the task of management of them to some voluntary agencies like the Salvation Army, American Baptist Mission, Chief Khalsa Diwan, Deo Samaj and Arya Samaj. In addition to these, Adimajati Sevak Sangh was also put in charge of the management of some settlements. These were assisting government in the moral uplift of criminal tribes.

The social experience of denotified tribes still adds to their lurking fears of being dominated by more vociferous strata of society. Unless society provides equal opportunities and treatment with others in every sphere of life, these people are not willing to come out of their shell. What we ought to do is to develop a sense of oneness with these people, a sense of unity and understanding. It necessarily involves a psychological approach.

Tribal communities are considered as early settlers or autochthonous groups of people. It is at the same time true that they are also non-static or itinerant groups owing to many compelling circumstances. For thousands of years, these tribes lived in their sylvan setting without having any intercourse with the outside world (Gandhi 2006).

The problem of crime in society has been a gigantic and complex phenomenon. In recent times, crime rate, as a whole is increasing very rapidly all over the world. Crime thrives wherever economic deprivations, social disruptions and radical discriminations prevail. Inequality, economic exploitation, unhealthy greed for possessing material goods and rapid change in the standards of morality in society constitute the breeding ground of crime in society. Criminality is not hereditary and the criminal propensity of many castes and tribes is due to the disintegration of their social moorings under economic and territorial displacements from time to time. The most important cause of their deprivation is the loss of their traditional means of livelihood. No human is a criminal by birth. The term 'criminal tribe' is a misnomer, because some castes and other communities are classified as criminal tribes in India. Some of them would be found to be members of Scheduled Castes or other communities. For example, in Srikakulam district of Andhra Pradesh Rellis are considered to be a criminal tribe. Even now they live only in two small villages, Pullota and Thallota, and carry agriculture or coolie labour work as their occupation. Kopotipalem Malas of Nellore district and Malas of Anneboyinipalli of Prakasam district are also wage labourers who are put under the current classification (Gandhi 2008).

Criminal tribes are distributed in almost all states of India. Many of them still lead a primitive style of life; some still retain food gathering or hunting or pastoral habits. In 1937, the Criminal Tribes committee headed by Tiwari opined that *criminal tribes were a legacy of unhealthy social environments and wrong methods pursued through many centuries in dealing with them. They are not the sinners, they have been sinned against* (Report of the Criminal Tribes Enquiry Committee1948). A vital aspect of the entire question is how to wean them away from crime and make them an integral part of mainstream society. In spite of their innumerable depredations, settlers are still in the clutches of poverty. Fruits of their hard work are being snatched by a section of people like rich landlords, merchants, moneylenders, politicians, lawyers and corrupt police officers. The ex-settlements have become a vicious circle in which stolen property dealers, corrupt police officials, investors in crime and greedy criminal lawyers form a part and parcel of exploitative situation (Singh 1976a).

The patterns of rehabilitation under missionaries were of different nature. They started agricultural settlements, industrial settlements, reformatory settlements and penal settlements. In these settlements, inmates were carefully supervised and given employment for making an honest living. Children were put in schools where training in one craft or the other was imparted to them. During the day time, they were allowed to work and at night they were put under a strict guard. The whole idea was to reclaim them to honest life. With the passage of time, ex-criminal or denotified communities have to face a number of problems. Important among them are:

- *Economic and territorial displacements.*
- *Loss of livelihood followed by loss of organised life.*

- *Stigma of criminality and subsequent loss of self-respect in society.*
- *Police oppression, harassment, harsh treatment and torture.*
- *Long durations of stay in jails and disconnect with family relations.*
- *Poverty and force of habit goading them to take up undesirable activities.*
- *Negative role of civil society (stolen property dealers, police officials, criminal lawyers).*
- *Sub-standards of living.*

(Lalitha 1995: 95)

Due to all the above-mentioned factors they were isolated and recoiled into the shell of their own life patterns. After the repeal of the Criminal Tribes Act, a large number of criminals were freed from the stigma of criminality. The Backward Class Enquiry Commission which was appointed in 1955 by the Government of India suggested ameliorative measures to enable them to turn over a new leaf in their lives and make them good citizens.

1   *Criminal tribes should be called denotified communities or Vimukta Jatis.*
2   *They should be included in scheduled castes, tribes and backward classes.*
3   *They should be resettled in batches and integrated with the larger society.*
4   *Proper education should be imparted to them.*
5   *Reformatory activities should be undertaken.*
6   *Distinction to be made between collective criminal activities and individual acts.*
7   *Suitable employment for children should be provided.*
8   *Simultaneous economic rehabilitation should be ensured simultaneously.*

The new nomenclatural protocol viz., denotified tribes too is misleading. It does not make any qualitative difference to call them criminal or ex-criminal or denotified communities. All these words need to be removed and make them as free citizens of this country. They should be included in the categories of Scheduled Castes, tribes and backward class communities. It is the responsibility of the nation to absorb them slowly into the fold and make them believe that they are a very important segment of society. As. J.J. Panackal said *no reformation of the denotified communities is complete until the society accepts them in their fold without distinction* (Lavanam and Hemalatha 1974: 12).

The prime reason for their living at the subsistence level is their unstable occupations with uncertain income and disproportionate expenditure. They are now much worried about the future of their children. Opportunity should be given to them to intermix socially with the children of higher castes. Krishnalal (1978: 9) rightly pointed out that *family is the spring board of the child's social and personal growth*. Education is an effective weapon and instrument of social change. It plays a significant role in changing the fortune and lifestyle of these children. So the entire gamut of reforming these communities depends on how best educational facilities can be provided to these children. Education helps to channel their energies into productive purposes. Comparing them to the rest of society, they are bound to suffer from an inferiority complex and parents are afraid that their children could not reach higher echelons of society because of psychological barriers they suffer from. Children may be educated in a healthy and proper environment free from oppression, fear, harassment and suspicion. Well-known and reputed social reformers of South India, Hemalata and Lavanam who spent most of their life in affecting reform and change among Yerukala DNTs and their children across various settlements in Andhra, said in this context that *transformation is now taking place from the culture of crime to the culture of sociability; from anti-social means to social means of livelihood, from inferiority complex to cooperative spirit and from harsh behaviour to reason and understanding*(Lavanam and Hemalatha 1974: 13).

Many communities among the NT and DNTs are pastoralists. The Backward Classes Enquiry Committee under Kaka Kalekar had made certain recommendations for the upliftment of these communities. However, no serious efforts have been made since 1955 by the state and central governments to implement measures recommended by the various commissions and committees for the development of the youth. Even the recent Scheduled Tribes Forest Bill does not cover grazing rights of NT and DNT population in the country. Therefore, there is an urgent need to prepare a road map for the development of youth among these sections of the people. Their land rights, forest rights, grazing rights and passage rights across the states have to be recognised.

Majority percentage of the DNTs is illiterates. Government authorities don't show statistical figures of enrolment and retention among children of these sections. The drop-out rate of children in the schools is very high. Government did not provide schools for nomadic and denotified tribal communities. Children are still attending missionary schools in some ex-settlement areas. Curriculum in education system should address issues of the NTs and DNTs. Education programmes concerning these sections should bridge gaps between traditional knowledge and livelihood practices. A comprehensive educational support should be provided to members of the youth. Residential schools exclusively for DNT children are recommended by many activists. Primary, secondary and vocational training institutes should be opened at appropriate locations for the benefit of youth. Health awareness among NT/DNTs is very much lacking. Medical facilities are scanty and many members are totally unaware of health hazards. They are so poor that they cannot afford to go to qualified doctors or better hospitals. They are totally dependent on quacks. Children in growing age are vulnerable to contamination of various diseases due to malnutrition (Simhadri 1979).

NT/DNT communities have a rich cultural heritage. They have intimate knowledge of various handicrafts. Over a period of time some of the communities have developed expertise in artisanship and handicrafts. Various handicraft materials made by them are very popular in the country. There is a great demand for these items in international markets. There needs to be in place proper encouragement for their creativity and craftsmanship. The NT and DNT communities who are involved in the music and puppetry and other traditional martial arts should be resettled in tourist centres so that they could attract tourists and provide their experience and expertise. The National Science and Technology Commission should provide measures for extending the umbrella of modern science and technology and higher scientific technological research (Simhadri 2000).

Youth among these communities should be provided with domicile certificates by the competent local authorities. That is due to the special occupational conditions of these people. State and central government authorities should initiate dialogues with forest department authorities and evolve a policy that ensures their rights over forest products. For example some Yerukalas and Waddars are living in Lingala village (Mahbubnagar district, Telangana) and Siddhapuram Village (Kurnool District, Andhra Pradesh). Their villages are surrounded by thick forests. They heavily depend on forest products. But the government authorities are preventing them to do so. In the absence of work availability, young members of various settlements are forced into illicit liquor trade in order to eke out their livelihood. A small section of youth is also involved in petty offences like pocket-picking, chain-snatching, suitcase lifting, shop-snatching etc. They are victims of the local police. Young women among NT and DNT communities are vulnerable to sexual harassment, rape and murder. Special cells should be created to allow women of these communities to come forward and give voice to their grievances. Many a member of these communities possess knowledge about herbs and medicinal plants. Their expertise can be utilised to collect, develop herbs and medicinal plants which are in a great demand in the country and outside. They also possess good sportsman ship. Some of the talented youth can be selected for national and international sports in order to boost up their confidence (Government of India 2010).

## V

In recent times, Andhra Pradesh witnessed a good deal of awakening and awareness among the denotified communities. Impact of neighbouring villages and towns was much felt on these people in the fields of education, employment and political awareness. For example, Yerukalas, Yanadis, Sugalis, Waddars, Dasaris, Poosalas and Dommaras have started their associations and emerged as strong social organisations. They do conduct annual meetings in order to resolve their problems. There are district and *taluk* associations in which social workers, educated members of the community, employees, politicians and youth are actively involved. They are working actively for the advancement of their socio-economic conditions. Some of them within the community have become graduates and post-graduates. Some of the community members are working in the all India Services. In the political sphere women are in the forefront than the males. A woman had become a member of parliament (Lok Sabha) and served as minister of state in P.V. Narasimha Rao's cabinet. In Stuartpuram ex-settlement, Yerukalas participated in national movement and were inspired by national leaders to fight for the abolition of criminal tribes act. Committed social workers and few government officials strove hard for the upliftment of some sections of people among these communities. This has been the result of the activities of progressive thinkers, reform leaders and left intellectuals which highlighted the plight of denotified communities since 1950s. Consequently, a cadre from denotified communities has emerged in the state (Government of Madras 1953).

Various societies like Bharatiya Adimajati Sevak Sangh, Andhra Rastra Adimajati Sevak Sangh and Andhra Rastra Yerukala, Yanadi,

Sugali, Woddar Sanghams (associations) came forward to constantly address the issues related to these communities. Thakkar Bapa was the pioneering social worker who professed a philosophy and technique with a missionary approach to their welfare. Bharatiya Adimjati Sevak Sangh held various conferences under the leadership of Thakkar Bapa. Andhra Rastra Adimjati Sevak Sangh took its birth in 1948 under his leadership of Vennelakanti Raghavaiah. Chadala Janakiram, Devarakonda Hanumantha Rao, Ramesam Nagaiah, Palaparthi Verraiah and others were its members. Prior to this, Andhra Rastra Yanadi Sangh came into existence. It was started in 1927 in Nellore district in Andhra Pradesh. Colonisation, liberation from slavery, education and political awakening were the main aims of the Sangh. It worked for political upliftment of denotified communities through the formulation of colonies in Chittoor, Nellore, Guntur, Krishna, Godavari and other districts. Mobilising community members, opening of schools, female education, abolition of nomadic and wandering habits, formation of cooperative societies etc. formed part of the organisation's activities (Haikerwal 1934).

One of the means of raising awareness has been literature. The literature of denotified communities was modelled on the lines of Dalit literature. Tribal literature in Andhra Pradesh not only gave a vent to miserable sorrows and happenings of Adivasis and denotified communities but also opened up new vistas of tribal activism. It also enlightened and educated several people into mainstream society. The literary expression of the denotified communities and writers began with the publication of *Kallumunta* by Palaparthi Veeraiah and Ramesam Nagaiah. Since then various types of books, magazines, newspapers and articles were published in Telugu and English. The best examples are *Kallumunta, Ramarajyam* and *Yekalavya. Yerukula, Adivasi, Dalit Marg, Penal Reformer Patrika* and *Harijanodharana* are some of the newspapers published by the Andhra Rastra Adimjati Sevak Sangh and Andhra Rastra Yerukala Sangh. These literary works and papers depicted life in ex-settlements, harassment meted out to them by criminal tribes acts, their professions, community cultural activities, meetings organised in different parts of the state, crimes committed by them, folk songs, police and public activities and welfare activities undertaken. However, due to lack of leadership and financial help publication of these periodicals stopped. Research work and advocacy too were undertaken by the Sangh. Vennelakanti Raghavaiah endeavoured hard for the upliftment of denotified communities in the state. His motive was for the repeal of criminal tribes act in the state. He started Andhra Rastra Yerukala Mahasangham in Epurupalem village, Prakasam district of Andhra Pradesh during 1947–48. The Sangh has a prolonged history. It had organised its caste association meetings at Chittoor, Vijayawada, Tadikonda, Nellore, Guntur, Nandigama, Palnadu and other places (Singh 1976b). Literature of denotified communities played an important role in sensitising their society. Their journalistic and autobiographical expressions have a limited utility in changing their socio-economic conditions. What is presently required is the engagement in serious social research, especially in the native languages is a progressive step towards this direction. Denotified communities must be mobilised politically and socially. Their caste associations must be empowered to sensitise them. Toady most of these communities have their caste associations without proper guidance and vision. They however, conduct meetings, conventions and agitate for their basic rights. During the 1950s and 1960s their caste associations emerged under the pervasive impact of national leaders. It is also important to note that caste associations among these communities do not have the required strength, unity, identity, financial power, political support etc. Due to lack of leadership, proper ideology and agenda, ego-centric approaches and vested interests these associations became week and were unable to show their strength in society. Political elite in Andhra Pradesh had been unable to quickly co-opt the emerging leadership among the denotified communities. At best they are used as political vote banks. The community leaders are also not able to maintain decent public life, integrity and honesty. As a result, despite widespread politicisation, the denotified communities have not emerged as a successful pressure group (Radhakrishna 1992).

Integration of the denotified communities is a challenging task before the policy framers, administrators and government. Social integration is an important aspect for the development of denotified communities of Andhra Pradesh. In the Indian social system, weaker sections such as scheduled castes, scheduled tribes and other backward classes though suffered a great deal of social oppression and discrimination they are included in Indian Society. Some of the smaller scheduled tribal groups have formed their own villages and societies (Mullaly 1912). Though the denotified tribes had links with village society, they were never allowed to be a part and parcel of local village society. They remained excluded from mainstream society for a long time and their transitory existence, paralytic, inferior lifestyles, poverty-stricken conditions, illiteracy, peculiar behaviour, wandering habits, culture and panchayat system are hindering their integration. The first step towards this direction is social, economic, political, physical and cultural integration. Government should provide them with housing facilities at the locations preferred by them. Rehabilitation measures initiated by successive governments did not register considerable progress in achieving the objectives of development (Panakal 1973).

Social integration of denotified warrants a total change in the attitudes of dominant society towards these communities. They should be provided with opportunities to participate in panchayats, municipalities, local self-government bodies and other decision-making bodies. No doubt this is a stupendous task. At present, development activities and upliftment programmes are confined only to certain voluntary organisations and agencies. The idea of development of denotified tribes must be spread widely. Communities such as Nakkalas, Dommaras and Nirshikaris are small and scattered communities. Government should make all efforts to integrate them into surrounding society. The issue of social integration of the denotified communities had not been adequately addressed so far. Social integration has selective applications. Sometimes, social integration leads to troubles also. The denotified communities have to face many challenges in this regard. Some nomadic and denotified communities such as Yerukulas and Sugalis have been reasonably well integrated. But their number is very negligible. Spatial and temporal dimensions also need to be considered. Integrating the denotified communities in the towns, districts and urban centres is relatively easier than in the rural villages (Guha and Madhav 1989). Villages, smaller towns and rural areas are not favourably disposed to accepting members of denotified communities. There is also some resistance in the districts already. It is only in the metropolitan cities that the denotified communities can peacefully settle and mingle with local populace with their art and crafts. There is a demand for their talent and performances in the cities rather than in the remote villages. However, in the cities, they have to work very hard and lead a secluded life. There is also a problem of disintegration of family members and individual life. Their community traits, culture and characteristic features will be lost. Separate colonies with modern facilities may be conducive for their social and cultural integration (Nigam 1990).

A broader social consensus must emerge towards the integration of denotified communities. Very often NT, DNT Communities are isolated. There is a need to break the isolation. Their individual desire is to equip themselves with various skills and improve their own functioning as the members of civil society. The burden of past must be thrown out from their youth. Government should propose area development plans keeping in mind various developmental activities. Though it is stupendous task, efforts should be made through committed social workers and NGOs. The ultimate aim is to socialise the DNTs, readjust them to society, rehabilitate and change them. The whole issue of rehabilitation hinges totally on the complex process of convincing them and transforming them into people who can eke out their livelihood through the sweat of their brows. Since their problems originate in social and economic issues the main thrust of rehabilitation should be socio-economic in nature. Rehabilitation has to be anointed with a human approach (Thurston 1909).

In view of the problems faced by NT-DNTs and the issues nagging them during colonial and post-colonial India, scholars and social activists have suggested various ameliorative measures to address development challenges of denotified communities. Some of the important recommendations that have been pending for quite some time are as follows:

- Conduct of sample surveys to assess their present socio-economic.
- Adequate funds should be spent on their economic development.
- D form pattas be made eligible for bank loans.
- Labour contract societies should be organised in consultation.
- Vocational trades like brick-making, mat-weaving, dress-making be established.
- Self-employment schemes need to be organised on the cooperative basis.
- DNT youth should be provided suitable public employment to enhance their social status.
- Sanction of generous bank loans to educated unemployed youth in settlements.
- Continuous engagement of youth in public activities and keep them away crime.
- Undue police harassment shall be done away with.
- DC (Dossier Criminals) sheets shall be lifted in case of good conduct ex-criminals.
- Stolen property dealers, corrupt officials and greedy criminal lawyers to be counselled.
- Educational facilities and special scholarships to be extended to all eligible students.

(Report on the Conditions of Nomadic and Denotified Tribes of India 2006: 21)

## Note

1 *Files of the Superintendent of Police, Crime Branch, Hyderabad*, vide *No.1185/ CIB/58 dated 27.2.21958*. These tribes are as follows: Telaga Pamulas, Dandasis, Konda Doras, Rellis, Paids, Kintil, Kalinga, Nakkalas, Piriki Mukkalas, Donga Yalhas, Vedurupaka Malas, Boyas, Netti Kothalas, Reddikas, Yanadis, Dommaras, Anipi Malas, Vaddi Upparas, Buda Bukkalas, Lambadas, Waddars, Kemparis, Pamulas, Reddy Yanadis, Jarugumalli Madigas, Donga Dasari, Mondi Banda, Jogula, Nawabpeta Korcha, Amagunta Palegars, Paraya, Thota Naiks, Bhathu, Turaka, Pedda Boya, Dabbala Vagula, Nirshhikari, Iranis, Kanjar Bhatt, Jatur mixed gang.

## References

Aiyappan, Ayinapalli. 1948. *Report on the Socio-Economic Conditions of the Aboriginal Tribes of the Province of Madras*. Madras: Government Press.

Arnold, David. 1979. 'Dacoity and Rural Crime in Madras, 1860–1940', *Journal of Peasant Studies*, 6(2), January.

Bhargava, B. S. 1949. *The Criminal Tribes of India*. Lucknow: United Publishers.

Bhowmick, P. K. 1963. *The Lodhas of West Bengal*. Calcutta: Punthi Pustak.

Bhowmick, P. K. 1975. *Essential Primary Consideration Schemes*. New Delhi: Bharatiya Adimajathi Sevak Sang.

Devy, G. N. 2005. *A Nomad Called Thief*. Hyderabad: Orient Longman.

Fuches, Stephen. 1972. *The Aboriginal Tribes of India*. New Delhi: Macmillan.

Gandhi, Malli. 2006. *Development of Denotified Tribes: Policy and Practice*. New Delhi: Sarup and Sons.

Gandhi, Malli. 2008. *Denotified Tribes: Dimensions of Change*. New Delhi: Kanishka.

Guha, Ramachandra and Madhav Gadgil. 1989. 'State Forestry and Social Conflict in British India', *Past and Present*, 122(123).

Haikerwal, B. S. 1934. *Economic and Social Aspects of Crime in India*. London: George Allen & Unwin Ltd.

Hunter, William Wilson. 1881. *England's Work in India*. Smith, London: Elder and Company.

Government of India. 2010. *NT-DNT Rag: Report on the Conditions of Nomadic and Denotified Tribes of India*. New Delhi: Ministry of Social Justice and Empowerment.

Government of Madras. 1953. *Home Department Proceedings, 1937–1952*. Madras: Government Central Press (Tamil Nadu State Archives).

Lalitha, V. 1995. *The Making of Criminal Tribes: Patterns and Transition*. Madras: New Era Publications.

Lavanam and Hemalatha Lavanam. 1974. *Notes and Reflections of Our Work in the Rehabilitation of Ex-Criminal Tribes People in the Settlements*. Vijayawada: Gandhi Peace Foundation.

Mullaly, Frederick S. 1892. *The Criminal Class of Madras Presidency*. Madras: Superintendent Government Press.

Nigam, Sanjay. 1990. 'Disciplining and Policing the Criminals By Birth', *Indian Economic and Social History Review*, 27(2).

Panakal, J. J. 1973. 'An Agenda for Criminology', *Indian Journal of Criminology*, 1: 51–67.

Radhakrishna, Meena. 1992. 'Surveillance and Settlement Under the Criminal Tribes Act in Madras', *Indian Economic and Social History Review*, 24(2).

Radhakrishna, Meena. 2001. *Dishonoured By History: Criminal Tribes and British Colonial Policy*. Hyderabad: Orient Blackswan.

*Report on the Conditions of Nomadic and Denotified Tribes of India*. 2006. New Delhi: Ministry of Social Justice and Empowerment.

Simhadri, Y. C. 1979. *The Ex-Criminal Tribes of India*. New Delhi: National Publishing House.

Simhadri, Y. C. 2000. *The Denotified Tribes of India: A Sociological Analysis*. New Delhi: Classical Publishing Company.

Singh, Jaspal. 1976a. *Crime in India, Reformation of Ex-Criminals*. London: Unpublished Key Note Address.

Singh, Jaspal. 1976b. *Reformation of Ex-Criminal Tribes*. New Delhi: Unpublished Monograph.

Thurston, Edgar. 1909. *Castes and Tribes of South India*, Volume III. Madras: Government Press.

# 16
# DECENTRALISED GOVERNANCE AND IMPLEMENTATION OF PESA IN TRIBAL AREAS
Evidences from the western tribal belt of India

*Yatindra Singh Sisodia and Tapas K. Dalapati*

I

After Independence, persistent efforts have been made to make rural local self-government viable and self-sustainable on the lines portrayed by Mahatma Gandhi. Unfortunately, the response of the state governments was of very different nature and as a result the pace and pattern of establishment of rural local political institutions was not very enthusiastic in the initial phase. The state governments showed very little interest to empower the village level institutions and transfer of power to these institutions was almost negligible. Though political leader of some Indian states like Kerala, Karnataka, Maharashtra and West Bengal came forward to establish panchayats at local level, on the whole the actual and functional pace of decentralisation was very slow in India. Champions of local self-government have been argued that the development planning was faulty at grassroots level and fruits of development programmes not reaching to the people despite plethora of schemes have been implemented and massive funds have been pumped into the rural sector. People's participation was rarely seen and the development model was of 'top-down approach'. Accountability of the delivery mechanism was nominal as it rested with the bureaucratic hierarchy that viewed rural masses as mere recipients.

Almost after 45 years, the Central Government realised this hard truth that the delivery system in the tribal/rural area was not effectively operational; it was realised that without functional participation people through panchayats, development of rural and tribal areas will not be sustained. As a result, the introduction of 73rd Constitutional Amendment Act was enacted in 1993. The execution of the Act was made mandatory for all the Indian states and panchayats have been provided a constitutional status. A special chapter (Part IX) has been added to the Indian Constitution on Panchayats. The 73rd Amendment has provided uniformity and formal structure to these traditional institutions of self-governance for the sake of their effective functioning. The 73rd Amendment has initiated a fundamental restructuring of governance and administrative system of the country, based on the philosophy of decentralisation and power to the people. Policy planners have realised by now that the new Panchayat Raj institutions have the potential to usher in a new era of change and development in accordance with people's needs and priorities, and to revitalise a deeply troubled system of democracy (Behar and Kumar 2002) at grassroots level.

The idea that produced the 73rd Amendment Act was not a response to pressure from the grassroots but it was due to an increasing recognition that the institutional initiatives of the preceding decades had not delivered, that the extent of rural poverty was still high and thus the existing structure of government needed to be reformed. It is interesting to note that this idea evolved from the Centre and the State Governments. It was a political drive to see panchayat raj Institutions (PRIs) as a solution to the governmental crises that India was experiencing (World Bank 2000) at grassroots level. The institution of panchayat raj in its rejuvenated form seeks to achieve the objectives of democratic decentralisation to accelerate socio-economic development and usher in equity and social justice in rural and tribal areas.

The enactments of the 73rd Constitutional Amendment Act and the subsequent state-wise panchayat raj Acts in India have brought to frontline the significance of grassroots democratic processes. This change in the Indian political system is the result of a growing conviction that the distantly placed and centralised governance cannot achieve growth and development in a society without people's direct participation and initiative. This experience has brought the lesson that the success of the new panchayat raj system largely depends on the congruence of perception and commitment of the people, their leaders and of the officials, about the role to be played by them in the new system. Contextually and theoretically too, the new panchayat raj system has been created as new a model of self-governance (Sisodia 2002). The objectives of the new panchayat raj is to execute and implement schemes and programmes to meet the real local needs, to mobilise people, to channelise their energies towards rural reconstruction through the new institutions. Its objectives include reducing the influence of the higher and intermediate level bureaucracy and leaving the responsibility to the local people to decide their destiny as per their aspiration.

A decade and a half of new panchayat raj in India has been a matter of debate and speculation about its performance and impact. All the major states have completed at least two rounds of panchayat elections and in majority of cases at least three successive rounds. Almost 3 million people including 1 million women and a sizeable number of SCs/STs took part in these elections. The sizeable presence of underprivileged and the poor as people's representatives through reservations for the grassroots political institutions is a landmark development in the rural politics of the country. This significant development has special meaning because a decade earlier in most parts of rural India these groups were excluded from public life and political participation. This is also a matter of serious debate as how this excluded lot after their inclusion in active politics at grassroots would effectively participate and tackle local power equations and set the agenda for development. Yet the fact remains that these backward and so far ignored classes have heralded their arrival on the political stage of the country in the countryside.

The responses of the state governments towards new panchayat raj varied significantly and it is very difficult to generalise about this issue on the basis of their functioning for the last one decade or so. Only a few states like Maharashtra, Gujarat, Kerala, Karnataka and West Bengal have had a track record of Panchayats since the 1950s and the exemplary lead taken by the state of Madhya Pradesh after 1993 brings together a total of six states only that took steps to strengthen PRIs. On the other hand, states of Bihar, Jharkhand and Jammu & Kashmir are considered prominent examples among states where little or no progress had taken place over the last one decade; even regular panchayat elections were inordinately delayed in these states.

A perusal of state profiles would show that panchayat raj reforms have certainly taken place with vigour and zeal in some western and southern parts of the country that are relatively sound from the point of view of economy, are socially vibrant, and have active civil societies. On the contrary, the northern states with the greatest degree of poverty, inequality and deep schisms of caste and low pace of governance resulted in weak panchayats (Robinson 2005).

In this scenario of decentralised governance, exemplary reforms have taken place in Kerala and Madhya Pradesh due to the strong political will of the political leadership of these states after the implementation of the 73rd Amendment Act. In Kerala, the people's planning campaign was predicted on a high level of popular mobilisation that was made possible by high level of literacy and professional support with a mass base of social movement (Issac and Franke 2000). In Madhya Pradesh, the then Chief Minister Digvijay Singh had introduced a series of reforms and amendments in panchayat raj system to strengthen the grassroots institutions, specially the Gram Sabha. The example of West Bengal is well-known where the CPM government used the PRIs as a political support base in rural areas with a significant degree of success. The success of land reforms initiatives in West Bengal could take place due to Panchayat Raj (Webster 1992).

## II

### 73rd Amendment and implementation of PESA

Tribal communities are most marginalised section of the Indian society. They have remained comparatively isolated from the mainstream development process and maintain an uninterrupted long tradition of well knit, cohesive social structure and value system backed their own custom and traditions. They have also several indigenous traditional institutions to resolve their conflict and manage their resources and socio-political life. When the institution of new panchayat raj was planned to be introduced in the tribal areas it was felt that there was an urgent need to protect the tribal from the marginalisation in the age of globalisation. The Working Group (1996) of the Ninth Five Year Plan suggested participatory planning as a necessary prelude for growth and equity in tribal areas which have not gained significance from the development process since Independence. In order to strengthen the grassroots level local bodies and to provide self-rule of tribals, the Part IX of the Constitution that deals with Panchayats has been specially extended through an Act of Parliament called Panchayats Extension to Scheduled V Areas Act (PESA) 1996. Prior to this Act, a committee was constituted under Shri Dilip Singh Bhuria to examine various dimensions of self-rule of tribal and the constitutional requirement for extension of the Panchayats provision in the Scheduled Areas. The suggestions made by the committee assimilated various provisions of Scheduled V and Scheduled VI areas and 73rd Constitutional Amendment. Under PESA special treatment has been given to the social, political, cultural and economic aspects of tribal life.

One of the highlighting features of PESA is its suggestion that 'every Gram Sabha shall be competent to safeguard and preserve the traditions and customs of the people, their cultural identity, community resources and the customary mode of dispute resolution'. In addition to this, the Central Act of 1996 provides extensive powers to Gram Sabha in the Scheduled Areas in the following sectors: (1) Approval of plans, programmes and projects for social and economic development prior to their implementation; (2) Identification of beneficiaries of anti-poverty programmes; and (3) Certify utilisation of fund spent by the Panchayat.

PESA after giving the above exclusive powers to the lowest unit of grassroots democracy has further provided that the Gram Sabha or Panchayats at appropriate level shall have the following powers: (1) to be consulted on matters of land acquisition and resettlement; (2) grant prospecting licence for mining lease for minor minerals and concessions for such activities, (3) planning and management of minor water bodies, (4) the power to enforce prohibition or to regulate or restrict the sale and consumption of any intoxicant, (5) the ownership of minor forest produces, (6) the power to prevent alienation of land and to restore any unlawfully alienated land of a scheduled tribe, (7) the power to manage village markets, (8) the power to exercise control over moneylending to scheduled tribes, (9) the power to exercise controls over institutions and functionaries in all social sectors and (10) the power to control local plans and resources.

While prescribing such wide ranging powers to 'Gram Sabhas or Panchayats at appropriate level', PESA has further warned that, 'the State legislation that may endow Panchayats with powers and authority as may be necessary to enable them to function as institutions of self-government. It also contains safeguards to ensure that Panchayats at higher level do not assume the powers and authority of any panchayats at the lower level or the Gram Sabha'. The states were suggested to amend their respective Panchayat Acts to extend the provisions of the Panchayat to Scheduled Areas of their respective States within a year keeping in mind the letter and the spirit of the Central Act of 1996.

Three different forces are influencing the process of decentralised governance- the state, the civil society and the community. The interaction between these forces and its intensity, govern the pace and pattern of implementation of PESA. Although at surface, the state aims to decentralise the governance, the political economy of decentralisation restrict intense interaction between the state, the civil society and the community.

Efforts have been made to empower people through legislation in Scheduled Areas but there are indications that the level of participation of people at grassroots level is very low. The grassroots institutions like gram sabhas are almost a formal institution with no role in various development works at the level of village. It is unfortunate that both the grassroots leadership and grassroots bureaucracy have not been able to strengthen the gram sabha in Scheduled Areas. The responsibility of natural resource management (land/water/forest) lies with village level institutions but there still exists discrepancies regarding minor minerals/minor forest produce and therefore the direct control of the tribal community over NRM is far from reality. All the plans including tribal sub plan are to be implemented through grassroots level institutions but lack of information is a major bottleneck in this regard. Decision-making at grassroots level is of typical nature where elected representatives are more genuinely involved in the process of decision-making whereas the community is at large ignorantly out of this process.

So far as financial status of panchayats is concerned, it is completely dependent on the grants from government. Revenue generation at local level could not become possible because of lack of resources to generate revenue in tribal regions; taxation is also not possible because lack of basic amenities needed for day to day life; majority of the people live in acute shortage of livelihood bases which in turn leads to a situation where basic survival is a major question among majority people. The grants and funds percolating to grassroots institutions through governments are mainly for welfare programmes and development works and hence the panchayats lack total control over such resources and local planning; prioritisation of such funds for the community is ignored.

In tribal regions, there is a stronghold of traditional leadership which creates hindrances to the smooth functioning of panchayats. Nevertheless, there are examples where the traditional and panchayat leadership is the same, and in such a situation the functioning of panchayat is much better. Low level of people's participation can be mainly attributed to a strong and invincible social and economic stratification existed in villages. Sarpanch and other influential people tend to dominate the decision-making process. There are generally two prominent and sharply contrasting groups leading the panchayats (1) the traditional influential representatives and (2) the other of new entrants. The performance and efficacy of panchayat members is strongly influenced by the social stratification and class distinctions.

Moreover, gram panchayats are not adequately accountable to gram sabha. The gram sabha is not aware of the gram panchayat functioning. The idea of participation as an important part of panchayat raj has rarely been observed in practice. In fact, in retrospect, it seems inevitable that persons of influence would look at larger community participation with hostility.

In Scheduled Areas of Madhya Pradesh, Rajasthan and Gujarat, the village level situation is different from the high expectations created by PESA. State Acts are also confronting with the provisions of PESA. The issue of tribal non-tribal leadership in Scheduled Areas has created new political equations. The political dynamics at grassroots level has different dimensions it has many players in the circles and they throw their weight according their influences in the local power dynamics. As a matter of fact, it can be argued that despite the specific provision provided through PESA, there is a gap between macro-level decisions and grassroots level reality. Tribal regions have their own peculiarities. The main actors in panchayats are traditional leader, new entrants, local bureaucracy, non-tribal society and government departments' like- forest and revenue. The traditional leadership generally looks at the decentralised process as a rival parallel institution and challenge to their natural stronghold and in this circumstance need for awareness generation and sensitisation of people regarding new panchayats raj very much necessary. The new entrants to Panchayats are not fully acquainted with the provisions of PESA and therefore their understanding of this aspect needs to be broadened. Planning and management of minor water bodies is entrusted to gram sabha but there are other institutions as well like- watershed mission to look into this matter hence it is necessary to create coordination among traditional system with new schemes. Amendments have been made in Acts for mining lease, exploitation of minor minerals, minor forest produce, to prevent alienation of land but still there are dilemmas of sharing the stronghold in implementation process. Non-tribal leadership has been very strong in tribal regions; they work as middleman/agents for development schemes. They have established good network with local bureaucracy and influence decision-making process in their favour negating the tribal leadership at the grassroots level.

Against this backdrop, this chapter attempts to find out the processes and mechanisms working in the implementation of PESA in Madhya Pradesh, Rajasthan and Gujarat.

## III

### *Fieldwork: methodology and context*

The main focus of this research was the implementation of PESA in the contiguous scheduled V areas of Madhya Pradesh, Gujarat and Rajasthan. The issues of panchayat representatives were considered for observation within the study so as to comprehend the dynamics of its working, nature of changes and development. The study also strived to understand the interplay, inter-linkages and conflict between these actors. Western tribal belt of Madhya Pradesh, southern tribal belt of Rajasthan and northern tribal belt of Gujarat have many social and cultural similarities. The political and social movements in these regions have also been very close in these parts at times. Looking into these similarities one district from each tribal belt of the States was selected for the micro-level study. The selected districts were Jhabua from Madhya Pradesh, Banswara from Rajasthan and Dahod from Gujarat. For a representative coverage, two blocks were selected from each selected districts and from each block five gram tribal panchayats are purposively selected for the study. In this selection due representation is ensured for women headed Panchayats. Therefore, ten tribal villages were purposively selected from each district and the total number of villages included in sample was 30. From each selected Gram Panchayats 10 Gram Sabha members (five male and five female) and seven panchayat representatives (one sarpanch, one upsarpanch and five panchs) were interviewed regarding implementation of PESA in their gram panchayats and its impact upon the governance after implementation of PESA in their socio-economic and political life.

## IV

### *Panchayat Raj representative's participation, attitudes and perceptions regarding implementation of PESA: an analysis*

#### Socio-economic characteristics

The study was carried out in 30 villages of three states viz. Madhya Pradesh, Rajasthan and Gujarat. As per the dispensation of 73rd Amendment, one-third seats are reserved for females and in sample selection; this important aspect has been kept in consideration. In this study it is found that majority of the respondents are below the age of 45. If we look at the data with a viewpoint of respondents from different states, it is quite clear that the representation in all the age groups is almost similar to that of the total age group wise representation. Overwhelming majority of the respondents is married and state specific data also endorses the same situation. The sub-caste factor plays a significant role when elections take place at grassroots level and during the meetings where important decisions are to be taken. Damor and Katara are most represented sub-castes in the sample. Almost half of the respondents are illiterate. State-wise representation of data makes it very clear that the maximum illiterate respondents are from Madhya Pradesh. This is also a bitter truth that the educational attainment among the tribals is very less and this is reflected through the sample respondents as well. However, the situation of panchayat representatives is much better as compared to villagers in this regard.

The tribal respondents of this region have both nuclear and joint family structure. Majority of the respondents have a family size of five to eight and interestingly the state specific data also supports this reality. Majority of the respondents do agriculture work. This is also because agriculture is their first occupation and in lean months, they do labour work as well. The state specific data also reiterates the similar pattern. There are hardly few respondents who have big landholding otherwise majority of the respondents fall in the category up to two acres and field experiences suggest that the piece of land owned by individual household is very small and at times economically unviable for agriculture purposes. Majority of the respondents fall in the lowest income category, which denotes that majority of them belong to below poverty line group. This situation is almost similar which is visible in all the three states.

### *Exposure towards PESA*

It is indeed a matter of concern that overwhelming majority of the respondents has no exposure towards special status of Panchayats in V Scheduled Areas. It makes a significant meaning since this particular message was repeatedly percolated down to the representatives and a small group could at least know about this. Broadly very superficial information is available with the respondents. If we look at the data in terms of specific states, the scenario remains more or less the same. Operationalisation of Gram Sabha

## Operationalisation of Gram Sabha

There is almost no change in the perception of respondents regarding gram sabha. This is also because the level of exposure among the tribals is very low and one-third of the respondents are women who have hardly any understanding of these issues. Overwhelming majority of the respondents who are panchayat representatives, have no exposure to special rights and this situation remains almost similar in all the three states. There is meagre knowledge about the special rights of Gram Sabha in Scheduled Areas among the Gram Sabha members. Only some prominent issues are known to a few respondents regarding special rights of Gram Sabha.

A significant percentage of respondents know the number of meetings to be held in a year. It is a very negative situation to note that overwhelming majority of the respondents does not know the right quorum required for gram sabha meetings. This situation is almost similar in all states. The number of respondents is higher who know the mandatory presence of women as compared to the respondents who know the required number for quorum. This is because for quorum, the exact number was asked and here only mandatory presence was asked. Significant aspect of PESA regarding composition of more than one Gram Sabha in one gram panchayat is known to less than half of the respondents. The presence of government officials is regular; this is because the Gram Sabha is a platform where from all the government schemes are initiated and the decisions and programmes of the government are percolated down; this is one of the reasons that presence of members is regular.

The wish of sarpanch is very prominent in the opinion of majority and the very important dimension of selection of person for presiding over among the tribals is missing. In the opinion of overwhelming majority, sarpanch presides over the meeting and the responses from Rajasthan are highest in this category. Another important category that of a tribal villager elected by the majority for this purpose presides over the gram sabha meeting, this is second highest response and the responses from Madhya Pradesh are highest in this category and as per the rule, this is the right answer. Important aspect of PESA regarding tribal person can be nominated to preside over the gram sabha meeting is known to a limited number despite the fact that respondents are panchayat representatives. The information about meeting is received in majority cases through a peon/chowkidar/kotwar. Panchayat representatives and secretary are also a very important source of information so far as meetings are concerned.

It is indeed very important that in majority of cases the information is made available about the gram sabha meetings. The availability of information significantly varies and it does not have state specific phenomenon. It is interesting to note that overwhelming majority of the respondents do know about one or another very important work of gram sabha. Overwhelming majority of the respondents make efforts to inform, motivate and inspire villagers to attend the Gram Sabha meeting. State-wise, variation in responses is very limited. It is indeed very important that in majority cases, the respondents feel that one should participate in the gram sabha meeting.

The major reasons for the participation are related to make the tribals aware about the problems of the village and appraise them regarding different schemes and solution of their problem. It is indeed very important that a sizable number of respondents have negative point of view for attending Gram Sabha meeting knowing the fact that it is of no benefit to them hence nobody listens in the meeting. Around two-third of the respondents do participate in gram sabha meetings regularly which is very significant from the view of tribal situation. However, since the participants are panchayat representatives and if one-third of them are not regular, it becomes a matter of concern. Agriculture/ labour work is most significant reason of irregularity in gram sabha meetings. It is indeed a matter of concern that though being Panchayat member only half of the respondents have presented their point of view which is not in the interest of the development of the new system.

Significant number has found the work done/in process in response to the point of view presented in gram sabha meetings. It is a very encouraging situation that despite having the social audit, only half of the respondents who are panchayat representatives know the information with regard to the stages of work. Sizeable number of respondents have expressed their views that the role played by them is mostly related to submission of proposals, giving suggestions and discuss proposals; in fact, these are the main roles assigned to panchayat members. Only more than one-third respondents try to know the problems of villagers and put them in Gram Sabha meetings for the simple reason that it is significant from the point of view of implementation of PESA. Drinking water, irrigation and employment opportunities are the major problems shared by villagers with panchayat representatives.

Decisions in Gram Sabha are rested either with majority or with sarpanch. Majority of respondents receive information related to all important aspects. Overwhelming majority of respondents have knowledge about the provision that the gram sabha's decisions are mandatory to implement. Majority of the respondents are of the opinion that sarpanch plays the vital role in selection of beneficiaries. Another important role is cited as gram sabha and this is exactly the institution assigned for selection of beneficiaries. A very significant number is aware of this important fact that the selection of beneficiaries for the welfare schemes is to be done through gram sabha. Almost two-third respondents feel that there is benefit to BPL families through gram sabha. In majority opinion, the time needed to get the benefit is usually one to two months. Overwhelming majority of respondents know that there is benefit to village from the institution of the of gram sabha. In majority opinion, the village development is most important benefit in attending gram sabha and also the issues related to benefit are employment, agriculture and infrastructure. More than half of the selected respondents have knowledge of execution of the suggestions of gram sabha. It shows that a significant number has understanding of this important provision.

Half of the respondents feel that the wishes and suggestions of gram sabha are considered by gram panchayat. Looking into the innovation and its technicality, a sizeable number is coming closer to the understanding of the system. One very important aspect of selection of village development through gram sabha is endorsed by almost two-third of the respondents. Nevertheless, sarpanch has still a very important say in selection and operation of village development work.

## Operationalisation of Gram Panchayat

Gram Panchayat is the main executing institution of all the work at the grassroots level. Three-fifth of the respondents know the exact interval of organisation of gram panchayat meeting while the remaining respondents refer different periods because of different level of understanding among panchayat members. Overwhelming majority of the respondents do participate in gram panchayat meetings regularly which is very significant from the point of view of tribal situation. Non-understanding of the proceedings and the husband representing women representatives are the main reasons of irregularity in meeting. Proposal discussion is most important task in gram panchayat meetings. Decisions are rested either with unanimity or with recommendation of gram sabha. Overwhelming majority of the respondents inspect the ongoing construction work in the village. The respondents do visit different offices for inspection purposes; however, the schools and anganwadies are mostly under inspection of respondents. Villages are still in demand of basic amenities like drinking water, electricity, road/bridge etc. on priority basis.

Almost half of the respondents present a very negative picture as gram panchayat has no role in solving village problems whereas a large number of them are of the opinion that they do forward the proposal. This is because the respondents are gram panchayat members who have already aired the problems in gram panchayat meetings repeatedly. Despite such efforts, there are no positive or concrete results coming out. As a result of this villagers have lost faith so far as the care of solution of these problems through gram panchayat is concerned.

## Natural resource management

Management of natural resource according to indigenous knowledge of tribal is one of the main activities under PESA. Less than half of the respondents do know one of the very important tasks assigned by PESA Act of management of natural resources (land, water and forest) through gram sabha. 50 per cent tribal villages have the availability of forest and minor forest produce. As far as control over forest is concerned, all the respondents are categorically of the view that government/forest department has control over it. Only a very small number of villages have minor minerals. Overwhelming majority of villages have water bodies. Gujarat has the highest number of institutions to control this problem. Committee system is functional to manage the water bodies. However, a considerable number of respondents find no arrangement for water body in their villages.

## Conservation and protection of traditions and rituals

Overwhelming majority of the respondents believe in local traditions and rituals. Gram Sabha has the responsibility of conservation and protection of traditions, rituals and cultural identity. Surprisingly, this fact is not known to majority of the respondents. Issues of conservation and protection of traditions, rituals and cultural identity in gram sabha are discussed by a limited number of respondents. Knowledge about traditions and rituals is confined to very superficial issues and no specific details are discussed in terms of traditions and rituals to be protected by the gram sabha like traditional pattern of dispute resolution, worshipping natural resources, traditional method of natural resource management, livelihood patterns etc. In the majority of cases,

Gram Sabha/jati Panchayat/sarpanch looks after the question of dispute resolution. Gram sabha and jati panchayats are considered as most effective institutions in conservation and protection of traditions, rituals and cultural identities. Conservation and protection through gram sabha has got hold of sarpanch's decision in majority cases, while a substantial number favours the villagers' consent in this matter. The respondents who have made their point of view in favour of jati panchayat for the conservation and protection of traditions and rituals have supported the acceptance of the role of tadvi/patel in all these matters. Social evils in tribal society are plenty which ultimately leads the life of many to miserable conditions. The PESA Act has provision of including this matter in discussion of gram sabha; a large number of members endorse this fact which is indeed good for the tribal society. Almost all major social evils need to be reformed/curbed by Gram Sabha as this is the opinion of majority of the respondents. Dowry and use of liquor are considered as the major social evils that need to be banned. Overwhelming majority of the respondents are of the view that there is no harm to local culture and traditions because of Gram Sabha. Almost three-fourth respondents are of the opinion that the present panchayat system is different from the earlier one. Since the PESA Act has categorically empowered the gram sabha with enormous power and majority of the respondents have accepted this change, this is a positive contribution to the system. As a change from earlier panchayat system, more development works are taking place and there is a direct involvement of the villagers in village matters after the creation of Gram Sabha under PESA.

It is interesting to note that there is a very constructive role of the Gram Sabha in many important aspects related to village development work; however, the number of persons having this opinion is limited. Even then, this is definitely a positive indication that involving weaker sections of society and women members in the gram sabha has raised the status of this institution. It is clear and very positive from the above interpretation that overwhelming majority of respondents feel that non-tribal people have cooperative attitude towards scheduled area panchayat. Illiteracy has been termed as one of the most crucial significant problems faced by the panchayat members. Training, an essential tool of equipping the people with capacity to run panchayat affairs, has not been carried out to make the panchayat representatives aware about the importance of PESA and the procedural aspects of Panchayat Raj institutions. Respondents have received training mainly from block headquarters. The respondents have mainly received the training related to working of panchayat, information/knowledge about the basics of panchayat and understanding of rules and regulation through training. The suggestions given to improve the system are related to regular holding of meetings, more powers, more finances etc. In fact the real issues which create hurdles against smooth functioning of panchayat raj in schedules areas are not suggested by the respondents; thus positive efforts are needed for the improvement. This is also because the level of understanding and exposure among tribal representatives is comparatively low.

V

*Conclusion*

It has been evident from the working experience of PESA and also as the above mentioned responses of respondents indicate that the level of participation of people at grassroots level has been relatively low. Despite knowing the procedural aspects, gram sabhas are almost a formal institution. The state governments did not transfer all the powers through conformity acts. The village experiences suggest that considerable number of the panchayat representatives and villagers are aware about the procedural aspects of gram sabha meetings.

It seems that only amendment in the State Acts and specific provisions for new system will not change the scenario. There is an urgent need to opt for an effective device whereby maximum people can be informed, made aware and motivated to come forward for the proper implementation and execution of PESA. There is an urgent need to break the culture of silence among tribal and to strive for capacity building, sensitisation and orientation to improve the tribal self-rule scenario.

The prevailing circumstances clearly define that betterment in this situation is the need of the hour. Awareness generation and capacity building are required to generate understanding among the tribal community and for this NGOs (Non-Governmental Organisation) and voluntary organisations (VOs) should play a significant role. There is a need to sensitise local bureaucracy and non-tribal leadership to fully understand the significance of PESA and cooperate with tribal community in smooth functioning of Panchayats. All the laws and rules confronting PESA need to be amended accordingly. The civil society has a significant role in awareness generation and capacity building.

There are some successful/constructive pockets in Madhya Pradesh, Rajasthan and Gujarat where efforts have been made in this regard. The situation is, however, significantly different in tribal regions where the civil society's intervention is conspicuously absent. The interference between the community and bureaucracy can be transparent if it is linked with non-governmental organisations. Constructive interactions between the state, the civil society and the community shall bring much-needed awareness about the rights of the people along with transparency in planning, execution and monitoring of the programmes. In this process, the benefits of PESA could be distributed equitably, which in its turn, can reinstall community's faith in the PRIs.

## References

Behar, Amitabh and Kumar, Yogesh. 2002. 'Decentralisation in Madhya Pradesh, India: From Panchayati Raj to Gram Swaraj (1995 to 2001)', *Working Paper 170*. London: ODI.

Issac, Thomas T. M. and Franke, Richard W. 2000. *Local Democracy and Development: People's Campaign for Decentralised Planning in Kerala*. New Delhi: Leftword.

Robinson, Mark. 2005. 'A Decade of Panchayat Raj Reforms: The Challenge of Democratic Decentralisation in India', in L. C. Jain (ed.), *Decentralisation and Local Governance*. New Delhi: Orient Longman.

Sisodia, Yatindra Singh. 2002. 'Decentralised Governance in Madhya Pradesh: Experiences of the Gram Sabha in Scheduled Areas', *Economic and Political Weekly*, 37(40): 4100–4.

Webster, Neil. 1992. 'Panchayat Raj in West Bengal: Participation for the People or the Party?', *Development and Change*, 23(4): 129–63.

World Bank. 2000. 'Overview of Rural Decentralisation in India, Volume 3', *Working Paper No. 28014*. New Delhi: World Bank, 24.

# INDEX

Adivasi Mulya Adivasi Sangha 157
adverse possession (AP):
 conflagration over 86–8;
 Framework Agreement on
 Cooperation for Development 88–9;
 life in enclaves 84–6; nations in
 enclaves 79–84, 89–91
affirmative action programmes:
 development projects/schemes
 35–40; ineffective implementation
 of 35–7; integrated tribal
 development projects 34; other
 forms of 33–5; tribal subplan 34;
 types 32; use by tribes 32–3
Akram, Muhammed 70
All-India Coordination Committee of
 Communist Revolutionaries 121
Andhra Pradesh: atrocities 222–3,
 226, 231; criminal tribes in 321;
 development schemes 287; DNT
 communities 312, 315, 324–9;
 ex-criminal tribes in 315; GCC
 of 193; gender issues 95; militant
 land-rights movement 122;
 NTFP collection 186; peace talks
 138–9
Anganwadi Kendra (AK) 45, 59–60
anti-Posco movement 127, 160
Arunachali tribe 73
Arunachal Pradesh 76–7
atrocities: access to justice 224–7,
 238–9; against Dalits 9–10,
 236–9; forms of 221; NT-DNT
 communities 319; patterns of
 9–10, 219; power and dominance
 by local leaders/village council
 234–6; regional variations 221–4;
 repression under laws 228–30;
 terrorisation by police and
 security forces 230–1; against
 women 105–6, 231–4
auxiliary nurse mid-wife (ANM)
 58–9, 64

Balaghat tribe 43
Bangladesh: division of tribes
 72–5; enclaves 79–91; Framework
 Agreement on Cooperation for
 Development 88–9
Bapa, Thakkar 326
Baster tribe 42
Bawari tribe 320
Bengal Commission 70
Bhaduri, Amit 126, 166
Bhantu tribe 320
Bhil tribe 277
Bhoodan movement 117
big capital 149–52
Bihar 223, 277, 334
Bihari, Batke 53–6
Bilaspur tribe 42
Bisoyi, Chakra 118
Bisthapan Birodhi Jan Manch
 (People's Platform Against
 Displacement) 160
Biswas, C.K. 70
borewell technology 205–9
Bose, Jeevan 137
Boundary Commission 70–1
Boya tribe 315

348

# INDEX

capital 182–3
Chakkala tribe 315
Chakma tribe 72, 75–9
Chhattisgarh 94–106, 135, 171, 221–3, 226, 231, 232, 254, 277
Chhattisgarh Energy Policy (Chhattisgarh Urja Neeti 2001) 104
Chhattisgarh Women's Policy (Chhattisgarh Mahila Neeti 2000) 103
Chittagong Hill Tracts (CHT) 75–9
citizenship 28, 31–2, 73, 76–8
civil rights 31
colonial administration 274
colonial rule 29, 113, 269–70
Communist Party of India (CPI) 121
Communist Party of India-Maoist (CPI-ML-Maoist) 128
Communist Party of India-Marxist-Leninist (CPI-ML) 121
Communist Party of India-Marxist-Leninist-Liberation (CPI-ML-Liberation) 124, 125
Communist Party of India-Marxist-Leninist-New-Democracy (CPI-ML-New-Democracy) 124, 125
community development programmes 34
Community Forest Management (CFM) 120
Community Health Centre 43, 59–60, 63–6
Constitution of India 3, 28, 31–2, 94, 104, 156, 192–3, 276, 287, 288, 300, 303–6, 319
corporate social responsibility (CSR) 158
criminal law 314–15
Criminal Tribes Act of 1871 316
Criminal Tribes Act of 1911 315–16
Criminal Tribes Act of 1924 318, 320, 322
criminal tribes (CTs): denotification of 315; impact of criminal law on 315–16; labeling 311; reformation/rehabilitation of 316, 321–2; seasonal migration of 316–17; social experience of 320–2; unstable occupations 323

cultivation practices 187–8
cultural appropriation 109–13, 127

Dalits: atrocities against 9–10, 236–9; investment-induced displacement of 155; in Odisha 108, 113–17, 119, 123, 125–6, 144; untouchability of 9–10
dams 160–1, 163–4, 168
Dasari tribe 315, 325
debt 162–8
'decentralised responsive governance' 103
Deen Dayal Mobile Hospital (DDMH) 61–2
denotified tribes (DNTs): cultural heritage of 324; growth rate of population 312; history of 312–13; recommendations to address development challenges 329; reformation/rehabilitation of 321–2; role in long distance trade 312–13; social experience of 320–2; social organisations 325–6; state-wise lists of 315; threat to 313–14; unstable occupations 323; welfare measures initiated for the development of 317–19
development: national 37–8; projects/schemes 35–40; regional 37–8
development-induced displacement 37–40, 76, 155; see also investment-induced displacement
Dhar tribe 42
dispossession 29–31, 109–13, 156–62, 284
doctors 63–6
Dommara tribe 315, 320, 325
Dom tribe 315
Dongria Kandh Development Agency (DKDA) 125
Dongria Kandh tribe 124, 158
Dungdung, Gladson 169

ecological collective 148–9
eco-socio-political environment 272
education: equal 299; functions of 298; home language 298, 307–8;

# INDEX

mother tongue 300–1; NT-DNT children 324; right to 297, 308; school language 308
Elwin, Verrier 120, 278
employment 182
Employment Assurance Scheme (EAS) 35
Employment Guarantee Scheme (EGS) 35
enclaves: life in 84–6; nations in 79–84
Eshwari 137
ethnic collective 148–9
ethno development 290–1
excluded areas 274, 276
exclusion 5–10, 27–8
expenditure 181–2

farming 187–8
fifth five-year plan 34, 193
financial capital 182–3
five-year plans 34, 193, 284, 312, 317
Food for Work Programme (FWP) 35
Forest Conservation Act 135
forest policy 39–40, 270–1
forest rights 4–5
fourth five-year plan 34
Framework Agreement on Cooperation for Development between India and Bangladesh 88–9
Fundamental Right to Freedom 192–3

Gangaulu, Tadangi 135
Garo tribe 72–3, 81
Geithner, Timothy 165
gender issues 95
Girijan Cooperative Corporation (GCC) 193
Gokul 137
Gond tribe: colonial administration 277; harras marriage 100–2; health and disease management practices among 41–66; inclusions and exclusions of women 94–107; social organisation 94; social world of women 98–102; spiritual life world 98–9
Government of India Act of 1919 274

Government of India (Excluded and Partially Excluded Areas) Order of 1936 274
gram panchayat 338–9, 341, 343–4
gram sabha 337–8, 341–6
Greenspan, Alan 165
groundwater market 202–3
Gujarat: atrocities in 221, 223, 226; colonial administration 277; groundwater market 202–3; implementation of PESA in 338–47; poverty incidence 254; PRI in 334; scheduled areas of 338, 339; tubewell partnerships 202–3; water exchange in Mathnaa village 197–8, 203–10; water scarcity 198, 199–203

Habitual Offenders Act of 1952 315
Hajong tribe 72, 75–9
Haragopal, G. 133
harras marriage 100–2
Hastings, Warren 270
health/disease: action agenda for inclusive health management 65–6; Anganwadi Kendra in Pathai 59–60; Community Health Centre in Sahpur 43, 59–60, 63–6; Deen Dayal Mobile Hospital 61–2; Janani Suraksha Yojana 61; modern treatment methods 43–5, 50–6; perception of villagers and health workers working in Pathai and Sahpur 41–5, 46–7; preventive measures 56; Primary Health Centre in Pathai 43, 45, 50, 58–9, 63, 65–6; private doctors at Sahpur 63–6; safe drinking water 57; Total Sanitation Campaign 56; traditional treatment methods 41–3, 47–50; treatment facilities 63; treatment methods 41–5, 47–56
Herman, Edward 166
home language 307–8
Ho tribe 270
human rights 2–5

inclusive society 31–2
income 181

# INDEX

Indira-Mujib Pact of 1974 82, 86
integrated action plans 170-3
Integrated Tribal Development Projects/Agencies (ITDPs/ITDAs) 34, 193, 278-81
International Monetary Fund (IMF) 164-5, 168
investment-induced displacement: escalating dispossession and 156-62; integrated action plans 170-3; investment from financial system based on debt 162-8; process of 155-6; resistance movements and 160-2; voices of people against 168-70; see also development-induced displacement

Jacob, M.M. 76
Jaintia tribe 72
Jambuvandai tribe 315
Jammu 334
Janakiram, Chadala 326
Janani Suraksha Yojana (JSY) 61
Jawahar Rojgar Yojna (JRY) 35
Jharkhand 103, 135, 221-3, 254, 334
Jhodia, Mukta 147-8
Jhodia tribe 145
Jogi tribe 315
Joint Forest Management (JFM) 120-1

Kalinganagar movement 160
Kaller tribe 320
Kalundia, Dabur 146-7
Kanjar tribe 320
Kaptai Hydel Project 76
Karnataka 222-3, 226, 334
Kashmir 334
Kawal tribe 320
Kerala 334-5
Khasi tribe 72-3, 81, 94
kidnap episode 132-40
Kintali Kalinga tribe 315
Kols tribe 270
Konda Dora tribe 315
Kondha tribe 145
Koraput farming system 188
Korava tribe 320
Krishna, R. Vineel 132-40

Lambadi tribe 320
land acquisition 288
Land Boundary Agreement of 1974 81
land legislation 116-17, 289-90
land policy 37-8
land-rights movements: armed militant land-rights movement 121-2; early campaigns 118-19; Narayanpatna land-rights struggle 122-3; Niyamgiri anti-mining struggle 123-6; non-violent militant land-rights movement 123; reclaiming forests 119-21; resistance movements 157
language: community and 299-300; culture and 299-300; Eighth Schedule of 303-6; home 298, 308; language policy issues 301-2; mother tongue education 300-1; national 297; official 297; policy issues 301-2; political economy of 303-7; regional 298-301, 307; school 308
Laxman, Majhi 146
livelihoods: characteristics livelihoods 181-2; context 183; continuum 191-2; eroding tribal identity 192; farming 187-8; framework 181-3; major 183-95; for market 189; NRLM 194; NTFP collection 184-7, 188, 193-4; PDS 195; resource alienation 189-91; resources/capitals 182-3; seasonal migration and MGNREGA 188-9, 194; special provisions to tribal communities 192-4
Lodha tribe 320
Lombardi tribe 315

Madhya Pradesh: atrocities in 221-3, 226, 229, 233, 235; colonial administration 277-8; creation of Chhattisgarh 103; dispossession of land 163; implementation of PESA in 338-47; Land Revenue Code and PESA 290; medical treatment methods 42-3, 45-66; poverty incidence

351

244, 251, 254; PRI in 334–5; scheduled areas of 338, 339
Maharashtra 103, 221–3, 226, 277, 334
Mahatma Gandhi National Rural Employment Guarantee Act (MGNREGA) 184, 188–9, 194
Mahji, Tilka 269
Majhi, Bhagaban 157
Majhi, Laxman 118
Majhi, Maharaja 146
Majhi, Pabitra Mohan 132–40
Majhi, Rendo 118
Mandla tribe 42
Maoist movement: government counteroffensive 170; kidnap episode 132–40; resource wars 159–60; spread of 128–30; supporters 287
Mathnaa village: groundwater market: 207–10; land ownership 206; resident status of households 203–4; social fabric 203–7, 210; use of borewell technology 205–9; water exchange 197–8, 203–10; well ownership 206
media 149–52
Meena tribe 320
militant land-rights movement 121–2, 123
Mizo tribe 73–5
Modified Area Development Approach (MADA) 34
Mohan, Radha 137, 139
Mohanty, Dandapani 133
Mondi Vagula tribe 315
moneylender colonialism 163
mother tongue education 300
Mukerjee, Bijan Kumar 70
Mutharacha tribe 315
Myanmar 73–5

Nagaiah, Ramesam 326
Naga tribe 73–5
Narayanpatna land-rights struggle 122–3
National Counter Terrorism Centre 151
national language 297
National Rural Employment Guarantee Act 35, 156
National Rural Employment Programme (NREP) 35
National Rural Livelihoods Mission (NRLM) 194
National Scheduled Tribes Financial Development Corporation (NSTFDC) 193
Nat tribe 320
natural capital 182
natural resource management 344
Nayak, Gana 137
Nehru, Jawaharlal 37, 78, 274, 278
New Economic Policy 164
Niyamgiri anti-mining struggle 123–6
non-timber forest produce (NTFP) collection 184–7, 188, 193–4
notified tribes (NTs): atrocities 319; cultural heritage of 324; growth rate of population 312; recommendations to address development challenges 329; unstable occupations 323; welfare measures initiated for the development of 317–19

Objectives Resolution of 1946 274–5
Odisha: atrocities in 222, 223; border with Chhattisgarh 103; under British rule 113–14; cultural appropriation 109–13; dispossession of land 111–13; Kandhamal violence in 162; kidnap of R. Vineel Krishna and Pabitra Mohan Majhi 132–40; land legislation 116–17; land-rights movements 157; land-rights movements in 118–26; as most indebted state 163; people's resistance movements 126–8; random outline 109; socio-cultural history of the region 110–11; spread of Maoist movement 128–30
official language 297
Operation Green Hunt 151, 159, 170
orality 272

# INDEX

Oraon tribe 270
Orissa 221, 254, 278
Orissa Scheduled Areas Transfer of Immovable Property Regulation of 1956 (OSATIP) 156

Paidi tribe 315
Pakhiwar tribe 320
Panchayati Raj (Extension to Scheduled Areas) Act 104
Panchayat Raj Institutions (PRI) 333–4
Panchayats Extension to the Scheduled Areas Act (PESA): 73rd Amendment and 288–90, 332–3, 335–8; challenges 346–7; civil rights and citizenship issues of indigenous women and 98; conservation and protection of traditions and rituals under 344–5; criticism of 287; exposure towards 340; implementation of 11, 156, 170–1, 173, 335–8; natural resource management under 344; operationalisation of gram panchayat 343–4; operationalisation of gram sabha 341–3; passage of 4; use in kidnap episode 135
Panchsheel Policy 278–9, 284
Pathai village: Anganwadi Kendra 45, 59–60; demographics 45; Janani Suraksha Yojana 61; perception about health and disease 46–7; Primary Health Centre 43, 45, 48, 50, 58–9, 63, 65–6
Patnaik, Nagabhushan 122
Patnaik, Naveen 138
Patnaik, Sudhakar 137, 139
Paulson, Henry 165
Permanent Settlement Act 114
physical capital 182
political rights 31
Poosala tribe 325
poverty incidence study: data-related issues 243–4; district level calculations of consumption and poverty 251–4; impact of growth on reducing poverty 254–7; macro picture of consumption and poverty incidence 246–51; measures of deprivation 245–6; policy issues 258; sample size 245
Pradesh, Madhya 163
Prasadam, Ganti 133, 137, 139
Primary Health Centre (PHC) 43, 48, 50, 58–9, 63, 65–6
Protection of Civil Rights (PCR) Act of 1976 217
Public Distribution System (PDS) 195
public distribution system (PDS) 57
Pyrdiwah issue 86–8

Radcliffe, Cyril 70, 79
Radcliffe Line of 1947: areas of dispute 80–4, 86–8; creation of 71–2, 80, 82; failure of 79–80; objective of 72–5
Raipur tribe 42
Rajasthan 221, 226, 254, 277, 338–47
Ramesh, Jairam 169
Rammohan, E.N. 170
Rao, Devakonda Hanumantha 326
Rao, R.S. 133
Rao, Varavara 137, 139
Reagan, Ronald 165
Reddika tribe 315
regional language 298–301, 307
Regulation Act of 1834 274
Rehman, S.R. 70
Relli tribe 315, 321
reservation 32–3
resistance movements 126–8, 132–40, 157, 160–2, 269–71, 285, 287
resource alienation 189–91
Right of Children to Free and Compulsory Education Act of 2009 297, 308
rights: citizenship 31–2, 73, 76–8, 98; civil 31, 98; ecological collective versus ethnic collective and 148–9; education 297, 308; forest 4–5; Fundamental Right to Freedom 192–3; human 2–5; land-rights movements 118–26, 157; political

# INDEX

31; social 31; special 32; status of tribal people 31–2; tribal 143–5
risks 182
Roubini, Nouriel 168
Rowbotham, Michael 167
Rural Landless Employment Guarantee Programme (RLEGP) 35

safe drinking water 57
Saleh, Abu 70
Salwa Judum (Purification hunt) programme 105
Sampurna Gramin Rojgar Yojna (SGRY) 35
Sansiya tribe 320
Sarita 137
Sayeed, P.M. 77
Scheduled Castes and Scheduled Tribes (Prevention of Atrocities) Act of 1989 217, 218, 220, 223–4, 225, 238
Scheduled Castes and Scheduled Tribes (Prevention of Atrocities) Act of 2006 319
Scheduled Castes and Scheduled Tribes (Prevention of Atrocities) Act Rules of 1995 217
Scheduled Castes (SCs) 61, 93, 242–58
Scheduled Districts Act 274
Scheduled Tribes and Other Traditional Forest Dwellers (Recognition of Forest Rights) Act 0f 2006 4–5, 120, 135, 156, 238
Scheduled Tribes (STs) 4–5, 61, 178–95, 242–58
school language 308
seasonal migration 188–9, 316–17
Sen, Ashtosh 137
sexual relationships 99–102
sexual violence 105–6
Shahpur Development Block: Community Health Centre 59–60, 63–6; Community Health Centre in Sahpur 43; Deen Dayal Mobile Hospital 61–2; perception about health and disease 46–7; private doctors 63–6
Shankar Lal, Dhurve 52–3
Sidhi tribe 42

Sikoka, Lado 159
Singh, Manmohan 164
Sirike, Ratana 135
Sirisha 137
slash and burn cultivation 187–8
social capital 182
social exclusion 5–10
social forestry 57–8
social rights 31
special rights 32
spiritual capital 183
Sreenivasulu, Sriramalu 137
structural violence 156, 313
subprime mortgage crisis 165
Sugali tribe 325
sustainable development 158
Swanjayanti Gram Swayrojgar Yojna (SGSY) 35

Tagu tribe 320
Tandari Mandalam tribe 315
Telaga Pamula tribe 315
Total Sanitation Campaign (TSC) 56
tribal communities: betrayal of 276–7, 282–5; eco-socio-political environment 272; livelihoods 178–95; profile 179–80; role of orality 272; social inclusion and exclusion 28–31; societal construct 271–2; special provisions 192–4
Tribal Cooperative Marketing Developing Federation (TRIFED) 193
tribal development 278–81, 287
Tribal Development Cooperative Corporation (TDCC) 193
tribal identity: big capital and the media 149–52; blunders in history burdening 142–5; ecological collective versus ethnic collective and 148–9; eroding 192; history of continuity 149; redefining 145–8
tribal literature 326–7
tribal rights 143–5
tribal subplan (TSP) 34–5, 193, 278–81
tubewell partnerships 202–3

# INDEX

Umbrey, Lacta 76
Universal Declaration of Human Rights 3
Universal Declaration of the Rights of Mother Earth 172
untouchability 9–10
Urali Goudar tribe 315
Uttar Pradesh 103

Varna system 9
Vedanta Resources PLC 123–6
Verma, J.S. 4
Verraiah, Palaparthi 326

Waddar tribe 315, 320, 324, 325
water exchange: in Gujarat 197–210; Mathnaa village 197–8, 203–10
West Bengal 80–2, 180, 222–3, 283, 332, 334–5
witchcraft 98–9

women: atrocities against 105–6, 231–4; civil rights and citizenship issues of 98; current crisis in development and impact on 104–5; gender issues in tribal societies 95; NT-DNT communities 325; regulation of sexual relationships 99–102; role in food production and other livelihoods 96–7; sexual violence 105–6; social world of 98; witchcraft and 98
World Bank 163–5, 168, 169
World Health Organization (WHO) 44

Yanadi tribe 315, 325
Yerukala tribe 312–15, 323, 324, 325–7
Yonggam, Nadek 77

zamindari system 113, 121

Printed in the United States
By Bookmasters